Anthropology of Contemporary Issues

A SERIES EDITED BY
ROGER SANJEK

Between Two Worlds

ETHNOGRAPHIC ESSAYS
ON AMERICAN JEWRY

EDITED BY

Jack Kugelmass

Cornell University Press

Ithaca and London

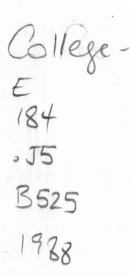
First published 1988 by Cornell University Press.

International Standard Book Number (cloth) 0-8014-2084-9
Internation Standard Book Number (paper) 0-8014-9408-7
Library of Congress Catalog Card Number 88-47735

Printed in the United States of America

*Librarians: Library of Congress cataloging information
appears on the last page of the book.*

*The paper in this book is acid-free and meets the guidelines for
permanence and durability of the Committee on Production Guidelines
for Book Longevity of the Council on Library Resources.*

Contents

Contents

Acknowledgments

Collecting and editing the essays in this volume took several years. I am very grateful to the authors for their patience and willingness to endure numerous requests for revisions. I believe that the final product will have made those efforts worthwhile.

Special thanks are due to Roger Sanjek for suggesting this project to me and to Peter Agree at Cornell University Press for nurturing this book and waiting patiently for it to reach its current form.

I also thank Marc Kaminsky for agreeing to edit Barbara Myerhoff's essay, which she completed shortly before her death. Her work has been an inspiration to many, and I believe I am speaking for us all in dedicating *Between Two Worlds* to her.

J. K.

New York, New York

Between Two Worlds

Introduction

Jack Kugelmass

This collection of original essays on the ethnography of American Jewry is intended as a reflection both on the subject of study, American Jewry, and on the object of study, anthropologists and anthropology. But because almost all the anthropologists conducting these studies are extremely intimate with their subjects, there is a dialogue here that is not always made explicit in anthropological inquiry: the dialogue between the anthropologist as outsider and the anthropologist as insider. Moreover, it is a dialogue in which the boundaries separating one from the other constantly shift, as perspectives, emotional ties, informants, and personal histories change.

The need for a self-reflexive volume, particularly on the subject of American Jewish ethnography, stems in part from current recognition of the value of reflexivity in anthropological research (Ruby 1982) and in part from the special conditions of the ethnography of American Jewry, which, very much like the sociology of American Jewry, as Samuel Heilman (1982) notes, consists for the most part of research done by Jews to be read chiefly by Jews. If this is so, then to what end do we do our work? Although it would be difficult to suggest one single answer here, it does seem rather clear that the ethnographic study of American Jewry is integrally related to the general issue of ethnic identity as an alternative to hegemonic ideologies, or as Michael Fischer argues in regard to ethnicity, "as alternatives to the melting pot rhetoric of assimilation to the bland, neutral style of the conformist 1950s" (1986:196). Indeed, the search for that identity is particularly acute within the postmodern world of fragmented cultural universes. In this sense, the personal quest for authenticity and communal needs compete deep within the heart of the anthropologist with interests that are purely scientific. And this is a unifying theme in all of these essays: the common approach evident in them speaks less to the purely methodological value that self-reflectivity has come to play in anthropological research and much more to the ethnotherapeutic value, the search for wholeness, that ethnography can bring to bear in postmodern society (hence the continuing interest of modern man in primitive or premodern cultures).

I do not mean to lessen the importance of this book for the scientific study of American Jewry or even to suggest that its intended audience is only a small circle of like-minded anthropologists. Quite the contrary. This book is about American Jewry, and although it is by no means a complete inventory, it tells us a great deal about the culture, or perhaps better stated the cultures of the group. But it is not intended as a reader, covering all the parameters of the subject: there is no introductory essay in this volume on the history of American Jewry, nor are there essays on the group's demographics, its economic structure, or on its political culture. There are already many excellent books on these and similar subjects and there is no need to replicate material well documented by others.[1] Instead, the reader will find here vignettes, among the many small segments that make up American Jewry: each may be seen as a paradigmatic representation of a larger picture or, if the reader prefers, as a fascinating example of the permutations possible when people agree to share an identity and yet are organized only informally, that is, as the anthropologist Abner Cohen (1974) argues, outside of official state organizations. Although the bonds that join group members to one another may be used to gain competitive advantage in trade and commerce, the fact remains that the bonds are by custom rather than by law. Since the group cannot impose mandatory codes of behavior on its members, it lacks a coherent identity—a fact that may be as troubling to the social scientist studying the group as it certainly is to the lay or religious leaders determined to preserve or enhance the group's identity. Of course, the diversity of American Jewry stems not only from the informal nature of the group's social organization but also from its history as an immigrant community formed through successive waves of immigration.

[2]

The roots of American Jewry may very well extend back to or derive from the European discovery of the New World in 1492.[2] Spanish exiles were the first Jewish settlers of the New World, some of whom eventually made their way to Peter Stuyvesant's colony, New Amsterdam. Despite the very early Jewish presence in America, for the most part, pre-nineteenth-century Jewish migration was small and piecemeal. It was only the migrations first of German Jews in the first half of the nineteenth century and then of East European Jews from the 1880s through the 1920s that led to American Jewry's emergence as a significant community.

Today there are just under six million Jews in the United States, less than 3 percent of the total American population. These figures are in some ways misleading, for despite the small number of Jews here, the Jewish presence in America is rather pronounced, in large measure because Jews are not randomly distributed throughout the country but tend to cluster within certain regions and localities. More than two-thirds of all Jews live in the northeast and northcentral states, with the largest concentration (over two million) living in the New York metropolitan area. Chicago and Los Angeles, America's second and third largest cities, are both major Jewish centers. Moreover, the strong Jewish presence in the electronic and print media as well as in high-status professions and academic institutions (Cohen 1983:90–92) contributes to a highly visible group profile. These attributes perhaps account for the fact that Jews have come to occupy a central position within contemporary American culture, having traveled a considerable distance away from the periphery in only a few decades. Examples of this change are everywhere in evidence, not only in residential patterns and clubs but even in American language and culture: numerous Yiddish words have been incorporated into American English and are now used in the media by Jews and non-Jews alike; Jewish subjects and non-stereotyped Jewish characters are commonplace in books, the press, films, and television.[3] Indeed, the decision to build a Holocaust museum on the mall in Washington, in Battery Park City, in New York and in a number of other cities throughout the country is further testimony to the status of Jews within American society and culture.[4]

Although they came from every corner of the world, the overwhelming majority of contemporary American Jews are Central and particularly Eastern European Jews. To the degree that one can speak of normative Judaism in America (regional and even local variations in behavior are factors among others that weigh against a concept of normative American Judaism), it is an offshoot of Ashkenazic, particularly eastern Ashkenazic culture: American Judaism is the religion practiced by second-, third-, and fourth-generation descendants of the mass migration from Eastern Europe at the turn of the century. Even Reform Judaism, once the dominant Jewish expression in America, has in recent years tried to reestablish itself within that context—a shift away from its origins within German Reform Judaism.[5] Indeed, if we could define American Judaism, it would be in terms of a religious expression or expressions that for the most part seeks some balance between the need to legitimize behavior internally, that is with reference to Judaism's rabbinic and folk traditions, and the very pronounced tendency to accommodate behavior to the surrounding world. Such a religious expression stands in direct opposition to attempts made particularly in the nineteenth century to remove that conflict by legitimizing Judaism through a non-Jewish worldview, such as German liberalism or a revolutionary ideology, and seeking to dispense with those "archaic" aspects of Judaism that contradict the legitimizing worldview.[6]

For a religious elite, establishing such a balance is frought with tension: on what basis can deviation from Orthodox religious observance be justified? What should be done about intermarriage, sexual promiscuity, or the flagrant disregard of ritual and religious commandments? The nonelite have much less trouble finding a balance, perhaps because they have given over to the elite the role of being exemplary Jews. Little wonder, then, why American Jews have developed such strong sympathetic feelings toward Hasidim, the most obvious of exemplary Jews. Less compelled, therefore, to establish an explicit rationale for violating religious law, the nonelite establish albeit implicitly a folk expression of Judaism.

Charles Liebman suggests that we distinguish between a folk and an elite religion and argues that in the assimilation of East European Jewry to American society the persistence of religious practices has not been in accordance with the place of those practices within the hierarchy of religious traditions as defined by the elite. They reflect, rather, the persistence of a cultural lifestyle: "The laws pertaining to permissable and forbidden foods survived longer than Sabbath observance, though in an attenuated form. The parts which survived were rooted in the folk, rather than in the elitist aspect of Judaism" (1971:242). Kosher "style" has replaced the shunning of *treyf* or ritu-

[4]

ally proscribed foods. The folk also distinguished between "disguised" *treyf* such as Chinese food, and shell fish and ham or pork, the latter being less permissible than the former. No such distinction is made in rabbinic reckoning. For most American Jews, Judaism is practiced less as a religion than as a cultural lifestyle and a social affiliation. Liebman also argues that the abandonment of religiously sanctioned observances is governed less by genuine desires to assimilate than by convenience. Contemporary Jews, for example, see intermarriage as the most damaging of all violation of religious proscriptions, an attitude that is not in keeping with elite religious reckoning, but one that is conducive to maintaining Jewish ethnicity, conforming to the folk's own hierarchy of what violates Jewish law: "The distinguishing mark of American Jews is less and less how they behave and is certainly not what they believe: it is that they associate primarily with other Jews" (243). The degree to which American Jews restrict their principal ties to other Jews is made clear in Steven Cohen's (1983) survey. Thirty-nine percent of the respondents indicated that all or almost all of their closest friends are Jewish; only 15 percent of the respondents indicated that less than half their closest friends are Jewish. These findings are corroborated in William Mitchell's essay in this volume. Mitchell, a non-Jewish ethnographer who studied Jewish family clubs in New York City, writes:

> In some of the Jewish homes I visited, I was something of an "event" because I was the first *goy* guest. . . . After a pleasant visit with a Jewish family accompanied by an informant, I learned that I was the first "wasp" to have entered the home. My informant's comments about our hostess was, "I bet she sighed a sigh of relief when you went out the door!"

In addition to showing that Jews restrict their social contacts to fellow Jews, Cohen's study also shows that 77 percent of Jews attend Passover seders, 67 percent light Hanukkah candles, while 54 percent fast on Yom Kippur, 22 percent light Sabbath candles, and only 5 percent observe the Sabbath proscriptions on work or commerce. The figures bear out the results of Sidney Goldstein and Calvin Goldscheider's study of the Jews of Providence, Rhode Island, which demonstrate that among third-generation American Jews there has been a decline in Sabbath observance and the laws of *kashres* [ritually proscribed food], but there has been an increased significance of halakhically, that is, rabbinically defined less significant holidays such as Hanukkah and the Passover seder. The home- rather than the synagogue-centeredness of both of these holidays make them less onerous to celebrate for those not well versed in esoteric ritual. At the same time, the ready association of both holidays with key American symbols of freedom from tyranny and revolution lend themselves to celebration, even for those who otherwise eschew religious ritual. Indeed, as Anita Schwartz illustrates in her essay in this volume, a modified Passover seder is the only "religious" ritual that had made its way into the left-wing coops established in the Bronx among radical Jewish workers.

Certainly an important element in the ritual and iconic repertoire of the nonelite revolves around "external symbols that identify them as Jews" (Sklare 1974). The use of symbols of identification is an area well worth investigating. Even a cursory look indicates at least two very different kinds of symbols: those that are symmetrical with the symbols of the host culture and those that are asymmetrical. While one set serves to integrate American Jewry into mainstream "hyphenated" Americanism (for example, Jewish-American and Italo-American), the other sets up definable boundaries between Jews and the host culture or even among various Jewish subgroups. Yarmulkes, *peyes* [sidelocks], *arbe kanfes* [ritual fringes], and strict Sabbath observance characterize asymmetrical symbols; *khays* and Stars of David as neckchains, and electric Hanukkah lights as window decorations, characterize symmetrical symbols. And there are shades of gray between the two, suggesting that Liebman's model of elite and folk Judaism may have limited value, particularly for categorizing the great variety of American Jewish subcultures. The fact is that much of the expressive behavior surrounding the articulation of ethnic identity stems not so much from the internal traditions of the group as from an affective tie made all the more emphatic by the awareness of symbols and expressive behavior of other ethnic groups. After all, how much do most second- and third-generation ethnics know about their ethnic culture? As the folklorist Barbara Kirshenblatt-Gimblett suggests, "The folklore of ethnicity may be defined as expressive behaviour on and about cultural boundaries. The folklore of ethnicity grows out of a heightened awareness of cultural diversity and ambiguity, out of mastery of multiple cultural repertoires and the ability to choose and switch among them" (1987:88). Elliott Oring's study, in this volume, of a modern Orthodox musical group specializing in songs satirizing the ultra-Orthodox indicates the complexity of the division between

[6]

traditionalist and nontraditionalist Judaism, and through it we can see the degree of fine tuning of symbols of asymmetry among the various subgroups of American Jewry.

Most studies of American Jewry rely upon the denominational divisions of Judaism between the Orthodox, Conservative, and Reform wings. Since these divisions, for the most part, reflect associational rather than behavioral patterns, their heuristic value is somewhat limited. Strictly for the purposes of anthropological inquiry, I would subdivide American Jewry into three main categories, using as a key criterion in each case the degree to which social relations are likely to be restricted to other Jews. What I am advocating is not a definition of American Jewry but a research strategy with varying points of entry and criteria for comparison. I should also point out that this model needs to be modified to incorporate regional variation, local ethnic diversity, urban ecology, and the culture of origin for particular ethnic communities (see Deborah Dash Moore 1987), all of which have considerable impact on the culture of a particular Jewish community. Moreover, the differentiation of social relations and cultural commitment along the lines of gender is a particularly underexamined factor that determines the character of local, regional, and national American Jewish culture.

In the model I am proposing, category one is the ultra-Orthodox, or those Jews commited to the principle of legitimizing their normative behavior almost exclusively through rabbinic precedent and law. They are suspicious of modernity, tend to be residentially segregated, and though closely interwoven with the modern world through business, they see themselves as in this world but not of this world.

Category two comprises the so-called modern Orthodox and Conservative Jews, certain Reform Jews, and various politically oriented Jewish secular groups, too, for whom Judaism and modernity, although they remain to a degree antithetical to one another, can be brought into balance. They see themselves, therefore, both in this world and of this world. They associate almost exclusively with Jews, read mainly Jewish books, and are affiliated with Jewish institutions. Jewish religion or secular Judaism is a cornerstone of their identity, but it is not the only aspect of their Jewishness.

Category three are those Jews who identify themselves as Jews but who define their Jewishness within larger legitimizing principles of American democracy or other universalist principles rather than within the principles that are internal to Judaism as defined by the elite.

[7]

To them, Judaism is a universal religion. If they shun Judaism, they do it for the same reasons they reject any religion. If they attend synagogue, it is for purposes of partaking in life cycle rituals such as weddings and bar mitzvahs and sometimes prayers for the dead, although at least some members of this category may attend some High Holy Day services, particularly *yizkor* [memorial] services. For them Judaism and Jewish culture are "styles" of behavior, devoid of deep ritual commitment or allegiance to elite proscriptions, but very much associated with affective ties. Although many and perhaps most American Jews would fall in this category, an excellent example of the type can be seen in Fran Baskin's description in this volume of recent Russian immigrants to Brighton Beach.

These categories may cover the range of American Jewish beliefs and practices but they are not rigid divisions. Not only do people cross over among the three categories, particularly at various stages of the life cycle (e.g., parents whose children reach bar mitzvah age and affiliate with synagogues, the elderly who become regular minyan members because they seek both companionship and spiritual sustenance), but numerous groups and individuals inhabit gray areas between any two categories. The Havurah movement, as described by Riv-Ellen Prell in this volume, is a case in point: in practice it is close to Conservative Judaism, with some influence from the hasidic prayer style, particularly the atmosphere of the *shtibl;* in theory, it is liberal and reformist—far more committed to equality for women within Jewish ritual than any other subgroup, aside, perhaps, from Reform.

The plethora of ways of being Jewish in America speaks to two critical facets of Jewish life: since the Emancipation in Western Europe and the Enlightenment in Eastern Europe, Jews have had to establish their own definitions of who they are vis-à-vis the surrounding non-Jewish world. And this enterprise is particularly risky for the immigrant communities upon which American Jewry is built, which arrived in this country torn from long-established ties to patriarchal families and tight-knit communities. Together the young immigrants had to invent, so to speak, a New World Judaism. As Deborah Dash Moore suggests, "Migration created peer group Jewish societies lacking the constraints of a parental generation and, temporarily the needs of children. Migration helped reorient the locus of Jewish identity from tradition, the past and the religious community, to ethnicity, the future and the secular individual. Though not abrogating the past and its values, the communities established by Jewish immigrants reinterpreted tradition, seeking a usable past that foreshadowed the future and legitimated their claim to Jewish authenticity" (1987:108).

The common element among these various subgroups is the belief each of them has of being Jewish, not only by choice but also through birth and ancestry. Within that belief lies a very broad range of distinct ideological strands and behavior, giving each of the subgroups that appear in this volume such distinct personae that one sometimes needs to be reminded that they are indeed part of a single ethnic group. Ethnicity can be seen, then, as a broad category definable principally as a means of circumscribing affective ties and, whenever possible, marriage alliances, and as a label of contradistinction between groups. Moreover, these groups understand their differentness largely synchronically—that is, in relation to current conflicts and divisions—although they generally construct a diachronic dimension to ethnic divisions by attributing historical or even mythical reasons for ongoing conflicts and exclusivity, or for the opposite, namely intergroup alliances. In contrast to the divisions of ethnicity, divisions among various Jewish subgroups such as Sephardim and Ashkenazim are largely a function of different historical experiences. However, they may articulate an identity that increases rather than decreases their differentness from other Jewish subgroups either for reasons of class or more simply as an extention of family pride and place of origin. Whenever unequal social status is combined with pride of family or place of origin, the possibility of ethnic cleavage is probably very great. Perhaps the most telling reason for stressing the synchronic dimension in ethnic exclusiveness stems from the scant knowledge that most second- and third-generation ethnics have of their own traditions. In the American context it seems rather evident that ethnic groups establish their identities as much through interaction and conflict with other ethnic groups and the establishment of symbolic criteria for group exclusivity as they do through a desire or in most cases ability to conserve so-called traditional values. If the latter were the principal determinant in ethnicity, Jews would long ago have ceased functioning as a single ethnic entity.

There are both centrifugal and centripetal forces affecting ethnicity. Individuals are far more complex than the broad ethnic categories into which they are born. They are, after all, refractions of group ideals through the prism of personal and particular socioeconomic and political circumstances. And not always does ethnicity have a paramount place in the articulation either of a group's or of an individual's identity. At the same time, local and family ties tend to create centrifugal forces pulling away from the larger group identity. The breakdown of Hasidism into numerous and sometimes mutually antagonistic sects is a case in point, and the great variation in styles of expressive behavior among the sects is a rich area for ethnographic research (Kirshenblatt-Gimblett 1987:87–88). I remember listening with astonishment as a Pupa Hasid explained to me that the reason his group was relocating to Ossining had to do with the presence within Williamsburg of other hasidic sects: for the ultra-Orthodox, sectarian pluralism threatens the legitimacy of the claim each group makes of being the most authentic bearer of tradition.

There are also centripetal forces at work to balance the tendency toward localism. The ethnic category of common identity is one such force and it quickly overtakes the more local identities in crises. But even under normal conditions, the sheer multiplicity of localized identities reinforces the need for an overarching identity revolving around certain key symbols. The central text of Judaism, the Torah, provides a single overarching symbol (Goldberg 1987). A Yugoslavian-born Sephardic folksinger tells Ruth Fredman Cernea: "I don't know if it's better [to attend a Moroccan rather than an Ashkenazic synagogue]. What can you expect when we're a minority in a minority. I think the answer is to do what I did. Just [assimilate with the Ashkenazim] be one of them, do what they do, because Jewish is Jewish." Indeed, this centripetal aspect of Jewish ethnicity, namely Judaism, goes to the very core of Jewish ethnicity. The combination of group identity with religious particularism gives Jewry a unique character, qualitatively different from that of ethnic or religious groups. As Eugene Borowitz notes, despite their covenant with God, Jews "never gave up their essentially ethnic character. Thus, the absence of dogma in Judaism is but another sign that the Jews continued to maintain themselves as a people and not as a church" (1973:10).

Given the relative newness of American Jewry (most are descendants of immigrants who arrived only a hundred years ago or less), it is not surprising to see such wide diversity among the various Jewish subgroups, and it therefore might be fairest to look at American Jewry as a cultural fabric in the making,[7] the seams of which are still very much in evidence. Moreover, the pattern and texture of the fabric varies a great deal from place to place. If we can use Fredman Cernea's study of the Washington Sephardic community as a case in point, then we can see that localized identities are not viable in a city where small numbers and residential dispersion weigh against communal solidarity. Consequently, an overarching Sephardic identity revolving around a single ritual is emerging to substitute for identities based on the countries of origin. By contrast, the sheer volume of New York Jewry fosters a great range of Jewish subgroups, some of which exhibit a degree of proscriptive attitudes toward marriage alliances outside the group.

Although their descendants' roots are now firmly planted in American soil, Ashkenazic Jews still exhibit various attachments to their Central and Eastern European places of origin, evident either in the form of genealogical research or in the resurgence of interest in Old World Jewish culture and customs, including a considerable amount of travel to Poland, for example, in the past few years. Will a more unified American Jewish culture and identity emerge over time? Perhaps. But certainly if we follow Abner Cohen's theory of ethnicity as dramatizing "the processes by which the symbolic patterns of behavior implicit in the style of life, or the 'sub-culture' of a group . . . develop to articulate organizational functions that cannot be formally institutionalized" (1971:xxi), the inner conditions in American society for the most part do not mandate a single, uniform Jewish ethnicity. Jewish identity in America therefore serves primarily cultural and psychological functions, not social and political ones. This voluntaristic quality also promotes Jewish heterogeneity. If American Judaism serves personal rather than political needs, the range of possible Jewish expressions is quite large indeed.

All cultures provide a set of myths or stories to explain appropriate behavior and to give the prescribed behavior a level of meaning that makes it into a personal and a group challenge to chaos. But in contemporary culture, all myths are subject to considerable dispute: not all members of a group accept the same myths as the central ones upon which the culture is based; if they do, they do not necessarily interpret them the same way. For centuries various groups of Jews have sought to reestablish a link to authentic Judaism, and various groups within American Jewry today continue that search. Some see their roots in their own image of a "primitive" past. Others see their roots in the pioneering spirit of Zionism's kibbutz movement and the resettlement of the ancient Jewish homeland. For others, the Eastern European Jewish past has reemerged as the bulwark against assimilation as evidenced by the recent revival of *klezmer* music (Slobin 1987) and current attitudes towards Yiddish. Little wonder, too, that

[11]

Hasidism has come to have such an enormous impact on popular Jewish culture. By laying claim to an understanding of the authentic expression of Judaism, it crosses over the barriers of localization among Jews of various national origins. Moreover, it is an approach that at least according to popular lore traditionally valued intent as much as behavior, in a sense bringing the possibility of righteousness within the grasp of the nonerudite and even those whose formal level of observance is limited. This very quality gives it remarkable appeal, particularly as ritual observance lessens while Judaism as a discrete and symbolic identity remains. I am referring, of course, not so much to Hasidism's ability to recruit, which seems, at least at surface level, impressive, as to how the idea of Hasidism has become part of popular Jewish culture. Examples are Elie Wiesel's novels, many of which posit Hasidism as a response to the Holocaust; Shlomo Carlbach's music; retold hasidic tales; kitsch paintings or drawings of hasidic men dancing—all these have become a part of contemporary American Jewish culture.

Various observers have pointed out the dramatic impact that Israel's Six-Day War had upon American Jewry. Not only did the war and its aftermath make Israel a central focus of Jewish communal organizational activities, but also, as Yakov Evantov and Cvi Rotem observe, it brought Israel to occupy, "an important place in synagogue activities, sermons and various religious celebrations" (Waxman 1983:119). For American Jews, Israel is less a potential place of refuge than a broad collective focus of Jewish identity. Trips to Israel are frequently highly charged pilgrimages, which include visits to significant monuments in Jewish popular history or what some sociologists of religion refer to as Judaism's civil religion—Masada and Yad Vashem.

Quite recently, the Holocaust has been incorporated into the ritual life of American Judaism. Perhaps this too is an outgrowth of the search for roots, an expression of a newly discovered loss of an irretrievable past. Today Holocaust memorial centers are being established throughout North America. These institutions are particularly interesting for anthropology, because they tend to be a cross between a museum and a shrine, suggesting something deeper as institutions than repositories of information. Given the place the Holocaust has assumed in American Jewish life (the sociologist Chaim Waxman (1983:123) argues that, like the Six-Day War, the Holocaust has become part of the core of civil Judaism in America, one can expect the subject eventually to generate some very important studies.

Considerable evidence indicates the recent upswing in the number of Jews attracted to Orthodoxy. With fifteen hundred synagogues in North America, Orthodoxy is a powerful force in American Jewish life and one that shows every indication of growing (Gittelson 1984). Some argue that the phenomenon was predictable, given the sociology of immigration. The earlier waves of Jewish migration around the turn of the century did not, for the most part, include the Orthodox rabbinic elite, while most of these Jewish immigrants themselves were less ideologically commited to Orthodoxy than synagogue affiliation might indicate. Between 1937 and 1948 a quarter-of-a-million Jewish refugees arrived here from Eastern Europe. Among them were a large number of Orthodox rabbis and their followers. They provided, according to Chaim Waxman, "the numbers and manpower for the renaissance that was to manifest itself more than a quarter of a century later" (1983:123). Other factors are at work here, too, including changes in American life, particularly the rise in religious consciousness and public ethnicity (ibid.). I suspect another reason here, too. Orthodoxy represents a turning inward, a response to an increasingly cynical world in which Jews feel particularly vulnerable. If Israel represents a political bulwark against persecution, religion represents solace in the face of disaster. And historically, only the latter has withstood the test of time.

These then are some of the areas that need to be considered in an ethnography of American Jewry. This volume covers some of them, but many topics must await the work of other researchers. I raise these issues in the hope that others will pay them due attention.

Why were these selections included and not others? In part, the answer is chance. Much depended upon my network of friends and colleagues for acquiring these essays. And chance interfered again when important topics had to be left out because certain studies are still in progress. For example, essays on Jewish cultists in California, and *baley-tshuve* ("returnees" to Orthodoxy). Other studies, too, belong in this volume, such as ones concerned with Israelis in New York, Syrians in Brooklyn, Iranians in Los Angeles, and Cubans in Miami; some studies, equally important and I think very much within the purview of anthropology or at least its sister field, folklore, have not yet been done: What is a more characteristic feature of American Jewry than the ever-changing styles of suburban bar mitzvah celebrations (a Jewish version of the potlatch)? Or United Jewish Appeal trips (what Victor Turner might term pilgrimages) to Poland and Israel, or

[13]

Israel bond drives (what Clifford Geertz might see, because of the competitive nature of giving, as analogues to Balinese cockfighting)? What is more Jewish than Jewish summer camps? Or the Catskill Mountain Jewish resorts with their discussion groups, diningroom banter and nightclub acts? On a more serious level, Israel Day parades, Holocaust memorial services, survivor groups, and the so-called second-generation or survivor's children's groups all constitute important aspects of American Jewish life that ought to be studied. I am not aware of any such studies and was not able therefore to include them in this book. By the same token, there is a surprising range of material here, both in terms of countries of origin (as diverse as Yemen and Poland) and in terms of styles of Jewish experience (from ultra-Orthodox Hasidim to agnostic elderly), despite the limited number of essays that could be included. The volume's contents reflect the remarkable range and diversity of American Jewry and suggest the tremendous depth and richness of the subject. Indeed, one would hope that these essays might sensitize anthropologists to the wealth of good and highly accessible study material right at hand yet hardly touched by other researchers.

On a more practical level, one purpose of this volume is to introduce anthropologists to some of the special problems and considerations the ethnography of American Jewry presents for "entering the field" and completing a successful project. Jews in general, and American Jews in particular, are a quintessential urban group.[8] Though urban residence makes Jews particularly accessible to anthropologists tied to academic institutions, urban groups do present problems as subjects of study. Not the least of these is finding a suitably discrete unit comparable to the village community that traditionally defined the parameters of an anthropological study (Foster and Kemper 1980). Fortunately, American Jews often constitute discrete units that are, if not quite comparable to an isolated village, at least suitable for study: community centers, synagogues, schools, old-age homes, family clubs, and *landsmanshaftn* all provide excellent fieldwork venues. Moreover, the lack of isolation may have its advantages: a good ethnographer should be sensitive to the special situation of multicultural interaction. The study of Ashkenazic Jewry is the study of a minority group in constant contact with the host society (Weinreich 1980). Every aspect of its culture, from its language to its peculiar religious expressions, indicates the scope of such contact. Neither American nor European Jewry lived in isolated communities.

Even that quintessential Jewish community, the *shtetl*, was Jewish only insofar as Jews resided there, not that only Jews resided there.

Most ethnographers, especially in urban settings, encounter a typical problem: how to make contact with elusive informants. Even in the case of a highly visible group like the Hasidim, identifying a discrete subgroup is complicated by the fact that different groups sometimes look rather similar to one another, particularly to an untrained eye. In the case of Boro Park or Williamsburg, Brooklyn, many different sects live side by side. Eventually, the nature of the community and its membership becomes apparent. The two simplest ways of locating informants, as Janet Belcove-Shalin notes, are through "networking," that is, through branching out to new informants via old ones and by making the most of chance encounters:

> Late one afternoon as I was taking the B-subway line from Manhattan during rush hour, the train stalled. I noticed an elderly hasidic man who seemed to be having difficulty understanding the garbled messages about alternative routes relayed over the P.A. system. After a moment of hesitation, I walked over to him and offered help, which to my surprise, he graciously accepted.
>
> Since this man had recently come to the U.S. from Bnei Brak, an ultra-orthodox suburb of Tel Aviv, and spoke virtually no English, I suggested that he, his wife, and I, get together for joint Yiddish-English lessons. He accepted the offer and we exchanged phone numbers. A week later I was invited over to their apartment for *shabes*. This was the beginning of a productive and warm relationship. (personal communication)

Audacity is an indispensable part of fieldwork.

Some hasidic groups present special problems because of their relative isolation and their desire to disconnect themselves from the outside world. So they are discrete enough as a unit for study but alas quite unwilling to be the subject of study. Even those who are relatively open are reluctant, at best, to cooperate fully with a project whose aim is solely to enhance scientific knowledge. "Arranging an interview was one thing," writes Belcove-Shalin in her essay in this volume, "The real challenge was directing my informants toward the subjects of interest to me. The problem that dogged me throughout my fieldwork was the Hasidim's negative perception of me as someone radically different from themselves. For Hasidim, I was a *goyish Yid* (gentile Jew)—someone viewed with a combination of contempt and

[15]

incredulity." Fortunately for Belcove-Shalin, being classified as an *amorets* or religious ignoramus allowed her to ask questions about beliefs that an insider could not pose without running the risk of being labeled an *epikores* or nonbeliever. Still, it wasn't the anthropologist who gained acceptance within this group. It was the potential convert to an Orthodox way of life. Hasidim are not alone in objecting to being studied by anthropologists. In his essay on his research on Jewish family clubs, Mitchell writes:

> To be "studied" is seen by some as demeaning: that one is being treated as an object rather than as a human being. I occasionally ran into this type of resistance, especially when I tried to gain access to family social events and was turned away because some family members didn't want to be "studied." Family affairs, including meetings of family clubs, were generally considered private activities where relatives could relax and have fun. The presence of a researcher, I was once told, would be "a damper" on the festivities.

In establishing an initial rapport with informants, ethnographers frequently use "impression management," that is, they foster an image of who they are and what they are doing in the community. The "line" they give may sometimes be a critical element in dispelling mistrust, particularly during early stages of the research. "Impression management" may be useful as a technique in starting field research, but it cannot guarantee the success of the project. Ultimately, the ethnographic encounter is a meeting of two people attempting to come to terms with each other.[9] Indeed, the very success of a field research project ultimately stems from the quality of the relationship established between the ethnographer and his chief informants, more so than any other factor, including prior familiarity with the culture. There are some who would argue otherwise. Samuel Heilman (1980) cites an example of how his own familiarity with Jewish liturgy enabled him to recognize the implicit meaning behind certain synagogue behavior. Heilman argues that an observer who lacked such a background would not have retrieved this data by questioning informants, since they could only convey the explicit meaning of their behavior. The essays in this volume suggest a counterargument: for anthropological fieldwork, lack of prior familiarity is the kind of vice that can readily become a virtue. It causes gaffes and potential breeches in the subject-object relationship that, when worked through and resolved, become extremely helpful in interpreting a culture. Moreover, lack of prior knowledge places the ethnographer in a relationship to his informants very much like that of an apprentice to a master, and this "apprenticeship" has a crucial impact on the quality of the study as an emerging dialogue between two views of the world—the ethnographer's and the informant's.

Several essays (those by Belcove-Shalin, Kugelmass, and Myerhoff) indicate the ethical dilemmas inherent in doing Jewish ethnography. Given recent discussions in anthropology on the ethics of fieldwork, particularly fieldwork conducted on minority groups by members of the white middle class, it may be useful for us all to recognize that ethical problems always come with the turf. Research on human subjects is a tricky business, no matter how closely related the subject may be to the researcher. Indeed, the ethical dilemmas may be exacerbated in the study of "one's own" culture, if only because the ethnographer assumes that there is little need to be vigilant in protecting the rights of people he sees as belonging to his "own" culture. Jonathan Boyarin, for example, recalls: "As a student of anthropology, I learned that 'natives' do not always want to be studied. I reasoned that if I concentrate on Jewish culture, no one will accuse me of cultural imperialism." And yet most Jewish ethnographers working among Hasidim, for example, disguise the intent of their work by at least feigning an interest beyond scientific inquiry. According to Belcove-Shalin, "Hasidim believe that Judaism cannot be viewed objectively nor can it be understood through rational study alone [consequently] it was only after I encouraged . . . their belief that one day I might become more observant that they began to take me seriously and open the door to me." Would a non-Jewish ethnographer feel comfortable in disguising his real motivations in quite the same way? Probably not. A non-Jew would probably assume that the distance between his own and his informant's culture was too vast. Nor would he or she be likely to be offered the chance.

For the most part, the ethnographic encounter generates the idea that Clifford Geertz (1968) critiques as a "common moral community" that enables the separate agendas of the ethnographer and informants to succeed. When groups know that they are being studied, they try to exert some influence over the observer and they often expect something in return—whether material goods, gifts, affection, attention, confirmation, or recognition. In the tug of war that sometimes occurs, the anthropologist may sometimes find herself using the very same strategies she has observed her informants using on others. This is all

[17]

the more possible when their common ethnicity establishes certain "familial" bonds. Here is a description of my own efforts to get a reluctant chief informant to participate in the making of a documentary film:

> As an anthropologist I might have had reservations about interfering in the life of an informant, pressuring him to do what he so adamantly refused to do; it wasn't the anthropologist who pressured, it was the part of me that felt like "family." I felt justified in crossing certain bounds of professional propriety since I felt like I was apprenticing in the "family business" of finagling God, Jewish relief organizations, and city agencies. Sacks's uncooperativeness was a test of my new-found skills against an arch finagler.

Sometimes the demands informants make on the ethnographer can be as much of a nuisance as the anthropologist's demands on informants. Groups may have a proprietary interest in the person conducting the study. How does the ethnographer establish the boundaries between herself and her informants? If an anthropologist becomes a member of a minyan (the ten adult Jewish men who constitute a ritual quorum) or is active in a senior citizens' center where his presence comes to be counted on, how does he arrange his time to meet other needs—including leisure? Moreover, how does she pull away from the community altogether to pursue other projects? In her essay Barbara Myerhoff relates how she encountered this dilemma each time she and the director of the film "Number Our Days" returned to visit the senior citizens' center in Venice, California: "And there is always their anger if we have stayed away too long, accusations of infidelity (who had replaced them in our affections? Now that we were 'rich and famous,' did we no longer need them?) The rush of grateful familiarity and sense of belonging, always accompanied by floods of guilt. We are children again eager for their approval, achingly imperfect and vulnerable." Nor is guilt the only factor operating here. Anthropological studies are remarkably open-ended. As Myerhoff notes, "And for me, the anthropologist, there is always the problem of having missed information as well as people whenever I am away. It is only our monographs that end. The lives of our subjects perdure after we have stopped looking and listening." Belcove-Shalin encountered a comical side to the dilemma of separating oneself from one's informant's designs when she had to ward off the good intentions of an informant matchmaker. Upon reviewing the written request she had made to present at an audience with the Bobover rebbe, the matchmaker advised, "You've forgotten the most important thing . . . to find a husband!" In such cases, the entire enthnographic enterprise becomes a peculiar tug of war in which neither side plays entirely above board. Is dissembling legitimate, if it is the only way in which a group will allow the presence of an ethnographer? My own feeling is that context defines the level of significance; there are times when dissembling is legitimate and there are times when it is not. Sh. Ansky, the father of Jewish ethnography, in his ethnographic expedition to the Jewish towns in the Ukraine from 1912 to 1914 made extensive use of deception in order to gather certain kinds of information. For example, elderly women who recited various charms, incantations, or other spells against the "evil-eye" or various sorts of disorders were forbidden to disclose their formulas even to close family members, because they believed that to pass such information on to someone who does not believe in their efficacy would cause the charm to lose its potency and might even cause a deleterious effect on the reciter. A member of the expedition, Avrom Rekhtman, described how the prohibition was circumvented:

> We made use of various means and ways to elicit from the excorcists their incantations. Often one of us would feign illness, lie in bed and send for an excorcist. Sometimes they used wax divination, sometimes they excorcized an evil eye or the like. One of us would sit in a corner and as much as he could catch, he would note the woman's incantations. The photographer, however, could almost always take pictures.
>
> Many times Ansky would go to one of these women and complain to her about his terrible luck; he would relate that he had previously been a wealthy man, a merchant and now he was impoverished, destitute, without any means of eking out a living. He had, therefore, come to her, so she should teach him some of her incantations, give him some of her remedies and amulets, so that through them he might be able to earn a living. Ansky, at the same time, let them know that he wasn't expecting these things gratis, but was prepared to pay a small sum. Ansky's quivering voice and simple words usually brought results. The women let themselves be convinced—showing pity and seeing earnings, too, they tried to haggle for more. Finally coming to terms, Ansky wrote down the incantations they related to him. (1958:291–92)

Was Ansky correct to behave this way? I think so. But in using this method the ethnographer needs to take great care not to cause damage to his informants—a possibility all the greater when dealing

[19]

with a literate culture whose members may read the published work. Moreover, insensitive behavior of a single ethnographer, whether a flagrant violation of traditional custom or an indiscrete disclosure of confidential information, might have very serious consequences for future research among certain groups.

Fortunately, there is more to ethnography than problems of an ethical or methodological nature. The anthropological encounter does at times bridge the gap between two worlds. Not only did Mitchell learn a different style of speech interaction than he had been prepared for growing up in New England, but, "Perhaps of even more significance, I learned something my Jewish informants and their families have known for centuries: how it feels to be a dangerous outsider." Jewish ethnographers, too, experience a bridging of the gap between two cultures while studying other Jewish groups. As Myerhoff notes, "The elders have somehow become our touchstones, the fixed and reliable planets by which we navigate our lives and morality. After a particularly materialistic and vulgar bar mitzvah or a skeptical, shallowly felt religious service, I find myself rushing back to the center, to reground myself in their changeless, fully lived, deeply embedded form of Jewish practice." Boyarin suggests another byproduct of anthropological research that stands him in good stead for his current participation as a nonobserver, that is, as a member of a neighborhood shul: "Anthropology has helped me to come to belong at the shul: to withhold my opinions when it seems necessary, without feeling the guilt of self-compromise; to accept instruction and gentle reprimands with good humor, to believe it is worthwhile preserving something that might otherwise be lost."

For informants, too, ethnography has a special meaning, particularly when the products of the research reach an audience. One curious feature about research among American Jewry is that the subjects of the studies are likely consumers of the finished products. Whereas anthropologists generally disguise the names and identities of their informants in order to protect their identities and rights to privacy, Myerhoff felt later that having done so in her book *Number our Days* (1979) was a disservice to her informants. Indeed, Myerhoff's reasoning is that she had to play a different role with these elderly people than simply one of scientific observer. In working with the elderly, the anthropologist "is a witness, must bear witness when no one else is available." She eventually discovered that informants "would rather be seen than be invisible, even if they disagreed with the portrait."

[20]

Myerhoff notes one informant's attitude toward the fictional name she had been given in the book *Number Our Days:* "She could remain anonymous or call herself Rebekkah Goldman since she could not write, publish, and distribute her own interpretation of herself. Thus whenever I brought a stranger or guest to the Center, she introduced herself not by her real name but as Shmuel Goldman's widow, Rebekkah, so she would be 'recognized.'" Concerned about their own mortality, some elderly informants are quite eager to see their names in print or their faces on the screen. Literate informants create peculiar situations. Indeed, I sometimes found myself almost cast by my informants in the role of scribe:

> Sacks is an avid reader. He subscribes to some of the magazines in which I've published articles. He listens to the radio while he works and he tunes in when I do broadcasts. He has a strong critical sense and he says what he thinks. As he has been my main informant, most of what I write is about him. And I increasingly have the feeling that he uses me as his personal scribe. If I miss one of his witticisms or anecdotes, he fills me in later. Mrs. Miroff, my other key informant, does the same thing. Each Saturday she provides me with a running commentary on her interaction with the "bums," the street people she feeds, and she frequently opens with a teaser: "I have a story to give you could write a book. It's a story of a life."

There are times, though, when discretion is important. Still weary from the surveillance and persecution they experienced during the McCarthy era, members of the left-wing residential coop Anita Schwartz studied are reluctant to have their identities revealed in print, lest they suffer political repercussions. But whether or not real names are used, the fieldworker's presence, as Richard Schechner notes, gives "the society an additional significance to itself and to others: a sense that someone else is interested, is listening, and, consequently, an encouragement for people within the society to be reflexive" (1977:80).

What, one might ask, could anthropology contribute to the study of American Jewry? Most Jewish anthropologists are not trained in Judaism's great tradition—the various rabbinic commentaries on the Torah. North American Jewish studies departments rarely have anthropologists on the full-time faculty. I find this to be a particularly disturbing fact, given Robert Alter's (1982) assertion that the scholarship of American Jewry is becoming America's Jewish "culture."

Just how correct he is is evident by the place that *Number Our Days* has assumed in American Jewish life. Venice, California, has become a place of pilgrimage for those familiar with the book, and the community center in which the study was based has received considerable financial support as a result of its current fame. Yet from the standpoint of most Jewish Studies programs, anthropology is relevant only insofar as it generates certain models that can be used for literary criticism. Jewish Studies is a text-oriented discipline: it has a long way to go before it can accept culture, rather than Culture, as a proper domain of study. Should anthropology meet the challenge of its near exclusion from Jewish Studies by turning inward and studying the lore of rabbinic texts? Joshua Trachtenberg, Hayyim Schauss, Theodor Gaster, and Raphael Patai are all practitioners of this sort of anthropological research. Though perfectly fine, these are studies of Judaism, rather than Jewry. Let the experts on rabbinic lore and archival research do their work. Anthropology's domain is in the field, and it is there that its strength lies. Anthropology looks to the little tradition. It seeks culture not in the minds of the few but in the lives of the many. Moreover, no field can match the intensity of anthropological fieldwork, nor for that matter the very close relationships that it engenders between an ethnographer and her or his key informants. Consequently the studies that anthropologists generate on contemporary American Jewry are significant documents whose value can only increase with time. Riv-Ellen Prell's study of ritual humor and ritual change in a Havurah is a case in point. The study pinpoints the tensions inherent in religious beliefs as social changes, particularly equality between the sexes, are integrated into religious practices. Her work can be looked at as a reading of a culture at a given point in time, as well as a valuable deciphering of the contradictory sentiments that go hand in hand with religious change. The same is true for Anita Schwartz's work on the left-wing coops. Through years of fieldwork observation, we can witness cultural change and the peculiar forces at work within individual families that cause people to veer off in different directions. And the value of an ethnography as a document of a culture at a point in time is true for Fran Baskin's study of the ritual behavior of Soviet Jewry. How will these groups look in the future? We don't really know. But perhaps we may want to know in the future how they looked in the past, so that we might better understand how they got to their current state.

There are many stories within this volume. Although some of them are presented in a more self-reflexive way than others, there is every-where here a sense of quest, an interest in learning more about Juda-ism (Belcove-Shalin; Myerhoff; Prell), of rediscovering one's personal past (Boyarin), or of trying to understand personal identity by looking, as Richard Schechner suggests, at people who are simultaneously "me" and "not me." Belcove-Shalin describes the hasidic synagogue she attended as "a threatening and difficult milieu for someone with a secular background like mine." She sometimes found herself being "on the verge of tears . . . as a Jew feeling so utterly alien in another Jewish environment." For their part, the Hasidim looked at her, too, "as someone radically different from themselves." Young middle-class researchers studying the elderly poor, a cool New England Wasp studying hot Jewish family clubs, an observant Jew really interested in Yemeni Jews studying Yemeni Muslims, a feminist within a male-dominated minyan—these are all confrontations between people who are simultaneously "me" and "not me." Prell notes in describing a Havurah minyan:

> I watched these events with volatile emotions. The anthropologist in me was delighted at finding rites of reversals. The feminist in me was sensitive to women's responses. They laughed less heartily. Some looked very uncomfortable. Only a few commented under their breaths. The pain and anger I heard subsequently made it even clearer to me that I could not uncritically see the apparent fun of the key participants. These events were painful for half the room. Women were not included. Had I been a member, I would also have sat on the sidelines, silenced and awkward. As the anthropologist of the group, I had often identified very closely with the most powerful men of the group, who had dominated the joking. They had much to tell me and I was an eager listener. But I was also a Jewish woman, and had to realize that I would have had none of the power necessary to dominate the Torah and the humor that morning.

In every case, either explicit or implicit, an encounter is made with a "not me" in which the "me" seeking to carry through the study must somehow assume the role of the "not me." Shalom Staub in his essay reflects on how very complex that new identity can be:

> In the presence of Yemeni Muslims and Jews together, my own status shifted in ways it never had with either Muslims or Jews alone. Al-though the Yemeni Jews were puzzled by my presence at first, I quickly became their confidant. Our speaking Hebrew was a private commu-

nication, and they revealed attitudes that at times openly contradicted the appearances they fostered in their conversations in Arabic. It was a confidance that left me uncomfortable, as if I were betraying the Yemeni Muslims, who had taken me within the community. When Qa'id served the broth, I knew I had to make a public choice between honoring my host and demonstrating my observance of *kashrut*.

And it is precisely the coming to terms with this "not me" that constitutes the dramatic tension within the fieldwork study. As Myerhoff notes: "A new creation is constituted by two points of view examining one life. It has its own integrity but should not be mistaken for the spontaneous, unframed life-as-lived person who existed before the interview began. This could be called an "ethno-person," the third person who is born by virtue of the collusion between interlocutor and subject." Just how interwoven the identities of ethnographer and informant can become is demonstrated by the following discussion with my chief informant, Moishe Sacks, concerning who will say what at the discussion following the screening of the documentary film that was based on our work together:

A few days before a sneak preview of the film in New York, I asked Sacks what he planned to say to the audience when he gets up to speak. "That's easy. I'll just tell them the story of the Khofets Khayim who was traveling from town to town with a *balegule* [coachman]. After hearing the Khofets Khayim give the same speech in town after town, the *balegule* says to him, 'You know what you do isn't so hard. At the next town let me do what you do and you be the *balegule*.' So they switch places. When they come to the town, someone comes to the 'Khofets Khayim' and asks him a very difficult question on the Talmud. The 'Khofets Khayim' has no idea how to answer the question. So he thinks for a moment, then he answers the man, 'You know that question is so easy that I'm not even going to bother with it. I'll just let this simple coachman over here answer it.' So you see, if anyone asks me something that I can't answer, I'll just tell them that it's too simple for me to bother with and I'll tell them they should ask you." That night when I was asked to say a few words following the screening, I stole Sacks's lines from him. I told the audience the story of the Khofets Khayim and the coachman and then I introduced Sacks as the simple coachman. Never one to be upstaged, Sacks later told me that he knew that I would do that and that's why he told me the story.

As complex as the relationships are that stem from the ethnographic encounter, the tension within them is critical for the success of the study: the ethnographer must strive to comprehend another person or culture. If there is no desire to create a third person—what Schechner refers to as the "not-not-me"—there is no dramatic tension, there is no attempt to understand another, and consequently the situation is not an ethnographic one. Replication rather than ethnography is the result. As Boyarin notes regarding a possible fieldwork project close to home: "I doubt it would be the Eighth Street shul. There, I am trying to belong. I have little desire to retain the distance that an anthropologist needs in order to see a situation clearly." One of the principle lessons of ethnography is that it forces a confrontation with the self by holding up a mirror to the observer and forcing him to see his own culture with the critical eye of another. Mitchell, for example, writes about the peculiar impact his Jewish informants had upon him:

> It seemed as if I could do nothing right and that nothing was sacred; if they had a view, it existed to be expressed. Even my own cultural background did not escape critical commentary. Once, in an interview on Jewish weddings, I commented that the giftgiving of money was different from my family's custom:
>
> MRS. X: "Well, you're not Jewish, or no?"
> WM: "No."
> MRS. X: "No, then that's the difference. The style is entirely different! I know in your case they usually bring gifts in their display."
> WM: "That's right."
> MRS. X: "And everyone brings a piece of junk, and by the time you get through, half the stuff is thrown out. You don't even use it. Am I right?"

Besides discomfort, the realization of the existence and power of another cultural universe also generates curiosity. What better way is there to realize another possibility then to play at being another, to dance with Yemenis as Staub did, and for just that brief moment to act as if one were indeed someone else. And yet, for an anthropologist, that realization can only be fleeting. She does return. And by returning, a statement is made about whose story this is. From the anthropologist's viewpoint, it is her story, her coming to terms with Otherness. But from the natives' point of view, the study should tell their story. All the greater is the struggle if the project becomes well known. As Myerhoff relates concerning the response of center members to the film's Academy Award, "Everyone was happy about the Academy Award and the public validation of them it offered. But

[25]

Lynn [the director] and I were urged not to become too inflated about it. They had, after all, told us on the first day we began filming that if we did our work well, we would get an Oscar. It was clear that we were only the recorders, and it was their lives, their survival, that was the material to be acclaimed. (And of course if we had failed to get the award, it would have been just as clear whose fault that was!)."

In reality the successes and failures of ethnography are always joint responsibilities. After all, ethnography is all about dialogue: the story told by informants through the prodding of the ethnographer and then the story retold by the anthropologist.

In an informally organized community without an enforceable normative code of behavior, each Jewish subgroup is allowed to tell its own story about who it is and how it sees itself within the mainstream of Jewish tradition. This is no less true for anthropologists as a group. Little wonder then that when the two communities meet they engage in a lengthy dialogue aimed as much at identifying the other as identifying the self. For both, the presence of an Other is crucial in making that definition possible. That dialogue is anthropology.

This volume is divided into three sections. Section one, "The Search" (the essays by Kugelmass, Boyarin, Belcove-Shalin) examines the complexity of the anthropological endeavor, particularly when it is intertwined with the search for an authentic self; the essays of section two, "Subcultures" (the essays of Schwartz, Markowitz, Oring, Fredman Cernea, and Prell), which explore a wide range of American Jewish subcultures, are less concerned with the self than they are with the relationship between individual subcultures and the larger Jewish community; the essays of section three, "Us and Them" (the essays of Mitchell, Staub, Myerhoff, and Kugelmass), explore the relationship that develops between ethnographers and informants and its impact on the identities of both.

The system of transliterating Yiddish and Hebrew words in these essays is loosely based on the YIVO system with allowance made for more readily recognized spellings for certain terms and holy days. Although preference is generally given to the Ashkenazic pronunciation of Hebrew terms, in the case of those essays which pertain to speech communities that use either Sephardic or modern Hebrew pronunciation, the system of transliteration reflects the actual usage.

Notes

1. Readers should consult Marshall Sklare's various readers on American Jewry. For specifically sociological studies, see Heilman (1982).
2. Luis de Torres, the interpreter who accompanied Columbus on his first voyage, was baptized just before setting sail. Marranos apparently served as *conquistadores* under Cortès (*Encyclopedia Judaica,* 2:808).
3. The use of Jewish characters and Yiddish words on television is particularly common, as evidenced by such hit dramatic shows as "Hill Street Blues" and "L.A. Law." In his description of the film industry, the writer David McLintock relates the following: "Contrary to popular notions about bland financiers, most important executive positions in the entertainment business today are occupied by high-spirited, entrepreneurial Jews who emigrated to Hollywood from New York and other points in the East and Midwest. And Yiddish remains the second language of Hollywood" (1982:49).
4. This is a particularly ironic development given how the event itself was treated in the American press at the time it occurred. According to David Wyman: "Strong popular pressure for action would have brought a much fuller government commitment to rescue and would have produced it sooner. Several factors hampered the growth of public pressure. Among them were anti-Semitism and anti-immigration attitudes, both widespread in American society in that era and both entrenched in Congress; the mass media's failure to publicize Holocaust news, even though the wire services and other news sources made most of the information available to them; the near silence of the Christian churches and almost all of their leadership; the indifference of most of the nation's political and intellectual leaders; and the President's failure to speak out on the issue" (1984:x–xi).
5. See for example the *New York Times,* 25 June 1985 coverage of a conference of reform rabbis.
6. The refutation of religion as blind superstition was a prominent part of the political and cultural program of many Jewish radical groups, particularly the anarchists who were active at the turn of the century. But even they, their beliefs of internationalism notwithstanding, had wanted, as Irving Howe notes, "to keep within the familiar bounds of immigrant culture, for even when scoffed at on the East Side, it was still the place where they felt most at home. The great world they dreamed of conquering was actually the world they were least prepared to visit" (1976:105).
7. Ethnicity, like all aspects of culture, is constantly evolving. Michael Fischer, for example, talks about ethnicity as "something reinvented and reinterpreted in each generation" (1986:195).
8. Although Jews in various parts of the world, including some Jews in Eastern and Central Europe, have adapted quite well to living in rural areas. See, for example, descriptions of rural Jews in prewar Poland in Kugelmass (1980).
9. For additional discussion of this subject, see Shaffir (1985).

REFERENCES

Alter, Robert. 1982. "The Jew Who Didn't Get Away: On the Possibility of an American Jewish Culture." *Judaism* 31:274–86.

Borowitz, Eugene. 1973. *The Masks Jews Wear: The Self-Deception of American Jewry*. New York: Simon & Shuster.

Cohen, Abner. 1974. *Urban Ethnicity*. New York: Tavistock Press.

Cohen, Steven Martin. 1983. "The 1981–1982 National Survey of American Jews." In *American Jewish Yearbook* 83:89–110. Philadelphia: The American Jewish Committee and the Jewish Publication Society.

Dash Moore, Deborah. 1987. "The Construction of Community: Jewish Migration and Ethnicity in the United States." In *The Jews of North America,* ed. Moses Rischin. Detroit: Wayne State University Press, 105–17.

Encyclopedia Judaica. 1972. Jerusalem: Keter Publishing House.

Fischer, Michael. 1986. "Ethnicity and the Art of Memory." In *Writing Culture,* ed. James Clifford and George Marcus. Berkeley and Los Angeles: University of California Press, 194–233.

Foster, George, and Robert Kemper. 1980. "Anthropological Fieldwork in Cities." In *Urban Life,* ed. George Gmelch and Walter Zenner. New York: St. Martin's Press, 315–28.

Gaster, Theodor. 1955. *Customs and Folkways of Jewish Life*. New York: Apollo Editions.

Geertz, Clifford. 1968. "Thinking as a Moral Act: Ethical Dimensions of Anthropological Field Work in the New States." *Antioch Review* 28, 2:139–58.

Gittelson, Natalie. 1984. "American Jews Rediscover Orthodoxy." *New York Times,* Sunday Magazine, 30 September.

Goldberg, Harvey. 1987. *Judaism Viewed from Within and from Without*. Albany: S.U.N.Y. Press.

Heilman, Samuel. 1980. "Jewish Sociologist: Native as Stranger." *American Sociologist* 15, 2:100–8.

———. 1981. "The Sociology of American Jewry: The Last Ten Years." *Annual Review of Sociology* 8:135–60.

Howe, Irving. 1976. *World of Our Fathers*. New York: Touchstone.

Kirshenblatt-Gimblett, Barbara. 1987. "The Folk Culture of Jewish Immigrant Communities." In *The Jews of North America,* ed. Moses Rischin. Detroit: Wayne State University Press, 79–94.

Kugelmass, Jack. 1980. *Native Aliens: The Jews of Poland as a Middleman Minority*. Ann Arbor: University Microfilms.

Liebman, Charles. 1974. "The Religion of American Jews." In *The Jew in American Society,* ed. Marshall Sklare. New York: Behrman House, 222–52.

McClintock, David. 1982. *Indecent Exposure*. New York: Dell.

Myerhoff, Barbara. 1979. *Number Our Days*. New York: Dutton.

Patai, Raphael. 1977. *The Jewish Mind*. New York: Jason Aronson.

Rekhtman, Avrom. 1958. *Yidishe etnografye un folklor*. Buenos Aires: YIVO.

Ruby, Jay. 1982. *A Crack in the Mirror*. Philadelphia: University of Pennsylvania Press.

Schauss, Hayyim. 1970. *Guide to Jewish Holy Days*. New York: Schocken Books.

Schechner, Richard. 1982. "Restoration of Behavior." In *A Crack in the Mirror,* ed. Jay Ruby. Philadelphia: Temple University Press, 39–81.

Shaffir, William. 1985. "Some Reflections on Approaches to Fieldwork in Hassidic Communities." *Jewish Journal of Sociology* 22, 2:115–34.

Sklare, Marshall. 1974. *The Jew in American Society*. New York: Behrman House.

Slobin, Mark. 1987. "Fiddler off the Roof: Klezmer Music as an Ethnic Musical Style." In *The Jews of North America*, ed. Moses Rischin. Detroit: Wayne State University Press, 95–104.

Trachtenberg, Joshua. 1961. *Jewish Magic and Superstition*. Cleveland and New York: Meridian Books.

Waxman, Chaim. 1983. *America's Jews in Transition*. Philadelphia: Temple University Press.

Weinreich, Max. 1980. *The History of the Yiddish Language*. Chicago: University of Chicago Press.

Wyman, David. 1984. *The Abandonment of the Jews*. New York: Pantheon Books.

SECTION ONE

The Search

[1]

Between Two Worlds: Notes on the Celebration of Purim among New York Jews, March 1985

Jack Kugelmass

It is Wednesday afternoon. The holiday of Purim begins this evening and I have made no plans to attend a reading of the *Megillat Esther* [Book of Esther]. My own shul, or perhaps I should say the synagogue I am studying, is in the South Bronx, and for reasons of safety the Megillah reading there is held only on the following morning. Since I attend synagogue more for research than pleasure, I derive some comfort from knowing that I am free to do as I please with my evening. For the moment I have other concerns. A coworker is producing a special Purim issue of the YIVO's newsletter. The institute is one of a diminishing number of remnants of the *haskole* or enlightenment, the great East European thrust toward the end of the nineteenth century to create a secular Judaism. My colleague, a young filmmaker and a member of a well-known Yiddishist family, is busy with the Yiddish section of the newsletter but he needs someone else to write the English parodies. I tell him I am too busy, but even as I say the words, ideas mysteriously flow from my mouth. He pushes me into a chair and rolls over an ancient typewriter. I promise only a few minutes of my time. An hour later, I am still writing, even though my colleague begs me to stop because the building is about to close and we are in danger of being locked inside. Somehow the thought of remaining here overnight amid the documentary remains of East European Jewry does not appeal to me. There is talk of ghosts. A former researcher now deceased, who long boasted of his exploits as a fighter in the French Foreign Legion and as a lover on the streets of Paris, always struck me as a restless soul: a likely candidate to return from the grave. I grab my coat and leave. Once again I think about *Megillat Esther;* but by now something in me has stirred, perhaps the anthropologist who is becoming increasingly interested in the ethnography of American Jewry and is therefore curious to know how Jews celebrate a holiday that for most hardly figures in the hierarchy of significant ritual observances. Or perhaps I have simply been seduced by the spirit of the holiday. Whatever the cause, I am determined to find some place where I can listen to the reading.

In this city of two million Jews, there are many readings to choose from. Many waves of migration beginning almost at the founding of New Amsterdam have given rise to a complex and highly variegated community in which there are many ways of being Jewish and many ways of celebrating Jewish festivals. A colleague has invited me to visit the Reform Temple he is studying, now temporarily located in a Lutheran church. I can still visualize from his descriptions the *sukkah* built inside the church's nave. The community is desperately trying to reestablish itself after some internal friction resulted in the defection of half the congregation and the selling of its former sanctuary. It now faces the uneasy prospect of recruitment and self-definition in a neighborhood in which Orthodoxy not only has gained the upper hand, but by drawing upon its resurgence within the larger context of American Jewry is becoming increasingly militant and contemptuous of Reform's innovations in rituals. The festival has already been billed as a major celebration of Judaism, an affirmation of the temple's Jewishness. I am interested. After all, there is a larger drama going on here concerning the way American Jewry defines itself, the nature of *minhag America,* the unique and highly flexible approach to religious law that American Jews abide by.[1] But the issue is much too serious for my mood. And having recently visited the temple, I am anxious to see something new. A friend suggests I go to Anshei Chessed, the home of the so-called West Side minyan, the "who's who" of the young New York Jewish intelligentsia. "To be a member," someone once commented, only partly in jest, "you have to have at least one published book." The reading, I am told, is followed by a klezmer revival band concert and hasidic-style dancing. I am reluctant to attend. There is the question of money: tickets are ten dollars. I check my pocket and realize that attending will mean yet another trip to an instant cash machine: a sobering thought. And there is the question of

[34]

identity and commitment: participants are expected to display an un-self-conscious expression of Jewishness, which I seem unable to affect. It never feels right. I rule out Anshei Chessed. It is not a wise decision, because I learn later that the minyan members produced an elaborate Purim play. In accordance with folk tradition, the plays and much of the behavior surrounding Purim have strong parodic qualities, including role reversals: the *Purim rov* [rabbi] in traditional Ashkenazic communities was a clown, elected rabbi for the day, who presided over mock ceremonies. Combining the more ancient parodic traditions and its own iconoclasm, Anshei Chessed's Purim play is produced by a psychoanalyst: the story of Queen Esther and her uncle Mordechai is retold with distinctly Freudian connotations. This year, fortunately, the play is to be videotaped by an ABC cameraman, an indication that American Jewry's intelligentsia has begun to take its culture seriously. Robert Alter (1982) has suggested that without its own language, American Jewish culture is the product of its literati. But in this case the literati reflect a larger cultural pattern because the play is one of countless folk dramas performed by elite and nonelite alike. At any rate I am grateful for the videotape because I can see the play another time.

I recall an invitation from another colleague to visit his shul on the Lower East Side. The offer has been made many times since he joined the synagogue, but each time I have declined. Tonight's the night, I think to myself. I hurry to the subway, anxious as time slips away, push people aside as I exit, then race to a tall, narrow, beige brick building that stands propped between two Lower East Side tenements.

I arrive just as the *megillah* reading begins. Far too humble to attract more than a score of people, the tiny shul creates a sense of intimacy despite the scattered seating of the congregants, and a feeling of fullness despite the small numbers. Like so many old synagogues in this area, this one too wears its age poorly: exposed plaster and peeling paint overwhelm the decor. I take a seat next to my colleague and listen for the cues from the other congregants for when to stamp my feet at the sound of Haman's name. My colleague pays careful attention to the reading, but I do not. Instead I watch the others and consider who they are. A few are his friends. Not Orthodox themselves, they have become regulars at his urging. Others he has met in the shul. More and more, he is beginning to resemble them, even to look and talk like them. While they were raised to be observant Jews, he has chosen to be one. I wonder what will come of it. A book perhaps. But will it be a book about an anthropologist's encounter with Orthodoxy in a marginal Orthodox area, or a book about becoming an Orthodox Jew? Later, I realize that the latter is far more likely than the former. That realization occurs on another holy day, this one, the second to the last day of Passover. We are invited to a luncheon at a local rabbi's apartment on the Lower East Side. The man lives on the sixth floor. When we enter the lobby my colleague wheels his son's baby carriage past the elevator and stops at the staircase. He suggests that we divide the task of carrying the baby carriage up the stairs. I respond with a sharp silent glance that communicates much: I do not intend to exert myself for what I see as religious extremism. He carries the carriage up the stairs. It suddenly strikes me how vulnerable we are, those of us who study Jews. We approach them somewhat naively as academics. But they are like a vortex, determined to suck us in so they might see their own future in our eyes.

My colleague and his wife have arranged the kiddush following the *megillah* reading. When they encourage us to break our fast, I realize that I have already done so many times today. Like most of my non-Orthodox colleagues, I do not observe the Fast of Esther, but rather use it as an occasion to distribute and devour humentashen.

The Day of Purim

The following morning I spend at the Intervale Jewish Center in the Bronx. I arrive with a box of humentashen, having been warned by the shul's leader that now that his bakery has closed, he will not be bringing any. The baker asks where I purchased them. I realize the question relates to whether animal fat or butter was used in making them. I assure him they are kosher. He accepts the gift but I feel hurt that he would ask: it reveals a certain lack of trust between us. Only a handful of men are present. Thinking that food will not be served, most congregants have not bothered to come. We read the *megillah* and spin the *gragers* [noisemakers] but it is a rather sad Purim, all of us painfully aware that time is not on the side of this last outpost of Jewish life in the South Bronx.

I return to my office in Manhattan, where I receive some pointers from an Orthodox secretary at YIVO on where to see costumed children delivering *shalekhmones* (the fruits and candies that religious Jews exchange on the day of Purim). She suggests I wear a yarmulke "to fit in better." When I pull one out of my pocket and place it on my head, she begins to giggle. How strange I must appear to her, masquerading as an observant Jew. How strange, too, that having long ago abandoned her disdain for non-Orthodox men, she has now become my coconspirator, teaching me how to infiltrate her world. Only later do I learn that as a non-Hasid and a daughter of Polish Jews, she too is an outsider in Williamsburg. I learn this only through a conversation I have with her about television. She wants to know what I watch and then reveals she has one at home, too: "I keep it in the bedroom. This way if a neighbor comes by, they don't need to know I have one. I wouldn't say no. But I don't need to advertise it also." "What do you watch?" I ask. "*Dynasty* I like. And I like *The Newlywed Game.*"

I head out to Williamsburg, the home of the seemingly reclusive Hungarian Hasidim. With me is an Israeli who has come to America to make a film on Yiddish for the BBC. We emerge from the elevated train and, seeing the many bearded Jews surrounded by a cityscape of shop signs in Yiddish and Hebrew, my Israeli friend comments jokingly: "There are only Jews in America!" We spot some children in costume and begin to take photographs. Someone advises us to head to Lee Avenue. We do so and see scores of hasidic children in costume: bears, witches, hump backs, trolls, Arabs, Ronald Reagan, policemen, miniature Hasidim, Torah scrolls, Disney characters. Perhaps, on this day, we will not be conspicuous in this forest of long black coats, with their foliage of fur-trimmed hats. We follow the crowds along Lee Avenue, photographing as we go. Some people move away from the camera; here and there someone warns us not to take pictures: "It's not permitted." A few pose. Others ask why we are shooting: "For somebody or just for yourself?" "For myself," I reply. "Good. *A gut Purim* to you." Just like other Jews, I think to myself: two opinions even here, in this ultra-Orthodox community.

I continue photographing. A young Hasid in costume, holding a large wad of dollar bills, approaches and asks for money. The proceeds, I later learn, are for charitable work here and in Israel. He is very aggressive in his approach, the result of a deeply rooted Jewish belief that since the giving of alms saves one from death, charity is a gift of sorts from the recipient to the donor. The costumes are apparently closely linked to soliciting alms. Jews believe that the highest form of charity is when neither the giver nor the recipient know one another; the masks promote anonymity. But charity on Purim has a special meaning. Haman, the ancient persecutor of Persian Jews, offered the king a large sum of money for the privilege of killing the Jews. The giving of charity is an inversion of that act, a transformation of a profane cause into a holy deed. Later in the evening I will visit the Satmar *besmedresh* (study hall) to witness the rebbe *firn a tish* (conduct a ritual meal). Even the much-cherished voice of a rebbe cannot silence these solicitors, armed to the teeth with zeal, displaying ever-growing wads of bills. Not all who beg do so in the name of others. Outside the Satmar *besmedresh* sits a beggar. Today he is king: all who enter or leave are obliged to greet his outstretched hand with money. Him I avoid, but the young boys with their wads of bills are relentless. I give the one who hounds me two quarters. He pockets the money and stares at the camera: "What kind is it?" "A Minolta." "How much does it cost?" Something deep within causes me to flaunt an extravagance, a gentile's pleasure: "Six hundred." "Six hundred?" The astonishment in his voice betrays the fact that the revelation has had the intended effect. "So it's a professional?" "Yes." "I have a Cannon Program. It's good?" "Yes. It's good." "Where did you buy this, at 47th St.?" "No." "Why not?" "They don't sell it there." The question sounded like an accusation. I guess his thoughts: What kind of Jew buys retail? A real Jew purchases cameras and electronic products from 47th St. Photo, the hasidic discount emporium located in the heart of the hasidic-dominated diamond exchange in midtown Manhattan. Perhaps he thinks I am so deracinated that I lack even this bit of knowledge. And I wonder about him and the community. Why does he have a camera? And such costumes among people who shun television—do the children know anything about the cartoon characters they masquerade? I photograph a husband and wife walking with a large fruit basket for *shalekhmones*. Trailing a few feet behind them is their little girl, clad head to toe in a witch costume.

Later I notice a hasidic family out for a stroll. The woman pushing a baby stroller, as all hasidic women seem to do, greets others, while the man is busy videotaping the children in costume. A non-hasidic Orthodox young man approaches. "Are you here for a magazine or just for yourself?" "Just for myself." "That's good. I suppose you came to take pictures of the burning?" "What burning?" "Burning the Israeli flag! Every year Satmar burns the Israeli flag. I took about ten pictures. Just to document it." The man proudly waves his Instamatic camera in my face, as if I could verify somehow that inside it he has captured a still-flickering flame of heresy in Jewish cultural history, anti-Zionism. A Skverer Hasid I meet later whose apartment is decorated with Israeli "folk art" depicting Jerusalem and the Western Wall would not consider a Satmar for a son-in-law because he has trouble with anyone who would look down on him. "They make a religion out of anti-Zionism." He explains that the protest, although done by extremists, has its merits: "Should a state insist that corpses be defiled with autopsies? Should it allow missionaries to build a campus on Mount Scopus?" I respond with diplomatic silence. The Hasid insists the protest is against the policies of the state, not against its existence. I, however, see it differently: this is a public demonstration. Satmar's protest is probably aimed directly at American Jewish "false gods," the so-called civil religion implicitly guiding American Jewish beliefs and behavior. The sociologist Jonathan Woocher (1985) argues that there are seven elements to that civil religion: among them are charity, mutual aid, a sense that there is an ever-present threat to group survival, the Holocaust, and the centrality of the State of Israel. I, the anthropologist, absorbed in the harmless masquerade of children, missed the serious spectacle of adult men burning a flag in protest. Had I spoken to someone sooner, I too could have documented it. The camera, I realize, sets a barrier between me and this community. Only dialogue will give me entry into their world. Fortunately I am running out of film. And fortunately too, as the folklorist Barbara Kirshenblatt-Gimblett has noted, the "spontaneous" demonstration is an annual event at 3:00 P.M. on the day of Purim. This too I will see another year.

My new acquaintance has no more time for conversation. His ride comes for him and he is on his way back to Boro Park. "If you come tonight to Boro Park, perhaps I will see you," he shouts as the car drives off. Later that night I and a photographer friend stand by the side of an access road to the Brooklyn Queens Expressway and hitch a ride. This is a common way of commuting between the two neighborhoods. We are picked up by a Hasid wearing a plastic fireman's helmet. When we reach Boro Park it is nearly 1:00 A.M. The Hasid drives his other passengers to their destinations. Then, using a bullhorn, he announces to an inebriated pedestrian that he is looking for the Bobov *besmedresh*. The startled pedestrian, it turns out, is the Hasid's brother. He wobbles into the van and slumps into the front passenger seat. The Hasid looks at us and says with a mixture of sarcasm and apology, "Don't mind him. He's a little under the influence." "It's Purim," I respond. "It's O.K. to be stoned." "Oh, I wouldn't call him stoned. He's more like pebbled." Purim is one of the few times each year when drunkenness is prescribed, and the more zealous Hasidim assume the task with such vigor that in a short time they are quite unable to carry themselves and move about only if they are supported by their friends.

Boro Park is the turf of the non-Hungarian hasidic groups, and many ultra-Orthodox non-Hasidim. It is a thriving neighborhood. With its strip of kosher pizza parlors, dairy restaurants, and discount electronic equipment emporia it is less charming and more worldly than Williamsburg. (There are smaller electronic shops in Williamsburg—local places that cater to natives rather than strangers. The only pizza in Williamsburg is served in a drab felafel joint. Watching a Hasid twirling dough in the air may be the only redeeming feature of dining out in the area.) What Boro Park lacks in physical charm is more than made up for by the annual Purim plays performed inside the study houses of the hasidic courts of Munkacz and Bobov. The former boasts a huge new building with a Jerusalem stonelike interior; the latter is held in a drab fifties-style building, its grand new headquarters still under construction (the many failings of the contractor have already made their way into the play). The performance begins well after midnight, only after the completion of the *tish*, the ritual meal over which the rebbe presides, and continues until the early hours of the morning. By then I will have tired of the event, the pushing for a place to stand, the craning of the neck to see above the fur-trimmed hats, and the terrible feeling that my academic Yiddish will not suffice, that I can have only a peek at a culture's innermost presentation of itself.

In Williamsburg I continue along Lee Avenue, alone now, having lost my Israeli friend. Here and there I see young hasidic men in costumes less elaborate than the childrens': a police baton and matching hat, a Mexican bandana, a straw hat. One or two look inebriated. A few Hasidim carry ghetto blasters blaring pop renditions of hasidic and religious music. The same music can be heard emanating from the projects, occupied in this area by Jews more than by blacks and Puerto Ricans. I learn later from a Puerto Rican director of a non-Jewish YMCA about the formula the respective communities have worked out with the city for distributing available public housing. There is room for compromise: Hasidim prefer to live on lower-level floors because they will not ride in elevators on *shabes;* Puerto Ricans believe that

[40]

Hasidim are better able to wield political clout than they are, so having them in the building guarantees better maintenance.

The loud music contributes to the sense of cultural reversal. Now Puerto Rican neighbors are accosted by loud strange-sounding music. Couples accompanied by children are out for a stroll, with pre-packaged parcels of *shalekhmones* wrapped in bright yellow, orange, or green cellophane. I follow them as they head away from the main avenue onto the side streets. Here the beautiful old brownstones, the once fashionable homes of a nineteenth-century gentry, are being transformed into dwellings more suited to Jewish life. Balconies are being added onto the façades, making space to construct the outdoor makeshift abodes for the annual Sukkot festival. They are strangely asymetrical, since, to open toward the sky, they cannot be stacked one upon the other. Other changes are for style and comfort, and they reflect, too, the impact of the outside world.

Each hasidic neighborhood has its own social ecology. Williamsburg is home to Puerto Ricans as well as Hasidim. Crown Heights, the Lubavitcher's turf, is home to a large West Indian community. Boro Park is entirely occupied by Jews, but it borders on a middle-class Italian neighborhood. The transformation of simple brick or clapboard structures into gaudy flat stone facades is a design conspiracy of Southern Italian contractors and Jewish homeowners. In Williamsburg, the changes reflect the encroachment of suburban design on an ancient city neighborhood; Satmar has relocated part of its community to Monsey; Skver to New Square; Pupa to Ossining. Old narrow windows with classical fennils are being replaced by wide picture windows. As it turns dark, I can see inside the homes, each with a long table covered with a white lace tablecloth, itself covered with clear plastic. Two lit candles are perched on top of tall silver candelsticks. A challah and bottles of kosher wine and Slivovitz are on the table. Although most Jews treat Purim as a minor holiday, Purim is a major festival for Hasidim and they celebrate it accordingly, with ritual garb, festive meal, and a rebbe's *tish*. I, a secular Jew, envy them. I would like to enter one of those homes and wash my hands in preparation for the Purim *sude* [feast].

I return to Lee Avenue, where I see my old friend Joel Cahen busily snapping photographs. Joel and I were graduate students together: he, a Dutchman, and I, a Canadian, had both come to New York to study the language and culture of East European Jewry. Joel in Amsterdam, where he codirects the Jewish Historical Museum. He is in New York this week on official business (New York, after all, was once called New Amsterdam and the Jewish connection with the city's European namesake is kept alive in archives and cemetery tombstones), and he had agreed to look for me in Williamsburg. We continue together. The sun has gone down, and I am now freezing and famished; I insist on entering a bakery in search of warmth and food. The store is everything a kosher bakery should be: it is dark, with antiquated wood and metal shelving, and a pungent smell of fresh pastry wafts through the room. I point to some danish pastries and in Yiddish ask for two. The old, hunched-over baker mumbles something and then, in a stiff cranelike movement that betrays the countless times he has done the same task today, scoops them up with a piece of waxed paper. He begins hunting for a bag, but I tell him there is no need. Once outside the store we devour the danish as we walk. Another year I went to the same bakery with a friend. We ordered coffee, and the owner's son put each container into a medium-sized white paper bag. Once outside, I tossed the bag into a garbage bin, but my friend examined it carefully while she sipped her coffee, then held it up to my face so I could read the blue print that read "FOR MOTION SICKNESS, CAPITOL AIRLINES." This rather unaesthetic juxtaposition made me think of a nearby store: one side had counters of freshly slaughtered meat, the other side had shelves of luggage.

A degree of sensual coarseness finds its way into undainty Jewish renditions of Polish pirogi and Chinese eggrolls. But baking is another matter and simple Jewish breads and pastries offer welcome relief from an otherwise ordinary cuisine.

Kosher baked goods often do not contain dairy products; they then can be served together with meat without violating religious proscriptions. The chocolate filling of the pastry Joel and I eat is rich and dark, conforming to both the laws of *kashres* and contemporary tastes. Taking great pleasure in the food, I am oblivious now to my surroundings and I am taken completely by surprise when we are suddenly accosted by a hefty Hasid, unsteady on his feet, accompanied by two children. The man is in his late thirties. He is stout, with a full brown beard streaked with gray. His mouth seems to foam as Yiddish sentences splatter off his lips. "Have you made the blessings for the holiday?" "Yes, we have," I lie. Apparently shared ethnicity permits this invasion of each other's turf. The question he poses is designed to make a stranger conform to his way. I, feeling a little guilty on account of the

lie, ease my conscience by reminding myself that such small decep-
tions for the sake of Jewish ethnography are hardly my own invention.
When the Yiddish playwright and folklorist Sh. Ansky conducted his
ethnographic expedition to the small Jewish towns in the Ukraine
shortly before World War I, lying became a prime way of eliciting data
from otherwise difficult informants, particularly the elderly women
who provided charms and incantations to people in need (Rekhtman
1958). Besides, Joel and I are both wearing yarmulkes. To admit to not
making the blessings would betray the masquerade. I pray that the
Hasid does not probe. Apparently God is listening because the Hasid
accepts what I tell him at face value. "Good," the Hasid responds.
"Our rebbe, Rabbi Teitleboim, has explained the importance of Jews
reciting the blessings. That's how to bring the Messiah. Not Peres or
Begin you should believe in. They're just like the Amelikites. You
must believe in God and recite the blessings. When the Messiah
comes then we'll all be in the land of Israel."

As the man talks the two children tug at his sleeve. They are in a
hurry to go somewhere. The father is in no hurry to leave. He has a
message he wants to relate to us. "Where do you live?" he asks.
"Amsterdam," my friend answers first. "Amsterdam? Do you know
rabbi so and so?" "Yes." An instant bond. "And you, too, are from
Amsterdam?" "No, no. I live in New York." "New York? What part of
New York?" "Manhattan. The Village." "Manhattan?" But this time
there is no connection. Manhattan is a remote island, much farther
from this hasidic enclave in Brooklyn than far away Amsterdam is.
One day a cartoonist will draw a map of the world as seen through
hasidic eyes. Manhattan will be reduced to a small sliver labeled "47th
St.", the heart of the hasidic-dominated diamond exchange. Brooklyn
will loom large, only slightly smaller than Jerusalem. Between them
will be Paris and London (very small by comparison with the more
illustrious American and Israeli cities), then Antwerp. Here and there
a city will appear because within it resides a great rabbi.

Fortunately, the *skhus* (merit) of a great rabbi of Amsterdam Jewry
seems to apply to me too. Friends of the Hasid stop to greet him. He
introduces both Joel and me as "Jews from Amsterdam." "Where is
everyone off to?" I ask, watching scores of people heading down Lee
Avenue. "Home." "Are they off to a *sude* [festive meal]?" "Yes, to a
sude." "Could we see one?" "You want to see a *sude*? Of course!
Come with me I'll take you to a *sude*." The Hasid grabs us both by the
arm and pulls us in the direction he was headed. "Come. I will take

you to my father-in-law's." The Hasid has called my bluff. I would like
to see a *sude*, not take part in one. I look at Joel, hoping that he will
intervene and invent some excuse, a previous engagement perhaps.
Joel does no such thing. He, after all, is here to experience American
Jewry. This will be an event, a souvenir to take back with him to
Amsterdam, to heighten the meaning of the snapshots he is taking.
Together they will form a collection, a private museum on contemporary Judaism. After all, he is a curator, and assembling dioramas of
oddities is his stock in trade. But for me, the anthropologist, there is a
great sense of risk here. I feel less secure about the nature of the
enterprise because anthropology does not lend itself to casual encounters. Besides, I am worried that my ruse will be exposed, that the
Hasid will see who I am behind the yarmulke mask. But the Hasid
insists we go with him. And so I go, to please him and to please Joel,
and much to my surprise, to please myself too.

We turn off Lee Avenue, then head down a side street, entering the
first apartment building we come to. I tell the Hasid that we can stay
only for a few minutes. "Maybe just for a kiddush," I suggest. "As long
as you like. As long as you like." The Hasid is breathing heavily,
panting as he climbs the flights of stairs in this old five-story walk-up.
"No one's going to keep you here. Maybe you think I'm a little strange
because I am drunk. So I want to apologize. Today is Purim and we
are supposed to get drunk. I've had maybe a liter and a half of wine.
But now it's wearing off and I'm not so drunk anymore." At the end of
a dark corridor there is a tan-colored door smeared with shellac for a
wood-grain look. He pushes open the unlocked door, marches us
down a hallway covered in badly frayed linoleum, and announces to
the women preparing food in the kitchen and to his father-in-law
seated at the dining table that he has brought guests for dinner. The
old man cuts a striking image, ensconced in a seat at the head of the
table. He smiles approvingly and with such benevolence that, with his
flowing white beard and ruddy complexion, he's a deadringer for
Santa Claus. The illusion is shattered the moment the old man speaks
his Hungarian Yiddish. I do not understand the question he asks. The
son-in-law explains: "He wants to know if you want to wash your
hands." I understand that he is referring to ritual, not hygiene. I say
yes, and we head to the kitchen, where one of the children fills a silver
two-handled container with water and leaves it in the sink. I pour the
water over the fingers of each hand three times. I refill the container
and leave it in the sink for Joel. He repeats the ceremony. The boy

points to a roll of paper towels hanging from a wall, then he escorts us back to the dining room. The father recites the blessings over challah, cuts it, dips it into salt, then bites off a piece. We are instructed to do the same and although I have seen and performed this very simple ceremony many times before, I am uncomfortably aware now that there are details that I am not sure of. Must the challah be dipped in the salt, or may the salt be sprinkled on the challah? Can I ask questions now or must I be silent until all the men have performed the ritual? I dip without asking questions. I resent my ignorance, less because it impedes my work than because it demands constant vigilance. I cannot hide behind a mask of knowing. That too has its advantages. I must accept my lot as inferior to my host. I am to be his apprentice. We sit down and the food is brought out, the father served first, the guests second, and the family next. The women do not sit at the table. They serve, then eat separately in a second room adjacent to the dining room. My initial fear that we have usurped their places recedes as I realize that besides the ritually prescribed separation of men and women, logistics alone make the two rooms necessary. Even without us, the house is overflowing with people. My hasidic friend has nine children, not unusual in this community, and we are joined shortly by his brother-in-law with the same number of children. I am curious to know more about these people and I ask if I might pose some questions. My Hasid friend explains that Passover is the holiday when questions are asked, but I can ask now, too; he is referring to the questions the youngest child asks at the seder. And he is referring, too, to the fact that Purim and Passover are closely linked, both temporally and thematically. Both signal the special relationship between God and Israel, that peculiar combination of nationhood and religion that characterizes Judaism. More ignorant than the children of the household, I am now the youngest. I accept the demotion in age because through it I can dispense entirely with the masquerade and become a harmless ignoramus rather than a dangerous skeptic.[2] This meal will be a seder for me. The questions go only one way. The Hasid has little interest in me and the world I live in. "Were you born here?" I ask. "No. In Rumania. Then I lived in Israel for twenty years. I came here four years ago." "You live in Williamsburg?" "No. In Monroe. We have a Satmar community there." "What kind of work do you do?" "I correct manuscripts of holy books that are being published." "A proofreader?" "No. Not a proofreader. I have to check the original to make sure there are no mistakes in the manuscript and I

[45]

check the typeset copy to see that it, too, is accurate. I also write for our newspaper, *Der Yid.*" I tell him that we have something in common, that I, too, do some journalism. He gives no response, an indication that he sees no connection between his sacred work and the profane work I do. But that realization comes to me much later. On this night I am caught within the magic spell of the encounter, and I take the lack of response as a positive response. The attempt to establish a common bond between us is unnecessary, I tell myself. It is already evident by the invitation to join the family for the *sude*, and by the gracious way we are being treated. Our hosts insist that we pour ourselves soda, or wine, that we cut off pieces of challah, and they offer us additional helpings. More food is out of the question. Both Joel and I are big eaters, but even our prodigious appetites are appeased by what we are given: an hors-d'oeuvre of dense, salty gefilte fish, chicken soup with thin noodles, and meat *kreplakh,* an entree of boiled chicken, roast beef, stuffed cabbage, and a spicy stuffed derma side dish, followed by a dessert of stewed fruit. The stuffed cabbage and *kreplakh* are traditional Purim dishes but my hosts are unable to explain why: "Why? Cabbage is the season." What does this mean? I repeat the question but I make no further progress. Later, another Hasid will explain the meaning: Purim has none of the restrictions that normally accompany a Jewish holy day. One can work, cook, and travel. Yet is is a significant holiday for Hasidim, its importance hidden, and therefore it is proper to eat foods that likewise hide their inner selves. Tonight, despite my questions, I cannot turn the occasion into an ethnographic interview. What for me is an entry into an exotic world is for my host a chance to fulfill the *mitzvah* of hospitality to a sojourner. So I must accept the fact and be grateful for it, and be grateful, too, for their otherness, for it is that which draws me to them.

Between courses my Hasid prods his children into joining him in singing hasidic songs. They sing loudly: their voices are meant to reach the ears of neighboring families and perhaps with luck or just force of will of God, too. The melody is simple and the voices pounce upon it like swimmers to a wave. Now they ride with it and a harmony emerges. Then they fall back into the ebb and it seems as if their voices are about to be swept out to sea. Content to listen and accept my lot as their Purim *mitzvah,* I think: here we are, Jews from Canada, from Holland, from Hungary, from Rumania and Israel, celebrating together in America the holiday of Purim. We are as different from each other as night is from day and yet I, the non-Jewish Jew, feel perfectly entitled to sit here with them. I try without success to make the encounter serve my own purpose. They, Jews from a faraway time, enveloped within a world very much of their own fabrication, feel entitled to use me, too, for their own ends, to have me say the holiday blessings and work with them to bring on the Messiah. How odd it seems that this ethnographic encounter should join together Judaism's disparate segments. And yet through the encounter the parameters of the whole are defined not as a unified thing, for that American Jewry cannot be (nor could any ethnic group be that in modern society), but rather at certain moments such as these, as an emerging dialogue of the parts about what it means to be a Jew. Like all ethnicity within contemporary society, Jewishness is a turning inward, an alternate system of meaning in which "power" and "wealth" are constructed fictively through a system quite different from that used by the outer world, the normative majority. But Judaism is also a text. And all of us bring to it our separate social universes through which we interpret the text's meaning.[3] What unites us is the commitment to dialogue, the belief that we are entitled to infringe upon each other's autonomy as if one could, indeed, as if one were compelled to define through argument what is a Jew: the observant Jew feels he has a mission to reach out to a fellow Jew and bring him into the fold, his way of bringing on the Messiah; the secular Jew seeks the "quintessential" Jew in the Hasid, turning to him, in part perhaps in much the same way that American Jews turn to the rabbis to be the exemplary Jews, the guarantors that Judaism will continue to exist despite the assimilation of the many. And there is in part, too, a quality here of going back in time, a turning inward on a temporal dimension, to an "older," that is, an authentic Judaism. Anthropology may never entirely shed its sense that the subject of its study is separated from the field's practitioners through time, that one is more "primitive" than the other (Fabian 1983). Nor are we who study Jews less time-bound in our formulations. Indeed, herein lies the great dilemma of Jewish ethnography: the problematic nature of encountering the Other cannot be transcended, no matter how close the observer feels himself to be to the subject of study. As James Clifford (1986) suggests, ethnography has an allegorical quality to it. We are looking for a more authentic self and who more so than those who would study their own? But if making subjects into historical relics is our way of making sense out of otherness, they, that is, our subjects, are not bound by such formulations, except when we have subjugated them politically. So they respond to us not as relics but as equals or as our betters, determined to define in ways that suit them the nature of our interaction, the point to our dialogue, sometimes even as cowriters of the ethnographic text so that they might tell their story to a broader world. The Hasid who has read Lis Harris's *Holy Days* welcomes my visits: perhaps he thinks I can do for his group what Lis Harris did for the Lubavitcher.

Strangely, it is through the dimension of time that the Hasid, too, sees himself bound to the secular Jew: if one seeks to reclaim the past, the other seeks to alter the future; when all Jews obey the commandments, the Messiah will appear. Argument between us is possible because of a deeply rooted belief on both our parts that even though we do not share a common present we share a common history, and in our separate ways we believe that we will share a common destiny. And there is another bond here. Judaism is a combination of blood and custom. But if custom involves problematical issues, given the great multiplicity of Judaisms in modern times, blood is less problematical. The Hasid has his own way of looking at this. When I tell a Skverer Hasid that my father's father came to Montreal from a small town in Galicia, he demands to know its name. I tell him that it's not a well-known place, that he's probably never heard of it. "How do you know?" he asks. "Horodenka," I respond expecting only a blank look. "Horodenka?" he responds animatedly. "You've heard of it?" I ask surprised. "Of course. I can even show you where it is on the map." Horodenka, he explains, figures prominently in hasidic rabbinic genealogy. "It is possible that your grandfather was a Skverer Hasid." I am a soul finding its way back to its long never-forgotten home. So I am accepted for an essential rather than existential me. The latter me, he, too, sees as a relic soon destined for the junkpile of social history. By his reckoning, secular Judaism is crumbling. A poor bulwark against the tide of assimilation, it will be replaced by his way of being Jewish, just as my way once replaced his. We are like fortune-tellers, gazing at the future.

So dialogue between us is fraught with tension. There are expectations that cannot be met, attempts to categorize experience that are not right. But the problem of dialogue has much to do with the matter of agenda. I do not wish to become the Jew that he would have me be;[4] he insists I engage him in debate, to express my opinion, so that he might use the opportunity to explain his world and undermine mine. Yet when two Satmar students arrive at the door to solicit alms on Purim, there is no debate. He invites them in, offers them wine, which they take, and pastry, which they do not. They offer in return a *dvar toyre* (homily). When they have finished he offers one of his own, and when he is finished, they leave. Only then do I realize that he is more comfortable with me than he is with them. I ask him what they said, explaining that between the ghetto blaster blaring hasidic music and their use of *loshn koydesh* [Hebrew-Aramaic], I picked up maybe 5 percent of the *dvar toyre*. "That's pretty good," he responds, "I picked up maybe 1 percent."

A friend who introduced me to the Skverer Hasid is asked by the man why he is a vegetarian. "Is it for moral reasons or because you don't like the taste of meat?" "What's the difference?" I ask. "Well," the Hasid explains, "if it's for moral reasons then you are guilty of arrogance." "Why?" "Because there are four levels of things on earth. Things like stones, for example, which have no life. Things like grass, which are alive but have no consciousness. Animals such as cows, which have a limited consciousness. And man. Each is higher than the other. When it consumes the lower form, it also raises it beyond what it would achieve on its own. So when a man eats the flesh of a cow and derives from it the strength to perform a *mitzvah*, the cow benefits from the *mitzvah*, too. So if you refuse to eat meat for supposedly moral reasons, you're actually denying the cow the benefits it would attain. But if you abstain because you don't like the taste, that you're entitled to do."

Mythopoesis, I think to myself. I like the metaphorical imprint, but I am wary, nonetheless. Am I the cow that must be consumed? Is there no way for us to be together without one of us consuming the other? And then I think that this is not our dilemma alone, it occurs whenever cultures are in contact, no less so when ethnographer and informant meet. But there is here another level of meaning, because the interaction and its significance does not emerge from a *tabula rasa*, it encapsulates rather the history of Jewry and attempts to assert control over it. Indeed, those attempts are the driving force behind the emergence of ideologically based Jewish subcultures. Because they are revivalistic, they are expansionist; their legitimacy derives in large measure from the number of their adherents, from the extent of the larger group they embrace. So they attempt a cultural hegemony: their Judaism is the real Judaism; mine is not, although my soul is. Can I resist them?

The singing is seductive. Joel adds his voice to the others, humming

[49]

when the words are not familiar. I am still hesitant to join in. Instead, I look around the room at these faces, the adults with their beards and cloaks, the children still displaying through greasepaint mustaches the fading traces of Purim. But I am entranced by a still-powerful sense of illusion: now I see in them not the strangeness of a separate existence but the almost familiar world of my own Galician ancestors, the grand-parents on Esplanade Street at the foot of Mount Royal, whom I once feared because of their oldness, their otherness. How strange it seems that a one-day fieldtrip should send me on such a long journey back-ward and rob me of a hard-won distance from the past. And yet I feel drawn to these Hasidim, not so much because of any real sense that through them I could reclaim a forgotten past, but rather out of admi-ration for their valor, for their suspension of disbelief. And then I think that I, too, must suspend disbelief—not so that I might become them—but because what exists between us is indeed meaningful, because the discomfort and the challenges have a purpose, because what we create in coming together represents a dialogue of cultures, a kind of bridge between two worlds, so that whatever the future holds in store, at the very least there remains through the work of this profession a trace of an old, vibrant, and cacaphonous universe.

Notes

1. Charles Liebman (1974), the sociologist of religion, has identified a distinct pattern of ritual behavior and belief—a folk religion—among the nonelite, that is, those outside of the rabbinate and Orthodox circles. Perhaps its most striking feature is the emergence of "kosher style" food, which for many takes the place of food that actually meets the laws of *kashres*. When the Jewish hero of a recent Woody Allen film decides to convert to Catholicism, among the icons of his new identity are Wonder Bread and Hellman's mayonnaise. Marshall Sklare (1979), another ob-server of American Judaism, suggests that the religion of American Jews has moved significantly away from Judaism's traditional stress on sacramentalism. Indeed, most Jews believe that being a good Jew inheres in what you believe rather than in what you do and, in this sense, the religion and their way of celebrating Jewish holy days closely resemble the religion of moralism practiced by the majority's Christian culture.
2. For further elaboration of the concept of skeptic versus ignoramus see Janet Belcove-Shalin's discussion in her essay in this volume.
3. For a discussion of this point in regard to the human sciences in general see Todorov (1984:17).
4. For a discussion of Bakhtin's notion of constitutive duality as a source of enrichment in the human sciences, see Todorov (1984:108–9).

REFERENCES

Alter, Robert. 1982. "The Jew Who Didn't Get Away: On the Possibility of an American Jewish Culture." *Judaism* 31:274–86.

Clifford, James. 1986. "On Ethnographic Allegory." In *Writing Culture: The Poetics and Politics of Ethnography*, ed. James Clifford and George Marcus. Berkeley: University of California Press.

Fabian, Johannes. 1983. *Time and the Other: How Anthropology Makes Its Object*. New York: Columbia University Press.

Harris, Lis. 1985. *Holy Days*. New York: Summit Books.

Liebman, Charles. 1974. "The Religion of American Jews." In *The Jew in American Society*, ed. Marshall Sklare. New York: Behrman House.

Rekhtman, Avrom. 1958. *Yidishe etnografye un folklor*. Buenos Aires: YIVO.

Sklare, Marshall, and J. Greenblum. 1979. *Jewish Identity on the Suburban Frontier*. Chicago: University of Chicago Press.

Todorov, Tzvetan. 1984. *Mikhail Bakhtin: The Dialogical Principle*. Minneapolis: University of Minnesota Press.

Woocher, Jonathan. 1985. "Sacred Survival." *Judaism* 34, 2:151–62.

Research for this essay was made possible by a grant from the Wenner-Gren Foundation for Anthropological Research, Inc.

[2]

Waiting for a Jew: Marginal Redemption at the Eighth Street Shul

Jonathan Boyarin

My story begins in a community with an illusion of wholeness. I am between the age when consciousness begins and the age of ten when my family leaves the community and my illusion is shattered. Our family lives on the edge of the Pine Barrens in Farmingdale, New Jersey, along with hundreds of other families of Jewish chicken farmers who have come from Europe and New York City in several waves, beginning just after World War I.

Among the farmers are present and former Communists, Bundists, Labor Zionists, German refugees who arrived in the 1930s, and Polish survivors of concentration camps. These, however, are not the distinctions I make among them as a child. Johannes Fabian has shown us that when we write ethnography we inevitably trap those about whom we write into a hypostatic, categorical, grammatical "present" (Fabian 1983). An autobiographer has the same power over the memory of himself and those he knew in prior times as the fieldworker who later obliterates the narrative aspect of his encounter with his subjects— the power to deny their autonomy in hindsight.[1] Those of the farming community whom I will later remember, I know therefore by their own names and places: my grandparents closer to Farmingdale proper; the Silbers off on Yellowbrook Road, with a tree nursery now instead of chickens; the Lindauers, stubbornly maintaining an egg-packing and distribution business, while others find different ways to earn a living.

My child's world is not exclusively Jewish, nor am I brought up to regard it as such. Across our road and down a few hundred yards is a tiny house built by Jewish farmers when they first came to settle here. It is now, incredibly, occupied by a black family of ten. Next to them lives an equally poor and large white family. Shortly before we leave Farmingdale, the old Jew in the farm next to ours passes away, and the property passes to a Japanese businessman. The young men he hires live in the farmhouse, growing oriental vegetables on the open field and bonsai in a converted chicken coop, and they introduce me to the game of Go. The nearest Jewish household is that of my great-uncle Yisroel and his wife Helen, the third house to the right of ours.

Yet we are near the heart of Jewish life in Farmingdale. Half a mile—but no, it must be less—down Peskin's Lane (the name my grandfather Israel Boyarin gave to what was a dirt road in the 1930s) is the Farmingdale Jewish Community Center, on the next plot of land after Uncle Yisroel's house. Just past the community center is the farm that once belonged to my father's uncle Peskin, the first Jew in Farmingdale. Fifteen years after Peskin's death, the bodies of two gangsters were found buried on the farm. The local papers noted: "Mr. Peskin was not available for comment."

Our own farm consists of eleven acres. Facing the road is the house my grandfather built, with a large front lawn and an apple tree in back. Farther back, four large chicken coops mark the slope of a hill ending in our field, behind which woods conceal the tiny Manasquan River. The field, well fertilized by chickens allowed to scratch freely on it during the day, is leased each summer by a dirt farmer who grows corn. My father has joined the insurance agency begun by my mother, and they have gotten rid of the birds. The coops stand empty by my fourth birthday. One day, though, while a friend and I chase each other through the coops in play, we are startled by a pair of chickens. Their presence in the stillness and the faint smell of ancient manure is inexplicable and unforgettable. Thus, on the abandoned farm, my first memories are tinged with a sense of traces, of mystery, of loss. Do all who eventually become anthropologists have this experience in some form, at some time in their early lives?

My mother's turn to business is wise: chicken farming as the basis for the community's livelihood is quickly becoming untenable. Nor is it surprising, as she had given up a career as a chemist to come live with my father on the farm—thus taking part in the process of Jewish dispersal from the immigrants' urban centers, which in the last quarter of the century would be mirrored by a shrinking of Jewish communities in small towns and a reconsolidation of the Orthodox centers. My mother's father, an Orthodox Jew from a leading Lithuanian rabbinical family, has struggled to learn English well and has gone into the insurance business himself. After his death, my mother tells me that he had originally resisted her desire to marry the son of a Jewish socialist, but he consented when he met my father's father's father, a Lubavitcher Hasid named Mordechai.

My grandfather's concern for his daughter's future as an observant Jew was well founded. The Sabbath is marked in our family only on Friday nights: by my mother's candle-lighting, and her chicken soup in winter; by the challah; by the presence of my grandfather. We do not keep kosher, nor do we go to shul on *shabes*.

The Jewish Community Center—with its various functions as social and meeting hall, synagogue, and school—is nevertheless a focus of our family's life. Most of the ten or so other children in these classes I see at other times during the week as well, either in public school or playing at one another's homes. I am there three times each week, first for Sunday School, and then for Hebrew School on Tuesday and Thursday afternoons. This odd distinction is no doubt a practical one, since some parents do not choose to send their children three times a week. But since Sunday School was first a Christian institution, it also reflects an accommodation to Christian church patterns, as evidenced by the fact that Sundays are devoted to teaching stories of the Bible. One Sunday School teacher we have in our kindergarten year captivates me with his skill in making these stories come to life, as when he imitates the distress of an Egyptian waking up to find his bed covered with frogs.

Another teacher, a young woman with a severe manner and a heavy black wig, the wife of a member of the Orthodox yeshiva in Lakewood, later causes general misery because of her inability to understand children, although I will later appreciate the prayers she teaches us to read. One time I come in to Hebrew School immediately after yet another in a series of martyred family dogs has been run over in front of our house. Her attempt to comfort me is like some malicious parody of Talmudic reasoning: "You shouldn't be so upset about an animal. If a chicken and a person both fell down a well, which one would you save first?"

In addition to this somewhat haphazard religious training, there is the local chapter of Habonim, the Labor Zionist Youth Organization, to which my older brother and sister belong. I tag along and am tolerated by their peers. Once I am given a minor role in a stage performance by the chapter. Though I am too young to remember quite what it is about, the phrase *"komets-aleph:aw"* stands in my memory.

Later I will learn that this phrase occurs in a famous and sentimental Yiddish folksong. It is the first letter of the Hebrew alphabet, the first thing countless generations of Jewish children have been taught. Here is an unusual case in which a traditional lesson—how to pronounce the alphabet—is successfully inculcated in the secularized framework of a dramatic performance about the traditional setting. Perhaps this is because of the necessary rehearsals, in which I must have heard, as the song puts it, "once more, over and over again, *komets-aleph:aw*." The memory reinforces my later preference for this older, European pronunciation of the Hebrew vowels, my sense of the Israeli *"kamets-aleph:ah"* as inauthentic.

Also memorable at the Jewish Community Center is the annual barbecue run by the Young Couples' Club. Though my father will assure me in an interview years later that its association with the Fourth of July was purely a matter of convenience, the atmosphere is certainly one of festival, even including "sacrifices" and "altars": My father and his friends set up huge charcoal pits with cement blocks, and broil vast amounts of chicken; corn is boiled in aluminum garbage cans to go with it.[2] For the children, a Purim-like element of riotous excess is added: This one time each year, we are allowed to drink as much soda as we want. One year "wild," blond-haired Richie L., whose parents have a luncheonette booth for a kitchen table and an attic filled with antiques, claims to drink fourteen bottles, thus adding to the mystique he holds for me.

But it is the days when the Community Center becomes a synagogue that leave the strongest impression on my memory. There must be services every Saturday morning, but I am completely unaware of them. What I will remember are the holidays: Purim, Rosh Hashanah, Yom Kippur, Simhat Torah, and a crowd of people who just a few years later will never be there again. On the fall holidays, the shul is full of movement, impatience, noise, and warmth. Except for a few moments such as the shofar blowing, we children are free to come and go: By the steps in front, tossing the juicy, poisonous red berries of a yew that was planted, I am told, in memory of my brother Aaron, whom I never knew; inside the main doors, to look left at

[55]

Walter Tenenbaum wrapped in a *talis* that covers his head, standing at a lectern by the Ark of the Torah as he leads the service, or to look right, along the first long row of folding chairs for our fathers; thence a few rows back to where our mothers sit separately from the men, although unlike most synagogues that look and sound as traditional as this one, there is no *mekhitse*, no barrier between women and men; and finally out through the side door and down a flight of wooden steps to the monkey bars, into the ditch where one miraculous day we found and drank an intact bottle of orange soda, or into the kitchen, social room, and classroom in the basement. Once each year we children are the center of attention, as we huddle under a huge *talis* in front of the Ark on Simhat Torah to be blessed.

In classic ethnographies of hunting and gathering groups, landscapes are described as personalized, integral elements of culture. This was true of the landscape of my childhood friendships, which today is as obliterated as any *shtetl* in Eastern Europe. Any marginal group in mass society may be subject without warning to the loss of its cultural landscape, and therefore those who are able to create portable landscapes for themselves are the most likely to endure.

The Jews have been doing so for thousands of years; the Simhat Torah *talis* can stand in front of any Ark, and the original Ark, in the biblical account, was itself transported from station to station in the desert. Yet the members of a community are orphaned when the naive intimacy of a living environment is torn away from them. Such a break appears often in Jewish literature—significantly with the emphasis not forward on the beginning of adulthood, as in the European *Bildungsroman*, but rather on the end of childhood.[3]

I suddenly discover the distance between the world and myself at the end of August in 1966. When my parents pick me up from camp, they take me to a new house. For the last time, we attend high holiday services in Farmingdale. It is the only time we will ever drive there, and our family's friends no longer join us during the afternoon break on Yom Kippur for a surreptitious glass of tea and a slice of challah. Farmingdale is no longer home, and though our new house is only ten miles away, it is another world.

We live now in an almost exclusively white, middle-class suburb with many Jews, but our older, brick house is isolated on a block of working-class cubes. While neighbors my age play football in our yard, I often retreat to my room and console myself with sports books for preadolescents. My new and bewildering sense of marginality leads me to develop an exquisite self-consciousness. It is manifested in an almost constant internal dialogue, which keeps me company and will interfere with my adolescent sexuality. Indeed, my journey toward adulthood will be defined by a search for dialogue with others.

Ostracism is often the fate of a new kid on the block, and it may last longer when his family is Jewish and his home better than those on either side. There is a custom in this part of New Jersey of tolerating petty vandalism on "mischief night," the night before Halloween. Pumpkins are smashed, and we, along with other unpopular families on the block, have the windows of our cars and house smeared with soap. One Halloween I wake up to see graffitti chalked in bold letters on the sidewalk in front of our house: "Jon the Jew, a real one too." My father summons the kids next door—whom we suspect of being the authors—to scrape the words off the sidewalk, as I burn with shame.

He and I never discuss the incident, but later I will compare it with a memory of Freud's: As a child, he was walking with his father, when a gentile knocked his father's hat off. Rather than confronting the man, Freud's father meekly bent over to pick up the hat, and his son's humiliation persisted into adulthood (Bakan 1958). The moral is that a victim is likely to view any response as adding insult to injury. In my case, as my father asserts the American principle of equality and "teaches a lesson" to my occasional and vindictive playmates by forcing them to erase what they have written, I feel as though he is inviting them to write the words again, this time making me watch my own degradation.

The new synagogue my parents join is only a partial refuge. It exemplifies the difference between a shul and a temple. Everything in Farmingdale had faced inward: little concern was paid for praying in unison, and though the *shames* would bang his hand on the table for silence, he was seldom heeded; even the cantor was alone with God, facing away from everyone else, rather than performing for the congregation. Calling a synagogue a temple, by contrast, is doubly revealing. On the one hand, it indicates a striving for the majesty of the ancient House in Jerusalem. On the other hand, just like the English term used to designate it, its trappings are borrowed from the Christian world, down to the black robes worn by the rabbi and cantor.

These robes lack the warm mystery of Walter Tenenbaum's *talis*. The responsive readings of Psalms in English seem ridiculously artificial to me from the first. And my mother, who still comes only on

[57]

the holidays though I sometimes drag my father to temple on Friday nights, complains of the rabbi's long-winded sermons and yearns aloud for the intimate conversations along the back wall of the Farmingdale Jewish Community Center.

Unlike some, I do not leave the synagogue immediately after my bar mitzvah. I teach the blessings of the Haftorah to two reluctant boys a year younger than me. I briefly experience religious inspiration, and for perhaps two weeks put on *tefillin* every morning. But the atmosphere is hollow, and the emptiness breeds cynicism in me in my teens.

The coldness of the building itself is symptomatic of the lack of sustenance I sense there. The pretense and bad taste of modern American synagogues are well-known yet puzzling phenomena, which deserve a sociological explanation of their own. Even the walls of the temple are dead concrete blocks, in contrast to the wood of the Farmingdale Jewish Community Center. Services are held in a "sanctuary," unlike the room at the Community Center where activities as varied as dances and political meetings were conducted when services were not being held. Aside from any question of Jewish law, there is a loss of community marked by the fact that everyone drives, rather than walk to the temple. It is a place separated from the home, without the strong and patient webs spun by leisurely strolling conversations to and from a shul.

Most generally, the temple is victim to the general alienation of the suburbs. What happens or fails to happen there is dependent on what the people who come there expect from each other. Those who belong (there are vastly more "members" than regular attendees) seem bound primarily by a vague desire to have Jewish grandchildren. The poor rabbi, typical of Conservative congregations, seems hired to be a stand-in Jew, to observe all the laws and contain all the knowledge they don't have the time for. They are not bound to each other by Jewish religious ways, nor do they share the common interests of everyday life—the same livelihood or language—that helped to make a complete community in Farmingdale.

I go off to college and slowly discover that my dismissal of Judaism leaves me isolated, with few resources. I had realized my individual difference on leaving Farmingdale. Now, much more removed from a Jewish environment than ever before, I become aware of my inescapable Jewishness. In the small northwestern college of my dreams, everyone around me seems "American" and different, though I have never thought of myself as anything but American. Even in the humanities curriculum on which the school prides itself, Jewish civilization is absent. It is as though Western cultural history were just a triumphant, straight line from the Greeks to Augustine and Michelangelo (with his horned Moses and uncircumcized David), confusion setting in at last only with Marx and Freud.

Five years too late to benefit me, a Jewish Studies position will in fact be established at the college. Such positions are usually funded by Jewish individuals or organizations, and hence they represent the growing acculturation (not assimilation) of Jews into American academic life. The fact that they are regarded as legitimate by the academic community, however, is part of a reintegration of Jewish thought into the concept of Western humanities. Jewish ethnographers can contribute to this movement—for example, by elucidating the dialectic of tradition and change as worked out in communities facing vastly different historical challenges. We may then move beyond efforts to explain the explosive presence of Jews in post-Enlightenment intellectual life as a result of their "primitive" encounter with "civility" (Cuddihy 1974) to explore how the Jewish belief that "Creation as the (active) speech or writing of God posits first of all that the Universe is essentially intelligible" (Faur 1986:7) provided a pathway from Torah to a restless, unifying modern impulse in the natural and social sciences.

Such notions are far beyond me as an undergraduate. At my college in the 1970s, the social scientists in their separate departments strive to separate themselves from their "objects of study"; the humanists treasure the peace of their cloisters; the artists, knowing they are intellectually suspect, cultivate a cliquish sense of superiority, and there is none of the give-and-take between learning and everyday experience I have come to associate with the best of Jewish scholarship.

I find a friend, a Jew from Long Island, and we begin to teach each other that we need to cultivate our Jewishness. We discuss the "Jewish mentality" of modern thinkers, and paraphrasing Lenny Bruce's category of the *goyish*, sarcastically reject all that is "white." "I am not 'white,'" my friend Martin proudly postures, "I am a Semite." Meanwhile, reflecting on my own dismissal of suburban Judaism, I decide not to end willingly an almost endless chain of Jewish cultural trans-

[59]

mission. I stake my future on the assumption that a tradition so old and varied must contain the seeds of a worthwhile life for me, and decide to begin to acquire them through study.

Besides, my reading as a student of anthropology leads me to reason that if I concentrate on Jewish culture, no one will accuse me of cultural imperialism (cf. Gough 1968). No doubt others in my generation who choose to do fieldwork with Jews are motivated by similar considerations. Jewish anthropologists as a class are privileged to belong to the world of academic discourse, and to have an entrée into a variety of unique communities that maintain cultural frameworks in opposition to mass society.

Something deeper than Marxist critiques of anthropology draws me to Yiddish in particular. Before leaving Farmingdale, my best friend had been a child of survivors from Lemberg. I remember being at his house once, and asking with a sense of wonder: "Ralph, do you really know Yiddish?"

Ralph told me that although he understood the language—which his parents still spoke to him—he had never learned to speak it. Still, I was impressed that he knew this secret code. And now, finished with college and looking to find my own way home, Yiddish seems to be the nearest link to which I can attach myself. It is the key to a sense of the life of the *shtetl*, that Jewish dreamtime that I inevitably associate with my lost Farmingdale.

The Farmingdale community has, by this point, completely disintegrated: Virtually no Jews in that part of New Jersey earn their living as chicken farmers anymore. Many of those who have gone into business have moved to nearby towns like Lakewood. The Torah scrolls of the Community Center have been ceremoniously transferred to a new synagogue near housing developments on the highway between Farmingdale and Lakewood. I have never considered becoming a chicken farmer myself.

So, when I finish my college courses, without waiting for graduation, I flee back to New York. "Flee": No one chases me out of Portland, Oregon, God forbid! "Back": The city, though a magnet and a refuge, has never been my home before. Yet for three years I have shaped my identity in opposition to the "American" world around me, and I reverted along with my close friends to what we imagined as an authentic New York accent—the "dese" and "dose" that were drilled out of my parents' repertoire in the days when New York public school teachers had to pass elocution exams.

[60]

Rejecting suburban Judaism, belatedly pursuing the image of the sixties' counterculture to the Pacific Northwest, and self-consciously affecting a "New York Jew" style were all successive attempts to shape a personal identity. In each case, the identity strategy was in opposition to the prevailing conventions of the immediate social order. Similarly, opposition to their parents' perceived bourgeois complacency may underlie the involvement of young people with Judaism. Yet as Dominique Schnapper (1983) has noted, for young, intellectual Jews becoming involved in Jewish religion, politics, or culture, there can be no question of canceling out prior experience and "becoming traditional." In fact, this is true even of the most seemingly Orthodox and insular Jewish communities. There is a difference between learning about great rabbis of the past through meetings with Jewish graybeards who knew them, and through reading about their merits in the Williamsburg newspaper *Der Yid*.

Of course, not only Jews are in the position of reconstituting interrupted tradition (cf. Clifford 1986:116 ff.) But since they have been in the business of reshaping tradition in a dialogue with written texts for thousands of years, Jews may benefit more directly than others from learning about what other Jews are doing with their common tradition. It is conceivable that individuals may choose to adopt traits from other communities or even join those communities based on what they read in ethnographies. Whether such cultural borrowings and recombinations are effected in an "authentic" manner will depend less on precedent than on the degree of self-confident cultural generosity that results.

Arriving in New York, I adopt a knitted yarmulke, although my hair still falls below my shoulders. I immediately begin a nine-week summer course in Yiddish at Columbia, and it seems as though the language were being brought out from deep inside me. When I go to visit my parents on weekends, my father remembers words he'd never noticed forgetting. When I take the IRT after class back down to the Village, it seems as if everybody on the train is speaking Yiddish. Most important for my sense of identity, phrases here and there in my own internal dialogue are now in Yiddish, and I find I can reflect on myself with a gentle irony that was never available to me in English.

Then, after my first year in graduate school, I am off to Europe the following summer, courtesy of my parents. I arrive at the Gare du Nord in Paris with the address of a friend and without a word of French. I am spotted wearing my yarmulke by a young North African

Jew who makes me understand, in broken English, that he studies at the Lubavitch yeshiva in Paris. He buys me a Paris guidebook and sets me on my way in the Metro. At the end of the summer, this meeting will stand as the first in a set of Parisian reactions to my yarmulke which crystallize in my memory:

—The reaction of the generous young Trotskyist with whom my friend had grown close and with whom I stayed for two weeks: She could see the yarmulke only as a symbol of Jewish nationalism and argued bitterly that it was inherently reactionary;

—Of a young North African Jew, selling carpets at the flea market at Clignoncourt, who grabbed my arm and cried, "*Haver! Haver!* Brother Jew!";

—Of another young man, minding a booth outside one of the great department stores, who asked me if I were Orthodox, and interrupted my complicated response to explain that, although he was Orthodox himself, he was afraid to wear a yarmulke in the street;

—Of an old man at the American Express office who spoke to me in Yiddish and complained that the recent North African migrants dominated the Jewish communal organizations, and that there was no place for a Polish Jew to go.

Those first, fragmentary encounters are my fieldwork juvenalia. In assuming the yarmulke, I perhaps do not stop to consider that neither my actions nor my knowledge match the standards that it symbolically represents. But it works effectively, almost dangerously, as a two-way sensor, inducing Jews to present themselves to me and forcing me to try to understand how I am reflected in their eyes.

Externally, I learn many things about the situation of French Jewry. From the patent discomfort my non-Jewish Trotskyist friend feels at my display of Jewish specificity, I gain some sense of the conflicts young French Jews—coming out of the universalist, antihistorical revolutionary apogee of May 1968—must have felt years later when they first began to distinguish themselves from their comrades and view the world from the vantage point of their specific history. From the young street peddlers, I learn about how much riskier public proclamation of oneself as a Jew is perceived as being in Paris than in New York, and a concomitant depth of instant identification of one Jew with another. My meeting with the old Polish Jew at American Express hints at the dynamics of dominant and declining ethnic groups within the Jewish community, so vastly different from those dynamics in the United States.

Internally, I begin to understand that an identifiably Jewish head-covering places its own claims on the one who wears it. The longer it stays put, the more its power to keep him out of nonkosher restaurants grows. More important, people want to know who he is as a Jew. And if he does not know, the desire for peace of mind will spur further his effort to shape an identity.

Returning from Paris, I find an apartment at Second Avenue and Fifth Street in Manhattan. I tell people, "After three generations, my family has finally made it back to the Lower East Side." In fact, none of my grandparents lived on the East Side for a long time after immigrating, even though my mother tells me she regrets having missed the Yiddish theater on Second Avenue during her girlhood. By the time I move in, there is no Yiddish theater left. The former Ratner's dairy restaurant on Second Avenue, where, I'm told, Trotsky was a lousy tipper, is now a supermarket. Though sometimes one still sees a white newspaper truck with the word *"Forverts"* in lovely blue Hebrew letters on its side drive by late at night, this neighborhood has been the East Village since the sixties, and I think of it as such.

A new friend, who devotes his time to a frustrating effort to rescue Lower East Side synagogues, tells me of a shul still in use on an otherwise abandoned block east of Tompkins Square Park. Though my friend has never been inside, he is sure that I will be welcomed, since such an isolated congregation must be looking for new blood.

The place is called the Eighth Street Shul, but its full name is Kehilas Bnei Moshe Yakov Anshei Zavichost veZosmer—Congregation Children of Moses and Jacob, People of Zavichost and Zosmer. It is owned by a *landsmanshaft* (hometown society) founded by émigrés and refugees from two towns in south central Poland. No one born in either town prays regularly at the shul now, and only one or two of the congregants are actually members of the society.

The shul is located in the center of what New York Hispanics call "Loisaida"—an area bounded by Avenue A on the east, Avenue D on the west, Houston Street on the south, and Fourteenth Street on the north. Once the blocks up to Tenth Street were almost exclusively Jewish, and on nearly every one stood a synagogue or a religious school. Now, two of those former synagogues stand abandoned, several more have become churches, and the rest have disappeared.

Eighth Street is a typical and not especially distinguished example of turn-of-the-century Lower East Side synagogue architecture.[4] It consists of five levels. The lowest contains a cranky and inadequate

[63]

boiler. The second is the *besmedresh* or study room, which was destroyed by a suspicious fire in August 1982. The third level is the main sanctuary, long and narrow like the tenements among which it was tucked when it was built. Two rows of simple pews are separated by an aisle, which is interrupted in the center of the room by the raised table from which the weekly Torah portion is read. At the very front is the Ark, surrounded by partially destroyed wooden carvings that are the most artistic aspect of the shul. The walls are decorated with representations of the traditional Jewish signs for the zodiac; the two in front on the left have been obliterated by water damage from the leaky roof. Covering most of this level, with roughly an eight-foot opening extending toward the back, is the women's gallery. The gallery is constructed in such a way that it is easier for women sitting on opposite sides of the opening to converse with one another than to see what the men are doing downstairs. Finally, upstairs from the women's gallery is an unused and cramped apartment that was once occupied by the shul's caretaker. In the roof behind it, an opening that was a skylight until there was a break-in is now covered with a solid wooden framework, allowing neither light nor vandals to enter.

Avenues B and C, which mark off the block, were once lively commerical streets with mostly Jewish storekeepers. There were also several smaller streets lined with tenements, right up to the edge of the East River. When the FDR Drive was built along the river, all the streets east of Avenue D disappeared, the tenements on the remaining available land were replaced by municipal housing, and the stores declined rapidly. During the same years, a massive middle-class housing cooperative, funded by a government mortgage, was built along Grand Street one mile to the south, and many of the remaining Jewish families moved into those houses, leaving virtually no Jews in the immediate area of the Eighth Street Shul.

Yet a minyan has continued to meet there every Saturday morning, with virtually no interruptions, throughout the years of the neighborhood's decline, while the block served as the Lower East Side's heaviest "shopping street" for hard drugs, and it lasted into the present, when buildings all around it are being speculated upon and renovated by both squatters and powerful real estate interests. It appears that until recently the main reason for this continuity was a felicitous rivalry between two men who were unwilling to abandon the synagogue because their fathers had both been presidents of it at one time. Perhaps if there had been only one, he would have given up and made peace with his conscience. Perhaps if the two men had naturally been friends they could have agreed to sell the building and officially merge their society with another still functioning further south in the neighborhood. If they had been able to agree on anything besides continuing to come to the shul, the shul might not have survived this long.

The first time I walk in, a clean-shaven, compact man in his sixties—younger than several of the congregants, who number perhaps seventeen in all—hurries forward to greet me. What's my name? Where do I live? Where am I from originally? And where do I usually go to pray on *shabes?* His name is Moshe Fogel, and he sees to it that I am called to the Torah, the honor accorded any guest who comes for the first time, without asking any questions as to his level of religious observance. Later, an older member explains to me: "Once upon a time, you wouldn't get called to the Torah unless you kept kosher and observed *shabes.*" Now, Moish prefers simply to leave those matters undiscussed.

The history of the East Side as a place where all types of Jews have lived together reinforces his discretion. Externalities such as proper or improper clothing are not essential criteria for participation. This is true of the entire Orthodox community on the East Side and has even become part of its mystique. Rabbi Reuven Feinstein, head of the Staten Island branch of the East Broadway-based yeshiva, Tifereth Jerusalem, noted in a recent speech the common reaction in Boro Park and other thriving Orthodox centers to the nonconformist dress of East Side visitors: "It's okay, you're from the East Side." The president at Eighth Street still wears a traditional *gartl* when he prays, a belt worn over his jacket to separate the pure from the base parts of his body, and no one has suggested that such old customs are out of place today. But partly because the older members at the Eighth Street Shul walked through the East Village in the 1960s and knew there were many young Jews among the longhairs—even if they were horrified at the thought—they were willing to include in the minyan a young man in the neighborhood, who when he first came wore dreadlocks under a Rastafarian-style knitted cap. It is also doubtless true that at that time there was no other Orthodox synagogue anywhere that he would have contemplated entering.

By contrast, it is impossible for any Jew raised in the middle of secular society (including a Jewish anthropologist) to join a traditionalist community without giving up major parts of his or her identi-

[65]

ty. The ways in which a researcher of contemporary hasidic life "becomes a Hasid" are much more dramatic than the way in which one
becomes a regular at Eighth Street—but they are probably more
transient as well. In order to gain the confidence of the traditionalist
communities, the fieldworker has to give the impression, whether
implicitly or explicitly, that he or she is likely eventually to accept
their standards in all areas of life (Belcove 1988). All one has to do at
Eighth Street is agree to come back—"a little earlier next time, if
possible."

Two things will draw me back to join this congregation, occasionally
referred to as "those holy souls who *daven* in the middle of the jungle."
The first pull is the memory of Farmingdale: the Ashkenazic accents
and melodies (though here they are Polish, whereas Walter Tenenbaum had prayed in his native Lithuanian accent); the smell of herring
on the old men's breath and hands; the burning sensation of whiskey,
which I must have tasted surreptitiously at the conclusion of Yom
Kippur one year in Farmingdale.

The second thing that draws me, though I do not come every week,
is a feeling that I am needed and missed when I am absent. It's hard
for me to get up early on Saturday mornings, after being out late
Friday nights. It still seems like a sacrifice, as though I were stealing
part of my weekend from myself. If I arrive in time for the *Shema*,
about half-an-hour into the service, I congratulate myself on my devotion. The summer before I marry, in 1981, I hardly come at all. When
I go with my brother to meet Moshe Fogel at the shul and give him
the provisions for the kiddush I am giving to celebrate my upcoming
wedding, I tell Dan that I usually arrive "around nine-thirty," to
which Moish retorts: "Even when you used to come, you didn't show
up at nine-thirty!" Though he says it with a smile, a message comes
through clearly: If I want to claim to belong, I should attend regularly
and arrive on time. Although I am always welcome, only if I can be
counted on am I part of the minyan. The mutual dependence of Jews
on each other—a theme running through biblical and rabbinic literature—is pressingly literal at Eighth Street.

Meanwhile, my feelings about Paris coalesce into a plan. I know I
want to live there for a time, but only if I will be among Jews. Since I
am at the point in my graduate school career when I must find a
dissertation topic, I decide to look for fieldwork situations with Jews in
Paris. I make an exploratory visit with my fiancée, Elissa. Will she
agree to a pause in her own career to follow me on this project? Will

the organizations of Polish Jewish immigrants whom I have chosen to study be willing to have me study them?

The answer is yes to both questions. Speaking Yiddish and appearing as a nice young Jewish couple seem to be the critical elements in our success. We are invited to sit in on board meetings, negotiations aimed at the reunification of societies split by political differences for over half-a-century. I am struck by the fact that these immigrants seem so much more marked by their political identification than the East European Jews I've met in New York. Also, I am impressed at the number of societies that remain in a country that has suffered Nazi occupation and that historically has shown little tolerance for immigrant cultural identifications.

But is is not so much the differences between these Yiddish speakers and those I know in New York that draws me, but rather encountering them in an environment that is otherwise so foreign. Speaking Yiddish to people with whom I have no other common language confirms its legitimacy and reinforces the sense of a distinctive Jewish identity that is shared between generations. I go for a trial interview of one activist, who is disappointed that I didn't bring "the girl," Elissa, along with me. When he discovers to my embarrassment that I have been secretly taping the interview, he is flattered.

Just before leaving Paris, Elissa and I climb the steps of Sacré Coeur. The cathedral itself is an ungracious mass, and the city looks gray and undifferentiated below us. I experience a moment of vertigo, as if I could tumble off Montmartre and drown. Part of my dream of Paris, "capital of the nineteenth century," is an infantile fantasy of becoming a universal intellectual—to be free both of the special knowledge and of the limitations of my knowledge that follow on my personal history. Yet I know I cannot come to Paris and immediately move among its confident, cliquish intellectual elite. Even less will I ever have contact with that "quintessentially French" petite bourgeoisie typified by the stolid Inspector Maigret. My first place will be with the immigrants, whose appearance, strange language, and crowded quarters provided material for unkind portraits by Maigret's creator Simenon in the 1930s.[5] If I am unable to come to see Paris as they have seen it, if I cannot make out a shared marginality a niche in the city for myself, I will be lost, as much as the "lost generation," and in a most unromantic way.

During the two years between our decision to spend a year in Paris and the beginning of that year, I attend the Eighth Street Shul more

[67]

and more regularly, and Elissa occasionally joins me. Gradually, my feelings when I miss a week shift from guilt to regret. One *shabes*, waking up late but not wanting to miss attending altogether, I arrive just in time for the kiddush, to the general amusement of the entire minyan. One February morning I wake up to see snow falling and force myself to go outside against my will, knowing that on a day like this I am truly needed.

Other incidents illustrate the gap in assumptions between myself and the other congregants. I try to bring friends into the shul, partly because it makes me more comfortable, and partly to build up the congregation. My friend, whose hair and demeanor reflect his love of reggae music and his connections with Jamaican Rastafarians, comes along one Yom Kippur. We reach the point in the service when pious men, remembering the priests in the days of the Temple, descend to their knees and touch their foreheads to the floor. Since no one wants to soil his good pants on the dirty floor, sheets of newspaper are provided as protection. Reb Simcha Taubenfeld, the senior member of the congregation, approaches my friend with newspaper in hand and asks in his heavy Yiddish accent: "Do you fall down?" The look of bewilderment on my friend's face graphically illustrates the term "frame of reference."

Another week, the same friend, failing to observe the discretion with regard to the expression of political opinions that I have learned to adopt at shul, gets into a bitter argument over the Palestinian question. Fishel Mandel, a social worker and one of the younger members of the congregation, calls me during the week to convey the message that "despite our political differences, your friend is still welcome."

After our wedding, I attend virtually every week. When Elissa comes, she is doubly welcome, since the only other woman who attends regularly is Goldie Brown, Moish Fogel's sister. Though Goldie doesn't complain about being isolated in the women's gallery one flight above the men, she seconds Elissa's suggestion that a *mekhitse* be set up downstairs. The suggestion gets nowhere, however: It would entail displacing one of the regular members of the congregation from his usual seat, and though there is no lack of available places (I myself usually wander from front to back during the course of the service), he refuses to consider moving.

I reason that I will have more of a voice concerning questions such as the seating of women if I formalize my relationship to the shul by becoming a member. My timid announcement that I would like to do so meets with initial confusion on the part of the older members of the society present. Then Fishel, ever the mediator and interpreter, explains to me that the shul is not organized like a suburban synagogue: "There's a *khevre,* a society, that owns the shul. In order to join, you have to be *shomer mitzves,* you have to keep kosher and strictly observe the Sabbath."

I drop my request. Shiye the president reassures me with a speech in his usual roundabout style to the effect that belonging to the *khevre* is a separate question from being a member of the minyan: "They send their money in from New Jersey and Long Island, but the shul couldn't exist without the people that actually come to pray here."

Meanwhile, our plans to go to Paris proceed. Our travel plans become a topic for discussion over kiddush at shul. One of the older, Polish-born members tells us for the first time that he lived in Paris for nine years after the war. We ask him why he came to America, and he answers, *"Vern a frantsoyz iz shver* [It's hard to become a Frenchman]", both to obtain citizenship and to be accepted by neighbors.

At the end of the summer, we expect to give a farewell kiddush at the shul. A few days before shabes, I get a phone call from Moish Fogel: "Don't get things for kiddush. We won't be able to daven at Eighth Street for a while. There's been a fire. Thank God, the Torah scrolls were rescued, but it's going to take a while to repair the damage." It is two weeks after Tisha B'Av, the fast commemorating the destruction of the Temple in Jerusalem.

Leaving New York without saying goodbye to the shul and its congregation, we fly overnight to Brussels and immediately *shlep* (the word "drag" would not do the burden justice) our seven heavy suitcases onto a Paris train. Arriving again at the Gare du Nord, I think of the thousands of Polish Jews who were greeted at the station in the twenties and thirties by fellow immigrants eager to hire workers. As soon as we get off the train, Elissa immediately "gets involved," demanding the credentials of two dark-skinned men who claim to be policemen and attempt to "confiscate" a carpet two Moroccan immigrants are carrying. Upon Elissa's challenge, the "policemen" demur.

We practice our French on the cab driver: I explain to him why we've come to Paris. He warns us that we shouldn't tell strangers we're Jewish. It is only a few weeks since the terrorist attack on Goldenberg's restaurant, and no one knows when the next anti-Semitic attack may come. I reply that if I hadn't said we were Jewish, we wouldn't have found out he was a Jew as well, adding that in New York the names of taxi drivers are posted inside the cabs. He says he wouldn't like that at all.

So we receive an early warning that ethnicity in Paris is not celebrated publicly as it is in New York, nor are ethnic mannerisms and phrases so prevalent as a deliberate element of personal style. This is the repressive underside of marginality. It appears wherever the individual or community think it is better not to flaunt their distinctiveness, even if they cannot fully participate in the host culture. It leads to suspicion and silence, to the taxi driver's desire for anonymity.

Arriving at our rented apartment, we meet our neighbor Isabel, who will be our only non-Jewish friend during the year in Paris, and who later explains that meeting us has helped dispel her prejudices about Jews. Over the next few days, we introduce ourselves to Jewish storekeepers in the neighborhood: Guy, the Tunisian kosher butcher; Chanah, the Polish baker's wife; Leon, the deli man from Lublin, who insists he didn't learn Yiddish until he came to Paris.

We have a harder time finding a synagogue where we feel at home. For Rosh Hashanah and Yom Kippur, we have purchased tickets at one of the "official" synagogues run by the Consistoire, the recognized religious body of French Jewry set up under Napoleon. Most synagogues run by the Consistoire are named after the streets on which they're located. Meeting a Hasid on the street, I ask him whether he happens to know when Rosh Hashanah services begin at "Notre Dame de Nazareth." He grimaces and makes as if spitting: "Don't say that name, ptu ptu ptu!"

The synagogue is strange to us as well. Most of the crowd seems if anything more secular than most American Jews, who go to the synagogue only on the high holidays. Many teenagers wear jeans or miniskirts. Because of the fear of terrorism, everyone is frisked on entering. Inside, the synagogue is picturesque with its nineteenth-century pseudo-Moorish motifs, but it is as religiously dissatisfying as the suburban American temple I used to attend. The services seem to be conducted in a traditional manner, but it is hard to tell from among the noisy throng in back. The *shames*, as a representative of the government, wears a Napoleonic hat, and the rabbi delivers his sermon from a high pulpit. When the synagogue was built, Offenbach was the choirmaster.

After Yom Kippur, I think idly about the need to find a more comfortable shul, and when I hear about an East European–style minyan within walking distance, I consider going on Simhat Torah. Watching television reports of terrorist attacks on Simhat Torah in other European capitals, I am consumed with shame at my own apathy, and thus I walk a kilometer or two to find the synagogue on the rue Basfroi the following *shabes*.

Going in, I am first shown into a side room, where men are reciting incomprehensible prayers with strange and beautiful melodies. Eventually I realize that they are North African Jews, and I venture into the main room to ask, "Is there an Ashkenazic minyan here?"

The man I ask replies in French, "We're not racists here! We're all Jews!" at which his friend points out:

"The young man spoke to you in Yiddish!" Continuing in Yiddish, he explains that while everyone is welcome in the main synagogue, the services there are in fact Ashkenazic, and so some of the North African men prefer to pray in their own style in the smaller room.

Gradually I settle in, though I have trouble following the prayers in the beginning. Remembering a particular turn in the melody for the reader's repetition of the Amidah that the president at Eighth Street uses, I listen for it from the cantor here at the rue Basfroi, and hear a satisfying similarity in his voice. I feel like a new immigrant coming to his *landsmanshaft's* shul to hear the melodies from his town.

Throughout our year in Paris, I attend this synagogue about as frequently as I had gone to Eighth Street at first. Although the congregation is not unfriendly, no one invites me home for lunch, partly out of French reserve, and perhaps also because it is clear that I'm not very observant. I feel "unobservant" here in another sense: I do not register the vast store of information obviously available here about the interaction of religious Jews from different ethnic backgrounds. It escapes me, as though I were "off duty." In contrast to my feelings at Eighth Street, I am not motivated by the desire to make myself a regular here. And this is not my fieldwork situation: Nothing external moves me to push my way through socially, to find out who these people really are and let them see me as well.

The Jews I encounter in the course of my research belong to an entirely different crowd. The *landsmanshaftn* to which they belong are secular organizations. If I wanted to observe the Sabbath closely, it would be difficult for me to do my fieldwork. The immigrants hold many meetings on Saturdays, including a series of *shabes-shmuesn*, afternoon discussions at which the main focus this year is the war in Lebanon.

I mention to one of my informants that I sometimes go to the synagogue. "I admire that," he responds. "I can't go back to the synagogue now. I've been away too long; it's too late for me." Toward the end of the year, we invited an autodidact historian of the immigrant community to dinner on Friday night, and ask him to say the blessing over the challah. "I can't," he refuses, and will not explain further. Though his intellectual curiosity has led him to become friendly with us, and he is considering doing research on the resurgence of Orthodoxy among young French Jews, his critical stance vis-à-vis his own secularist movement is insufficient to allow him to accept this religious honor. Enjoying the possibilities offered by marginality is sometimes impossible for those who are neither young nor well educated and who have often been deceived in their wholehearted commitments.

Throughout the year, Elissa has been growing stricter regarding *kashres*. She refuses to eat nonkosher meat and will order only fish in restaurants. She articulates our shared impression that Jewish secularism has failed to create everyday lifeways that can be transmitted from generation to generation, and that any lasting Judaism must be grounded in Jewish law and learning. Before parting for the summer—she to study Yiddish at Oxford, I to Jerusalem, to acquire the Hebrew that I will need to learn about Jewish law—we discuss the level of observance we want to adopt on our return to New York, but we come to no decision.

Elissa and I meet at the end of the summer in Los Angeles, for the bar mitzvah of her twin cousins. I am uncomfortable riding on *shabes;* after spending an entire summer in Jerusalem; for the first time, it seems like a violation of myself. The roast beef sandwich I eat at the reception is the first nonkosher food I've eaten since leaving Paris.

Thus, without having made a formal declaration, I join Elissa in observing *kashres* (save for occasional lapses that I call my "*treyf* of the month club" and that become less and less frequent), and she joins me in keeping *shabes*, albeit with some reluctance. Preparing to fulfill a promise made in a dream I had while in Paris, I take a further step: At the beginning of November, I begin attending daily services at another East Side shul and thus putting on tefillin again. One of my mother's cousins at the Telshe Yeshiva in Cleveland—whom I have never met—told me in the dream that I would always be welcome there, and I responded that if I got there, I would put on tefillin every day from then on. Later in November, Elissa and I fly to Cleveland for the weekend. Though we are welcomed warmly, it is clear that the rabbis and *rebetsins* at the yeshiva hoped for something more Jewish from me, the great-grandson of the Rosh Yeshiva's second wife, Miriam.

We return to the Eighth Street Shul as well, which has been secured and repaired sufficiently to make it usable once again. There are changes. Old Mr. Klapholz, with whom I hardly had exchanged a word, has passed away. Fishel's uncle Mr. Hochbaum, a congregant for half-a-century, no longer attends, since he is unable to walk all the way from Grand Street. On the other hand, my long-haired friend has moved into the neighborhood and attends regularly. Two of the younger members of the congregation have small children now, and they must go to a shul where there are other children for their son and daughter to play with. In February, our oldest member passes away, and after Shavuot, another member moves to Jerusalem. Two more young men eventually begin coming regularly and bring along their infant children. Now, in June 1986, the shul has thirteen regular male attendees. I am no longer free to sleep late on Saturday mornings, and fortunately I no longer want to.

All of this, to the extent it is of my own making, is the result of a search to realize that fragile illusion of wholeness which was destroyed when my family and almost all the others left Farmingdale. I will hazard a guess that Jewish anthropologists—perhaps anthropologists in general—are motivated by a sense of loss. Yet the seamless image of community is inevitably a child's image. We cannot regain what is lost, if only because it never existed as we remember it. Nothing in society is quite as harmonious as it seemed to me then, and I later learned about bitter political struggles that had taken place in Farmingdale, just as they had among the immigrants in Paris.

Our strategy, rather, should be to attempt to understand what it is we miss and need, which is available in still-living communities in another form. The image of wholeness which we share is foreshadowed by communities all of us stem from, however many generations back, and it can serve as a guide in the search for the reciprocal relationships of autonomous adulthood.

Anthropology is a tool for mediating between the self and the community. It has helped me to come to belong at the Eighth Street Shul:

[73]

to withhold my opinions when it seems necessary, without feeling the guilt of self-compromise; to accept instruction and gentle reprimands with good humor; to believe it is worthwhile preserving something that might otherwise disappear. But belonging at Eighth Street does not mean that I have dissolved myself into an ideal Orthodox Jew. If I attempted to do so, I would be unable to continue being an anthropologist. If I fit into any category, it may be what my friend Kugelmass calls the "funky Orthodox": that is, those who participate in the community but whose interests and values are not confined to the Orthodox world. In fact, there are no ideal Orthodox Jews at Eighth Street; it is our respective quirks that provide the *raison e'être* of this haphazard but now intentional once-a-week community.

The fact that I have found a religious community that needs me because of its marginality and will tolerate me because of a generosity born of tradition is what I mean by the marginal redemption of one Jew. Likewise, if the shul survives, it will be because of its very marginality, because of the many individuals who have recognized the creative possibilities of a situation that demands that they create a new unity, while allowing each of them to retain their otherness. Isn't this the dream of anthropologists? Whether attempting to communicate knowledge between different Jewish communities, or between communities much more distant in tradition and empathy, we are messengers. We spend our own lives in moving back and forth among the worlds of others. As we do so, in order to avoid getting lost along the way we must become cultural pioneers, learning to "get hold of our *trans*cultural selves (Wolff 1970:40). Communities on the edge of mass society, or even on the fringes of ethnic enclaves, seem to be among the most congenial fields for us to do so.

Let me finish with a parable:

Two Jews can afford to be fastidious about the dress, comportment, and erudition of a third. It gives them something to gossip about and identify against. Ten healthy Jews can have a similar luxury; an eleventh means competition for the ritual honors. It's nine Jews who are the most tolerant, as I learned one forlorn *shabes* at Eighth Street. It was almost ten o'clock, and there was no minyan. Since everyone seemed content to wait patiently, I assumed that someone else had promised to come, and asked, "Who are we waiting for?"

"A *yid*," our oldest member replied without hesitation.

Eventually a Jew came along.

Notes

1. Compare Pierre Bourdieu's critique of the structuralist theory of "reciprocal" gift exchange: "even if reversibility [i.e., the assumption that gifts entail countergifts of equivalent value] is the objective truth of the discrete acts which ordinary experience knows in discrete form and calls gift exchanges, it is not the whole truth of a practice which could not exist if it were consciously perceived in accordance with the model. The temporal structure of gift exchange, which objectivism ignores, is what makes possible the coexistence of two opposing truths, which defines the full truth of the gift" (1977:6).

   Similarly, in a narrative such as this one, because I, as author, already know the ending, it may seem as though each successive element fits into those that precede and follow it in such a way that their necessity is perfectly known. Actually my aim is to show how the background that nurtured me shaped in part my unpredictable responses to situations that in themselves were historically rather than culturally determined. See my conclusion, where I refer to one of the communities I now participate in as "haphazard but intentional."

2. Even if it was no more than a matter of convenience, this annual event demonstrates Jonathan Woocher's point that American Jewish "civil religion expects Jews to take advantage of the opportunities which America provides, and to use them to help fulfill their Jewish responsibilities" (1985:161).

3. This may seem an outrageously loose claim, and I am quite willing to be proven wrong by literary scholars. But compare the conclusion of James Joyce's *Portrait of the Artist as a Young Man:*

   > "Mother is putting my new secondhand clothes in order. She prays now, she says, that I may learn in my own life and away from home and friends what the heart is and what it feels. Amen. So be it. Welcome, O life! I go to encounter for the millionth time the reality of experience and to forge in the smithy of my soul the uncreated conscience of my race" (1968:252–3).

   with the end of Moshe Szulsztein's memoir of a Polish Jewish childhood:

   > "When the truck was already fairly far along Warsaw Street and Kurow was barely visible, two more relatives appeared in a great rush, wanting to take their leave. These were my grandfather's pair of pigeons. The pigeons knew me, and I knew them. I loved them, and perhaps they loved me as well. . . . But the truck is stronger than they are, it drives and drives further and further away from Jurow. My poor pigeons can't keep up, they remain behind. . . . Before they disappear altogether from my view I still discern them within the distant evening cloud, two small flying silver dots, one a bit behind the other. That, I know, is the male, and the second, a bit in front, is the female" (1982:352).

4. For photographs of Eighth Street and other Lower East Side shuls, both surviving and abandoned, see Fine and Wolfe (1978).

5. "In every corner, in every little patch of darkness, up the blind alleys and the corridors, one could sense the presence of a swarming mass of humanity, a sly, shameful life. Shadows slunk along the walls. The stores were selling goods unknown to French people even by name" (Simenon 1963:45).

[75]

REFERENCES

Bakan, David. 1958. *Sigmund Freud and the Jewish Mystical Tradition*. Princeton, N.J.: Van Nostrand.

Belcove-Shalin, Janet. 1988. "Becoming More of an Eskimo." In *Between Two Worlds: Ethnographic Essays on American Jewry*, ed. Jack Kugelmass. Ithaca: Cornell University Press.

Bourdieu, Pierre. 1977. *Outline of a Theory of Practice*. New York: Cambridge University Press.

Clifford, James. 1986. "On Ethnographic Allegory." In *Writing Culture: The Poetics and Politics of Ethnography*, ed. Clifford James and George E. Marcus. Berkeley: University of California Press.

Cuddihy, John Morrow. 1974. *The Ordeal of Civility: Freud, Marx, Lévi-Strauss and the Jewish Struggle with Modernity*. New York: Basic Books.

Fabian, Johannes. 1983. *Time and the Other: How Anthropology Makes Its Object*. New York: Columbia University Press.

Faur, José. 1986. *Golden Doves with Silver Dots*. Bloomington: Indiana University Press.

Fine, Jo Renée, and Gerard Wolfe. 1978. *The Synagogues of New York's Lower East Side*. New York: Washington Mews Books.

Gough, Kathleen. 1968. "Anthropology and Imperialism." *Monthly Review* 19, 11:12–27.

Joyce, James. 1968 [1916]. *Portrait of the Artist as a Young Man*. New York: Viking Press.

Schnapper, Dominique. 1983. *Jewish Identities in France: An Analysis of Contemporary French Jewry*. Trans. by Alan Goldhammer. Chicago: University of Chicago Press.

Simenon, Georges. 1963. *Maigret and the Enigmatic Lett*. Trans. by Daphne Woodward. New York: Penguin Books.

Szulsztein, Moshe. 1982. *Dort vu mayn vig iz geshtanen*. Paris: Published by a Committee.

Wolff, Kurt. 1970. "The Sociology of Knowledge and Sociological Theory." In *The Sociology of Sociology*, ed. Larry T. Reynolds and Janice M. Reynolds. New York: David McKay, 31–67.

Woocher, Jonathan. 1985. "Sacred Survival." *Judaism* 34, 2:151–62.

[3]

Becoming More of an Eskimo: Fieldwork among the Hasidim of Boro Park

Janet Belcove-Shalin

Long before I began fieldwork among the Hasidim, I knew how difficult my task would be. A single woman in a sex-segregated society, a non-Orthodox Jew in an ultra-Orthodox Jewish community, an exponent of cultural relativism in an ethnocentric milieu—I could hardly expect my informants to be forthcoming and accommodating. Having settled in the hasidic community of Boro Park, Brooklyn, I was relieved to discover that my fears were only partially justified. The very handicaps I had most feared proved at times to be hidden assets. No male anthropologist could establish nearly as good rapport with a *hasidiste* (a female Hasid), whose modesty must be safeguarded, as I could. A non-Orthodox Jew examining Orthodoxy, I presented a welcome opportunity for my hosts to try to intensify my religious observance. And even my research could be counted on to stimulate readers' interest in a religious way of life.

Of course all my vices and virtues were foremost in the minds of the informants who consented to be interviewed. This supposition was

This article is a revision of a paper presented at the 1982 Annual Meeting of the American Anthropological Association. It is part of a project supported by grants from the National Science Foundation, the Lucius N. Littauer Foundation, and the Memorial Foundation for Jewish Culture. I thank Zalman Alpert for his insightful remarks on the basement inhabitants of Boro Park, and Jack Kugelmass and Dmitri N. Shalin for detailed comments on the earlier drafts of the manuscript. Finally, I express my deepest gratitude to all those generous informants who shared with me their personal reflections.

underscored in a conversation with one of my key informants, Mr. Silverstein,[1] an enthusiastically upbeat, wry, intellectual Hasid, unusually generous with his time, who was always ready to help me, the naive anthropologist, unravel the meanings of the social fabric of his community. One afternoon while discussing the significance of the *tish*, a ritual meal presided over by the rebbe (a leader of a hasidic dynasty), Mr. Silverstein mentioned a conversation he recently had at a *tish* that involved his rebbe, the rebbe's son, and a friend, Mr. Feld. The conversation was about me:

"That evening at the *melave malke* [the fourth meal of the Sabbath, and a time of mystical significance], as we and the rebbe were honoring the outgoing *shabes* [Sabbath], telling a few stories of the *tsadikim* [righteous men] and eating some herring, one of our *khaverim* [comrades], Hershel Feld, remarked to me that an anthropologist [i.e., me] had approached him and requested an interview, mentioning my name as a reference. At that time, Mr. Feld had declined, but he was now wondering if he shouldn't reconsider. The rebbe's son interjected that he too had been approached by others, and was always wary about that sort of thing. Mr. Feld readily concurred: 'After all,' he asserted, 'What is the value of exposing ourselves to possible ridicule? Remember the woman who came on Lag b'Omer [a day's break in a period of mourning] researching Jewish music and dance, who wrote notes like mad in the *vayber shul* [women's area of the synagogue] and made everybody feel uncomfortable?'

"Challenging them, I retorted that even though we don't go out missionizing, if someone comes to us, it's an opportunity to explain ourselves. Since we are here with a mission, we have an obligation to explain . . . to bring *kedushe* [holiness] into the world. And if an opportunity comes to explain, to teach, to show while we are in control of the situation, then it is alright, it's part of our mission.

"Mr. Feld protested, recalling an interview he once gave in which his words were taken out of context, and since issues of mental health were involved, the misstatements were particularly regrettable.

"I was sympathetic but still of a different mind. 'Why,' I challenged, 'has a researcher picked this topic of all topics? What made *this* the topic? This is not so simple a question. It's *hashgokhe* [providence]! Every person can learn more about *yidishkeyt* [Judaism] somewhere. Research is an individual's opportunity to experience it *and* to make the choice—yes or no. And they can't say, "I never had the chance." Again, it's *hashgokhe!* . . . And who do you think is reading this anthropological stuff? Only the person with an interest. Who knows how they will connect with the material. I'm never afraid of exposing what I consider to be truth, what I consider to be *kedushe*, to scrutiny.'

"Finally, the rebbe raised his voice: 'Where does it all lead to? I must see committment on the part of the researcher or else I will not take up my own time and energy.' To this I replied that each informant also derives a personal gain from the experience because it helps to clarify issues in one's own mind. Once you express these issues you can survey them, possibly reevaluate, but you always see where you are.

"The rebbe's son retorted, 'How many people studying Eskimos actually become Eskimos?' I rejoined, 'How many Eskimos do you know doing this kind of research? Maybe if an Eskimo were studying Eskimo things, he would become more of an Eskimo!'

"That's when Hershel Feld finally gave in: 'Well,' he said, 'next time this woman anthropologist comes to me, perhaps I won't be so busy.'"

This is, in essence, the story of my predicament. I was a stranger, an intruder, a potential threat to the community, yet I was tolerated, even welcomed, as someone who could be shown the right way of living—the hasidic way. The context of my fieldwork, then, is best characterized as a struggle for dominance between my secular and religious selves; as the Hasidim tried to enflame my religious passions, I, the curious ethnographer and unobservant Jew, plumbed the mysterious depths of their faith.

This experience had distinct methodological implications for my research: participant observation, I discovered, was not mere method, unreflexively applied to achieve entrée into community life. It was rather an intricate process of interpretation and role-playing. The reflexive inquiry I intend to pursue here focusses on the dynamic relationship between the ethnographer and her informants,[2] making it the centerpiece of analysis. To this end I evoke what Erving Goffman has variably referred to as "face-work," "presentation of self," and "impression management" (1959, 1967). All of these concepts highlight the conscious and subconscious acts that help us to sustain appropriate appearances in public places and arrive at mutually agreeable definitions of the situation in personal encounters. The following account, then, explores the relationship between myself and members of the hasidic society from the standpoint of the interaction that spawned it.

[79]

My interest in Hasidism long predates my professional interest in anthropology. In retrospect, I trace my fascination with this folk to a Jewish school—a secular establishment favored by those parents who had drifted away from religious Judaism, yet retained a strong feeling for Jewish culture that they hoped to cultivate in their children. Each Sunday morning, transferred back into history, I would imagine myself at the helm of the Macabbees' revolt, suffer the torment of the Spanish Marranos forced to disown their faith, or rejoice in the victory of the heroic Esther and Mordechai over the evil Persian, Haman. All of these events had occurred so long ago, among people vastly different in culture, society, and even religious practices, yet bonded together by a belief in a single people, sharing a set of symbols so powerful that they stir the consciousness of people across time and space. These symbols were particularly vivid, I thought, in those marvelous little stories—hasidic tales, as I later realized, whose simple humanity and honesty awed me.

After an eighth-grade graduation, my forays into *yidishkeyt* came to an end, and it was not until I began my work as a graduate student at Cornell University that I stumbled upon an article about Hasidim. As I was reading it, it occurred to me that the hasidic movement was a textbook case for the problems with which anthropology has always been concerned and with which I was then grappling: "charismatic leadership," "revitalization," "routinization," "magic," "ritual," and "symbolism." These academic interests, coupled with a genuine desire to fathom the religious life so contrary to my secular upbringing, prompted this inquiry.[3]

My interest took me to the YIVO Institute for Jewish Research in Manhattan, where I studied Yiddish and gained a background in Eastern European culture. During the delightfully hectic year I spent there, I met people with complementary interests, discovered the incredible variety of Jewish life in New York City, read, among many other books, the compelling works of Max Weinreich on the cultural history of Yiddish and those of Abraham Joshua Heschel on hasidic thought, and I began to study the history of Hasidism.

In the history of Judaism, Hasidism is a relatively recent movement. It sprang to life in mid-eighteenth-century Eastern Europe as a revitalization movement—an organized and sustained effort to create a more satisfying culture. Hasidism was initiated by Rabbi Israel Baal Shem Tov (Master of the Good Name), also know as the Besht. A renowned storyteller and popular healer, he had a special appeal to the simple folk whom he taught to serve God through song, dance, and piety. The Besht's circle of followers became a bona fide movement under his successors. His spiritual heir, Dov Baer of Mezeritch, dispatched his disciples to instruct others in the Besht's teachings. As growing numbers of Jews were attracted to Hasidism, communities came under the stewardship of charismatic leaders, referred to as rebbes or *tsadikim,* who developed customs and traditions of their own. With time, their leadership became hereditary, and the numerous hasidic dynasties were formed. The eve of the twentieth century saw Hasidism dominating the lives of the majority of Jews in the Ukraine, Galicia, and Central Poland, and the movement had many followers in Belorussia, Lithuania, and Hungary.

Europe's political turmoil played havoc with Jewish life. During World War I many hasidic communities laying in the paths of warring armies were destroyed, their inhabitants scattered throughout Europe, leaving them isolated from their coreligionists and spiritual mentors. The Holocaust dealt a final blow to the remaining hasidic centers in Eastern Europe. The survivors of once-majestic hasidic courts resettled elsewhere in the Old and finally in the New World. Elie Wiesel characterizes these new habitats as inextricably bound to the obliterated communities of their old masters: "They live in America but they belong to Lizensk, Mezeritch, or Rishin. There are no more Jews in Wizsnitz, but there are Wizsnitzer Hasidim on both sides of the ocean. The same is true for the other Hasidic branches or dynasties. Ger, Kossov, Sadigor, Karlin—these kingdoms have but transferred their capitals. Lubavitch is everywhere except in Lubavitch; Sighet and Satmar are no longer in Transylvania but wherever Satmarer and Sigheter Hasidim live and remember" (1972:38).

Today, New York City is the major center of hasidic life in the New World. Williamsburg, Crown Heights, and Boro Park are the most prominent residential areas favored by Hasidim. Of these three, the communities of Williamsburg and Crown Heights are the oldest and most studied (Gersh and Miller 1959; Kranzler 1961; Levy 1975; Mintz 1968; Pinsker 1975; Poll 1965, 1969; Rubin 1972). Yet in the last decade, Boro Park has emerged as the newest stronghold of *yidish-keyt,* attracting to its middle-class neighborhood the ultra-Orthodox. Today Boro Park is home to many hasidic communities, tracing their roots to Poland, Hungary, Galicia, the Ukraine, and White Russia. Such legendary dynasties as Bobov, Ger, Karlin, Vishnitz, Munkacs, Breslov, Skver, Belz, Spinka, and Satmar live within little more than a

[81]

square mile of each other. My first forays into Boro Park readily confirmed the neighborhood's image as a thriving, heterogeneous community.[4]

Boro Park is a peculiar mixture of modernity and tradition. Yeshivas, shuls, and *shtiblekh*—hasidic places of study and prayer—are everywhere. Twice a day an armada of yellow school buses bearing the names of their yeshivas in Hebrew and English crisscrosses the avenues. As they bring the youngsters to school, their fathers gather in *shtiblekh* to *daven* (pray).

Shops with religious paraphernalia line the avenues selling silk and velvet yarmulkes (head coverings for males), paper child birth amulets, mezuzahs (a small cylinder containing a prayer), embroidered challah (ritual bread) coverings, religious books, and an assortment of records, produced, in part, by the neighborhood hasidic boys' choirs. During the holidays, window displays are dominated by Purim costumes (a holiday celebrating Jewish survival in ancient Persia), the special plants for Sukkot (a pilgrimage festival associated with the first fruits harvest), and Hanukkah (the festival marking the Maccabean victory) candles and oils.

The ubiquitous women's clothing stores sell fashionable, though modestly tailored apparel (i.e., skirts below the knee, tops that cover the elbow and the collar bone) befitting the community's sense of propriety. One can also find numerous *sheytlekh* stores that retail wigs—an important accessory of a married woman symbolizing piety—in a variety of popular styles. By contrast, the men's clothing stores stock the traditional Eastern European garb: the dark-colored double-breasted knee-length coats or *ibitsirs*, along with matching vests and baggy pleated trousers. Then there are the textured and sometimes iridescent *tish bekeshes* (coats), worn by males on a *yontev* (holiday), *shabes*, or special occasion, which contrast with the total inkiness of day-to-day male clothing. Black hats of various designs—the broad-rimmed headgear of the Hungarians, the smooth tall crowned hats of the Poles, or the medium-sized smooth crowned hats preferred by the Galicianers—complete every man's wardrobe and can be purchased in special millinery shops.

During my first visit I was struck by the abundance of food establishments in Boro Park. Besides the typical grocery stores, there was a profusion of kosher take-outs, fast-food establishments selling a wide variety of "Jewish" delectables, such as pizza, felafel, and knishes; butcher shops, bakeries, and dairy stores. Every store's showcase

[82]

window prominently displayed notice of its products' rabbinic super-vision.

Boro Park is also a major center for bargain-priced merchandise. Its electronic stores rival those of the Lower East Side and Midtown Manhattan, both of which are dominated by Hasidim. And in the basements of many apartments, small wholesale shops have sprout-ed, operated by Orthodox women selling everything from lingerie to linen. Some shops have become such substantial enterprises that their proprietors' husbands have quit their own jobs to assist their wives.

The profusion of construction sites, unusual in a borough as old and established as Brooklyn, is another sign of the neighborhood's vitality. In vacant lots once filled with single-family homes, three-story multi-family dwellings sprout. These new red brick structures with their ample balconies have become hallmarks of an increasingly hasidic Boro Park. On the Jewish holiday of Sukkot, most balconies shelter a sukkah (booth) constructed of wood, formica, or brightly colored can-vass. At Hanukkah, menorahs (nine-pronged candelabrums) illumi-nate the front windows, much the way Christmas decorations do in other neighborhoods. And nearly all homes display mezuzahs at-tached to the right doorpost.

In mid-September of 1980, just before the Jewish high holidays, I moved into a basement apartment in one of those red brick buildings several blocks from Thirteenth Avenue in the heart of the hasidic community. The two-room dwelling with a secluded backyard, shaded by a meandering grapevine and enclosed by rose bushes, became home for the next two years of my life.

I vividly recall those early days in Boro Park. The very first night I was awakened at four-thirty in the morning by the heavy footsteps of my upstairs neighbor. The pattern was repeated the next night and the night thereafter. Increasingly exhausted, I reluctantly trudged upstairs to "inquire" about the nocturnal noises. I rang the doorbell a few times and was about to leave when an elderly man opened the door a crack: "Who are you?" he barked. I identified myself as his new downstairs neighbor. "Are you *shomer shabes* [observant of the Sab-bath and other commandments]?" he then asked. The very directness of his question (which I would hear again and again from other Boro Parkers I barely knew) stunned me. I mumbled something about keeping kosher and trying to keep many of the commandments. Satis-fied that I was a *bas Yisroel* (daughter of Israel), he went on to explain to me that his wife was not home, and though he would have liked to invite me in, it would not be proper for him to do so until she returned. Then without giving me a pause to explain the nature of my visit, he asked if I had a place to eat for the upcoming holidays. Startled by this sudden gesture of hospitality, I reassured him that I already had somewhere to go, and then felt all the more embarrassed by having to state the reason for my visit. Apologetically, my neighbor explained that an elderly sick man like himself rattled about on the wooden floor when he got up that early to observe the morning prayer of *slikhes* (penitential prayers preceding the high holidays). I knew nothing about *slikhes* at the time, and feeling ashamed of my ignorance about religious law and out of deference to the infirmities of an old man, I tried to make light of my complaint. I told my neighbor that I would do my best to ignore the noise in the future. After all, I rationalized to myself, *slikhes* could not last forever. But to my dismay, the end of *slikhes* did not bring relief. On *shabes* and *yontev*, I could hear the deafening thuds of visiting grandchildren, jumping, running, and skipping above me, as well as the scratching noises of the furniture moved around in preparation for bedtime. Complaining about the noise was futile, for it simply reflected the inner rhythm of life in Boro Park. A week into my fieldwork, though, I was dreaming of attics.

When I moved into Boro Park in the Hebrew month of Tishri, it was a time of intense religious activity. All my efforts to arrange interviews were rebuffed with the typical remark "after *yontev!*" Having little else to do, I joined others in bringing in the New Year of 5741 on Rosh Hashanah (Jewish New Year). Nine days later we observed Yom Kippur (the Day of Atonement), the climax of this period of judgment. On the 15th of Tishri, Sukkot began. *Khol hamoyed*—a five-day break in this holiday season—brought a welcome respite to the community and to my weary self. The festivities resumed on Shemini Atzeret (a time when the bond between the people of Israel and God is honored), and these then were capped off by the merrymaking on Simhat Torah (a celebration for the annual completion of the reading of the Torah and the beginning of the new cycle).

The pounds I had gained from the many holiday meals at the homes of my generous hosts were no doubt shed in nervous energy when I experienced the exacting and formal confines of an ultra-Orthodox shul (synagogue), a threatening and difficult milieu for someone with a secular background like mine. A diary entry records my feelings during Kol Nidre (the beginning of the Yom Kippur service when all vows are annulled). At times I felt on the verge of tears—not so much for the "sins" I was renouncing, but as a Jew feeling so utterly alien in a Jewish environment. "How can I ever hope to understand these people?" But after a day or two spent outside the community with friends, my resolve returned, and I was once again eager to start interviewing—to make sense of what I had experienced the month before.

Networking, or branching out to meet new informants via old ones, was the most common way of meeting respondents. Having secured new names and telephone numbers, I would spend endless hours on the phone contacting prospective informants and scheduling interviews. Ethnography that is conducted from a basement apartment, some ways off the street, differs sharply from traditional fieldwork. In a small community, where the line between public and private space is not as sharply drawn as in the West, social drama unfolds virtually in the fieldworker's front yard; one's life inevitably becomes intertwined with that of the people being studied. By contrast, completely buried in the bowels of Boro Park, I had to work hard at networking and to make heroic attempts (or so it seemed at times) to gain access to my informants' more private lives. My ability to meet with Hasidim was further complicated by the fact that in such a bustling urban community as Boro Park, time is a precious commodity not easily parted with. Women's days would be consumed by the needs of their large families, and perhaps by jobs. Men worked throughout the day and usually studied Torah in the evenings. Normally I tried to interview women before their children returned home from school or after they were in bed, and men at their offices or at home right before they left for the *besmedresh* (a place of study and prayer). It was somewhat easier to connect with retired couples who had the time and willingness to chat with me. I also arranged appointments with neighborhood leaders, hasidic big wheels, and officials in the community health services, who provided valuable insight into the workings of the community.

Arranging an interview was one thing. The real challenge was turning the attention of informants toward the subjects of interest to me. The problem that dogged me throughout my fieldwork was overcoming the Hasidim's negative perception of me as someone radically different from themselves. For the Hasidim, I was a *goyishe yid* (Gentile Jew), someone viewed with a combination of contempt and incredulity. This perception reflected their general attitude toward non-

Orthodox Jews. Hasidim dismiss Reform Judaism outright for what they consider its total disregard of halakhah (Jewish law). If they find Reform Judaism so preposterous as not to merit serious rebuttal, they are adamant about Conservative Judaism, which they consider much more of a threat because of its selective approach to halakhah. Some Hasidim are even contemptuous of nonhasidic Orthodoxy. One of my informants related the story of an acquaintance of his who was tossed out of a *shtibl* by the same Hasidim he knew in his youth from Hungary, but who now regarded him as a *maskil*—an Orthdox Jew unduly preoccupied with secular wisdom. Understandably, my status as a gentile Jew was a source of irritation to many of my respondents, who had little to gain from our association.

Equally disturbing for some informants was the nature of my enterprise. Querying them about their social reality could potentially expose its problematic nature and thereby undermine it. Yet it is in the nature of anthropology to probe individuals about their attitudes and practices, particularly about the contradictions and inconsistencies that are ever-present in social life. In doing this with the Hasidim, however, I risked being accused of engaging in *loshn hore* (evil talk). Occasionally, my questioning would be abruptly interrupted with the declaration that such a topic is, in fact, *loshn hore*. "Talking about *anybody*, good or bad, is inexcusable," one lady told me in response to a query, and that was the end of our conversation. But if the topic could conceivably compromise an individual's reputation, or worse, tarnish the image of a harmonious community devoted to fulfilling God's commandments, my writings about it might be regarded as a *khilel ha-Shem* (the defamation of the divine name), a particularly heinous crime within a religious community. Moreover, since Jews in general and Hasidim in particular see themselves as a vulnerable and frequently persecuted minority, most Hasidim have a very low threshold for what they consider to be slander. As even mild criticism could provoke hostility, I had to be very careful phrasing my questions and explaining the purpose of my study.

The wariness some Hasidim displayed toward my research was in part a reflection of their low regard for anthropology. Like many other people, Hasidim frequently confused it with the theory of evolution. Religious fundamentalists, they flatly reject Darwinism as contrary to the biblical story of divine creation and therefore sacrilegious. On more than one occasion, a book by a prominent local rabbi ridiculing the theory of evolution was recommended to me. One particularly feisty woman thrust this opus upon me and demanded that I read it right then and there. As I skimmed through its pages, I was appalled by its cavalier attitude to scientific facts and its penchant for wrong-headed generalizations. All my knowledge of cultural relativity notwithstanding, I had found myself on the defensive. Apparently, the conventions of my own milieu with its high regard for science and its revered constructs such as the theory of evolution had a stronger emotional hold on me than I had realized. Indeed, of all the indignities I suffered in Boro Park—the cancelled appointments, postponed interviews, the downright snubbing—it was this encounter that offended me the most. My feeble attempts to point out the book's more egregious misstatements only prompted an irate response. Clearly, this was not an appropriate place to argue the merits of the theory of evolution. And so, I quickly learned to put a considerable distance between my project and the accepted truths of my culture.

An evolutionary perspective was not the only problem anthropology posed for Hasidim. Some of those who grasped the nature of my study found the idea of cultural relativism untenable, if not out-and-out insulting. Hasidim, like all Jews, regard themselves as the chosen people—those who accepted God's invitation to abide by the 613 *mitzvot* (divine commandments). If gentiles observe seven of the precepts incumbent upon all descendants of Noah, they too share a place in the world to come. Most Hasidim, however, do not see any evidence that these canons are, in fact, being practiced. The most adamant on this issue were often my elderly informants, most of whom are Holocaust survivors. Those who could bear to discuss their war experiences, regaled me with one horror story after another as proof of man's inhumanity to man. Others simply denied that non-Jews had made much contribution to civilization. One particularly chauvinistic *hasidiste,* convinced of her unparalleled heritage, demanded to know: "What did they ever do in Africa? And what about Italian history? Just look at their heroes and compare them to a *Moyshe rebeynu* [Moses, Our Teacher]. And the scalping and cannibalism by American Indians? What exactly is there to be so proud of?"

Given this attitude, it is understandable that Hasidim find coexistence with the radically different communities of Hispanics on their northeast fringes and blacks in nearby Flatbush to be problematical. Specifically, these neighborhoods' comparatively high unemployment and crime rates are seen as threats to the hasidic community's autono-

[87]

my and viability; fearful of felons, Boro Parkers have organized citizen's patrols to discourage criminal incursions into their neighborhood.

Likewise, the Hasidim's view of American society is highly critical.
They regard it as an overly anarchical society, in which liberty means
freedom from responsible and meaningful relationships. The pornog-
raphy and perversity of 42nd Street, the generation gap, the breakdown of the family are all, according to Hasidim, the logical outcome
of false or superficial values. Moreover, they see such values as the
antithesis of those in their own community, where freedom is understood as the choice to commit oneself to God's commandments.

The flip side of my "misguided" loyalty to ethnography in the eyes
of Hasidim was my objective stance toward them. From my own
vantage point, this perspective was required if I was to "bracket reality," to place into question nearly everything that was unquestionable
for the Hasidim. But from the hasidic point of view, it was precisely
this value-neutral stance that interfered with my perceptiveness.
Hasidim believe that Judaism cannot be viewed objectively, nor can it
be understood through rational study alone. Authentic understanding
of the hasidic soul, I was told, presupposes religious engagement; it
must be approached subjectively as passionate, personal commitment. Should an individual choose to have a relationship with God, he
must suspend the judgement of reason to make a leap of faith. Here,
then, lies the paradox of my fieldwork: if I refuse to embrace the
spiritual practices of my subjects, I risk missing the very essence of
hasidic life, for in the hasidic worldview, to understand a Hasid is to
be one.

Clearly, if I could not find the way to overcome some of their
negative perceptions of me, my fieldwork would never advance further than a preliminary research prospectus. I somehow had to transform an extremely marginal, almost stigmatized status into a more
positive identity. Indeed, it was only after I encouraged (or chose not
to actively discourage) their belief that one day I might become more
observant that they began to take me seriously and to open their doors
to me. This transition occurred gradually, and it began with my introduction, my presentation of self (Goffman 1959); I informed each
potential respondent that I was living in Boro Park for dual reasons:
although I was a student researching the hasidic community, my studies afforded me the chance to satisfy my deep interest in Judaism. By
causally relating my studies to my religious involvement, I was able to

vindicate (somewhat) my discipline by showing its best face, insofar as it guided me toward a religious way of life. Subsequent encounters further proved my good will, as each informant could witness personally my commitment and sincere desire to learn more about Orthodoxy. Only then was I able to overcome my "radical" otherness and attain the more acceptable status of a "liminal" other.

The concept of liminality helps to chart my trajectory from a *goyishe yid* to an observant Jew. The term liminal stems from the Latin word *limen* or threshold (Turner 1967). The liminal personality is situated somewhere on the threshold between a new and an old status, between membership and nonmembership. For the Hasidim, I was a person in transition, who would eventually become a bona fide member of the religious community; they defined me as a woman in search of her religious roots and waiting for a husband to be chosen from among the members of the community. Indeed, my basement residence symbolized these liminal traits. Apparently, I had moved into a niche long favored by other aspiring souls on their way to becoming full-fledged members of the religious community.

Basement apartments are additional lodgings built by landlords to generate extra income. These less-desirable underground homes attract tenants of modest means. Most of these basement dwellers, however, prefer to consider their housing arrangements as an interim solution. Essentially there are three kinds of people who live in these accommodations: single women, male yeshiva students, and *baley tshuve* (individual Jews who choose to join a religious community despite their nonreligious background).

Young women come from all over the world to live in Boro Park in order to marry a "religious boy." Instead of living alone—an arrangement strongly discouraged by the community—women will share an apartment with at least one roommate. Since the single life is an unacceptable lifestyle, the primary objective of these women is to make a successful match. Strictly speaking, marriage is not a religious requirement for women, the way it is for men. Nonetheless, a woman finds herself in a difficult social position if she does not marry; for although a man can engage himself in a worthwhile career or pursue Talmud study full-time, neither are deemed suitable vocations for a religious woman, who can be fulfilled only as a wife and mother.[5]

The single men occupying basement apartments are typically students, sent to Boro Park to attend one of the numerous yeshivas. Although the status of student is completely respectable, it is a transitory one, to be superceded by the roles of husband and father. The yeshiva student's faith is held to be fluid until he is married and subsequently entrenched in community life. When he begins to draw on his learning as a married adult, he is no longer regarded as "impressionable" in relation to the corrupting influences outside the community.

The *bal tshuve*, the third category of underground dweller, consists of individuals who for various reasons feel themselves drawn to the world of Orthodoxy. The position of such persons is seen as a tentative one, since all acknowledge that religious observance entails a commitment and education not easily attainable by the unresolved. Their marginal status is underscored by the fact that *baley tshuve* do not normally marry into prominent hasidic households. There are several reasons for this: *baley tshuve* are often regarded as unstable because they turn to religion to fill a nonreligious void in their lives. It is also assumed that their parents did not observe the *mitzvot* of family purity when they were conceived, hence their conceptions were less than pure. For Hasidim, *yikhes* (family pedigree) is another important consideration in arranging marriages. Not only do they look for compatible families, they also hope to marry into a prestigious one, one distinguished by scholars, affluence, and piety. Few *baley tshuve* can boast descent from a long line of great Jewish scholars. Moreover, since they are from outside the community, few if any Boro Parkers know anything about their family backgrounds. As a result, *baley tshuve* have considerable difficulties integrating themselves fully into hasidic society.

Clearly my role as an anthropologist did not have much legitimacy in the eyes of most respondents, yet my basement status—a single woman and a *bal tshuve*—did. These were my properties congruent with their own values, hence those worthy of reinforcement. And so I deliberately chose to follow hasidic norms: to dress modestly, to observe public commandments, to keep the dietary laws, to attend shul, to seek out the rebbe with a *kvitl* (request)—in short, to cultivate the image of an individual with a sincere interest in orthodoxy. Despite my willingness to conform to the cultural externalities of Orthodox life, some Hasidim most assuredly saw through this face, detecting a far greater willingness on my behalf to learn rather than to practice, for I could not, it turned out, observe those *mitzvot* that felt inauthentic. This is when my informant would quote the biblical passage "*naase venishma*, we will do and we will hear," which the Hebrews uttered at Sinai when they accepted the covenant. The phrase is interpreted to mean that studying or understanding the Lord's will is secondary to practicing it; action is always more important than understanding. The implication, of course, was that I should observe what I had learned, regardless of my comprehension. Understanding, I was told, would in all probability come later. In response I could only shrug my shoulders, entreating them to consider the background from which I came that made it impossible for me to abide entirely by their laws—at present.

The adjustment I finally had to make to my informants' sense of reality is part and parcel of the fieldwork process, because the role of the ethnographer is inevitably what the informants allow it to be. Clifford Geertz describes this collaboration as a "set of fictions, half seen through . . . [that] lies at the heart of successful anthropological research" (1968:151, 154), Both the ethnographer and the informant are engaged in this sense-making process in which certain characteristics are reinforced while others are discreetly downplayed or strategically concealed. In any case, both the Hasidim and I steered clear of sensitive topics that would expose the precarious nature of our selves. Goffman describes this posture as "defensive" face-work (1967:14), an avoidance practice that keeps one "from activities [or topics] that would lead to the expression of information that is inconsistent with the line he is maintaining" (ibid.). In the case of my fieldwork, I maintained an appropriate face by stressing my enthusiasm (and a genuine one at that) for learning about the religious life, downplaying my academic degrees (Hasidim scorn college), and not volunteering any information about my varied circle of friends and activities outside of Boro Park. The Hasidim, on the other hand, defended their face by overplaying their communal harmony, lilywhiting untoward facets of their existence, and covering up deviance in their midst. Using Goffman's model of "impression management," Gerald Berreman argues that this conduct is fundamental to the inner workings of ethnography: both the ethnographer and informant are performers, deliberately choosing which faces to present. The impressions the anthropologist's subjects have of him will in the final result determine their own availability, hence the quality and quantity of the ethnographer's data (1972:xxxiii).

Impression management should not be misconstrued as the anthropologist deliberately selling a false image of herself. In the thick of fieldwork, there are many roles to play. Which of these is the authentic self may be as unclear to the anthropologist as it is to the informants. What may appear as " 'me behaving as someone else,' [can, in fact, be] 'me in another state of feeling/being': performing my dream, re-experiencing my childhood trauma, showing what I did yesterday" (Schechner 1982:41). At times, I was truly bewildered as to which one of my selves was more authentic—a note-taking anthropologist out there in the field collecting data for the dissertation, or a Jew at a Passover gathering, celebrating the Israelite's exodus from Egypt with the rest of my *khaverim,* with the suddenly awakened childhood memories of the *brokhe* (blessing) over the wine and the jolly seder songs. But even more often, I felt the temptation to break with my ethnographic persona altogether and to express my wonderment at my hosts' uncanny ability to keep faith in the face of pervasive evil in the world. What particularly baffled me was how the Hasidim could pray daily to a "just, merciful, and all-wise God" who had led them to (or at least failed to save them from) the Holocaust, suffering of unknown magnitude He visited on His chosen people. This sentiment is what Max Weber calls the problem of meaning—the need of all people to come to grips with the evil and suffering in the world that appears so meaningless. How, he asks, can we harmonize pain, defeat, and loss, with the image of a loving and magnanimous God? Why must the righteous suffer along with the sinful? How, I wondered, is faith possible after the Holocaust? I ached to raise such questions with these pious Jews, sometimes against my better judgment as an anthropologist, fearing that my queries would be judged as blasphemous and cost me the contacts I had so carefully cultivated.

To my relief, my questions did not seem to alienate my informants. In fact, they struck a responsive cord; many Hasidim were more than eager to try to make sense of this most recent cataclysmic event. Their responses, I discovered, revolved around two biblical types, what I would call the Noah and the Job paradigms.

The bible tells us that God saved Noah, a virtuous man, from the flood he created to cleanse the earth of all evil. We are taught that while God punishes the guilty, he will nonetheless save the righteous. The bible also relates the story of Job, a prosperous, God-fearing man who unwittingly becomes the target of a bet between Satan and God. Satan argues that if Job were to lose his worldly possessions, God would lose Job as his obedient servant. When the deal is struck, Job is put to the test: his possessions are destroyed, his family is lost, he himself is afflicted by diseases, but he still holds to his faith. This story teaches us that the innocent can suffer for reasons beyond their comprehension. Suffering, though, is not meaningless; it becomes a test of our fidelity to the Almighty.

Akin to their understanding of the flood story, some of my informants blamed the Holocaust squarely on fellow Jews. "Jewish people," said Mr. Silverstein, "can reach the heights of holiness, but just as well, they can sink to the depths of sin. . . . We didn't learn, we didn't repent, some Jews even turned their backs on their faith," he told me. "And it is precisely because we were so important to God that he chose to punish us, like a dear child."

Other informants, many of them Holocaust survivors, made peace with their past sufferings and, like Job, refused to second-guess God's reasons or to impute to Him malicious intent. Once I asked my landlady how she could call God "all-merciful" after having witnessed Auschwitz. "There is no contradiction," she retorted. "If I could understand everything, there would be no reason to have faith." Still another Hasid recalled the Klausenberger rebbe who was forced to witness his wife and eleven children being gunned down by the SS. "If anybody had asked me," the rebbe told my informant, "I would say they were innocent. *He* [God] saw otherwise. Let it be His way!"

The subject of keeping faith in a senseless world came up in a conversation with a hasidic gentleman, Mr. Schiff, I had met on a stalled subway. Our cordial ties had encouraged him to ask me some personal questions about my family's faith. I had to admit that my father found it particularly difficult to believe in God after the Holocaust. "Why would God multiply Job by six million?" both he and I wondered. Mr. Schiff reacted to my father's agnosticism with utter bewilderment: "But if he does not believe in God," he probed, *"what does he believe in?"* Mr. Schiff's total commitment to God was truly stunning! Absurd as it might seem to some to keep one's faith after the Holocaust, it was even more absurd for Mr. Schiff to give it up and embrace a meaningless universe. The world without a supreme judge and a sacred law was, for him, total anarchy; it is God who makes the insufferable sufferable. Whatever fate God had in store for him, he, like Job, was ready to accept the Almighty's wish with *simkhe* (joy)—a sigh and a smile with which the pious submit to and celebrate God's infinite wisdom.

While satisfying my hunger for personal knowledge, I had to be

[93]

careful not to overstep the invisible borderline that separates curiosity from tactlessness. Fortunately, I was aided in my efforts by the institutionalized role of the *amorets* (a person ignorant of Jewish law and custom). This role afforded me the welcome opportunity to make even the most elementary queries without incurring stigma. For the Hasidim, the *amorets* is not completely negative in connotation: the founder of the movement, the Baal Shem Tov, had a particular fondness, even respect, for the unschooled yet pious. On the other hand, once I had learned the way, I had to be very cautious not to breach it, for then I would be cast as an *epikoyres* (a nonbeliever or skeptic who knowingly disobeys the law) and risk total ostracism.

It was never quite clear to me, though, where one role ended and the other began. If I did not perform a mitzvah I had presumably learned, would I still be regarded as too ignorant to comprehend its tacit sacredness and hence as exempt from responsible religious action? Or would my inactivity be interpreted as a rejection of the mitzvah and thus constitute a flagrant violation? In point of fact, because the Hasidim saw me as a sympathetic outsider with little Jewish education, they employed a "protective orientation toward saving the others' face" (Goffman 1967:14), in this case my own, by casting me as an *amorets*. I am certain they would not have been so generous to an insider's nonparticipation, and I can only wonder how long the Hasidim would have allowed me to play this part.

My role as a single woman was also a source of constant concern to my informants. I was continually reminded about the proper station of the sexes, a topic of paramount interest for Boro Parkers. In fact, one of the features that distinguishes the Hasidim from the nonhasidic Orthodox is the stringent observance of the commandments of *tsneus* (modesty) and *tahares hamishpokhe* (family purity). These commandments are reflected in hasidic society by a well-defined division of public and private domains, and in the radical separation of the sexes.

Although I was constantly reminded of gender differences, I found that to discuss sexual matters was generally deemed inappropriate, even with women. It was not just a question of sex being an embarrassing topic. Many simply thought that an unmarried and unengaged woman had no business knowing what was of no use to her. Hasidic men and women apparently get their "sex education" when they are engaged: men—from an older, wiser man; women—in "*kale*" (bride) classes. In practice, many facts of life are learned after marriage, essentially by trial and error. My attempts to join a number of *kale* classes in Boro Park were rebuffed by the teachers, who gently told me that I would be welcome to participate, but all in good time.

The requirements of modesty and family purity proved to be a particularly serious problem in my dealings with male informants. I had to be extra-cautious to avoid transgressing the law to secure their cooperation. Hasidim believe that the separation of men from women other than their wives (though in some instances wives are not exempt), keeps a man directed toward God, away from his *yeytser hore* (evil inclination). Hence, all direct contacts between nonspouses are eschewed: men will not receive an object directly from a woman's hand; they will not listen to a woman sing; nor will they gaze directly at her. When, for example, I finally met with the rebbe, he had his male secretary on hand for the duration of the audience and never once looked in my direction. As long as I strictly adhered to these norms and kept all my interactions with men public, I did not have problems interviewing them. As a matter of fact, some of my best informants turned out to be men. My rapport with hasidic women, by contrast, proved to be more difficult than I had originally expected. I soon discovered that I had the least affinity with some of my own peers. Born and bred in Brooklyn, married, burdened with large families, forever lacking my social mobility, these women were very unlike myself. In retrospect, I think their discomfort may have stemmed from their ambivalent attitude toward the freedoms my status as a secular woman afforded me, a status they could occasionally envy, but had been socialized to disdain. On the other hand, I had a certain kinship with their mothers—a vital, can-do lot, whose wealth of life experiences before and after the Holocaust fascinated me, and whose grandmotherly warmth made me feel welcome.

Despite my ability to interview both male and female Hasidim, in a community such as Boro Park where sex and lifestyles articulate so strongly, my gender carved out for me a well-defined niche. I had to resign myself to the fact that I could not pray or study with men or attend storytelling gatherings. On *shabes, yontev,* and other ritual occasions, I was consigned to a place behind the *mekhitse* (a barrier dividing the sexes in the synagogue) with the women. As an unmarried woman, I was the subject of well-intentioned, albeit unwelcome, attempts to find an appropriate mate for me. For only as a married woman, according to the Hasidim, could I experience the joys of motherhood as well as observe the three positive mitzvahs incumbent upon women: *hadlakes haneyr* (the lighting of holiday and Sabbath candles), challah (breaking off the tiny piece of challah from the un-baked loaf), and *nide tivile* (the laws of family purity pertaining to menses).

To remedy what for them was an unenviable plight, well-wishers tried to arrange numerous matches for me. The instigator of most of my *shidukhim* (matches) was Rabbi Heyland—the *gabbe* (assistant) for a local rebbe. Rabbi Heyland was also an accomplished *shadkhn* (matchmaker). On more than one occasion I became the subject of his matchmaking ministries, when he took it upon himself to find for me a "nice religious boy." Once he even arranged for another *shadkhn* to call me up with a prospective groom. On another occasion he confided to me that a fellow from a yeshiva in Cleveland had come the day before and that he was interested in meeting someone nice. "Perhaps the next time he is in town you can meet him?" he added. And then there was the mathematician *bal tshuve* who called me one evening at Rabbi Heyland's prompting. The subject of my future mate was never far from Rabbi Heyland's mind. This became all the more evident the day I went to visit him at work to arrange an audience with the rebbe. It turned out that the only way I could meet the rebbe was by writing a *kvitl* (request), which he as the *gabbe* helped to prepare. Rabbi Heyland started the procedure by writing the initials of *borekh ha-Shem* (blessed be God) on the top of an unlined piece of paper. He then wrote in Yiddish my name (he always called me Sheyne): *Sheyne Sore bas Brine Rivke*, which literally means Sheyne Sore daughter of Brine Rivke (my mother's Yiddish name). I then showed him the requests I had prepared in Yiddish, the vernacular of the community. He proceeded to translate what I had written into Hebrew. Unable to restrain himself, he also revised my requests, some of which were overly esoteric or were on behalf of other people in general. "It's no good asking for others without specifying who they are," he explained to me. "Also, why ask to see the beauty in the world? It's there for everybody to see. But Sheyne—you have forgotten the most impor-tant thing—to find a husband!" And so it went. . .

Not everyone, of course, who consented to an interview did so to further my religious training or to marry me off. Some were simply curious about the non-Orthodox world and seized the chance to learn more about it from a not-so-alien other. Others just considered help-ing a person in need to be a mitzvah. For those more intellectually inclined, this was a rare opportunity to articulate concepts long ago learned in yeshiva. Some of the most fascinating interviews I had were with two appreciative and inquisitive informants, Isaac Tanner and Mordechai Zion, a Litvak (Orthodox, nonhasidic Jew) and a Hasid who worked together in a community office. Although these men had been colleagues for years, my questions nonetheless highlighted world-views of each of which the other was unaware, and often dissonant. At times, when the conversation was becoming increasingly intense, I would sit back and with some satisfaction quietly listen as these two men debated and grilled one another. Other office workers, their curiosity piqued by the controversy, would oftentimes stop by to enhance a view or simply add another. Our sessions, I now realize, were times in which these men could make better sense of their own traditions. Furthermore, by answering those questions pertinent to a social scientist, they recast and synthesized principles that had been all but taken for granted until our acquaintance. It was as if our hours together served as a time of study (commanded twice a day by the Torah), a time to deliberate and reexamine the tenets that guided their lives; I posed the questions, raised the exemptions, as they—a modern-day Abbaye and Rava—eagerly clarified, expounded, rein-terpreted from their unique perspectives.

One more group of people with whom I enjoyed rapport deserves to be singled out for mention. I discovered that my status as a liminal personality in Boro Park attracted other liminal characters who felt at ease with me and chose me as a confident. These people were usually my best informants, because although they were often deeply com-mitted to the hasidic ethos, they were able to assume a more detached and critical posture than most. This, however, was not without per-sonal consequences for the informant. Mr. Lerner was one such lim-inal personality. My first impression of this remarkable man is re-corded in my diary:

> My two conversations with Hillel Lerner have given me wings. My kabbalistic friend Yitzhak is right—when you meet a beautiful person, you do meet God! Mr. Lerner appeals to me greatly; his sensitivity, generosity, and appreciation for the ironies and paradoxes of life capti-vate me. I feel I am with a person who has had to make hard choices so often in his life that his existence is filled with intensity and passion. He alludes to the fact that his past is studded with heartache, yet he insists that pain is necessary for an authentic life.

Mr. Lerner was born of an assimilated immigrant family from the Ukraine. His father, now dead and buried in a non-Jewish cemetery, was an atheist. His sister married a Catholic. Not until he was seven did Mr. Lerner understand what it means to be a Jew. Prompted to get a traditional Jewish education, he was enrolled at the ultra-Orthodox school in Williamsburg, Brooklyn. It was here that he first encountered Hasidim. Their *nigunim* (melodies) captivated him. Every *shabes* he and his classmates would go from one hasidic shul to another in search of new melodies. Hasidim's appeal was cemented by a hasidic rebbe who came to Brooklyn following World War II. He was "everything a rebbe should be," Mr. Lerner told me. "Clever, passionate, clean—he had an aura of royalty to him, and he *deeply cared* about his Hasidim." When the rebbe moved to Israel, Mr. Lerner followed him. In Israel he married a young hasidic woman from another hasidic community, "a beautiful girl from a good family." He and his wife eventually had a brood of children, now scattered throughout the world. At the time of our friendship, Mr. and Mrs. Lerner were estranged, although he did not give up hope for a reconciliation.

As his family continued to grow, Mr. Lerner was compelled to augment his salary. He decided to acquire a certificate as a teacher of secular studies, enrolling in a university where he eventually studied sociology. His enthusiasm for the discipline led to graduate school and a dissertation that he never defended. At the time of my research, Mr. Lerner worked in the secular programs of neighborhood hasidic schools in the mornings and spent his entire afternoons at the *besmedresh*.

Mr. Lerner is acutely aware of his marginality. Living in North America, he dreams of being in Israel; well versed in secular literature, he shuns it for his religious studies; in a community that is family-oriented, he is estranged from his wife; but perhaps most significantly, he is a Hasid without a rebbe. After his rebbe died, he found it difficult to transfer his devotion to either of the rebbe's sons. These days he occasionally visits another rebbe, and prays without a *gartl* (a hasidic belt) at a *misnagdish* (nonhasidic Orthodox) shul. Despite his heartfelt alienation, Mr. Lerner was unwilling to change his conduct significantly. My comparatively free-wheeling life, which we discussed on occasion, was unappealing to him (save for the chance to view a Broadway play or two). Not only did my sort of lifestyle fail to captivate him, it repelled him; after he met me he retreated further into his world, a measure more secure in his own life's insecurities.

Mr. Lerner and other marginal Hasidim confounded the face of my more conventional informants by sensitizing me to the facets of hasidic life the latter preferred to gloss over. Theft, prostitution, even homosexuality, they claimed, were uncommon though not unknown to Boro Park. This is not to say that other members of the hasidic community were unaware of deviance in their midst. "Under the beard may be a *geluakh*" (nonkosher, shaven face; an amoral individual hiding behind the mask of piety), one *rebetsn* (the wife of a rabbi or rebbe) cautioned me. Yet I remember how naively staggered I was when two months into my fieldwork, a respectable member of the community, married into a prominent rabbinic family and teaching at a local yeshiva, confided to me, a virtual stranger, that he had committed the sin of adultery: "You should not think that everybody who looks like a Hasid is in fact one. A Hasid is a state of mind, a way of doing things—good things the right way. I consider *you* more than me. . . . I was raised in a family that I should be more than I am, and I am not; and you were raised in a family where maybe you should be less than you are and you are more. So, you are more than me. I think everybody is more than me. I have a *yeytser hore* [evil inclination] and I can't help myself."

This statement and others similar to it had important consequences for my research. If fieldwork among the Hasidim highlighted my own hazy Jewish identity, encounters with individuals like this man had me discover how amorphous the hasidic identity could be. Being a Hasid, I realized, means more than appearing to be one, means more than speaking like one, or even worshiping like one. The bottom line of being a Hasid is having a pious consciousness, which may or may not correspond to any symbol of piety. Man, the Hasidim say, is not born a *tsadik* (saint); piety is a quality that must be nurtured. And it is the Hasid who quintessentially strives to achieve the ideal of *hesed* or lovingkindness, a concept from which the term "Hasid" was coined. Ironically, if this Hasid perceived me as more spiritual than himself, it was because he thought I strived to be better, while he, an adulterer, yielded to his baser instincts. At the same time, it should not be forgotten, other Hasidim perceived me less sympathetically as a skeptic who questioned the tenets of our faith. In point of fact, perhaps a more accurate portrayal of me includes both these perspectives. Likewise, a fully valid description of a Hasid and the hasidic community must include a panoply of characteristics, often in apparent contradic-

[99]

tion. As my research evolved, determining for myself what it meant to be a Jew became no less difficult a task than understanding who was a Hasid.

The enigmatic survival of the Jewish people has inspired a variety of explanations: some have attributed Jewry's endurance to their history of social organizations; others looked to their capacity to disregard the present for an illustrious future; still others to the special qualities of the Jewish faith. Most intriguing, however, is the literary critic Harold Bloom's argument that ties Judaism's endurance to its "text-centeredness" or "text-obsessiveness," a passion for reading and interpreting sacred texts (1982:319). For Hasidic men, as for all other Orthodox male Jews, the study of sacred texts is a mitzvah: men are required to interpret texts twice a day. This discourse is not to be construed as an exercise in scholasticism, some recondite mindgame, but the very matter of survival. For during the reading, discussion, and interpretation of a Talmudic passage, a Hasid may draw upon his life's experience and thereby bridge the gap between the all-too-fallible world of everyday life and the sacred ideals of Torah. But the type of textuality I specifically have in mind is not necessarily contingent on having any one text in hand. It constitutes a frame of reference by which the Hasid makes sense of the world and distills a plan of action. Jews are not called "the people of the book" only because of their devotion to Torah, but because of their hunger for knowledge, for divining sense out of obstruse texts, for reading meaning into an unintelligible world. Thinking back upon Mr. Silverstein's story of the *tish*, I see how the discussion was actually a meditation on texts, a way of reconciling the sacred and secular dimensions of the participants' lives, indeed, the most recent chapter in *Toyre she-balpe* (Oral Torah). So when his friends finally decided to accept me into their community, it was on their terms; they rendered my activity into one of the community's most enduring key symbols—the *bal tshuve*. But despite the Hasidim's blandishments to transform me into a "Torah true" Jew, I eventually came to appreciate how hard the sincere Hasid actually struggles with himself to enhance his own relationship with God. In this sense, he, too, is a *bal tshuve*—the one who eternally aspires to be a true "Hasid." This is the thrust of Mr. Silverstein's remark when he cautioned: "Recognize the community as one of human beings, but also one which is seeking to perfect all that humanity is capable of. The very fact that there is a need to search for perfection means that we are not there, but that we have committed ourselves to being there."

Precisely because the Hasidim are apt to convey the image of communal and personal harmony, it is necessary to do full justice to the fierce undercurrents of spiritual struggle among them. And so, I ironically conclude with the observation that far from being a trait of the intruder-ethnographer alone, liminality typifies as well the hasidic way of life, the everyday existence of these Boro Park residents who through their ongoing dialogue with texts attempt continuously to position themselves on new thresholds of spirituality.

Notes

1. All names of informants are pseudonyms.
2. In the wake of this approach, the classical subject-object antinomy—the hallmark of positivistic methodology—yields to the principle of subject-object relativity. The concept "Hasid," then, is an emergent social category in that it is the product of interaction between the ethnographer and the informant. The actual context of this category is one that is inextricably bound to the interpretive practices of the investigated and, ultimately, of the investigator.
3. In recent years, anthropology has become more self-reflexive, more aware of the cultural and social roots of its own practices. Having discovered the West in the East, the image of the occident reflected in Islam (Lévi-Strauss 1977:462), are we not poised to discover the exotic in ourselves? I consider my own research to be an instance of the paradigm that regards the unfamiliar and familiar to be as intertwined in ourselves and in everyday life as they are in our dreams. We have finally discovered a stranger—an Other—in our own backyard.
4. There are two works dealing specifically with some aspect of the Hasidim of Boro Park, both dissertations (Epstein 1979; Kamen 1975).
5. There are, of course, exceptions. I met several hasidic women pursuing professional careers, among them, a graduate student working for her Ph.D., a social worker, and a nurse. Most of the professional women I encountered, however, were *baley tshuve*.

REFERENCES

Berreman, Gerald D. 1972. *Hindus of the Himalayas.* Berkeley: University of California Press.
Birnbaum, Philip. 1979. *Encyclopedia of Jewish Concepts.* New York: Sanhedrin Press.
Bloom, Harold. 1982. "Free and Broken Tablets: The Cultural Prospects of American Jewry." In *Agon: Towards a Theory of Revisionism,* ed. Harold Bloom. New York: Oxford University Press.
Bosk, Charles L. 1979. "The Routinization of Charisma: The Case of the Zaddik." *Sociological Inquiry* 49:150–67.

Epstein, Shifra. 1979. *The Celebration of a Contemporary Purim in the Bobover Hasidic Community*. Ph.D. diss., University of Texas.

Freilich, Morris. 1977. *Marginal Natives at Work: Anthropologists in the Field*. New York: Schenkman.

Ganzfried, Solomon. 1961. *Code of Jewish Law*. Trans. Hyman E. Goldin. New York: Hebrew Publishing Co.

Gersh, Harry, and Sam Miller. 1959. "Satmar in Brooklyn." *Commentary* 28:389–99.

Geertz, Clifford. 1968. "Thinking as a Moral Act: Ethical Dimensions of Anthropological Fieldwork in the New States." *Antioch Review* 28:139–58.

Goffman, Erving. 1959. *The Presentation of Self in Everyday Life*. Garden City, N.Y.: Doubleday Anchor Books.

——. "On Face-Work." 1967. *Interaction Ritual*. Garden City, N.Y.: Doubleday Anchor Books.

Gutwirth, Jacques. 1978. "Fieldwork Method and the Sociology of Jews: Case Studies of Hassidic Communities." *Jewish Journal of Sociology* 20:49–58.

Kamen, Robert Mark. 1975. *Growing up Hasidic: Education and Socialization in the Bobover Hasidic Community*. Ph.D. diss., University of Pennsylvania.

Kranzler, George. 1961. *Williamsburg, A Jewish Community in Transition*. New York: Philipp Feldheim.

Lévi-Strauss, Claude. 1977. *Tristes Tropiques*. New York: Pocket Books.

Levy, Sydell B. 1975. "Shifting Patterns of Ethnic Identification among the Hassidim." In *The New Ethnicity: Perspectives from Ethnology*, ed. John Bennett. New York: West. 25–49.

Mintz, Jerome R. 1968. *Legends of the Hasidim*. Chicago: University of Chicago Press.

Mayer, Egon. 1979. *From Suburb to Shtetl: The Jews of Boro Park*. Philadelphia: Temple University Press.

Mitchell, Douglas, and Leonard Plotnicov. 1975. "The Lubavitch Movement: A Study in Contexts." *Urban Anthropology* 4:303–15.

Pinsker, Sanford. 1975. "Piety as Community: The Hasidic View." *Social Research* 42:230–46.

Poll, Solomon. 1969. *The Hasidic Community of Williamsburg: A Study in the Sociology of Religion*. New York: Schocken Books.

——. 1965. "The Role of Yiddish in American Ultra-Orthodox and Hasidic Communities." *YIVO Annual of Jewish Social Sciences* 13:125–52.

Rabinowitsch, Wolf Zeev. 1971. *Lithuanian Hasidim*. New York: Schocken Books.

Rubin, Israel. 1972. *Satmar: An Island in the City*. Chicago: Quadrangle Books.

Schechner, Richard. 1982. "Collective Reflexivity: Restoration of Behavior." In *A Crack in the Mirror*, ed. Jay Ruby. Philadelphia: University of Pennsylvania Press. 39–81.

Schick, Marvin. 1979. "Borough Park: A Jewish Settlement." *Jewish Life Magazine*, 23–35.

Turner, Victor. 1967. *The Forest of Symbols: Aspects of Ndembu Ritual*. Ithaca: Cornell University Press.

Wiesel, Elie. 1972. *Souls on Fire*. New York: Random House.

SECTION TWO

Subcultures

[4]

The Secular Seder: Continuity and Change among Left-Wing Jews

Anita Schwartz

I first began fieldwork among descendants of the Workers Cooperative Colony when there was still a cloud of fear hanging over its residents. This community had been formed by left-wing Jews in 1927 and they had not yet fully recovered from the disruptive effects of the McCarthy era, particularly the execution of Ethel and Julius Rosenberg. During the McCarthy era the colony was under constant surveillance, owing to the belief that sought-after communists were being hidden there. Close to each major entrance to the courtyards of the colony, federal agents were stationed in a parked car, watching the people as they came and went, and it was believed that those who participated in the annual May Day parade and similar events were photographed. Several individuals had to appear before the Senate Subcommittee on Un-American Activities and subsequently lost their jobs or were imprisoned. Indeed, the disruption of community and family life lingered for over a decade.

I thank Jack Kugelmass for inviting me to write the story about the secular seder as observed by descendants of the Workers Cooperative Colony, familiarly known as "the coops." I am especially grateful to Jack for his patience in reading the various drafts of this essay and for his constructive comments and creative ideas, which I have incorporated into the article. The ethnographic material is the result of fieldwork among residents of the colony, located in the Bronx, New York. Normally anthropologists do not identify the locale of the people they study and in previous works this practice was observed. Now, however, people from the colony want their way of life and ideology known. The practice of maintaining confidentiality and protecting the identity of individuals from the colony has been adhered to.

As a result of a history of contact with people of the colony and as a student of anthropology interested in recording a once-vital way of life that appeared to be on the wane, I gained entry into the homes of its residents. Sometimes in hushed tones and at other times quite boldly I heard members of the colony proudly recall how they had achieved the highest quality of life for their children. They were "progressive Jews" who raised their children with a social consciousness. Stories were told with pride about how they aided strikers, stopped evictions, demonstrated against segregation in public facilities, opposed the injustice commited against Sacco and Vanzetti, fought for unionism and social reforms, and participated in the annual May Day parade. However, the word "communism" was never uttered, and topics that might have linked anyone to "subversive" activities were avoided. This was an implicit understanding, not something that was open for discussion. Besides I wasn't interested in muckraking. I am not a journalist, and in line with standard anthropological practice, I assured people that the names I used would be fictitious and details about individuals would be changed to protect their identities.

I wanted to understand what happens to a people's ideas, values, and beliefs as their way of life changes. Sociologists of ethnicity in American life, such as Robert Park and Louis Wirth in the 1920s and 1930s saw ethnic groups in terms of assimilation and their ultimate absorbtion after several generations into the larger society. Contemporary observers of American Jewry are less certain of this. Although some see the group as an "endangered species" (see Glazer 1985), others take an opposite view, even suggesting that American Jewry is undergoing a major revitalization (Silverman 1985). I never found the concept of assimilation a helpful one because it did not explain the loss of certain traits and values or the retention and persistence of others. Do a people "just" assimilate? Often the extent to which a person was said to have assimilated was measured against so-called "objective" criteria, such as intermarriage or the frequency of religious observance. These criteria were established by the "outsider," the social scientist. A primary interest of anthropologists is to obtain the "insider's" view. Indeed, a group that is viewed as having such marginal associations with traditional Jewish practice offers an interesting case study. Based on the data I gathered in the 1960s from the people who lived there, I traced the history of the colony, noting the various transformations of its ideas, values, and beliefs. Given the memory of the political climate that lingered at the time, I was content not to publish my research and to let the manuscript I had written gather dust in the closet.

In 1977, however, sentiments had long since changed about the past. The McCarthy era was over. Individuals who had been black-listed were able to enter meaningful occupations. A decision to have a reunion made by just a few individuals of the second generation generated great interest. Through informal networking and announcements in the *Morgen Freiheit,* the left-wing Jewish press, and in *Jewish Currents,* a monthly secularist periodical, two thousand people gathered for a day in New York to recall, reminisce, and reestablish contacts. I actively participated in the planning of the bicentennial reunion and interviewed descendants from the colony. The years since have witnessed a resurgence of interest among the descendants in recapturing the colony's way of life and of concern that it be conveyed to their children. Once again in 1983 and continuing to the present, I conducted interviews and attended meetings to learn more about the continuity of ideas, values, and beliefs in the face of the enormous changes and discontinuities that separate the three generations whose lives were shaped by the colony and its culture (see Schwartz 1984).

Workers Cooperative Colony

The people who formed the Colony migrated from Russia and Poland between 1910 and 1922. Some came to the United States with an already well developed political consciousness because they had broken with traditional *shtetl* culture. News regarding the socialist and labor movements spread among Jews of the *shtetl* through traveling lecturers and labor organizers. Other Jews who had migrated to the cities of Eastern Europe to become industrial workers were attracted to the socialist movement there. Ideologically, the people who were to establish the colony traced their background to the Bund, which in 1897 formed a separate Jewish workers organization within the Socialist party. Bundists fostered antireligious views and at the same time were outspoken advocates for cultural continuity and the use of the Yiddish language. They also identified with the Leninist principle of an international working class. The leaders of the Bund perceived no contradiction between establishing a separate branch for Jewish workers within the Socialist party and the Leninist principle calling for unity of all workers (Levin 1977).

Many of the young Jewish immigrants who formed the colony became workers in the needle, fur, and millinery trades. There they encountered sweatshops, indiscriminate hiring and firing, extremely low wages, and long hours. Degrading experiences in the shops and rising dissatisfaction drew them to the picket lines. Those workers who did not have a socialist background soon joined the labor movement and working conditions made them easy converts to socialist ideology. At first they affiliated with a Jewish socialist association, the Workmen's Circle. Soon thereafter, factions formed within the membership. At the extreme left, were the *"linke"* or leftists, who were attracted to Leninism and who were labeled as communists. In 1930 the new left joined with the International Workers Order (IWO), which by 1940 had attained a membership of thirty-five thousand members in the Yiddish-speaking branches (Howe 1976:344). In 1922 they began to publish their own newspaper (*Freiheit*), and they formed separate culture clubs and many voluntary associations.

The colony was the inspiration of a small group from the left faction of the socialist labor movement. They believed that the colony would serve as a model for other working-class people and would demonstrate the supremacy of a working-class cooperative community over other communities in a capitalistic system. However, it was not to be merely a real estate investment; it was to be a consumers' cooperative. Based on Lenin's concept of cooperativism, approximately 25 percent of the money would go back to the people in the form of educational, social, and recreational services. In this manner they would achieve an ideal community, a community where equality and brotherhood reigned as supreme values and where the highest quality of life existed for the worker.

The idea of building a cooperative community emerged in 1922–1923 among young men and women who went on summer hiking trips. The idea of the colony was based on a vision of a workers' paradise. From the ugly and crowded railroad flats on New York's Lower East Side, the workers moved to houses facing Bronx Park, surrounded by beautiful flowers and landscaping. "There were no elevators in the colony, still we wanted to live on the highest floors so that we could look down into the courtyards at the magnificent assemblage of flowers, fruit trees, and plants," stated one woman. A second-generation descendant recalls, "I was five years old when we moved from the Bowery. The colony was like the country. I remember frolicking in the grass. There were no sidewalks. It was the wilderness."

At its inception, the colony was composed almost entirely of left-wing Yiddish-speaking people from Eastern Europe who worked in the same trades. They formed a relatively homogenous group, culturally, economically, and ideologically. As active members of unions and as advocates for social and economic reform within the working class, they had deep pride in being workers and a conviction that meaningful social reform could only be achieved by a united working class. Moreover, the Yiddish language was a cornerstone of their worldview. Rooted in Eastern European Jewish life, it was the language of the "folk" (Wisse 1985). Yiddish became associated with social class, particularly with the oppressed, and with social reform. Thus, it gave ready form to the ideas, values, and beliefs of the working-class movement.

Very much like traditional *shtetl* culture, the focuses of the colony were the numerous voluntary associations within which the worldview and values of the members of the colony found expression.[1] Evenings were a time for meetings, lectures, discussion groups, dance and music groups (a choral group, a music school, and balalaika and mandolin orchestras). Periodically there were concerts and banquets so that people who excelled in a particular area received special recognition. Through the arts, lectures, and discussion groups, creativity in thinking and expression was encouraged and stimulated. The voluntary associations provided the links in the network of overlapping relations between the individuals and groups in the colony.

The children of the colony were informally divided by ages. Each age cohort formed a different group and was characterized by a unique set of relationships centering on various clubs and interests. Major activities were associated with the *shule*, the Yiddish secular school, and the youth center, but children started their education in the all-day nursery-kindergarten. In the words of the colony's newsletter, *The Bulletin*, "There children learn that they are not the center of the world, but must share work materials and toys, must work together with their comrades" (1934:9–11). Values such as working together, building together, and sharing were constantly emphasized. "The colony produced a certain kind of person," recalls a second-generation descendant. "We had a tremendous feeling of self, and, at the same

[109]

time, tremendous ability to work with one another. . . . We were highly disciplined and self-motivated people in doing the right thing for one another and had the feeling of community, of consciousness, of not being destructive in any way" (*The United Workers Cooperative Colony Journal*, 1927–1977:31).

The next stage in the formal education of the child was the *shule*. Classes were held in reading, writing, Jewish history, black history, labor history, and current events. The books used in the *shule* were written by members of the left-wing movement to perpetuate a class-conscious ideology. The stories chosen depicted the oppression of the workers and the distrust and antagonism of the poor toward the petty bourgeois (merchants, property owners, and so forth). Derived from works from such classical Yiddish writers as I. L. Peretz and Sholem Aleichem, themes about poverty, the oppressive aspects of Orthodoxy, and the poor/rich dichotomy conveyed a picture of life in the *shtetl*. At the same time, there was humor and irony associated with life in the *shtetl,* and the children developed a deep love and appreciation of their parents' backgrounds through that literature. In the Yiddish stories, poetry, and songs about the new world, similar themes of the oppressed worker and socialist principles were conveyed to the children. Certain songs took on special emphasis as the music and lyrics provided a vehicle for strong identification of the themes of the colony. One song in particular, *Shnel loyfn di reder,*[2] was often performed at the children's concerts in the *shule:*

> The wheels spin rapidly,
> the machines clang wildly,
> the shop is filthy and hot. . . .
> The master runs about,
> an animal, a wild one, . . .
> O how long will you wait,
> how long will you endure;
> working brothers, wake up!

Classes in *shule* were held daily after public school. There were generally over thirty children in a class and each grade had two classes. The younger children went to *elementar shule* Monday through Thursday from 4:00 to 6:00 P.M. Chorus and dance classes were held on Saturday. The *mitlshule* for high school children held classes on Friday evening and all day on Saturday. They also had choral and dance instruction on Saturday. Songs were often international folk songs, for example: "My thoughts will not cater to duke or dictator, No man can deny, My thoughts will be free," are verses from "Die Gedanken Sind Frei," a German folk song. In addition they sang Red Army songs, Negro spirituals, union songs, and Yiddish songs about brotherhood and freedom.

Children were to grow up not only with social and moral messages but with a love for beauty and nature, often conveyed to them through lullabies. Birds, flowers, trees, and animals were used in lullabies to produce comforting and peaceful images. Poems by I. L. Peretz set to music were noteworthy. For example:

> In the field a sapling stands
> Green are its tiny branches
> There a tiny bird is sitting
> Sitting, while its eyes are closing.
> On a tiny branch,
> A golden apple's growing
> Close your eyes, my little child,
>
> A blessing on your little head.[3]

Eastern European folk dances were taught and modern dances were improvised reflecting the dominant themes of the colony. The drama of stories portrayed in dance and in plays emphasized the suffering of *all* the poor, not just Jews, and the hope that all people would eventually enjoy social and economic freedom in a peaceful world. At the same time, implicit were the love for Yiddish, the language that linked these themes together, and for the history of the Jewish people as they grew to know and understand it. A ten-year-old child writing in Yiddish in 1947 says, "I am not very old, but as long as I can remember, my father and mother told me, 'You are Jewish. Never forget. When you hear the word Jew, raise your head high and smile. When you talk Yiddish and read and write Yiddish you must remember that Yiddish is your language, your mother-tongue.' I will always remember these words." They believed that their way of life was the norm. The idea that their lives were different from other Jewish children did not really occur to them. "When I was growing up, the colony was the center of the universe; only after the war did I realize that the world was outside of the colony and we were just a small part of it."

The youth center was divided into a wide range of science, social, and athletic clubs. Although the center had a less formal structure than the *shule*, the dominant themes of the colony were repeated there: brotherhood, unionism, equality, and strength in unity. Most of the names of the various clubs reflected historical issues that were of concern to the people in the colony. Thus, the Roy Wrights club was named after one of the Scottsboro Boys. The Ella May Wiggins club was named after a murdered leader of textile strikers in the south. Formal discussions about historical events were led by the educational director. In addition to the activities provided by the center and the *shule*, there was a music school, an art school, several mandolin classes, and a drum and bugle corps. In 1934 an estimated 400 children actively participated in the voluntary associations; 235 children were registered in *shule* and the center had 250 participants (*Bulletin* 1934).

The *elementar shule* was attended by children of the colony as well as by other children living nearby. The original plan of the colony included three large housing units, but only two were built. As a result, many who had intended to join the colony moved into nearby houses and their children attended *shule*. Thus many of the activities based in the colony included people from the surrounding area. The students of high school age came from an even wider geographical area than those from the *elementar shule*. In the summer, activities continued in the Yiddish camp. Most campers came from New York and the northeastern area, although it also recruited campers from as far away as California. Buses to the camp departed from the colony, so in this and in many other ways the colony was the focal point for progressive Jews. A second-generation descendant commented, "Because of all these outlets and the chance to develop within the colony we were isolated from the outside world. . . . We had a lot of freedom. I was content within the confines of the colony. It had everything I wanted."

The way of life in the colony stimulated the childrens' thirst for knowledge. In every nook and corner, on the streets and in the parks, on the benches, in the stores, informal discussions were held on social and political issues, and plans for activities such as lectures and forums were constantly made. The members of the colony, young and old, were always aware of the talents of others through the various voluntary associations, their publications, concerts, dance recitals, plays, and poetry readings. By providing opportunities for educational, recreational, and creative expression, the voluntary associations reflected the desire of the first generation to elevate the life of working-class people.

[112]

They hoped that ultimately all working-class people would enjoy the personal satisfactions achieved by the members of the colony in a peaceful world.

The voluntary associations provided a major vehicle for perpetuating a common ideology. They also constituted a focal point in the day-to-day lives of people in the colony and served to structure the network of ongoing relations. The people of the colony perceived themselves as unique and took pride in their sensitivity to worldwide issues of poverty, hunger, war, and racism. They viewed their colony as providing a model for all workers in a world based not on difference but on unity, equality, and cooperation. The theme of a united working class recurred constantly in lectures, plays, and discussions. Indeed the theme was actualized in the colony's treatment of American blacks. Commited to equality and the unity of the working class, the colony recruited twenty-five black families. Some of the children who attended *shule* and summer camp along with children of black-Jewish marriages became fluent in Yiddish. Poetry, songs, and slogans reflected the black-Jewish alliance against oppression. Black history was integrated into the *shule* curriculum and certain historical and political events were highlighted to raise the sensitivity of the children to oppose injustices, particularly those that infringe on human rights. The song *"Brider"* by I. L. Peretz depicts this theme. It was taught in *shule* and was often sung when children and young adults gathered informally, as well as at performances given in the *shule* and at camp.

> White, brown, black, and yellow,
> stir and mix these hues together,
> human beings are all brothers,
> children all of the same parents.

In 1931 financial difficulties resulted in the bank foreclosure of the colony's mortgage, but the members continued to control the management of the colony through an elected board of directors and meetings of the membership. In 1943 there was an opportunity to refinance the mortgage, provided that the residents absorb a slight increase in monthly charges. Members in the colony were divided on this issue and a majority of the residents voted to let a private landlord buy the buildings. The board of directors became a tenants' organization. City law mandated that the landlord provide and maintain all services and facilities that had previously existed as long as the residents actively continued to use them. Thus the classrooms of the *shule,* the library, and the auditorium were still available free of charge to the tenants.

There were other changes. During World War II, nationalistic and patriotic ideology in large part replaced the emphasis on Leninism, and the members of the colony began to use the voluntary associations to help in the war effort. The major theme during the war as expressed in the colony's journal was "all-out aid to our government and our people in its grim decision to destroy Hitlerism and to build a better, happier world" *(Journal* 1942:5). The lectures in the colony were devoted primarily to discussions about the war. The themes of patriotism and a strong desire to end the war were repeated in the poems and compositions of the children in the *shule (Magazine* 1945:1–5). Children and adults became involved in scrap drives, air raid drills, Red Cross classes, bond selling, and civil defense. Consistent with these changes, the formal and informal education of the children in the colony no longer emphasized the class struggle but winning the war. A pledge from the youth in the colony's journal read, "We resolve to strengthen, educate and devote ourselves so that we will always be on the side of progress, fighting reaction and thereby insure peace and security for the peoples of the world." Someone else from the colony wrote: "The colony has always stood in the front lines of struggle for preservation of civil rights, for maintenance of decent working and living standards, for adequate aid to the underprivileged and oppressed. Many have enlisted in our armed forces—all eligibles willingly answer the draft call, the men and women that make up our colony are giving of their blood to the blood banks, they are buying defense bonds and stamps to the utmost of their financial capacity" *(Journal* 1942:5). The nursery-kindergarten ceased to exist, in part, because the first generation had passed the childbearing age, while the second generation, now married, were either scattered throughout the nation or were in the armed forces. During the war the *shule* remained active. Parents not living in the colony sent their children to the colony school so that they could obtain a progressive, Yiddish, secular education. Many activities in the youth center petered out as the senior boys went off to serve in the armed forces.

The "melting pot" ideology was a dominant theme of the larger society during the postwar era. Ideally, all ethnic differences would blur and melt away. Racial hatred and discrimination would disappear. "We were all brothers under the skin" was a recurring theme. The union movement reinforced the ideas of the melting pot with slogans of "solidarity forever, and the union makes us strong," building on the belief that workers, no matter what their background, can be united. Such ideas as equality, justice, human rights, and freedom are clearly part of the traditional American value system (Bellah 1967). Paradoxically, this ideology coexisted with ongoing if not escalated discrimination against American blacks. The colony's ideology differed from mainstream beliefs in certain respects, and it was particularly evident in the fact that first- and second-generation Jews from the colony continued to be active in the struggle for civil rights.

In other ways also, members of the colony perceived themselves as different. In 1943 left-wing Jews held the first annual ceremony honoring the resistance fighters of the Warsaw Ghetto. The resistance song "*Zog nit keynmol*"⁴ became their official anthem. It was sung at all formal gatherings, and it defined and symbolized the essence of who they were. This song, stated a second-generation descendant of the colony, "fired the imagination,—you felt deep emotion, moral strength and the obligation to continue to fight all oppression no matter where. That is the legacy of the Warsaw Ghetto uprising and through the song, we, as Jews, will always remember our commitment against tyranny and injustice." "*Zog nit keynmol*" legitimized and validated their continued commitment against injustice.

Significant changes in the colony were taking place among the people of succeeding generations. Instead of entering their parents' occupations and becoming leaders of the workers, the second generation focused their attention on professional careers. Only a small percentage of the colony's children opted for industrial jobs, and out of this small group most eventually left industry and returned to school. The second generation were raised with a thirst for knowledge stimulated by the environment in the colony. While many second-generation American Jews went into business, approximately 90 percent of the colony's children went on to graduate school and many obtained doctoral degrees. As one of the first-generation women stated, "In our days, if we needed more money we went out on strike—now if the children need more money they go on to get their Ph.Ds" (Schwartz 1968:83).

Many of the second generation became quite successful in their fields. Some moved to other urban centers, while others bought houses in the suburbs. In communities where other secular left-wing Jews lived, new *shules* were established for their children, the third generation. Whereas the second generation grew up in a bilingual community and could speak, read, and write Yiddish, they continued to use the language primarily when they did not want their children to understand what was being said. By the 1950s, children entering secular *shules* spoke only English. In 1966 only twenty-five children attended *shule* in the colony and none spoke Yiddish when admitted.

For the first generation of Eastern European Jews and the second generation who grew up in the colony, Yiddish symbolized their tradition, their ideology, their communality, their morality. Without Yiddish and without the primary relationships of overlapping fields of social interaction that characterized day-to-day life in the colony, the third generation were deprived of these meaningful references in their own lives. The nostalgic stories of their parents and grandparents were insufficient to define their sense of self. One second-generation woman, referring to her teen-aged daughter said: "She can't really identify with a religious group because we are not religious. She has no cultural group to identify with. I identified with a culture. I loved the language. I didn't reject any part of Jewishness as I had grown to know and love it. I didn't know or understand the Lower East Side Jew—our parents left the Lower East Side. To our parents everything seems to have an order, a reason." Although the cultural rift is most evident between the second and third generation, the transition between the first and second generation was not entirely smooth either. Some of the second generation look back at the colony in a critical manner and resent the fact that a certain ideology was thrust down their throats. One woman remarked: "We were not given the opportunity to make a choice. We grew up believing there was no God; no one even thought of questioning this as an established fact. Although we continue to believe that there is no God, we want our children to have a choice in deciding about this matter."

Nor does the criticism flow in one direction only. Although they derive a great deal of personal pleasure from their children's accomplishments, the older people claim that although they provided an environment within which learning and education were encouraged, the children on leaving the colony became preoccupied instead with their careers and with affluence.

Is to "Be Jewish" to Be Religious?

The people who formed the colony were not only dissatisfied with the values of American culture, they also rejected many of the beliefs and practices of the larger Jewish community. As a religion in which God is the sole cause of all, Judaism had little relevance to these young Jewish workers. They were outspoken atheists who ran from the restrictions of traditional Jewish culture. In the words of one member: "In the *shtetl* you could only read the Talmud. Religion ties you down, you can't do anything; without it you are free." In traditional Jewish culture, not only is Hebrew more valued than Yiddish because it is the language of sacred texts, but an Orthodox man would even be above reading a Yiddish book (Zborowski and Herzog 1952:46, 72).

Yiddish literature from the middle of the nineteenth century onward was rooted in the daily life of the East European Jewish poor. For young Jewish socialists, the distinction between Yiddish and Hebrew was a distinction between the proletariat and the bourgeoisie. They interpreted their struggle to make Yiddish the national language of the Jewish people as part of the international struggle for social justice (Wisse 1985). Ruth Wisse states rhetorically, "When the Jewish Workers Bund of Lithuania, Poland, and Russia affirmed its dedication to socialism within a specifically Jewish framework, what framework could it have in mind other than Yiddish and the culture of Yiddish?" (1985:32).

Hebrew was also denigrated because of its association with the Zionists. Indeed, the opposition to Zionism posed a significant barrier between left-wing Jews and the larger Jewish community (Howe 1976:330).[5] There were other differences too: Traditional Judaic *rites de passage* were not practiced among members of the colony. When a boy was born into the family, no ritual circumcision (*bris*) was performed; a doctor performed the circumcision in a hospital. Similarly, the thirteenth birthday marking the transition from boyhood into manhood, the bar mitzvah, was not observed. Children growing up in the colony did not believe in a supernatural being. Instead of the traditional religious ceremonies, they celebrated May Day and so were symbolically united with workers throughout the world. The days preceding May Day were characterized by growing excitement as banners, signs, costumes, and song sheets were prepared. "When you walked out of the house and saw all the children dressed up so beautifully and assembling for the parade you knew it was a world holiday" recalls one woman.

Traditional religious holidays were not just ignored, they were openly defied. On the Day of Atonement, traditionally observed as a day of fasting and prayer, antireligious drives were marked by parties and lectures. The left-wing Yiddish press, on holy days, published antireligious material. Passover, which recalls the story of the passage of the children of Israel from bondage to freedom, was rejected as a nationalistic and religious holiday. Members of the colony ate bread openly during Passover as a symbolic expression of freedom and enlightenment. They never saw such actions as anti-Jewish or even as a rejection of their Jewishness: "We were Jewish. . . . We were more Jewish than many Jews who went to synogogue. Many of them did not even know the language, literature, or music. We had a sense of history and tradition and we were fluent in Yiddish," recalled a second-generation descendant of the colony.[6] For the people of the colony, their nonobservance was in a sense a way of observance. But it was a way of observance that in time lost some of its force. Both the deliberate observance and nonobservance of rituals are symbolic statements that help define the self in time and space. Particularly when a group of people experiences significant incongruities in their lives, there is a tendency to select those sacred bits and pieces out of the past that are most suited for reassembling into a meaningful whole. In much the same way, nativistic and revivalistic movements attempt to bring the world under control and to introduce a sense of order in it by "reinventing" so to speak old rituals. Indeed, in later years, individuals from the colony did observe a modified Passover ritual, the seder. The secular seder originally began as a collective ceremony in the *shule*. In the late 1960s, however, it gradually became an annual home ritual.

The upward social mobility of the colony's second generation, their geographical dispersal, and their reduced daily experience of Yiddish culture resulted in a growing gap between the manifest ideology of members of the colony and their social reality. The following account illustrates the way one family experienced these discontinuities over three generations. Moreover, it indicates how the adoption of the annual seder, which previously had been eschewed, acted as a vehicle through which ideas, values, and beliefs were expressed and legitimized.

The S. Family

Mrs. S. came to New York from Russia at the age of seventeen in 1921. Her two brothers and a sister had already migrated to New York and were working in the garment industry. While she came from a traditional Jewish background, one of her brothers whom she greatly admired was very committed to socialist ideals and was involved in union organizing among the Jewish working class. On arriving in New York she moved in with him, his wife, and two children.

Since most of the people she met were from the left wing of the Jewish labor movement, she soon married someone from within this group. She was married in a civil ceremony, because Mr. S. refused to be married under a *khupe*, the ritually prescribed canopy under which a Jewish marriage ceremony is held. Her sister, however, forbade them to live and sleep together until a religious ceremony was held, and two months after the civil ceremony, Mr. S. was tricked into attending his own religious marriage ceremony so that the relationship could be consummated.

Mrs. S. worked in the garment industry and Mr. S. was in the fur trade. Both were faced with seasonal unemployment, so their joint income was viewed as necessary to maintain the household. At the same time, members of their circle placed considerable value on work. Indeed they felt that women, too, should be part of a productive labor force.

Their children were raised in the colony and went to *shule*. In the summer they attended a secular Yiddish camp. A son attended *shule* in the 1930s and the daughter (Amy) started *shule* in 1943 and attended until 1952. During this period, Passover was not observed in the colony. However, in *shule* Passover was treated as a historical event and interpreted in relation to contemporary issues. The pharoah of the traditional Haggadah, like Haman of the Book of Esther, was associated with Hitler. He had ordered the death of all newborn Jews. Moses was associated with contemporary freedom fighters. The story of Passover was used to draw linkages between Jews and blacks in their common struggle against discrimination and tyranny.

Mrs. S.'s son reached adulthood after the war and moved to a rural community where there were few Jews. Concerned about Jewish education for his children, he brought them to a nearby town on Sundays to attend Reform Sunday school. Mrs. S.'s daughter (Amy) also married and moved out of the colony. When Amy's daughter (Sylvia) was about ten years old, a progressive Jewish secular school was formed in their neighborhood and Sylvia was enrolled. Classes were held once a week in English. Children were taught to read and write Yiddish, and they were also taught Yiddish songs and Jewish history. The latter included biblical stories, stories of the Jewish labor movement, black history, and stories about the Eastern European culture of their grandparents. After-school activities also included art classes, music lessons, dance classes, drama, and sports. Living in a pluralist urban environment, Sylvia found that going to *shule* lacked the same significance it had for her mother. After graduating *elementar shule* with just a rudimentary knowledge of Yiddish, Sylvia begrudgingly enrolled in the *mitlshule*. Classes were held from nine to three on Saturday. Her Yiddish education was supplemented by attending the secular camp for several summers. Sylvia dropped out of *mitlshule* after two years and did not return to camp. When Sylvia reached her mid-teens she began arranging her own activities and *shule* was not part of it.

After being a widow for ten years, Mrs. S. remarried in 1973. Although her second husband was not religious, he did observe various Jewish holidays and in 1973 introduced the traditional Haggadah into the household of the S. family. Actually this was not the S. family's first seder. In 1972 the teacher of Sylvia's *shule* had consulted with the parents and it was decided to have a communal secular seder in recognition of the Passover holiday. Students, parents, and grandparents were invited. The food and preparation were done cooperatively by the parents. The Haggadah was put together by the teacher from one that was used in another *shule*. The story was told in English, but it contained numerous Yiddish songs and poems learned in *shule* which were part of the repertoire of the secular progressive *shules*. The seder was attended by about sixty people and Mrs. S. recalls that she met two of her friends there, whose grandchildren were attending *shule*.

Out of respect for her husband, Mrs. S. invited the family to a traditional seder the first year of her marriage. Her husband carefully supervised all of the preparations. Members of the household were of divided opinion on the seder. Mrs. S. was pleased with its introduction into the family. Amy, however, was annoyed that so much effort went into a traditional seder rather than a secular one. She was concerned that the progressive values of her heritage would be lost. Therefore she decided that the following year, 1974, there should be a secular seder. In deference to her mother's husband, she agreed that on the first night of Passover there would be a traditional seder, and on the second night, she would make a secular one. In 1974 the practice of having two seders, a traditional one in Mrs. S.'s home and a secular one in Amy's home, was adopted by the family as an annual practice.

In the summer of 1981, Amy's daughter Sylvia went to Israel for a year to attend college. She married an Israeli there and then returned to the United States to complete her schooling. The following year, Sylvia's husband attended his first secular seder. He enjoyed it, but for him it was "a civil rights play rather than a seder." In 1983 at the end of the seder in Mrs. S.'s home, she declared that at age seventy-nine she was too old to continue the tradition; it was too much work for her. She asked that her granddaughter take over. Sylvia's husband said that he and Sylvia would love to make a traditional seder. In 1985 Sylvia made a seder on the first night. The family had a secular seder on the second evening at Amy's house. At the end of the reading of the secular Haggadah, Sylvia began to reflect aloud on its significance. It was the first time she had experienced a seder as a mother and it created a heightened sense of value for her about her Jewish background. She was newly concerned as a parent that her daughter should have a progressive Jewish background. She wanted her husband to learn more about the Yiddish camp and the secular *shule,* thinking that perhaps she would look into sending her own child to one. She now sensed the value of both ways of being Jewish, the secular-progressive and the traditional. The songs and poems she learned in *shule* and camp became more meaningful to her as she began to see herself as the one who as a parent now has an additional role as a "transmitter of culture."

The Seder: A Paradigm of Continuity and Discontinuity

The Haggadahs used by descendants of the colony reflect variations on the themes of freedom, brotherhood, world peace, and resistance to tyranny and oppression.[7] Particular historical events and issues that have been emphasized consist chiefly of the Holocaust and of black-Jewish relations. Changes from the traditional Haggadah were made not merely in content but also in prescribed behavior. In the traditional seder, the participants remain seated throughout the entire ritual in a "reclining" position to symbolize their freedom from slavery. In the secular seder, participants stand while singing "*Zog nit keynmol,*" the song of the Warsaw Ghetto uprising. Participants also stand when singing "We Shall Overcome," considered by many to be the official song of the American black resistance movement. The joining together of black and Jewish struggles for freedom is probably the most salient feature of the secular seder. Whereas the traditional seder highlights God's relationship with His people, the secular seder uses poems and songs to dramatize the suffering of the Jewish people. For example:

> In the country of the Pharoahs
> Where the pyramids rise grim
> Lived a wicked king, who ordered
> All the Jews to slave for him.
>
> Day and night the Jews all labored
> Making bricks without a sound
> While the cruel Egyptians beat them
> Till they fell upon the ground
>
> Then a leader arose among them
> And he taught them how to fight
> For the freedom stolen from them,
> In the dark Egyptian night
>
> Let us all be brave like Moses
> Saying NO to slavery,
> Lifting high the flag of freedom
> Over land and over sea.[8]

This poem, which is sung in Yiddish and recited in English, is then followed by "When Israel Was in Egypt Land" and "Oh Freedom," both of which are American Negro freedom songs and serve as a bridge between the Jewish and black peoples.

The Passover story for the left-wing Jew is the story of all people who have once been and who continue to be in bondage. Some left-wing Jews have introduced new issues into the seder, such as American intervention in South America and apartheid in South Africa. For most Jews, the story points to the particularism of the Jew, the chosenness. Indeed it was during the Exodus that God gave the Jews the Torah. For them, the suffering of the Jews is part of an age-old pattern of hatred and envy, a sign of the Jews' special nature. Members of the colony, however, view anti-Semitism and racism as one and the same thing. To them, the story of Passover is a universal story about equality and peace. So they light a candle for Martin Luther

King, Jr., whom they link to Moses and Abraham Lincoln, and participants stand to sing "We Shall Overcome." Although there are particularist aspects to the seder, such as lighting six candles in memory of the six million Jews who died in the Holocaust, and recalling the Warsaw Ghetto uprising, which began on the day of the first seder, the overt ideology expressed in the ritual is universalist. They retain the four cups of wine from the traditional seder, here in the form of four toasts. The first two are for freedom and brotherhood. The third toast is to the resistors of Nazism and to those who gave their lives for freedom and dignity. The final toast is to peace in the world for all time. A father who wrote a Haggadah for his children stated: "There are three aspects which provide a model for the Haggadah. You identify the oppressors on the one hand, the oppressed on the other, and the goal of freedom and justice. By identifying these three themes you can link the story of Passover to modern times."

Despite the various additions, the left-wing secular seder in many ways follows the traditional Haggadah. The symbolic foods of the Passover seder are retained and are set aside on special plates. The Haggadah for the secular seder does not specify that kosher foods should be used. But since such special foods as the wine and matzah are specifically purchased for the seder, they tend to be "kosher for Passover." At the same time, other foods such as meat are generally not kosher. Other elements of the seder are retained. Matzah, the unleavened bread, is eaten to remember the liberation of Jews from slavery. Three special matzahs are set aside on the table. Half of the middle matzah is called the *afikomen*. *Karpus*, a green vegetable, is used to remind Jews that Passover was a spring holiday before it became a holiday of freedom. *Morer* are the bitter herbs to remind one of the bitterness of slavery. *Khahroyses* is a mixture of apples, nuts, cinnamon, and wine and is eaten to remember the clay or mortar that Jews were forced to use to make bricks in Egypt. *Beytso*, is the hardboiled egg, which is a symbol of spring and fertility. *Zroah*, the shank bone of a lamb, is set aside to remember the custom of sacrificing the first-born animal in the spring. A special cup of wine is also set aside for Elijah, the Prophet, who according to legend visits Jewish homes at Passover disguised as a poor man.

Like its traditional counterpart, the secular seder has several different functions. It is a "traditionalizing" event serving as a vehicle for cultural transmission from one generation to the next. At the same time, it is something new in the sense that it provides a format for introducing comtemporary issues and events within a traditional contex{

Perhaps the most important feature of the secular seder is that it provides a public means for defining and acting out a collective ideology. The 1960s was a period of dispersal for members of the colony, and it was during this period that the practice of the secular seder was adopted by colony families in their homes. Like the *shules* that sprung up in various suburban and urban centers, it was a response to the concern for cultural continuity and the survival of basic values that were part of the way of life in the colony. This dispersion is akin to the diaspora. While secular Jews did not hope for a return to the biblical homeland, they could return through ritual, to a highly valued way of life, to collective beliefs and sentiments that have a sacred, almost religious character.[9]

Subcultures do not exist in isolation; they react to social historical events in the dominant culture. Such events, national and international in scope, in a sense determine the subculture's form, content, and style of expression (Hebdige 1979). The people of the colony saw striking parallels between themselves and American blacks in their struggle against oppression and exploitation. Indeed, black-Jewish relations and the desire for true brotherhood and equal opportunity was a salient theme in the colony's ideology. Yet social and historical events in the 1960s replaced the melting-pot ideology with cultural pluralism. In terms of the dominant culture, gaps between blacks and Jews widened (Waxman 1983). The Black Panthers' ideology of separatism, the Six-Day War in Israel, the Yom Kippur War of 1973, and the growing identification of blacks with Third World cultures and their hostility toward Israel all contributed to this gap. The murder of Martin Luther King, Jr., appeared to end an era of peaceful, nonviolent, civil rights activism with which left-wing Jews had closely identified themselves. In 1949 busloads of youths from the colony went to Peekskill, New York, in order to form a protective circle around Paul Robeson, a black singer and known communist, so that he could perform unharmed. Many returned to the colony with smashed and bloodied heads. How was this event to be interpreted in the late sixties and early seventies?

The genius of a people's ability to maintain their subculture involves finding new ways for expressing their worldview or manipulating old ways that reflect the subculture's difference and uniqueness, which are validated by the larger society. Within an ideology of cultural pluralism, what better way is there to legitimate such values as brotherhood, freedom, justice, equality than through the story of the exodus of Jews from Egypt? The dramatic telling of the story through ritual legitimizes and authenticate these values (Moore and Myerhoff 1977). Through the secular seder, the black-Jewish alliance is reestablished and the belief confirmed that Jews and blacks are part of the same struggle for justice and freedom. Indeed, through ritual, there is continuity in the very ideas and values upon which the colony was built, despite the assaults that time and history have made upon it.

Notes

1. In the *shtetl*, however, the voluntary associations called *khevres* reflected the value placed on religious education; see Levitats 1943.
2. The songs of Jacob Schaefer are an important part of the rich cultural heritage of left-wing secular Jews, and when he died in 1937 the colony honored its fellow cooperator by creating a Schaefer Memorial Room so that Schaefer's works could be available for loan or study.
3. This poem, "Sapling in the Field," and the others that are referred to in this article appear in *Lets Sing a Yiddish Song* (New York: Kinderbuch Publications, 1970).
4. Hirsh Glik, a poet in Vilna, upon hearing the news of the Warsaw Ghetto uprising, wrote this song. It immediately became the official hymn of the Jewish underground partisan brigades.

> We must never lose our courage in the fight,
> Though skies of lead turn days of sunshine into night.
> Because the hour for which we've yearned will yet arrive,
> And our marching steps will thunder: we survive!
>
> From land of palm trees to the land of distant snow,
> We have come with our deep sorrow and our woe,
> And everywhere our blood was innocently shed,
> Our fighting spirits will again avenge our dead.
>
> Not lead, but blood inscribed this song which now we sing,
> Its not a caroling of birds upon the wing,
> But a people midst the crashing fires of hell,
> Sang this song and fought courageous till it fell!
>
> So we must never lose our courage in the fight,
> Though skies of lead turn days of sunshine into night.
> Because the hour for which we've yearned will yet arrive,
> And our marching steps will thunder:
>   We survive!

5. It is the one position postulated in recent decades that has received continuous responses of disapproval and outrage from other American Jews. In other aspects, such as their concern for Jewish cultural survival, the image of themselves as a people who are unique intellectually and morally, and their commitment to social

concerns and social justice, left-wing Jews can readily be placed within the general framework of American Jewish civil religion (Woocher 1985:157).
6. Charles Silberman addresses this issue. He notes that "in 1909, when immigration from Eastern Europe was at flood tide and New York was a predominantly first-generation community, only 25 percent of Jewish elementary school-age children were receiving any Jewish education at all. . . . Twenty-five years later . . . the proportion was no higher" (1985:172). Thus, children of the colony were significantly different from the larger Jewish community in regard to their all-encompassing Jewish upbringing, even though they did not observe religious holidays.
7. Silver (1980) traces the Haggadah, the story of the exodus of Jews from Egypt, historically and notes that since its appearance as a book on its own in the thirteenth century, its prayers and liturgical poems have not changed. On the other hand, customs and rites have changed as a reaction to social historical events. For example, the change from using red wine as recommended in the Talmud to white wine during the fifteenth and sixteenth centuries was related to the belief by non-Jews that the red wine used at the seder was the blood of slaughtered Christian children. With the end of pogroms, however, red wine was reintroduced into the seder. Secular Haggadahs are not merely an American phenomenon. In Israel secular Haggadahs were used to convey dominant political and ideological themes. Whereas, in the traditional view of Passover, God performed miracles and gave freedom to the Jews, in the Israeli secular Haggadahs, references to God are avoided or are substituted for by references to the people of Israel. The Passover story stresses courage, heroism, and the continuing struggle for national honor and freedom. In the socialist kibbutzim, the traditional Haggadah is transformed into a collection of songs and poems celebrating Jewish nationhood (Liebman 1982:60–65).
8. Text of "In the Land of Pyramids" was written by David Edelshtadt.
9. Charles Liebman (1982) has argued that religion is a "meaning system, a set of symbols which root cultural conceptions into the general order of the universe. . . . The major symbols through which religion is conveyed are rituals on the one hand and beliefs and myths on the other." Liebman underscores the importance of ritual in creating the experience of community and of myth as a vehicle for projecting images and telling the story of one's origin (see also Turner 1969).

REFERENCES

Bellah, Robert N. 1967. "Civil Religion in America." *Daedalus* (Winter):1–21.
Bulletin. 1934. New York: A Colony Publication.
Glazer, Nathan. 1985. "On Jewish Forebodings." *Commentary* 80, 2:32–36.
Hebdige, Dick. 1979. *Subculture: The Meaning of Style*. London: Methuen.
Howe, Irving. 1976. *World of Our Fathers*. New York: Harcourt Brace Jovanovich.
Journal. 1942. Fifteenth Anniversary Edition. New York: A Colony Publication.
Levin, Nora. 1977. *While Messiah Tarried: Jewish Socialist Movements, 1871–1917*. New York: Schocken Books.
Levitats, Isaac. 1943. *The Jewish Community in Russia 1771–1884*. New York: Columbia University Press.
Liebman, Charles S. 1982. "The Religious Life of American Jewry." In *Understanding American Jewry*, ed. Marshall Sklare. New Brunswick, N.J.: Transaction Books. 96–124.

Moore, Sally F., and Barbara G. Myerhoff. 1977. "Introduction: Forms and Meanings." In *Secular Ritual*, ed. Sally F. Moore and Barbara G. Myerhoff. Amsterdam: Van Gorcum.

Schwartz, Anita. 1968. "The Colony: A Study of the Process of Culture Change." Masters' thesis, New York University.

———. 1984. "Ethnic Identity among Left-Wing American Jews." *Ethnic Groups* 6:65–84.

Silberman, Charles E. 1985. *A Certain People: American Jews and Their Lives Today*. New York: Summit Books.

Silver, Arthur M. 1980. *Passover Haggadah: The Complete Seder*. New York: Menorah Publishing Co.

The United Workers Cooperative Colony Journal, 1927–1977. 1977. New York.

Turner, Victor. 1969. *The Ritual Process: Structure and Anti-Structure*. Chicago: Aldine Books.

Waxman, Chaim I. 1983. *America's Jews in Transition*. Philadelphia: Temple University Press.

Wisse, Ruth, R. 1985. "The Politics of Yiddish." *Commentary* 80, 1:29–35.

Woocher, Jonathan S. 1985. "Sacred Survival: American Jewry's Civil Religion." *Judaism* 34, 2 (Spring):151–62.

Zborowski, Mark, and Elizabeth Herzog. 1952. *Life Is with People: The Culture of the Shtetl*. New York: Schocken Books.

[5]

Rituals as Keys to Soviet Immigrants' Jewish Identity

Fran Markowitz

Under the elevated railway, clustered together in aging stone tenements, shiny new shops decorated with multicolored pennants and bright signs in Cyrillic script attract a steady clientèle of fur-clad matrons and potbellied men. Flashing gold-toothed smiles, store clerks and shoppers exchange sentences in rapid-fire Russian as herring, caviar, and black bread, along with news items and local gossip, change hands.

These Russian sights and sounds are found not in a faraway Moscow neighborhood but in Brighton Beach, an oceanfront community in Brooklyn, New York. Since the early 1970s, more than one hundred thousand Soviet Jews have made new homes in the United States, and about half of them live in New York City. Brighton Beach, once home to earlier waves of East European Jews, attracted several thousand immigrant families. Although the area lost a great deal of its residen-

Funding for the research reported herein was generously provided by a FLAS fellowship from the Center for Russian and East European Studies, University of Michigan, a Grant-in-Aid from the Wenner-Gren Foundation for Anthropological Research, and by a predoctoral fellowship, NRSA No. 3 F31 MH09168–01S1, from the National Institute of Mental Health.

I am very grateful to all the gracious people who patiently answered my many questions, and especially to those who included me in their family and friendship networks. A special word of thanks goes to Zhenya, *dorogaya podruga moya.* Aram A. Yengoyan, Sergei Kan, and Jack Kugelmass read earlier drafts of this essay. Their careful readings and helpful comments added much to the final version of this essay.

tial and commercial population to the suburbs in the 1960s, during the 1970s its low rents, seaside location, and business opportunities made Brighton Beach a hospitable environment for recently arrived Soviet émigrés. Moreover, the neighborhood's long-term residents, elderly Jews who remained behind after their children fled, initially welcomed the newcomers, seeing them as catalysts for rejuvenating and re-Judaizing their crumbling neighborhood. In the 1980s Brighton Beach has indeed been revitalized, but kosher butchers and bakeries continue to shut their doors as Russian groceries, restaurants, fashionable boutiques, and shoe stores spring up in their place. Now long-term residents grumble that their old Jewish neighborhood has been turned into a Russian ghetto.

Soviet émigrés see it differently. They view themselves first and foremost as Jews, not as Russians, and they are astonished that Americans attach to them a Russian identity that eluded them all their lives in the USSR. Adamantly claiming equal status with their American counterparts, Soviet immigrants recognize as well that having lived in the Soviet Union under the influence of Russian culture has made them a different kind of Jew than their Brooklyn neighbors.

Labeled as different because of their language, their mode of dress, their patterns of consumption and food preferences, Soviet émigrés remain removed from and not quite "Jewish enough", for the mainstream American Jewish community (Gitelman 1984:97; Baskin 1985). Soviet immigrants thus confront two dimensions of otherness in their postmigration experiences. They face not only the task of learning and adapting to the linguistic, political, and economic workings of the United States but also that of becoming part of and feeling a sense of belonging with the American Jewish community in whose midst they live.

This essay attempts to uncover the dynamics of culture change among Soviet Jewish immigrants and its effects on their Jewish identity through an examination of their lifecycle rituals. The investigation is implicitly guided by two questions: (1) How different in fact are Soviet Jewish immigrants from American Jews? and (2) Through the ritual process, in what ways do these immigrants alter or emphasize particular aspects of their Jewish identity to come closer to—or to delineate themselves from—American Jewish expectations for "Jewish enough" Jewish behavior?

Rituals, because they encapsulate, demonstrate, and play with central symbols of a social system can be used as keys to unlock the unconscious workings of a culture (see Ortner 1978:1–2). In this paper I describe and analyze Soviet émigrés' bar mitzvah and funeral rites. I have chosen these rituals for two major reasons: (1) their juxtaposition in the lifecycle, and (2) the difference between their frequency of performance in the Soviet Union and the United States. These rituals therefore provide contrasting points of entry into Soviet émigré culture, and, taken in concert, they reveal much about the immigrants' specific Jewish identity.

In the Soviet Union, bar and bat mitzvah are rarely celebrated, but burial in a Jewish cemetery is a persistent practice. In a country where religion is viewed as backward superstition, and sometimes even as sedition, there are virtually no ritual specialists to oversee a child's preparation, and the bar/bat mitzvah has become a thing of the past. Ironically, although the Soviet government has shut down churches and synagogues, it has not forbidden the separation of Christian and Jewish burial grounds. Old men stand outside cemeteries and for a ruble intone a benediction over the grave. "You know how my parents are atheists and how dedicated my grandmother was to the Revolution, but when she died, we had an old man say prayers at her graveside." Thus, while Jewish funerals are part of the tradition these immigrants bring with them, the bar/bat mitzvah is a rite that has been introduced only after emigration.

During fieldwork, from January 1984 to September 1985 and in June 1986, I attended two bat mitzvahs and one bar mitzvah ceremony and witnessed three funerals. In addition, many informants described other bar or bat mitzvahs they had been to, and several spoke to me at length about their experiences with deaths of loved ones in America and in the Soviet Union.

Historical Background

Ashkenazi Jews began settling in Russia during the middle ages (Dubnow 1916 1:38, 41; Ettinger 1970:36–37), where they occupied interstitial positions between the Christian nobility and gentry and their peasants. Jews served as tax collectors and moneylenders and sometimes were the focus of hatred in Slavic lands. As their numbers grew, they formed their own communities in which everyday life was regulated by Talmudic law as interpreted by governing boards of local rabbis.

Official restrictions on Jews increased with the consolidation of the Russian Empire (Greenberg 1976 1:4–11; 2:31–54). Jews, with few exceptions, were forbidden residences outside of the small towns in the Pale of Settlement, restricted by a harsh quota system in their desire for university education, and denied entry into the civil service and other professions. These official prohibitions notwithstanding, during the nineteenth century the Jewish population of major Russian and Ukrainian cities swelled; either by studying abroad in France or Germany, gaining the few seats available in Russian universities, or by changing their documents, some Jews found their way into the professions and gained the right to urban residences. The 1897 census reveals that 49 percent of Russian Jews were urban dwellers then and that although 97 percent of the Jewish population claimed Yiddish as their mother tongue, 29 percent were literate in Russian as well.

Informants note with a mixture of pride and irony that Jews were very active in the overthrow of the tsars and in the revolution of 1917. During the latter part of the nineteenth century, it was not uncommon for young people to break with the traditions of their families and join secular Jewish movements. Zionism, socialism, and communism in a variety of groups and forms were seen as ways to improve the lot of mankind in general and of the Jewish people in particular.[1] After the revolution, as a literate, mobilized diaspora (Armstrong 1968:8–9), Jews quickly filled key positions in the new government. Jewish youth took great advantage of the opportunities to receive higher education and they trained for the professions. In so doing, many freed themselves from what they perceived to be a parochial and oppressive past. In the early days of revolutionary fervor, Jewish radicals staged anti-rituals on major Jewish holidays, often outside the synagogue doors.

Internal factors within Russian Jewry coupled of course with external stresses led to the dissolution of the traditional, religiously based Jewish life in the early part of the twentieth century. Yet it is important to keep in mind that Jews, whether secularized communists or those who maintained some religious or cultural traditions, did not lose sight of their Jewish identities (Baron 1964:210–14). In 1933, the Soviet state ensured that they never would by means of the institutionalization of an internal passport system. From that time forward, whether a person is born in Georgia, Latvia, Russia, or the Ukraine, his or her Jewish "nationality" is written on line five of his or her passport. Thus, although Jews are urban residents, highly educated native speakers of Russian who have experienced between forty and seventy years of Sovietization,[2] they and those around them are still well aware of their Jewish identity.

By the mid-1970s, Jews were not only hearing loud outcries of anti-Zionism in the official press after the two most recent Arab-Israeli wars, but they were also finding their opportunities in the workplace curtailed. Institutes of higher learning became more difficult for Jews to enter, and an increasing number of Soviet Jews came to realize that "we (as a family, as a people) have no future here in the Soviet Union." For some, this dissonance was pushed to the limit when they found themselves blacklisted, unable to work at all in their professions because someone with their same last name had emigrated. They were left with no choice but to emigrate themselves, having lost not only their means of livelihood but also their identities.

Once in the United States, these new immigrants were assisted by Jewish social service agencies that administered resettlement funds, helped them find work and learn English, and encouraged them to take part in American Jewish life. While Soviet Jews did not flock to the synagogues and, with few but notable exceptions, did not become religious Jews overnight, they do take pride in their Jewish heritage. They now celebrate important holidays and key rites of passage in ways they were unable to do in the Soviet Union.

Bar/Bat Mitzvah

Survey data from several cities in the United States consistently show the commitment of immigrant parents to keeping their children within the Jewish fold (see Simon 1983), with a significant proportion of children attending Jewish schools (Federation of Jewish Philanthropies 1985:34–35—35 percent; Gitelman 1984:97—49 percent; Gilison 1981:21—39 percent). After coming to America, many parents have increasingly opted to have bar/bat mitzvah celebrations to mark the passage of their children into Jewish adulthood (38 percent of those questioned in New York City by the Federation of Jewish Philanthropies 1985:30–31). For many of these parents and their guests, these ceremonies are their first encounter with Judaism in a public arena.

In New York City, particularly in Brighton Beach, immigrants have the option of celebrating their childrens' bar and bat mitzvahs in any one of eleven Russian restaurants.

Despite some differences in decor, menu, and orchestra, the restaurants are very similar to one another: dining on weekend nights is by reservation only. The six-hour meals combine Russian conviviality—food, drink, and song—with American opulence. Even the most modest of the restaurants provides an impressive table of *zakuski* (appetizers) and several additional courses throughout the night. There is no shortage of vodka and brandy, and spirits already high are made more so by the orchestra's repertoire of Russian, Ukrainian, Georgian, Uzbek, Jewish (Yiddish and Israeli), Italian, and American popular melodies.

Many of these restaurants advertise "Have your birthday, anniversary, wedding, bar mitzvah here with us!" None of the restaurants is kosher, and although Jewish specialties (such as gefilte fish and *ptsha*) are always served, they are placed on the table along with crab salad and pork-based cold cuts. Establishment owners provide a list of rabbis who will perform Jewish ceremonies in their restaurants. Not surprisingly, however, the list of participating clergy is small and confined to liberal Reform rabbis. Nonjudgmental about the everyday life of the immigrants, the rabbis allow and even encourage them to express their Jewishness in a style appropriate to their own background:

"You know, the main reason, one of the reasons, I picked the Russian restaurant is because I felt—I can't go to a synagogue and then put on a face like I lived this way my whole life. Do you see what I mean? Like our temple—it's Conservative, and I didn't feel I could go there and have the ceremony there because that's not me. And I couldn't ask that rabbi to come to the restaurant because it's non-kosher. So how could I go to a synagogue and do it there if it didn't feel right?

"This rabbi . . . was on the list [the restaurant owner] gave us of rabbis who work with them. He was the third one I called. As soon as I talked with him on the phone I liked him. I want to tell you that he is a great businessman too, because he understood that in a Russian ceremony you shouldn't get too involved and you shouldn't mind is it kosher or not. He knew that this is the only way to deal with us.

"When I met with the rabbi I was very uptight, and I was afraid he would ask all these questions [about religious practices]. But he didn't, and after he came to the house and talked to me, my husband and the children, he understood what we wanted. We did it exactly as we wanted."

In another case, where the parents chose to separate the religious ceremony, held in a synagogue, from the celebration, held in a Russian restaurant on Rosh Hashanah eve, the rabbi, this time Orthodox, instructed the child in his *haftorah* reading (the portion from *Prophets* a boy chants as part of a traditional bar mitzvah service) without posing questions about how, when, and where the family would have a party to celebrate this event.

Immigrants select a rabbi to instruct a child in preparation for bar/bat mitzvah not according to his credentials as a scholar and teacher but according to his personality and his attitude toward the family's manner of observance of religious traditions.

To many Soviet Jewish immigrants, celebrating the bar or bat mitzvah is not only a rite of passage for the child but a rite of expurgation for the entire family, ridding them of a negative Jewish identity and receiving in exchange a positive one: "You know, I told you this, in the Soviet Union being Jewish is something you hide. Here I know that being Jewish is something to be proud of. Now I am a little less outspoken about this than right when we came and I don't broadcast so much that I am Jewish, but I am very proud of this and I want my girls to be proud too. . . . You know I'm not religious, but that's not the point." The ceremony itself promotes among parents and children not only pride in a still shaky identity but also a sense that this newly rediscovered religion can be fun.

How is this done? Below, with slight modifications to ensure the privacy of the family,[3] I will describe a bat mitzvah that was celebrated in a Russian restaurant on a Sunday afternoon during the summer of 1985:

With a four-piece band set up on stage, a clean-shaven, gray-haired rabbi stands at the far end of the dance floor dressed in a black robe, a black yarmulke, and a thin *talis* (prayer shawl). He stands behind a table on which a white and red frosted cake, decorated with a gold facsimile of the Ten Commandments in its center and several large glass candleholders filled with tall white candles placed around it, is on display.

The rabbi, standing alone, says, "Please take your seats." Then, with a strong American accent, he repeats this phrase in Russian. He continues in English, "The ceremony is about to begin, and there will be no talking during the ceremony."

"I would like to welcome you to the bat mitzvah celebration of our beautiful, wonderful bat mitzvah girl, Leah (using her Hebrew name instead of the Russian, Lina). Let's give her a big hand!" and Lina walks out to join the rabbi as the orchestra plays a melody in a minor key. "And now—her wonderful parents—Bella and Alex!" who walk in side by side as the orchestra plays "Sunrise, Sunset."

"Today, in celebrating her bat mitzvah," the rabbi continues, "Leah is confirming her commitment to live by the laws of the Torah, to live as a member of the Jewish people. Now, in her sweet, beautiful voice, she will recite the *Shema Yisroel*—our statement that there is one God and no other gods before Him. Now to you, Lina!" And Lina chanted this one-line proclamation in Hebrew and immediately recited it in English, "Hear o Israel, the Lord is our God, the Lord is One."

The rabbi resumed, "Let's have a round of applause for this wonderful girl, for her sweet voice. Let's hear it for her!" And all two hundred or so guests applauded.

"Now very close friends of this beautiful bat mitzvah girl, Irene and Danny, will bring the Torah scroll to us." These children walked in together accompanied by Jewish music, carrying a small, velvet-covered Torah. The rabbi instructed them to place it on the table and then asked for "some applause for these sweet, wonderful friends—Irene and Danny!"

As the guests clapped and the children unceremoniously took their seats, the rabbi took off its velvet cover and unrolled the scroll. "Now, with your sweet little finger, touch the place in the Torah where we are going to read," the rabbi instructed the bat mitzvah girl. "Now she will kiss her finger to show us all how much she loves the Torah, the gift of God to the Jewish people. Now our lovely, beautiful, wonderful bat mitzvah girl will sing her bat mitzvah prayer over the Torah." This is a short Hebrew chant, after which the rabbi again asked for "a round of applause for her sweet and wonderful voice."

"Not only is this girl beautiful and sweet, she is also smart," he continues. "Now she will read to you a speech she has prepared for the occasion of her bat mitzvah celebration. I give to you now—Lina!"

Lina began reading in a clear, deliberate voice, "My dear parents, family, and friends. I am very happy that you all came to be with me to celebrate my bat mitzvah. I am very happy today to celebrate my bat mitzvah and to show my belonging to the Jewish people. . . ." The speech was short, three or four more sentences, focusing on family,

[135]

friends, and her gratitude to America for being able to express pride in being Jewish. At its conclusion the rabbi asked, "Wasn't that a wonderful speech from our beautiful, wonderful bat mitzvah girl?"

"Now, Leah, bend your head. I am now going to give her the bat mitzvah blessing, to confirm her, as her mother, her grandmothers, and great-grandmothers, as a Jewish woman. *Barukh ato . . . ,*" and he touched her on the head and intoned this Hebrew blessing. "Now this beautiful, wonderful girl has become a Jewish woman. Papa, today I will ask you to say something," the rabbi continues, addressing Alex. "Mama, today you have nothing to say because on all other days you do all the talking and papa stays quiet." The audience laughed and applauded at this remark. "Papa," the rabbi continues, "come here and repeat after me," and he intoned a short Hebrew chant, translating it into English for Alex to repeat, "And today—I am no longer responsible—for the Jewish education—of my daughter. I *am*—still responsible—for her support—until the day—that she gets married," to which he adds *"kin ayne hore"* and spits over his shoulder three time, "tfu, tfu, tfu,"[4] for which he receives appreciative laughter from the audience. "Let's have a big hand for Papa Alex—and what a wonderful papa he is! And for Mama Bella! It is no wonder that their daughter Lina is so sweet, smart, and beautiful—look at her wonderful parents! Let's have a round of applause for these wonderful parents—Bella and Alex!"

"We will now conclude the religious portion of the ceremony by making the final blessing—the *shehekhiyanu.*" The orchestra strikes up a fanfare and accompanies the rabbi as he sings this blessing. Then they play and sing the festive Yiddish song *"Mazel tov, simen tov."* The rabbi sings in a loud voice, and the guests join in rhythmic clapping.

"We have now concluded the religious portion of the bat mitzvah ceremony, and Leah has taken her place as a Jewish woman, like her mother, grandmothers, and great-grandmothers," the rabbi resumes. "A bat mitzvah is also a birthday celebration, and now we will call upon family and friends to help light the candles on this beautiful birthday cake for our wonderful birthday, bat mitzvah girl. First, I want to call *bube* Khane and *tante*[5] Mila to join us. We have a wonderful grandmother and beautiful aunt to light the first candle on our wonderful birthday cake." As the rabbi speaks and hands the taper to the grandmother, she starts to cry and dabs at her eyes as he says kind things about her. She lights the candle and kisses her granddaughter, crying all the time. "Let's have a round of applause for this wonderful grandmother and beautiful aunt!"

Several more names are called until all thirteen candles on the cake are lit. The band plays Jewish melodies throughout the candlelighting ceremony. The parents' close friends and business associates are called upon as well as family members to participate. When all the candles have been lit, the rabbi asks all the guests to join in singing "Happy Birthday to our beautiful bat mitzvah girl." The orchestra plays, the guests all sing, and Lina blows out her birthday candles. The band then strikes up a reprise of "*Mazel tov, simen tov,*" all the participants in the candlelighting ceremony take their seats, waiters remove the cake and table from the middle of the dance floor, and the rabbi disappears just as dinner is to begin.

This bat mitzvah ceremony elicited strong emotional responses from all the immigrant guests: "I was all choked up. It was really touching, moving, being up there. I cannot explain how or in what way—it just was—very touching." Another, through her tears, was able to explain the emotion she felt: "This was the first, the very first, bar or bat mitzvah I've ever been to. It was really nice to see— especially for us who, you know, in the Soviet Union were Jewish but hid it. We just wanted to be like everyone else. So we had no ceremonies, no rituals. This was really beautiful." "It was great! Wasn't the rabbi terrific?" exclaimed Alex and several of the guests.

Why did this ceremony elicit such positive heartfelt reactions? This bat mitzvah is radically different from those held in synagogues, and on the surface at least has little connection with normative Judaic practice: Although the bar mitzvah ceremony has deep roots in Jewish religious practice, bat mitzvah is a recent innovation, and its popularity is limited to Conservative and Reform synagogues, which unlike the Orthodox provide identical initiation rites for boys and girls. The rite signifies one's initial participation in prayer and in the Jewish community as a full-fledged adult. At age twelve for girls and thirteen for boys, the child is assigned a place of honor in the synagogue for all to see and takes part in the Sabbath service wrapped for the first time in a prayer shawl. During the normal course of prayer, the child, who has prepared many months for this moment, is called to the Torah to chant that day's portion of the *Prophets* and thus becomes a son or daughter of the law (bar/bat mitzvah). At the conclusion of the service, the child's family usually sponsors a reception for the congregation.

That night after the Sabbath, parents often throw gala birthday parties, spending thousands of dollars to celebrate their son's or daughter's passage into Jewish adulthood.

American bar and bat mitzvahs separate the sacred from the secular. At the last two bar mitzvahs I attended, one Reform, the other Conservative, I remember thinking that with these celebrations American Jews were sending messages to themselves that say: Although our daily lives are no longer intimately connected to the precepts of Judaism and the obligations of Jewish law, we have not forgotten our religion. In New York, Jews play a major role in all spheres of social, economic, political, and cultural life. Being Jewish is not only unstigmatized but aspects of Jewish ethnicity, such as Yiddishisms and Jewish food, have found their way into the cultural mainstream. Judaism, however, remains the sole provenance of Jews.

For Soviet immigrants, religion is not the linchpin of their Jewish identity. Jewish ethnicity or "nationality" remains stigmatized in the USSR, although Soviet Jews are, in the main, not religious. A rite that emphasizes the retention of Judaism in the face of the acculturation and acceptance by American society of secular ethnicity would only be a painful reminder that they, lacking Judaic knowledge, are not in fact "Jewish enough."

The bat mitzvah ceremony that Soviet Jewish immigrants perform in their restaurants works as ritual precisely because it blends and reconciles, rather than disconnects, three powerful aspects of their sense of self—their Jewish, Russian, and American identities. The rabbi, as a key symbol of Judaism, plays a crucial role in this identity resolution. As a modern, clean-shaven English speaker willing to come to "their" restaurant, he embodies Judaism in a positive and accommodating light, both as a committed Jew as well as a man of the world. Indeed, the rabbi represents precisely the way Soviet Jews see themselves—as educated, cosmopolitan, and Jewish. Moreover, the rabbi also possesses knowledge of Judaism and its ritual practices, something the immigrants recognize they have lost and would like to regain (through their children).

The bat mitzvah ritual itself, combining English prose with Hebrew chants in a public setting, is for the girl and her parents a cathartic experience that symbolically frees them from the stigma that their Jewish identity had in Soviet society. The girl's mother said, "In Russia every night I used to sleep with a kerchief tightly wrapped around my head to get rid of this Jewish [curly] hair of mine." Others told of their children's dread of going to school on the day they had to bring in their birth certificates for fear that "now everyone will know that I am a Jew." One girl, after insisting to no avail that she was not Jewish, became "blood sisters" with a Russian friend. She returned from school and demanded that her parents now change her birth certificate because now she had "Russian blood." The rabbi's frequent use of the words, "beautiful," "wonderful," "sweet" in reference to the bat mitzvah girl and her family confirmed and reconfirmed that Jews are indeed good, nice people.

The bat mitzvah was as much a rite of explication as it was an individual rite of passage. It reviewed the meaning of a tradition dating back thousands of years, a set of holy laws, sacred texts, and an ancient language that unite Jews throughout the world. The rabbi's restructuring of the bat mitzvah into a rite of explication allowed Soviet Jewish immigrants to understand and appreciate these traditions. It also made the rite a common ritual, a group rite of passage. The rabbi's explanations included the guests in the ritual. Without condescension, he fed them knowledge to foster their identification with the bat mitzvah girl, her family, and the entire Jewish people.

This ceremony, it must be kept in mind, took place in a specific context—a Russian restaurant in America. Not only was the bat mitzvah a proclamation of Jewish identity, but it was a demonstration of being both American and Russian as well. By means of the ritual in this context, these three facets of the self were reconciled and relegated to their proper places.

Although the restaurant is "Russian," its staff and musical repertoire proclaim that it is also Jewish, and its luxurious furnishings and the opulent dress of its patrons testify to its being in America. Performance of the rite in English underscores the Americanness of the event and of the people involved. While most immigrants are at least competent in English (Federation of Jewish Philanthropies 1985:15), there is no doubt that they feel most comfortable expressing themselves in Russian. Knowledge of English is a source of pride, especially the "perfect English" spoken by their children. The childrens' display of being "real Americans" through their language is read by the parents, who readily concede that they themselves will always feel themselves to be strangers, as confirmation of the fact that they did indeed make the right choice by coming to America.

Thus, Jewish identity as expressed through the bar/bat mitzvah is one in which cosmopolitanism and modernity take their places alongside the traditions and symbols of Judaism. It is a rite of confirmation, not only for the child involved but for the guests as well because their image of themselves as Jews is publicly and joyfully acknowledged. It is a rite of acceptance—not only the child's acceptance of her Jewish identity but also the acceptance of American Jews, represented by an American Jewish rabbi, of Soviet immigrants as Jews, legitimate bearers of this ethnic-religious identity.[6] It is also a rite of expurgation—a symbolic passage from a stigmatized identity to a positive identity. It is this combination of highly charged passages that make the bat mitzvah of one girl into a cathartic moment for all those involved. In clarifying and resolving competing strands of the identity for these immigrants, the bat mitzvah tells them that they did in fact achieve the goal that many cited for having left the Soviet Union in the first place, "to live normally, to be rid of that fear (of anti-Semitism), to breathe easy, to be free, to be myself."

The Funeral

Jewish funerals, in contrast to a bat mitzvah, are generally performed in the Soviet Union, and immigrants are forthcoming in discussing their impressions of these rites. "When somebody dies in Russia, they become better than they really are," explained one recent immigrant. "You can't even recognize the person from the eulogy." Others, in recounting their experiences at funerals in the USSR, did not even mention eulogies. They stressed instead the lack of pageantry and the modesty of the service and the importance of Jewish prayers:

"It is very unusual to have no Hebrew or any kind of Jewish prayer read. This is out of the ordinary. Even my family which is completely atheistic, and you know what atheists my parents are, when my grandfather died, and then my grandmother—and others I have seen like them, party members, revolutionaries—at death they always have someone. We didn't have a rabbi at my grandparents' [funerals] but someone who knew these prayers came and chanted them. At their graves, he was there. And then, right after the burial, we returned home with my parents. And that was it."

When death occurs in America, the immigrants can have the deceased picked up from home or the hospital, washed, dressed, buried, eulogized, and prayed for by calling one of the several Jewish funeral homes that advertise in New York's Russian daily newspaper. One newly bereaved widow had her daughter-in-law call a funeral home to make the burial arrangements: "He was a Jew and he lived as a Jew—I want it done according to Jewish custom—they know what this is." The family's responsibility was to choose a gravesite, talk briefly to the rabbi about the deceased's life, inform friends and family about the death, and, of course, pay the bill.

This reliance on funeral parlors stands in sharp contrast to the way burial arrangements are made in the Soviet Union:

"My mother called and got my grandfather's body from the hospital. There you can't trust anyone to do anything right, and what they would do with a body if it was sent right from the hospital to be buried, you can't even imagine this. We took my grandfather's body home and placed it on the floor. Isn't it true that the body should stay on the floor and not be raised?

"We have the body on the floor, and then I remember a man from the Jewish community came to the house and washed the body and dressed it in that long white cloth. He was buried in the Jewish cemetery with the right prayers said for him. I was seventeen [1969] —I remember how afraid my mother was that it would not be done right, and how she had to bring the body home and find the right person to wash, dress, and pray over the body. Here you can breathe easy because they take the body right from the hospital and do everything right."

Two funerals I observed were both acclaimed to be "right, absolutely right," although they differed in content. In the first, the mourners came to the funeral home, where a service was conducted in the chapel. The deceased's body lay in state for viewing. Dressed in a white shirt, silk tie, and dark suit, he was placed in a polished wooden coffin engraved with a Jewish star. His widow and daughter sat at the coffin's side for the fifteen or twenty minutes of body-viewing that preceded the memorial service. As they sat and wept, the fifty or so members of the funeral party passed by to pay their respects. Each person's head was covered according to Jewish tradition. Women mourners stopped and sobbed; many of them hugged the widow and cried with her, some of them calling out, "Fima, my dear friend!" Men looked at the deceased, bowed their heads, and moved on to take their seats in the chapel.

The second funeral service occurred at graveside. The twenty-three mourners, of whom only three or four were elderly friends of the deceased, arrived at the burial site before the grave was completely prepared. The deceased's son distributed black yarmulkes to the men, and his wife gave kerchiefs to women without them. The rabbi remained in his car reading the newspaper for the fifteen minutes during which the grave was being dug.

Upon the completion of the grave digging, the rabbi joined the group and began the service. The coffin, a plain, closed wooden box, was poised on the edge of the grave. One of the elderly women turned to another and asked, "Aren't they going to open it? Aren't we going to see her?" "No," replied the other, "it isn't necessary [*eto ne nado*]."7

Both rabbis recited eulogies for the dead ones prior to their burials; in the first case, the eulogy was conducted in Yiddish in the funeral parlor. At the second funeral, in response to the rabbi's question "Yiddish or English?" the family replied, "English." Choice of language reflects the age of the mourners in each funeral party; neither language is considered more respectful than the other, because the eulogy, always presented in the vernacular (usually Russian in the USSR) is for all to understand. It is words of comfort for friends and family, not prayers.

In both services the rabbis concentrated on two interrelated themes—living long and difficult lives as Jews and being uprooted in old age to remain with the family emigrating to America. Both eulogies8 ended on an optimistic note, immortality:

"I will speak in Yiddish because I understand that almost all of you understand this, our mother tongue and because I don't speak Russian. Yefraim ben Dovid was a good husband, a good father, a good grandfather and a good friend. He lived a good Jewish life, surviving the harshness and terror of a Nazi concentration camp, where he lost his first family. After this terrible tragedy, he returned to his native city and married Anna and rebuilt his life, having two children, Grigory and Nina. Finally, he came to America, where he was able to see his daughter get married and his grandson born. Then he was reunited with his son, Grigory, daughter-in-law Viktoria, and his granddaughter Irina. And now, like a ship coming back to port, after lengthy travels here and yon, Yefraim ben Dovid has come home. What does it mean for a Jew to come home? It means to rest among Jews in the hereafter. To come home is the rest we deserve after a long life."

The second eulogy said: "As the Bible tells us, there is nothing so rare as a righteous woman. And although we mourn the loss of Marina Kogan, we know that a mother's love always stays in the hearts of her children and grandchildren and is never lost. She came to this country from Russia, leaving her friends and a way of life that she knew in order to remain with her children and grandchildren. She made this sacrifice for the sake of her family, for the future generations. And although she is gone, she remains in our hearts. The Lord is my Shepherd, I shall not want."

In both services, an unrelated mourner stepped forward to express his grief. At Yefim's funeral, an elderly man, a friend and *zemlyak* (person from the same town or city), came forth, and in a strong voice he chanted a benediction in honor of the deceased. In Ashkenazic Hebrew, leaning on his cane, this man poignantly intoned his prayer. During both the eulogy and the chant, the deceased's widow and a woman who was a lifetime friend and a fellow camp survivor, sobbed and cried out, *"Bozhe moy!* [Oh my God!] Fima! Fima!" and, *"Oy vey iz mir!"* [Oh woe is me!]." After the old man's chant, the rabbi motioned for all the mourners to file out. They left the funeral hall, got into several vehicles, and drove to the cemetery.

In the second case, the son of the deceased asked one of his friends, a respected member of the immigrant community, to say "a few words." He stepped into the place where the rabbi had stood and, in Russian, discussed the difficult life this woman had lived: "She lived in Russia through such famines, and then the war. Yet, despite all this, she raised a wonderful son and such grandchildren! Her last several days were especially difficult—she was all alone, she had no one, she couldn't make herself understood [in the hospital]; she had no one—except her son. But let us not talk of these things and those days. Let us just know that now it is easier for her. And, as our rabbi said, 'A mother's love is never lost. It continues to live in the hearts of her children and grandchildren.'" The friend then stepped back into the group of mourners. The rabbi reclaimed his position and motioned for the deceased's son to join him.

In neither case did the rabbi or the friend who delivered the eulogy personally know the deceased. Each speaker created his speech from information provided by next-of-kin. In both cases the difficult life of a Soviet Jew was invoked; in both cases World War II and its special terror for Jews was mentioned, and in both cases this difficult life was juxtaposed implicitly against Jews' comfortable lives in America, and explicitly against death. These deaths are occasions for relief; these old, weary people have "come home." And having led righteous lives, having been good parents, as their earthly sufferings cease, they live on in spirit through the memories of their children and grandchildren in America.

These comforting words are very important for the survivors, who, in both cases, were responsible for the uprooting of their elderly kin. Both deceaseds were in their late seventies when they arrived in America and in their eighties when they died. They came to be with their families, to witness the opportunities for future generations. The survivors understood that their parents had left behind the only lives they knew. It was a sacrifice that needed some spoken appreciation. At the same time, it is a source of comfort for survivors that their loved ones are buried here in America where they can oversee the maintenance of their graves and rest assured that they are being cared for "correctly."9

In structure, both services were identical, culminating with the lowering of the body into the grave as the *kaddish* is intoned. At both services too, mourners actively participated in the ritual not only by saying "amen" after prayers but by the physical involvement of each person in burying the dead, experiencing the feeling of the earth, back to which the deceased is returned.

The Jewish identity expressed in these funeral rites is one based on suffering and sorrow, a common history of lachrymosity (Zenner 1977). In discussions of the long but difficult life of the deceased, attention is directed to the particular experiences of Soviet Jews, specifically during the 1930s and 1940s when they endured terrible hardships. Despite the fact that many of their Jewish traditions were undermined and that outsiders might have expressed uncertainty about their Judaism, having suffered as Jews, in their view, more than entitles these elders to full Jewish status in life and in death.

Funeral rites for Soviet Jewish immigrants do not transform the deceased into unrecognizable saints. Instead, the rites stress their connection with the entire Jewish people by reviewing the many hardships Soviet Jews underwent. And they affirm the triumph of recent immigrants who could die knowing that they were fortunate enough to leave behind wonderful children and grandchildren to enjoy life in America. Death is marked as a respite from suffering, and as a final reunion with fellow Jews. This latter point is most important to the surviving family; their ability to have an absolutely correct Jewish funeral in America enables them to fulfill the last wishes of the departed. In so doing, they reaffirm their decision to emigrate and assure themselves that it was the "right" step to take.

Conclusions

The bar/bat mitzvah and funeral rites described above both evoke and are based on comparisons between being Jewish in the Soviet Union (bad, hard) and being a Jew in America (good, easy). These ritual acts attest to the changes Soviet Jews have made in their identities since emigration. In these public markings of passages, Soviet Jews transform themselves from a stigmatized group uncertain of their customs and traditions to a legitimate people.

While the bat mitzvah is a joyous ritual celebrating entry into adulthood, and the funeral is a sad moment marking the death of a loved one, both rituals enhance the immigrants' Jewish identity as they reconcile who they are with their new surroundings. The specific passage of a particular individual becomes, in a wider sense, a transition rite for the entire immigrant community.

Notes

1. Two other important social movements were occurring at this time as well, *Haskalah,* or the enlightenment, which modernized but did not in its essence challenge Orthodox Judaism, and, of course, mass emigration to America.
2. Census data from the Soviet Union (1979) reveal that over 80 percent of the Jewish population claims Russian as its native language. The westernmost portions of the Ukraine and the Baltic republics did not become incorporated into the USSR until 1939. It was not until after World War II and the near-annihilation of the Jewish population of these areas that they fell under Soviet sway.
3. Throughout the course of this paper, names and in some cases family composition have been changed. Both remain true to the spirit of these people, however, i.e., some common Russian first names such as Ivan and Nikolai, which are rarely if ever used by Jews, were not chosen to disguise informants.
4. Both the Hebrew verbal incantation and the Russian custom of spitting three times are devices to ward off the evil eye. Informants laughingly tell me that Russians—or is it Russian Jews, no one is really sure—believe that a little devil sits on everyone's left shoulder. And if you mention a good quality or happenstance about someone which you wish will persist, or if you express the hope that something good will happen to them in the future, spit three times over your left shoulder into the face of this devil and then, automatically, the evil eye is blinded as well.

[145]

5. Yiddish kin terms for grandmother and aunt.
6. As I have discussed in greater depth elsewhere (Baskin 1985), Soviet Jewish immigrants have been challenged, or at least feel that they have been challenged, by American Jews about the legitimacy of their Jewish identity. Having a bar or bat mitzvah performed by a rabbi who is himself an American Jew helps to cancel out their self-doubts.
7. I have been told that Russian funerals, including Jewish ones, are much warmer than American funerals. In Russia, family and friends give the deceased a last hug and kiss. Therefore, the coffin remains open during the eulogies. A procession often led by a large photograph of the deceased accompanies the coffin to the cemetery, and once the burial is completed, "lots and lots of flowers, no matter what time of year," are lain on the grave.

   According to the strict interpretation of Jewish law, a dead person must be washed, dressed in a plain white shroud, and buried within twenty-four hours. Once dressed, the deceased is placed in a plain wooden coffin, which is shut. No decorations, including flowers, are to be placed on the grave because the body, which is returning to the earth from where it came, is no longer of concern, only the spirit of the deceased.
8. Because of the inappropriateness of recording devices or note-taking of any kind at a funeral service, the eulogies quoted are not exactly verbatim. All translations from Yiddish and Russian are mine.
9. Many immigrants have expressed their anger at the Soviet Union's policy of forbidding former Soviet citizens the right to visit the USSR, explaining, "Such cruelty—forbidding us to visit and tend to our parents' graves. What I wouldn't give for two weeks [in Kiev] to fix up my mother's grave."

REFERENCES

Armstrong, John A. 1968. "The Ethnic Scene in the Soviet Union: The View of the Dictatorship." In *Ethnic Minorities in the Soviet Union,* ed. Erich Goldhagen. New York: Praeger, 3–49.
Baron, Salo W. 1964. *The Russian Jew under Tsars and Soviets.* New York: Macmillan.
Baskin, Fran Markowitz. 1985. "Jewish in the USSR, Russian in the USA: Social Context and Ethnic Identity." Paper presented at the Annual Meetings of the American Anthropological Association, Washington, D.C.
Dubnow, S. M. 1916. *The History of the Jews in Russia and Poland from the Earliest Times until the Present Day.* 3 vols. Philadelphia: The Jewish Publication Society of America, vol. 1.
Ettinger, S. 1970. "Russian Society and the Jews." *Bulletin on Soviet and East European Jewish Affairs* 5:36–42.
Federation of Jewish Philanthropies/ Fran Markowitz Baskin. 1985. *Jewish Identification and Affiliation of Soviet Jewish Immigrants in New York City—A Needs Assessment and Planning Study.* New York: Federation of Jewish Philanthropies of New York.
Gillison, Jerome. 1979. *Summary Report of the Survey of Soviet Jewish Emigrés in Baltimore,* rev. ed. Baltimore: Baltimore Hebrew College, Center for the Study of Jewish Emigration and Resettlement.

Gitelman, Zvi. 1984. "Soviet-Jewish Immigrants to the United States: Profile, Problems, Prospects." In *Soviet Jewry in the Decisive Decade, 1971–1980,* ed. Robert O. Freedman. Durham: Duke University Press, 89–98.

Greenberg, Louis. 1976. *The Jews in Russia.* 2 vols. New York: Schocken Books.

Ortner, Sherry B. 1978. *Sherpas through Their Rituals.* Cambridge: Cambridge University Press.

Russia. Tsentral'ny Statisticheskii Komitet. 1905. *Relève général pour tout l'Empire: Des résultats du dépouillement de la population en 1897.* 2 vols. St. Petersbourg, vol. 1.

Simon, Rita J. 1983. "The Jewish Identity of Soviet Immigrant Parents and Children." In *Culture, Ethnicity, and Identity,* ed. William C. McCready. New York: Academic Press, 327–39.

Zenner, Walter P. 1977. "Lachrymosity: A Cultural Reinforcement of Minority Status." *Ethnicity* 4:156–66.

[6]

Rechnitzer Rejects:
A Humor of Modern Orthodoxy

Elliott Oring

Although folklorists may behave very much like anthropologists and sociologists when they are conducting research—identifying problems, formulating hypotheses, selecting a research population, delineating a methodology, and doing fieldwork—folklorists have perhaps been more inclined than the others to view their own immediate environments and behaviors as material worthy of serious contemplation, analysis, and interpretation. In other words, folklore research may begin simply as an encounter with objects and behaviors in one's own living room. This essay is the result of just such an encounter. Several years ago, a friend bought me a Jewish comedy record as a present. At first, the record was merely entertaining. The more I listened to it, however, the more I began to wonder about the significance of this comedy and its relation to that larger question of "Jewish humor" (Oring 1983).

Students of American-Jewish humor have tended to focus on the analysis of jokes and anecdotes broadly circulated in the Jewish community and published in various compendia. Some have regarded these jokes and anecdotes as mechanisms for adaptation and assimilation to American culture (Katz and Katz 1971). Others have seen this humor as the reflection of the increasing aggressiveness of an emancipated community demanding parity with the social majority (Cray 1964). Still others regard such humor as an expression of concern over the maintenance of a Jewish identity, devoid of any religious or spiritual core (Rosenberg and Shapiro 1958:74).

[148]

Understanding the Jewish jokes and anecdotes on which these studies have been based required for the most part only a very catholic knowledge of Jewish character, tradition, and sociology. The jokes were often understood and appreciated by Jews with widely disparate levels of Jewish education, religious knowledge, and ritual participation. Indeed, many non-Jews are also appreciative auditors and raconteurs of such "Jewish" jokes and anecdotes.

The Jewish humor I was listening to on my phonograph record was entirely different. First, the humor was in the form of songs and comic routines rather than joking narratives. Second, these songs and routines were disseminated through commercial recordings rather than in oral face-to-face communications (although we should not forget the impact of printed collections on the spread of Jewish jokelore). Third, and perhaps most striking, these songs and skits, unlike most of the Jewish joke repertoire, presupposed a highly esoteric ethnic and religious knowledge for the comprehension and appreciation of the humor.

This record that generated so much enjoyment and puzzlement turned out to be only one in a series of records titled *Rechnitzer Rejects.*[1] The first volume of this series was issued in 1982 and a volume was issued in each subsequent year through 1985. Although no record has been released in 1986, a volume is currently in production. The volumes are the creation of Perfect Impressions, a "public relations and entertainment management" firm based in New York, which specializes in Jewish entertainment.

The four albums consist of sixty-five bands or selections. Forty-three of these selections are songs, while the remaining twenty-two selections are comic routines, many of which involve music. The great majority of the songs are parodies and most of these are based upon standard and contemporary popular tunes, including "Puttin' on the Ritz," "Thunderball," "Feelings," "Memories," "Saturday Night Fever," "Tie a Yellow Ribbon," "Home on the Range," "Shake, Rattle, and Roll," "Old Man River," the theme from "Flashdance," and others. A few of the songs are parodies of specifically ethnic material: of Yiddish songs such as *"Mayn shteytele Belz,"* "My Zadie," and "Roumania"; of contemporary pop-hasidic material such as "Just One Shabbos" and "The Time Is Now"; and of popular Israeli songs like *"Kakhol ve-lavan"* and *"Khay, khay, khay."*

The comic routines take several forms. A number involve *khazones* or cantorial renditions of liturgy, supplemented with appropriate sound effects. Three routines are telephone conversations that a *mesh-*

[149]

ulekh or Jewish fundraiser has with the English receptionist of a Jew-ish doctor, the minister of a black church, and the proprietor of an Oriental massage parlor. Three routines involve the delivery of inap-propriate sermons, while two others are mock-Yiddish language tu-torials. Two routines are commercials, one is a political announce-ment, one a radio talk-show interview, and yet another a filler by someone impersonating Henry Kissinger.

The most striking aspect of these records is the extraordinary range of cultural data that is required to interpret these performances. From a linguistic point of view, listeners are expected in addition to English to have a good knowledge of Yiddish and Hebrew as well as a smatter-ing of Aramaic. In addition, they should be able to recognize Yiddish and Hebrew dialects and accents as well as the voices of various leaders who have been involved in Middle Eastern affairs (e.g., Men-achem Begin, Ariel Sharon, Anwar Sadat, Henry Kissinger, Jimmy Carter, Ronald Reagan). They need to be familar with typical Jewish foods (cholent, kishka, *kneydlakh,* chopped liver, and bagels) as well as concepts of kosher and glatt kosher. Musically, listeners are ex-pected to be familiar with *khazones* or cantorial style and be able to identify exaggerated examples of that style. Listeners must also be grounded in contemporary trends in Jewish music, including the voices and specific performances of Mordechai ben David, Shlomo Carlbach, Avraham Fried, and Jo Amar. Other musical currents from Israel, the klezmer tradition, and Yiddish theater are also drawn upon.

From the perspective of religious observances and rituals, the songs and skits call for some knowledge of: putting on *tefillin* (phylacteries) and customs associated with reciting the *kris shema* ("Hear O Israel"); *dukhenen* (bestowing the priestly blessing) and the ritual washing of the hands performed by the Levites; the singing of *zmires* or hymns during the Sabbath eve meal as well as the names of particular hymns; *aliyes* or summonses to recite blessings over the Torah; the wearing of wigs or *sheytls* by observant Jewish women as an expression of modes-ty; the Talmud and the language and gestures associated with its study, as well as specific prayers from the Sabbath and high holiday liturgy.

Lastly, these songs and skits rely on a more general sociological knowledge of Jews and the Jewish community, including such customs as: the propensity of Jews to enjoy the *shvits* or steambath; the continued existence and operation of the figure of *shadkhn* or matchmaker; resort hotels that cater to an observant Jewish clientel during Jewish holidays; concepts of *yikhes* or pedigree and its relationship to the according of ritual honors in the synagogue; the requirement of ten men to form a minyan or quorum for communal prayer; the conflicts that traditionally exist between a rabbi and the congregation that employs him; and the names and locations of particular Jewish communities and their character.

In addition to all of this specifically Jewish knowledge, the humor of the *Rechnitzer Rejects* further requires considerable familiarity with American culture, particularly American popular music, but also other media forms and figures such as radio talk shows and hosts, commercials, language instruction records, and celebrities.

The musical presentation is a contributing element to both the aesthetic and comedic properties of the songs and routines. The musical arrangements are full and strong. The opening notes of a song are usually sufficient to identify the song being parodied because the music so faithfully reproduces the original popular recordings. Those tunes that are "Rechnitzer originals" are melodic or otherwise engaging. The *khazones* is equally accomplished and sung by talented *khazonim*. In listening to the record one can easily feel that the comedy does not merit such a degree of musical sophistication. But this disparity between the musical and comedic levels only serves to enhance the quality of the latter. The humor is heightened by the extraordinary musical attention that has been dedicated to the production of a broad humorous text.

It is not possible to survey each of the songs and routines that appear on *Rechnitzer Rejects*. Instead, I will present and comment on two songs, because songs form the majority of selections on these records. The first song, "Home on the Blatt," is sung to the tune of "Home on the Range":

I was in the *besmedresh* [Yid, Heb: house of study], learning for a change,
when I heard my *khavruse* [Aramaic: study group] singing "Home on the
  Range."
He sang it with ease, and *neshome* [Yid, Heb: soul] of course,
And when he was finished, he got off his horse.

Oh give me a *daf* [Heb: page], where the *sugye's* [issue] not taf [=tough],
Where the Rashi and Tosefos [two medieval commentaries] is small,
Where seldom is heard, an Aramaic word
And my rebbe [rabbi] is always on call.

[151]

Oh give me a *blat* [Yid: page, leaf]
Where I'm able to learn *pashut peshat* [Heb: simple literalism]
With *tanaim* [teachers of the Mishnaic period] report, an encouraging *vort*
    [Yid: word]
And *rishonim* [post-Talmudic codifiers and commentators of the late
    Middle Ages] don't argue alot.

Oh give me relief from *kashes* [difficulties] so deep,
That they threaten to fracture my thumb.
And bring someone keener, to the lone *have amine* [premise]
When it seems the *maskone* [conclusion] won't come.

A *kal va-khomer*'s [a hermeneutic principle] okay,
But his friend *tsad ha-shave* [Heb: common denominator; basis for another
    hermeneutic principle] "No way!"
But when *im timtse lomer* [Heb: "And if you should say" indicating the
    anticipation of counter arguments]
Is like *sefirat ha-omer* [counting the days between Passover and Pentecost;
    i.e., numerous],
I'm tempted to cry out *"Oy vay!"* [Yid: Woe!, My gosh]

Oh give me a page, where *makhloykes* [Heb: controversy] don't rage,
And Abbaye and Rava [two Amoraic sages] agree.
Where the *Mishnah* is *stam* [apparent], and the Rabbenu Tam [one of the
    masters of the Tosefos]
Doesn't need a *"ve-nire le-Ri"* ["And it appears to Rabbi Isaac"; a
    reference to another important figure of Tosefos activity]

A *talmid khokhem* [Heb: scholar] I'm not,
I pity the brain that I've got.
When the *shakle ve-tarye* [Aramaic: balance and throw: i.e., debate] is not
    out to scar ya,
That's when I feel home on the *blat* (*Rechnitzer Rejects:* vol. 2, 1983: Side
    2, Band 3)

This song should be completely enigmatic to those unfamiliar with the
Talmud. For those who are somewhat familiar with the Talmud, the
overall sense of the song probably comes through, although some
elements are likely to remain obscure. This song is likely to be completely intelligible only to someone who has actually studied the Talmud. Even the reference to the fractured thumb in the fourth verse,
which involves no obscure language or terminology, depends on familiarity with the traditional gestures associated with Talmudic analysis and argument. Thus, this song provides a good illustration of the
depth of Jewish knowledge often prerequisite to the appreciation of
the humor on *Rechnitzer Rejects.*

Jews are enjoined to study Torah, and one of the highest forms of this study is study of the Talmud. "Home on the Blatt" is essentially a complaint about the difficulties of Talmud study. The singer expresses his wish to study an issue that is clear, about which there is no controversy, and upon which the major medieval commentaries of Rashi and the Tosefos (which always appear on the page where the issue is presented and discussed) have little or nothing to say. Indeed, virtually all of the esoteric terminology in this song concerns the desire for a direct and uncomplicated study experience.

The use of the tune "Home on the Range" is not arbitrary or accidental. "Home on the Range" evokes images of pastoral simplicity. A home on the range is a home in the great outdoors, connoting a solitary existence in nature, a life in which "discouraging words" are never heard. The study of the Talmud, however, does not take place on the open plains but in an urban center. It is carried on indoors in crowded houses of study. This study is a loud and intense verbal and gestural interaction within small study groups (*khavruses*) where *only* discouraging words are to be heard in the exchange of arguments and counterarguments. A romantic image of the American West stands in direct opposition to the conception of traditional Jewish life as symbolized by the Talmud and its rituals of study. Thus, the parodying of "Home on the Range" involves much more than the utilization of a familiar tune, meter, and an occasional bit of phraseology. As with all successful parody, an awareness of the original song's images and messages is required for a complete appreciation of the comic mutation.

The quest for the simplicity and harmony of the American prairie in the pages of the Talmud is, of course, a ludicrous one. Although the Talmud is the basis of Jewish law, the study of the Talmud is not primarily an exercise in learning and memorizing law. Often an authoritative decision for the case under discussion is never arrived at or stated. Talmudic study is rather a process of examining traditional legal opinions, organizing them, searching for their consistencies, reconciling contradictory opinions, and asking new questions based upon changed historical circumstances and situations. This process has a life of its own, independent of what the actual legal decision may or may not be. This process is of the highest intellectual order. Complexity and controversy are its trademarks. Contrary to the wishes expressed in the second verse of the song, there is no issue devoid of Aramaic words, since the greater part of the Talmud involves the Aramaic discussion of earlier Hebrew legal teachings. The desire, in the last stanza, for an issue upon which the sages Abbaye and Rava agree is equally fantastic, because in the Talmud, Abbaye and Rava rarely agree; indeed, their traditional disputations have come to serve as a metaphor for the entire system of Talmudic dialectics.

"Home on the Blatt" sends a clear message about the ludicrousness of yearning for American simplifications of Jewish life. The attempt to distill Jewish traditions down to a simpler essence can result only in their evaporation altogether. One can never be at home in Jewish life in general, or on a page of the Talmud in particular, if being "at home" signifies being without complexity, conflict, and anxiety. The song clearly communicates the impossibility of a Jewish life that is zealously reconciled with the values of the dominant culture—with the modern, secular values of American society.

The second example I present is not a parody of a specific song, although its music is drawn from a recognizable musical style. The song is "*Makhmir*":

Shades of black and the Satmar's back,
Gartl [Yid: a ritual belt] tight and *peyes* [Yid. Heb: side curls] long;
Socks are white and you know they're right,
Satmar's never wrong.

Shades of blue, he's a special Jew,
Being watched by many eyes;
Shades of green and I know what you mean,
It's a *kherem* [Heb: ostracism, excommunication] otherwise.

Chorus:
Half the town they think they're crazy,
But that's nothing new;
To understand the holy plan,
Here's what you must do.
They're off to see,
The *rov* [Heb: rabbi] to see,
If strictness is their word.

Makhmir, makhmir [Heb: strict, severe]
Makh mir dus and *makh mir dat* [Yid. pun: Make me do this, make me do that];
Makhmir, makhmir,
It's Satmar's secret.

Eenie, meenie, meinie, moe,
Catch a Hasid by the toe;

[154]

If he *shukels* [Yid: ritual swaying gesture] let him go,
He'll go back to ole Monroe [Monroe, N.Y.].

Shades of pink with a *shnaps* [Yid: liquor] to drink,
Simkhes [Heb, Yid: joyous occasions] make the Satmar sing;
Shades of red like the rebbe [leader of Hasidim] said,
He sees everything.

Shades of brown and around the town,
All *misnagdim* [Heb, Yid: opponents of Hasidism] spurn the sect;
Shades of grey well there'll come a day,
That they'll get more respect. (ibid: Side 2, Band 1)

The Satmar are a group of Hasidim from a town in northwest Romania (before World War I, a part of Hungary) which settled in Williamsburg after World War II. In 1972 the late Satmar rebbe established a yeshiva and a self-contained community in Monroe, New York. In the eyes of most traditional Jews, the Satmar Hasidim are an extreme manifestation of halakhic or Orthodox Judaism. For example, based upon his interpretation of Jewish law, the leader of the Satmar Hasidim has opposed both Zionism and the state of Israel, claiming that they are sinful and delay the coming of the Messiah. Hasidim in general, and Satmar Hasidim in particular, are opposed to any reconciliation between Jewish tradition and modern society. They are strict (*makhmir*) in their interpretation of the law, leaving no room for the insinuation of alien influences. In every way they attempt to protect Jewish law by removing any potential temptations or occasions for its violation. Thus the traditional dress of the Hasidim, mentioned in the first verse of the song, of black coat, belt, hat, and white socks, insulates them from the wider community and creates an additional barrier against modern institutions and values.

Although the song is ostensibly about Satmar, it's real concern is strictness in the interpretation of Jewish law. The Satmar Hasidim are only an extreme representation of this tendency to strictness, but it is a tendency to be found in other segments of the Orthodox community. The suggestion in the last verse of the song that a day will come when the Satmar will get "more respect" for their strictness is a ludicrous one. In a certain way, it is as ludicrous as the wish in "Home on the Blatt" that the study of the Talmud should be straightforward and uncomplicated. This ludicrousness in *"Makhmir"* is highlighted by arranging this paean to the Satmar in an exaggerated disco/pop instrumental style.

[155]

Both the songs I have presented are similar in that they set lyrics of specifically Jewish content to American popular songs or musical styles. These songs, however, are diametrically opposite expressions. "Home on the Blatt" explores the possibility of simplifying Jewish tradition; *"Makhmir"* explores the possibility that Jewish observance and community will come to resemble that of the contemporary Satmar. From the perspective or stance of the songs, both possibilities are equally ludicrous.

Yet neither perspective is truly ludicrous in its own right. They are only made to seem ludicrous in the songs. Indeed, Reform Judaism, as well as large segments of the Conservative moment, is dedicated to the reconciliation of Jewish tradition with modern culture to the extent that modern values determine which elements of traditional Judaism may be rationally maintained. Traditional Orthodoxy, on the other hand, makes no concessions to the modern world if that compromises the observance of the halakhah. The halakhah rules supreme, no matter how severe the burden of its observance. It is the halakhah that must extend itself over modern life; not the other way around. As I have said, neither of these positions is inconsistent or ludicrous in its own right. What appears ludicrous, however, is a position that seeks to maintain both perspectives: one that seeks to live in modern society in accordance with modern values while at the same time attempting to remain halakhic Jews. Yet this is precisely the position of modern Orthodoxy. And it is this dilemma of modern Orthodoxy that is aptly reflected in the tension between the extremes of Satmar severity and feeling at "Home on the Blatt."[2]

Of course, it should come as no surprise that these songs reflect a dilemma of modern Orthodoxy. After all, the interpretion and appreciation of *Rechnitzer Rejects* is open only to those who have been immersed in the culture and concerns of halakhic Judaism *and* who have also had broad exposure to secular, American, popular culture. But the humor of *Rechnitzer Rejects* is not a modern Orthodox humor only because of the knowledge that is requisite for its understanding; it is an Orthodox humor because it repeatedly articulates a fundamental incongruity of modern Orthodox life.

One characteristic of modern Orthodoxy is its orientation toward more liberal interpretations of the halakhah. Modern Orthodox Jews have looked for rabbinic responsa that are *maykayl* (lenient), those that make use of legal loopholes that allow for an observance that does not inhibit the pursuit of modernity. They avoid the responsa that are *makhmir* (strict) and that require extreme personal adjustments in living. But the pursuit of this liberal position contributes to a sense of religious ambivalence in many modern Orthodox people. It creates a doubt about the sincerity of their own commitment to the halakhah. It engenders an uneasy feeling that the traditional Orthodox, who avoid the honors and rewards bestowed by modern society, are more authentic Jews than they are, and that modernist Reform and Conservative Jews are perhaps also not so inauthentic. This ambivalence and insecurity about their ritual status is expressed in endless conversations and evaluations of the statuses of other members of the community, which invariably manifest themselves in pronouncements about being "too *frum*" [Yid: pious] or "crazy *frum*" or "black hats" on the one hand, or "too modern" or "goyim" on the other (Heilman 1973: 12–29; Shapiro 1985:167). Invariably, it is only others who are characterized in this fashion; one's own degree of observance is usually just right, showing perhaps only minor deviations from some unstated ideal.

This contradiction in the self-identity of modern Orthodox Jews cannot be easily resolved or summarily dismissed. Elsewhere I have argued that when irresolvable contradictions exist in the definition of self, one method of mastering the conflict engendered by these contradictions is to exaggerate them, externalize them, and celebrate them (Oring 1981:129). And this is precisely what *Rechnitzer Rejects* does. Again and again within individual songs and in the interaction between different songs, the contradictions between traditional Jewish life and modern life are replayed and broadcast in all their permutations. Proposed solutions, if they are offered, are invariably more ludicrous than accepting and living the contradictions. Ultimately, *Rechnitzer Rejects* communicates the idea that the problems of identity and of conceptions of the self are not so much to be resolved as transcended, and that a major vehicle for this transcendence is to be found in the forms and techniques of humor.

The first volume of *Rechnitzer Rejects* sold more than ten thousand copies. The other volumes were also expected to sell ten thousand or more (Martin Davidson 1986: personal communication). These kind of sales' volumes indicate "platinum records" in the Jewish market. What accounts for this kind of popularity? Why should a humor of modern Orthodoxy emerge at this time and prove so popular?

Such questions need to be framed properly. In many respects, the humor of *Rechnitzer Rejects* in not new. For example, the songs of

Mickey Katz (Gans 1953) similarly celebrated the ludicrousness of the encounter between Jewish and American culture. His parodies of American popular songs, however, highlighted the encounter between American culture and Jewish ethnic culture, that is, the Yiddish-speaking culture of Eastern Europe. Unlike the songs of the *Rechnitzer Rejects* albums, his songs contained no Hebrew or Aramaic and were devoid of references to either Israel or Orthodox religious culture. Nevertheless, Katz's albums clearly demonstrate that a commercial tradition of popular song parodies on Jewish themes is no innovation.

Furthermore, popular song parodies based upon Orthodox Jewish tradition are also not new. Such parodies, however, tended to emerge in the folk culture of modern Orthodoxy rather than in popular and commercial formats. The following is a fragment of a song that was popular among the students of a modern Orthodox elementary school in New York City circa 1955. It was set to the then popular hit song "Black Denim Trousers":

> He wore black denim *tsitses* [fringed ritual garment],
> And *peyes* [sidecurls] two feet long;
> And a black leather yarmulke [skull cap],
> With a button on the top;
> He had a hopped-up *gemore* [Talmud],
> That took off like a gun;
> And he was the terror,
> Of *heder* [Heb: room] one-o-one (1986: personal communication).[3]

Although somewhat less sophisticated, this parody is not appreciably different from most of the parodies presented on the *Rechnitzer Rejects* albums. Nor do I believe this example to be idiosyncratic. There is evidence that such traditions of song parody (as well as comic routines) have existed for decades among the youth of modern Orthodox communities, although they have not been documented in any of the folklore or humor collections of which I am aware.

The scope of the questions about the *Rechnitzer Rejects* albums has been somewhat narrowed. A tradition of Jewish parody of American popular song on commercial recordings is not new. Nor does the subject matter of *Rechnitzer Rejects* appear to be entirely new; rather it seems to parallel the folk traditions of modern Orthodox youth of the past several decades. The question that remains is: Why does such material come to be deliberately composed and recorded in the 1980s and why does it meet with such astounding commercial success? If my interpretation of the basic message of *Rechnitzer Rejects* humor is accepted, the question may be formulated as follows: Why in the 1980s do significant portions of the modern Orthodox community feel the need to project and celebrate this conflict of identity?

I believe the answer to this question lies in the recent compression of the spectrum of Jewish religious practice. That is to say, the range of religious expression to be found in Jewish institutional contexts has narrowed considerably in recent years. Furthermore, this compression has been toward the "right"—toward traditional or halakhic forms of expression.

Today, classical Reform Judaism, with its disdain for tradition and ritual, has fewer adherents. No longer is the anecdote about a Christian lawyer who discovered quite accidentally in the midst of a Sunday service that he was in a Reform Synagogue likely to ring true. Today one is more likely to encounter Reform Jews who pray with a *talis* and observe Sabbath and dietary laws (Sarna 1982:30). Reform practices, in a return to traditional forms, are becoming indistinguishable from those of the Conservative or even Orthodox congregations. The 1984 call by New York Reform congregation Shaaray Tefila to "join us on Rosh Hashannah for our '*Tashlikh*' service (casting away of sins)" (Silberman 1985:257) is merely an extreme example of this movement toward traditionalism.

Similarly there has been movement to the right within Orthodoxy itself. This move to the right has been manifested in stricter interpetations of the halakhah and an increasing intolerance for deviation. Modern Orthodox attempts to reconcile the halakhah with modern life have less support and are viewed as mere facades for halakhic deviation (Liebman 1979:21–22). All in all, this compression of Jewish practice along with other developments such as the *havurah* (fellowship) movement (Silberman 1985:256–257), the *baley tshuve* (penitent) phenomenon (ibid.:244–253; Sarna 1982:31–32) and Jewish feminist expressions (Silberman 1985:262–67) have served to blur traditional denominational boundaries, and in doing so threaten the identity of a modern Orthodoxy that is rooted both in the halakhah and the values and attitudes of liberal democratic society. In this environment, the incongruity between commitments to both secular and religious forms and values is no longer merely a concomitant of modern Orthodox identity, it has become the distinguishing feature of that identity. To know the language of the Talmud and its methods of study, to recog-

Elliott Oring

nize the lyrics of "Home on the Range" and their expression of naive romanticism, and to be able to laugh at the conjunction of the two— that is the measure of modern Orthodoxy. In repeatedly playing upon the incongruity of sacred and secular values, *Rechnitzer Rejects* emerges as an important touchstone of modern Orthodox identity at a time when the elements of that identity are being challenged and no longer seem clearly in focus.

Notes

1. These records are *Rechnitzer Rejects*, vol. 1 (HP29561), vol. 2 (HP29565), vol. 3 (HP29568), vol. 4 (HP29572) (New York: Perfect Impressions, 1697 Broadway, New York, NY 10019). They are produced and written by Martin Davidson with Seymour Rockoff as a contributing writer. "Home on the Blatt" and *Makhmir* are reprinted here with the permission of Perfect Impressions.

   The name *"Rechnitzer Rejects"* seems to imply that these are songs or tunes rejected by some hasidic leader (rebbe) from the town of Rechnitz. A town of Rechnitz did exist in the Austrian Burgenland along the Hungarian border, but the "Rechnitzer" here seems to come from the term "rekht" or "rikhtik" meaning "right" or "correct," implying that this is a rebbe who sees his own way of doing things as the "right" way for everybody. The producer of the records recalled that as an adolescent he would tell people in synagogue he followed the custom of the Rechnitzer Rebbe when they tried to tell him the "correct" ritual observance (Davidson 1985: personal communication).
2. Charles S. Liebman has noted: "Orthodoxy has responded by compartmentalizing Judaism. . . . Orthodox Jews, by and large, do not search for consistency between their Jewish and non-Jewish life. On the contrary, *they make a virtue of their inconsistency*" [my emphasis] (1979:23). "Cosmopolitan parochialism" is how Samuel C. Heilman describes this same characteristic (1973:7–8).
3. Oral witticisms also reflect this conjunction of the sacred and the secular (Heilman 1973:203–04).

REFERENCES

Cray, Ed. 1964. "The Rabbi Trickster." *Journal of American Folklore* 77:331–45.
Gans, Herbert J. 1953. "The 'Yinglish' Music of Mickey Katz." *American Quarterly* 5:213–18.
Heilman, Samuel C. 1973. *Synagogue Life: A Study in Symbolic Interaction.* Chicago: University of Chicago Press.
Katz, Naomi, and Eli Katz. 1971. "Tradition and Adaptation in American Jewish Humor." *Journal of American Folklore* 84:215–20.
Liebman, Charles S. 1979. "Orthodox Judaism Today." *Midstream* 25:19–26.
Oring, Elliott. 1981. *Israeli Humor: The Content and Structure of the Chizbat of the Palmah.* Albany, N.Y.: State University of New York Press.

——. 1983. "The People of the Joke: On the Conceptualization of a Jewish Humor." *Western Folklore* 42:261–71.

Rechnitzer Rejects: vol. 2. 1983. New York: Perfect Impressions, HP29565.

Rosenberg, Bernard, and Gilbert Shapiro. 1958. "Marginality and Jewish Humor." *Midstream* 4:70–80.

Sarna, Jonathan D. 1982. "The Great American Jewish Awakening." *Midstream* 28:30–34.

Shapiro, Edward D. 1985. "Orthodoxy in Pleasantdale." *Judaism* 34:163–70.

Silberman, Charles E. 1985. *A Certain People: American Jews and Their Lives Today.* New York: Summit Books.

[7]

Flaming Prayers:
Hillula in a New Home

Ruth Fredman Cernea

Traditionally, a *hillula* is a pilgrimage by the Jews of western North Africa to the tombs of revered rabbis on the anniversaries of their deaths and at times of personal or social crisis. In Washington, D.C., a new pilgrimage is taking place, not in an ancient cemetery but in the bare, white community room of a suburban synagogue. Rather than talk by the lights of flickering oil lamps, the "pilgrims" pay homage to the holy men under chandeliers and florescent lights. The journey does not begin in Marrakesh, Meknes, or Casablanca but in seemingly less exotic places—Rockville, Maryland; Fairfax, Virginia; the District's Connecticut Avenue. That first May evening that I attended *hillula,* the setting seemed all wrong and the ritual seemed incongruous in this bureaucratic modern city. But then I did not understand how the ancient symbols could speak to a very different popula-

The discussion of *hillula* in this paper is based on fieldwork conducted primarily between 1977 and 1982, with further attendances at the ritual in subsequent years. Research continues into the present, with a special interest in observing changes in community dynamics and in *hillula* now that the congregation has realized its long-cherished dream of a building and a rabbi of its own. I am grateful to the many busy Washingtonians who have welcomed me so graciously into their homes to share their histories and, indeed, their lives with me. If I mention my particular debt to Ida Dana, Annie Totah, Gwen and Marc Zuares, Stella and Samy Ymar, Ginette Spier, Flory Jagoda, and Lucy Himey, it is with full awareness of the many other Sephardim whose reflections and friendship have enriched my own life. I also wish to thank Rabbi Samuel Z. Fishman and Michael M. Cernea for their valuable comments on this paper.

tion and, indeed, how it is that a ritual, by its very nature, cannot be frozen in time.

The Aramaic word *hillula* means "feast" or "wedding feast"; it is also translated as "celebration" or "joy." The word suggests the kabbalistic concept underlying the ritual: when a particularly pious man dies, his soul unites in a joyous, mystical marriage with God. Through this wedding of a pure soul and the Divine, God becomes extraordinarily immanent and unusually approachable; the holy men of the Maghreb—Morocco, Algeria, and Tunisia—have been perceived, therefore, as conduits to carry to God the deepest hopes and fears of the community.

The most important *hillula* has been the *hillula* of Rabbi Shimon bar Yochai, a second-century teacher and legendary author of the core book of Jewish mysticism, the Zohar or "Book of Radiance," which has been widely studied and has had great influence on Judaism in the Maghreb and elsewhere. It is not surprising that when Jews of this region migrated to the United States they brought with them Rabbi bar Yochai's great *hillula*. But this ancient custom has had to find a new form to suit the needs of a different community.

The community that hosts this new *hillula* is the Magen David Sephardi (from the Hebrew, "Sepharad," or Spain) Congregation of Washington, D.C., an association of individuals from widely diverse backgrounds who are slowly but surely overcoming their differences to achieve a more certain sense of community. My own presence at *hillula* has been part of my research into the meaning and structure of "community" in today's highly mobile society. I have also sought to understand the process of becoming an American. How do people integrate their past, present, and future lives?

Large urban areas such as Washington, D.C., have long been the destination of individuals seeking an improvement of their economic or political conditions. The cultural background these migrants have carried with them has provided a sense of home, and the ethnic neighborhoods in which so many have settled have offered social and economic support to cushion the transition to a new life. More recent years have seen the emergence of a new kind of transient, one whose cultural baggage is less obviously displayed. Whether moving from some other part of the country or some other part of the world, these individuals constitute an increasing proportion of many modern cities. The result is a very heterogeneous population of migrants who may, nevertheless, continue to identify themselves by a traditional and seemingly uniform ethnic label. However, this identification, which implies an enduring body of values, relationships, and attitudes, is often denied the social support offered to earlier migrants by the institutions and informal personal relationships found in the ethnic neighborhood.

The Washington, D.C., region is a logical place in which to examine the social patterns of white-collar ethnics because the city clearly demonstrates the increasing dependence of the American economy on technical, professional, and institutional services. It exemplifies a society that gives priority—or at least equal value—to professional achievement and social class in determining residence, friendships, and other associations; a society that imposes conformity in dress and lifestyle. Once the economic barriers to residence are removed (and housing laws written prohibiting discrimination), people are free to make their decisions about housing according to criteria that often outweigh ethnic factors, such as commuting distance and the quality of the public schools. Just as they expect to drive to work, to shopping, and to recreational activities, the new migrants expect to drive to ethnic and religious events. No longer are traditional values and cultural attitudes subtly and continually reinforced through casual interactions; no longer does the environment coerce the individual into conformity, either in personal mores or in public behavior.

Under these conditions, ethnic identity becomes elective, a matter of individual psychology, and it must now compete with other attractive and optional identities for time and commitment. One may be a Sephardi, but she may also be an American, a concert-goer, a lawyer, a civil rights activist, a tennis player, a parent, a Democrat, or a member of numerous other organizations. With physical and social distances between residences and ethnic center, the meaning of community becomes uncertain. How is this less immediate and more ephemeral sense of association created and maintained?

The Sephardic Jews of the Washington, D.C., area have been a natural population in which to pose these more general questions. Not only is the population quite diverse in terms of educational, economic, professional, and personal history, but the very term that appears to define and delimit the group is itself a word of many meanings—a polysemic, multivocal symbol that has its greatest social utility when it is not examined too closely.

[164]

A Brief History of the Sephardic Jews in Washington

The 1984 demographic study of the Federation of Greater Washington found that 157,000 Jews reside in the Washington metropolitan area. Of these, 55 percent or 87,000 live in Montgomery County, Maryland, 22 percent or 33,500 are in Northern Virginia, and 15 percent, 24,300 people, live in the District of Columbia. Perhaps a few thousand of these identify themselves as of Sephardic heritage; possibly a thousand are from North Africa. These numbers of the Sephardic population are my own "best guesstimates," based on discussions with several individuals concerned with organizing the community and on my own experience in frequently meeting people who have identified themselves to me as Sephardic Jews after learning of my interest, but who have no contact with the more organized community. Community leaders are much more conservative in their estimates, suggesting that there are only "six hundred" Sephardim in the area—approximately the number on their membership lists. They freely acknowledge that there are probably many other "undiscovered" Sephardim in the region.

The disparity between these estimates reflects the fact that it is extremely difficult, if not impossible, to arrive at an accurate count of American Sephardim in Washington or anywhere else in the nation.[1] In addition to the problems common to any urban demographic study, there is the recurrent problem of definition—whom to count.

For the purist, "Sephardic" indicates only those who can demonstrate a family history linked to Spain. Jews lived in Spain from approximately the third century B.C.E. until the expulsion in 1492, after the unification of Spain under Ferdinand and Isabella and the concurrent ascendency of the church. The vast majority of the Spanish Jews fled eastward to the lands of the Ottoman Empire, where they were welcomed for their professional and commercial skills. Others traveled different paths—to northern Europe and then to the Americas, to North Africa, and to even more distant lands. In some places, the Sephardim maintained separate, endogamous communities well into the twentieth century; in other places, they intermarried with the resident Jewish populations.

Estimates of numbers of Sephardim today often include anyone not of Ashkenazic ("German," but functionally Central or East European) Jewish heritage, whether or not the person claims ancestral ties to

[165]

Spain. This raises the question of whether Jews who trace their ancestry solely to North Africa, the Middle East, or India may be considered a subset of "Sephardim" or another category altogether—Oriental Jews. The question is further complicated by the fact that throughout the centuries, Jews often migrated across the Straits of Gibralter in response to periods of peace or peril in North Africa or Spain. This question of definition is a scholarly, demographic, and political issue today, as Jewish populations mix in Israel, Europe, and the Americas.

Ashkenazim often refer to all non-Ashkenazic populations by one term, either as Sephardim, as Oriental Jews, as Jews from Moslem lands, or as Afro-Asian Jews. These labels ignore the substantial (until the Holocaust) Sephardic populations of Europe and the Americas, and blur distinctions many Sephardim consider crucial. Estimates of Sephardic populations may include persons who were "born Sephardic" but who are "culturally Ashkenazic," that is, who have no association with Sephardic society, who are not familiar with Sephardic history, religious, or social forms, and who belong to Ashkenazic institutions and participate in Ashkenazic rituals. And then, of course, there are the children of Sephardic-Ashkenazic "intermarriages." It may be politically advantageous to spread the demographic net as widely as possible, but doing so raises the question of whether Sephardic—or Ashkenazic—definition is a matter of culture or of "blood." Many Washington Sephardim reject the idea that one can acquire Sephardic status; to them, "Sephardic" is an indelible identity, transmitted, like being a "Jew," through the mother. And yet some of the most prominent Sephardim in Washington do not meet this criterion.

Those who can comfortably trace their family history to Spain carefully guard the parameters of this definition. They look back to Spain with honor and pride, for it was in Spain that Jews achieved an unprecedented level of sophistication, learning, and social influence. The greatest period of cultural florescence came during the tenth to twelfth centuries, the "golden age of Spanish Jewry," when poets, philosophers, physicians, and financiers interacted intellectually and socially with their Arab counterparts. There were also many dark periods in Spanish Jewish history, especially the final century of persecution and plunder before Jews were banned from Spanish soil. In many ways, however, Sephardic history is mythic history, with periods of pain blurred and periods of beauty recalled in the ballads sung in exile and especially in the language of the Jews of Spain, Judeo-

Spanish, or, more commonly, Ladino. Through the centuries, the sounds of Spain suggested nobility and lost glory to communities now dispersed throughout the Mediterranean and sometimes even further from this second Jewish ancestral home. The social, ritual, and commercial use of this blend of medieval Spanish and Hebrew helped these new communities maintain their social cohesion and unified them across the distances; it also preserved them into the twentieth century as proud heirs to a great tradition.

Used secularly as the language of the home and of commerce, and in synagogue and home ritual as a second sacred language, Judeo-Spanish linked scattered communities not only with each other but also with God. To generations of Sephardim in the Balkans and across the rim of North Africa, "Spanish" became the mark of the Jew: there are many anecdotes about relatives being amazed to discover in the twentieth century that there are people other than Jews who speak "the Jewish language." As may be expected, the spoken form of the language, which was not restrained by the letters of the Hebrew alphabet, was influenced more extensively by the host culture than was the written form. Reflecting the diverse contexts in which Judeo-Spanish flourished, it has many other names: Judezmo, Espaniolít, Sefaradí, Spañiol, Romance, Jidyó, and Haketía.

Sephardic Jews first came to the District of Columbia in 1914 from the crumbling Ottoman Empire.[2] The burial society that they organized soon after their arrival, the Yom Tov or "Good Day" Society, continues to serve this purpose. The Yom Tov Society also met for religious services in Ladino under the leadership of Solomon Ereza, who served as the fledgling community's rabbi until his death in 1977. More than a man died in 1977: Solomon Ereza's leadership and the melodies of the Ladino liturgy provided the spiritual and emotional center—and a touchstone to a life left behind—for the Balkan migrants to the area. I often sit at *hillula* with a couple from Istanbul. A successful businessman with two American-born grandchildren, the husband yet laments that since Solomon Ereza's death, he cannot feel at home at any religious service in Washington.

Rabbi Ereza was so important to Balkan Sephardim because the composition of the Washington community has changed through the years. First, the community welcomed Syrian Jewish businessmen from New York and later other Jewish businessmen from Morocco. Since the World War II and the founding of the State of Israel, there has been a slow but steady immigration of Sephardim from the Balkans, but most of all, they have come from North Africa and the Middle East. At the same time, the children of the original settlers to the area have been absorbed into the dominant American Ashkenazic Jewish culture through education and intermarriage.

In 1972 the religious functions of the Yom Tov Society were replaced by the newly constituted Magen David Sephardi Congregation under the leadership of Albert Emsellem from Fez, who had come to America in 1928 and to Washington in 1941. At that time, the only other Moroccan Jewish family in Washington was that of Maurice Cadeaux, who had been in the United States since 1924. Cadeaux estimates that there were then some fifty Moroccan Jewish families in America (Schulter 1977:290). By the time the Magen David Congregation was established, the majority of its members were first-generation North African immigrants, mainly from Morocco.

Until 1986 the congregation did not have its own building, rabbi, or other permanent staff. It met and held *hillula* at a Conservative Ashkenazic synagogue, Ohr Kodesh in Chevy Chase, Maryland, and it moved to more spacious quarters at Ohev Shalom Congregation in the District for the High Holidays. At the Sabbath minyan, approximately forty people are usually present; more than four hundred attend services for the High Holidays. The congregation sponsors a variety of religious and social events, such as fairs, balls, and holiday celebrations. The new building and the recently hired rabbi now permit the realization of another dream: a school.

Magen David envisions itself as a center for all area Sephardim and therefore is comfortable with the most encompassing definition of "Sephardi." This broad definition is also dictated by practical considerations: it opens the door to a much larger potential membership than a more purist understanding would allow. Nevertheless, the imprecision of the term is challenged by some members from the Balkans or of Balkan Jewish descent who insist that a Sephardi is simply one who can trace his or her lineage to Spain and can verify that link through the use of Judeo-Spanish. Some of Washington's Moroccan Jews do speak Judeo-Spanish, but many more do not; this lack is seen by some Balkan Sephardim as confirmation of the belief that all Jews from Morocco are not true Sephardim but are instead "Arabs," linguisitically, genealogically, and culturally. The North African Jews flatly deny the label. I remember a heated exchange between an American-born Sephardi who spoke Judeo-Spanish as a child, but only in the home, and a sophisticated and articulate woman whose familiarity with the language came from a childhood spent in an almost exclusively Spanish Sephardic neighborhood in Rabat. When challenged that a Jew from Morocco could not possibly be a Sephardi, she yelled, "My ancestors left Spain on July 31, 1492!" The first woman merely shrugged her shoulders and remained doubtful that such an oddity—a bona fide North African Sephardi—could exist. I brought another doubter, a highly educated American foreign service officer born in Bulgaria, to meet this "prize exhibit." They talked for a while in their common ancient language, remarking on the dialectical differences. At the end of the evening, he at least was convinced.

A similar expression of discomfort with the definition's lack of precision was expressed at the congregation's fair and flea market held one May on the lawn of Rabbi Ereza's daughter's home. At the last minute the name was changed from a "Sephardic" to a "Moroccan" fair, because the former term was thought to be unfamiliar to potential customers. This logical marketing device annoyed a very active member from the Balkans, who said quietly to me, "If it's a 'Moroccan' fair, I don't know why I'm working here." At the same fair a customer told me that she knew immediately by my dark hair that I am a Sephardi.

Bypassing the historical argument by interpreting "Sephardic" to mean a complex of ritual forms or cultural practices raises as many problems as it solves. By now, the congregation includes representatives from a wide range of Sephardic cultures from all parts of the Mediterranean, Middle East, North Africa, and Europe. This kalaidoscope of cultures assumes an added dimension as the children, who still call themselves Sephardi, become culturally more and more indistinguishable from their American Ashkenazic friends. As may be expected, local variations of the traditional Sephardic liturgy—each carrying the authenticity of time and custom—have developed in these many scattered Sephardic homes and communities. The contemporary Sephardic congregation must find a way to synthesize these divergent experiences in a way that disquiets no one. Although intellectual disagreements about definitions may surface now and then, they do not strike as strong a note of discord or touch as deeply as an unfamiliar chant during religious services or the absence of a cherished family custom. "I die to hear music from Egypt," lamented one of Magen David's members.

The Washington area attracts a select population among all ethnic groups, both Jews and non-Jews. With few manufacturing or other blue-collar industries, the region primarily attracts "cosmopolitan migrants (Tilly 1970:156)," highly educated or technically trained workers pursuing jobs in government, in various international agencies, or in other white-collar positions that service these institutions. Such migrants define themselves first by their professional statuses and their links to corporate employment networks; their relations to their present locale are contingent, and their ethnic identities are generally subordinated to economic and professional aims and identities. Jews of Mediterranean descent are represented in all white-collar areas— in the State Department, the International Monetary Fund, the World Bank, and as doctors, lawyers, nuclear engineers, and in other high-status professions.

A second avenue of migration into the region has been through personal networks in which a friend or relative assists with housing or a job until the newcomer settles in. Those using this path are more likely to be either experienced business people or young people, largely unskilled and just starting their careers. As the result of such networks, Jews from Morocco with French (so-called elite) names now operate beauty shops in fashionable neighborhoods throughout the area, and Jews from other Mediterranean countries own a variety of small businesses.

A new arrival in the region, who often must make a quick decision about housing, is not immediately aware that a Sephardic community exists in Washington. The cosmopolitan migrant typically chooses his home according to its proximity to work; the traditional migrant by proximity to friends or family—assuming, of course, that he or she can afford to live in that particular neighborhood. A further difficulty in choosing a home is the fact that Washington's neighborhoods are defined by class rather than by ethnic group; members of white and Asian ethnic groups are scattered throughout the region, living among their economic, professional, and social equals.[3] Once settled, individuals drive long distances to work and to leisure, professional, and cultural activities, and even, perhaps, to maintain that other dimension of their identity, their ethnic heritage. Perhaps, for they find that instead of a natural, casual association of neighbors sharing a common heritage, ethnic identity has now become a private matter, a matter of will and a series of conscious, elective decisions to locate others of similar heritage and travel long distances to meet with them.

For the Sephardim, the problem of locating others is especially acute. The lack of a permanent building for the congregation has had serious consequences until recently: new arrivals have had no visible center about which to congregate and no immediate way to find information about ethnic associates or activities. Consequently they have frequently chosen homes a great distance from Magen David's meeting place. Even if the pull of primal identity is strong, the problem of distance and conflicts with other activities have forced them to join synagogues closer to home. Others put the ethnic component of their selves in the nostalgic past, savoring it on special occasions in the home. America represents the future. A folksinger from Yugoslavia, who proudly sings the Ladino songs of her youth, argues nevertheless:

"I don't know if it's better [to go to the Moroccan-oriented Magen David than to an Ashkenazic synagogue] because it's just as foreign. . . . You have no choice. What can you expect when we're a minority in a minority . . . ? I think the answer to it is to do what I did, just [assimilate], be one of them, do what they do, because Jewish is Jewish. It's not home, but that's gone. You can remember it, you can sing it, you can talk about it, but it's finished. . . . I made trips back to see it for myself; I did not want to believe it [but] it's true. It's finished.

"We have to be realistic and come to this country. There is so much richness, so much Judaism. It's a pleasure no matter what it is— Ashkenazic or South African or North African—whatever it is, it's Jewish."

The new arrival's dilemma is compounded by the mixed welcome Washington offers. The area's international focus, its high concentration of people born outside of Washington and outside of the United States, its many cultural events, ethnic restaurants, groceries, and folk festivals make it rather easy for recent migrants to adjust. A woman from Turkey, who made several stops on her way to Washington, summed up the feelings expressed frequently by others during the course of my fieldwork: "It's rare to find a native Washingtonian . . . so [it's easier] to be included. As opposed to France, a lot of strangers settle here. . . . You are like one of them . . . you don't see the difference."

But this freedom to be a stranger, so appealing to this woman, is for others just the silver lining of a threatening cloud. The Mediterranean-born Jews I met commonly described Americans and American Jews as "cold" and see themselves as "warm," "hospitable," and "cosmopolitan." They miss the proximate communities of their youth, where hospitality and neighborliness were experienced informally each day. They chafe at the formality America brings to social life—

[171]

the prearranged visits, the long car trips, "touching someone" by telephone. They are disturbed by the absence of an easily identifiable Jewish neighborhood with its institutions and nearby groceries, restaurants, and other communal services.

Unlike Montreal, New York, Atlanta, Seattle, and Los Angeles, Washington has never been the destination of large numbers of Jews from any one "Sephardic" region. In other cities, the migrations were large enough to establish community services and public institutions in the first few years. Within the buildings congregants could share the changes in ritual, social practice, and social identity generated by the American experience. Congregation Or VeShalom in Atlanta is certainly not the same institution today as the one that was founded fifty years ago by a relatively homogeneous Sephardic population from Rhodes. Even so, its building, school, and social clubs kept the change within the family and the children within the congregation. The grandchildren of Or VeShalom look and act like other Americans, but some still belong to the congregation and they call themselves "Sephardi." In Montreal the more recent, large Moroccan-born population is providing a similar crucible for containing the changes that life in Canada will demand. In Washington, however, the numbers have always been too small and the Sephardim too heterogeneous in background and adaptation to American life to permit them to have their own synagogue, let alone a separate neighborhood.

The congregation's problems are compounded by the fact that today's new migrant is likely to be favored financially or educationally. These are not people who are glued either to the past or to the present; they can readily change their fates and also question their ethnic loyalties. Many in Washington left their first homes in Turkey, Bulgaria, Yugoslavia, Lebanon, Greece, Egypt, Libya, Tunisia, Morocco, Iran, or Israel for France, Israel, South America, or another part of the United States. They came to Washington, therefore, after many moves, many decisions, and they will if necessary move again. A businessman from Egypt who considers Washington his home "definitely," also reminded me that "Jews are nomads."

Still, if these Jews are nomads, they are nomads who carry within their hearts and minds a profound loyalty to the homes of their childhoods and to the religion that nurtured them. This sense of a treasured past was expressed by a restauranteur from Casablanca who had come to Washington after stays in Marseilles and Israel. Sitting in the corner of his French café one afternoon, this seemingly content man, who said he loves life in America, told me softly: "I go to [the Congregation] because I was born in Morocco. I will never change, even if I am seventy-five years old. . . . I will like always the rite of the shul [a Yiddish word for school, or synagogue]. I speak Hebrew; I know when I make a prayer I understand maybe ninety-five percent of it . . . the sound of our things, I love it. When I go to Ashkenaz, I'm lost. To me they swallow words."

But the Moroccan tone of Magen David's liturgy and the rituals that cradle this man are alien to Jews from other parts of the Mediterranean. Some Sephardim abandon the effort to recreate Sephardic experience in America and become part of the equally alien but dominant Ashkenazic Judaism of America. For others, however, the Mediterranean and Middle Eastern "feel," "touch," "sense" of Magen David is comforting despite the "Moroccans'" sometimes unfamiliar ways. Still, they are left in the quandary expressed by a woman from Cairo, a loyal member of the congregation: "The sound of the prayer is different. When I go to the synagogue, when an Egyptian sings, I don't understand [the Hebrew], yet I have tears in my eyes. It reminds me . . . of Egypt."

Yet she will rarely hear such melodies in Washington. Sometimes she comes to *hillula,* for the congregation's members are now her friends, but the ritual is as new to her as it is to me. We come, and find new meaning and new fellowship—precisely as *hillula* is losing its meaning for many who actually experienced it in Morocco.

It is too soon to know just which changes a permanent location will bring to the form and composition of the community. The congregation is now easier to locate, and it is therefore in a better position to grow. However, the practical problems of maintaining and staffing the new institution may make explicit the divisions inherent in the community's diffuse definition, problems that were put aside while long-term decisions did not have to be made. For instance, the large financial commitment necessitated by the new building was achieved through donations that came from as far away as Istanbul. At the first service in the new building, I sat among the Turkish-born Sephardim who solicited this distant money, and was informed, with great delight, that the rabbi who was "auditioning" that day was chanting in familiar, comfortable Balkan tones. These intonations were far less exciting to the predominately Moroccan-born congregants.

Hillula

For Jews from the Maghreb, a *hillula* is not so much a religious ritual as a confirmation of a way of life. They remember the cemeteries outside cities such as Marrakesh where people came at the close of Sabbath to seek help during a personal crisis. When a visit to the cemetery was not possible, supplicants would invoke the name of the holy man, for the name and the presence were understood as one. Still today, in a high-rise apartment building a few miles north of the White House, a woman from Tunis lights a candle three times a week for the great kabbalist Rabbi Meir Baal HaNess. If, as it says in the Book of Proverbs, "The soul of man is the light of the Lord" (20:27), then each Monday, Thursday, and Saturday, the light of Rabbi Meir Baal HaNess resanctifies and protects this home in America. None of this woman's nine children in France or in America continues this ancient practice.

I spoke with another firm believer in the power of Rabbi Meir late one Friday afternoon. An Orthodox Jew, she returned my call just before the Sabbath began, when telephone use would be banned in her home. Speaking quickly, she told me that "it is unthinkable" to visit Israel without visiting the tombs of Rabbi Meir, Moses Maimonides, and other revered men: "It is our way." She described such a visit with her American-born daughter. Instructed to tell her wish to the great man, the child hesitated, then asked, "Does Rabbi Meir understand English?" Another woman remarked that her family in France still returns to Tunisia for the pilgrimages. Their point of departure in Tunisia is no longer their homes but the Club Mediterranée.

It may be more accurate to say that the "point of departure" for the pilgrimages is not Club Mediterranée or Marrakesh but a conceptualization of the universe indigenous and somewhat unique to North Africa. Jews from North Africa share what has been called the *marabout* tradition that infuses both Jewish and Moslem practices in the Maghreb. The French word *marabout* (from the Arabic *murabit*) means "bound or tied to God," and indicates an extraordinary relationship between man and the holy, that which is "set apart." The *marabout* is endowed with *baraka*, blessing or divine favor, allowing him to perform wonders. However, *maraboutism* is not merely magical manipulation; more crucially, it is a mode of conceiving the universe that assumes an actual, functional intrusion of the holy into daily

[174]

experience, allowing close communication between mankind and God, or less merciful spirits. In *Islam Observed,* anthropologist Clifford Geertz describes *maraboutism:*

> More exactly, it is a mode of construing—emotionally, morally, intellectually—human experience, a cultural gloss on life. And though this is a vast and intricate problem, what this construction, this gloss, comes down to, so at least it seems to me, is the proposition [again, of course, wholly tacit] that the sacred appears most directly in the world as an endowment—a talent and a capacity, a special ability—of particular individuals. Rather than electricity, the best (but still not very good) analogue for "baraka" is personal presence, force of character, moral vividness. Marabouts have baraka in the way that men have strength, courage, dignity, skills, beauty, or intelligence. Like these, though it is not the same as these, nor even all of them put together, it is a gift which some men have in greater degree than others, and which a few, marabouts have in superlative degree. (1968:44)

The presence of the otherworldly among the mundane is an ever-present aspect of life in the Maghreb. *Kubbas,* tombs of holy men, dot the countryside and cities. In *Tuhami,* the anthropologist Vincent Crapazano describes the vast population of saints and *jnun* (loosely, "demons") that constitute reality for the Moroccan tribesman. And the Algerian-born Jewish historian André Chouraqui said of life in North Africa, "Everything was holy. We lived intimately with God."[4]

Among Berber populations, the concept of spiritual endowment is institutionalized in tribal structure, producing hereditary lineages of individuals capable of working wonders (Gellner 1969). Among the Jews, the extraordinary did not derive from family endowment but from the holy man's ability to personify a state of perfection beyond the reach of the ordinary man.

To have reached a higher degree of perfection is not to become divine. One does not become a god but rather a clear channel between heaven and earth. This makes the word "saint," with its Christian connotations, a bit awkward when applied to North Africa and particularly to the relation of the Jews to their pious men. Placing this gloss from Europe on North African experience can produce an account such as this, from the 1906 travels of Nahum Slouschz through North Africa: "But of prime importance is the cult of the dead. The whole Mellah and the Jewish cemeteries are filled with saints, real or imaginary, who bring salvation to those who worship them and dam-

[175]

nation to those who neglect their cult. The living crowd the cemeteries and the grottoes" (1944:438).

The Christian connotations of the word "saint" must also be filtered
out of Chouraqui's account of the mutual experience of *maraboutism*
among the populations of North Africa:

> Judaism in general repudiated the veneration of saints and sacred im-
> ages as contrary to the Second Commandment, but nevertheless it was
> an integral, and vastly important element of Judaism in North Africa. It
> was obviously inspired by Moslem examples—among the Arabic-
> Berber population of North Africa the veneration of the *marabout*
> (monk or hermit) held a most important place in the faith. There were
> few villages and sites in the Maghreb that did not have the charac-
> teristic *kubba* of some local saintling to which the piety of the crowds
> was directed. The Jews adopted this Moslem custom. Moslem influ-
> ence on their devotion was so strong that frequently there were no
> sharp lines between the saints venerated by the Moslems and those
> venerated by the Jews. . . . A study of venerated tombs made by L.
> Voinot in 1948 in Morocco revealed the existence of thirty-one saints
> who were claimed at the same time by both Jews and Moslems, four-
> teen Moslem saints revered by the Jews and fifty (Jewish) saints revered
> by the Moslems. (1973:72)

Although the tombs may be visited at any time, the most important
pilgrimage takes place on the anniversary of Rabbi Shimon bar
Yochai's death, the eighteenth day of the Hebrew month of Iyar,
which usually falls in May. This date, also known as Lag B'Omer,
corresponds to the thirty-third day between the festivals of Passover
and Shavuot.

The days between the great festivals have traditionally been observed as a semi-mourning period. It may be that the solemnity of
these days reflects the concern in ancient times with the success of the
spring harvest. A more popular explanation comes from the Talmud.
According to legend, in the second century thousands of Rabbi Akiva's
students died of plague during the days following Passover. The
plague ceased miraculously on the thirty-third day; in memory of this
great event, the restrictions against shaving, music, and dancing are
temporarily lifted, and the penitential *tahanun* prayer is not recited.
Lag B'Omer has become a day of rejoicing and of weddings.

In Israel and in other Jewish communities around the world, Lag
B'Omer is celebrated as a scholar's holiday with bonfires, picnics, and
weddings. Kabbalists throughout the world rejoice on the anniversary

of their master's death. Since the sixteenth century, Ashkenazic adherents of Jewish mysticism have come to the grave of Rabbi bar Yochai at Meron, in the Galilee, to celebrate the holiday with music, feasting, and bonfires. At the opposite end of the Mediterranean, their North African counterparts honor the teachers in the cemeteries of the Maghreb.

There is some dispute about the actual authorship of the Zohar. Most scholars agree with Gershom Scholem that this core book of the Kabbalah was composed or compiled by Moses de Leon in thirteenth-century Spain. Nevertheless, the book takes the form of dialogues between Rabbi bar Yochai, the "Holy Lamp," and his pupils in second-century Palestine, and it is this sage, not de Leon, whom the North Africans thank for the Zohar. Whether they are actual or elaborated folk legend, the insights attributed to Rabbi bar Yochai have come to articulate a mode of religious experience that includes a wide range of possible avenues of relationship with the Holy. God may be reached through rational comprehension of the many shades of meaning in His Torah or He may be reached, just as validly, through more sensual, emotional paths. The two paths meet in the pilgrimages, for although the holy man is approached through faith, light, and music, he has earned his power to reach to God by his great learning, mystical insight, and exemplary life.

The talmudic legends of Rabbi bar Yochai illustrate this ideal confluence of cognitive and sensual approaches to the Divine. One story tells how Rabbi bar Yochai hid in a cave with his son Eleazar for thirteen years, forbidden by the Romans to study or teach the Torah. A spring of water and a carob tree appeared miraculously to sustain their bodies, and the radiance of the Torah—the essential meanings underlying the actual words—entered the darkness of the cave to nourish their souls (Shabbat II). The Talmud also connects Rabbi bar Yochai with the rainbow, the sign of the covenant between God and man in Genesis (9:12–17). The rainbow was a reassurance by God that He would never again send a flood to destroy the earth, no matter how sinful the people might be. But a truly saintly man was an equal guarantee: it was said that because of Rabbi bar Yochai's extreme righteousness, the rainbow did not appear in his lifetime (Yev Ber 9:2). Thus Rabbi bar Yochai is identified with the mystical image of refracted light as a medium for apprehending God.

In North Africa, this sensuous, aesthetic, immediate pathway to God was given full rein, complementing the more "intellectual" study of the Torah. The Zohar was placed beside the Torah in many syn-agogues, Zohar-reading societies read the special book twenty-four hours each day,[5] and God's "Radiance" was placed in the room of a sick person or one in childbirth.

The *hillula* of "The Great Illuminary" is still celebrated with com-munity-wide assembly. With great nostalgia, a Maryland woman born in Fez recalled the pilgrimages of her childhood:

"It was unusual to go to the cemetery at night. . . . We went with lanterns; it made the whole thing, it gave a character to the whole evening. . . . The lanterns lit the way to the tombs of the holy men and to those of family members. . . . Rabbis sat at tables that were set up at the gates of the cemetery, with bowls for donations for charity, and sellers of oil lamps and the poor lined the walls. As you go, with your lantern, you dropped coins in the bowls, gave a coin or two to each of the needy—a little bit to each person. In the cemetery, there were crowds, lights, darkness, dancing, singing. There is always a big crowd around the tombs, and fires around the tombs. Everyone who comes lights a candle at the tombs. It is a feeling of sadness, mixed with joy. You catch a completely different atmosphere. Everyone is there. . . . I have been told that at Ouzane there is a bush, a burning bush, with fire all the time. . . . People still come and put their candles by the bush."

Hillula in Washington

"We were secure in our beautiful tradition," remarked my Judeo-Spanish-speaking friend from Rabat. "Being a Jew was everything. . . . It was a country . . . it was a cocoon. . . . Here in America, it's differ-ent. The Jew is not so religious, so mystic."

The *hillula* of Rabbi Shimon bar Yochai starts shortly after dusk. Candles in silver holders line the long table in the front of the syn-agogue's large community room and behind them are rows of small candles in glass, the common memorial candles that Jews burn for twenty-four hours on the anniversary of a close relative's death. Scotchtaped to each candle or to the glass is a small piece of white paper with the name of a great rabbi or other great Jewish leader. There are two or three candles bearing the names of Rabbi bar Yochai, his teacher Rabbi Akiva, and Rabbi Meir Baal HaNess. Because he is believed to be a "miracle worker," the light of Rabbi Meir is often sought in behalf of a relative or friend who is gravely ill. The list is long and for some present, personal: the prophet Elijah—Eliyahu, King David—David HaMelekh, Moses Maimonides, Yehuda NaNasi, Yosef Caro, Yohannan ben Zakkai, Yosef HaTzaddik, Abu Hatzeira, Pinchas ben Yair, Itzhak Alfassi, Maklouf Emsellem. The son of Maklouf Emsellem waits to buy his father's candle; another man claims descent from the great Maimonides; others still carry the same tribal affiliation as King David. Many of the names are new to me, rabbis from small towns across the Maghreb, but they evoke love and loyalty in many persons who will wait patiently to purchase the candle of their favorite sage.

Slowly people assemble, greeting each other with kisses on both cheeks, inquiring in French about each other's health and family. There are a few children among the approximately 150 people present most years; except for a loyal core of some forty people, the composition of the *hillula* community fluctuates from year to year. During the years that I have been attending the *hillula*, the group has included persons born in Turkey, Lebanon, Syria, Israel, Egypt, Libya, Tunisia, Iran, Iraq, England, Argentina, America, and, of course, Morocco—Casablanca, Fez, Mogador, Meknes, Rabat, and Marrakesh. We sit at round tables. Along one wall of the room is an informal bar where we may help ourselves to soft drinks, juice, or whiskey. In fact, not much alcohol is drunk this evening.

The evening begins with the Arvit or Maariv (evening) service by the men. In the absence of a rabbi, an elder of the congregation from Casablanca often leads the service and presides with the other congregational leaders over the evening's activities. One year a Moroccan-born rabbi came from New York to participate in this displaced *hillula*. Several American-born children move restlessly about the room as the rabbi reminds the group of the importance of the celebration:

"We all traditionally kiss our hearts when we mention the name of Shimon bar Yochai.

"Apparently, as he was writing the Zohar, at the last moment of giving his soul to the Almighty, he said to his disciples, 'I proclaim that the day of my death be a day of celebration throughout all generations.' As soon as he died, his teachings and the light of the Zohar spread to all generations through his disciples.

"Now the Zohar is studied more and more. One of the signs that the *moshiakh* is coming is the increased intensity of the study of the

Kabbalah, which was based on the teachings of Rabbi Shimon bar Yochai. "For twelve years he studied in a cave, sustained by the fruit of a carob tree. As soon as he heard of passing the decree (that the Romans would not persecute him), he appeared to the world as totally spiritual, and he exclaimed, 'How come people are occupied with worldly occupations, not with Torah?' A legend in the Talmud says people whom he looked at died. He was not ready for this world, so he went to the cave for twelve more months. Now, when he came out, he was ready for this world. He saw an old man preparing for Shabbat, and realized that even in a simple Jew there could be greatness.

"Since then, humbled and ready for this world, his teachings spread. The world knows and loves him for his Zohar, and we go to the Zohar, and we see him and are protected by faith and the light of the Zohar. May the memory of Rabbi Shimon bar Yochai illuminate your hearts and your houses."

Each year a member of the congregation serves as an auctioneer, shouting the word *"misheberakh"* ("He who blesses") after each transaction. Although used in the sense of "sold!" at an auction, *misheberakh* is actually the traditional call to God asking His blessing for one who is to be honored or who is ill.

In English or French, the auctioneer seeks the highest price for each candle. Some wait for the candle of the man in whose power they have most faith; others wait until the bids—which may reach five or six hundred dollars—become lower. Each purchase, each kindling, is accompanied by the rabbi's chant in sacred Hebrew asking the Almighty to bless the person in whose honor the candle is being purchased. Each mitzvah, each good deed, also provokes an outpouring of song, traditional *piyytim*, or melodies suitable to the name on the candle: "Eliyahu HaNavi," "David Melekh Yisrael," or even merely "La, la, la." Above all, it is the strains of "bar Yochai . . . Ashrekha" which fill the room, when the several candles bearing his name are purchased and at other times. Sometimes the women ululate, adding their own, unique music—the shrill, piercing sound made by North African women at times of great emotion.

Throughout the evening, the concept of the reciprocal relationships of the individual and community and of the community and God are recognized both implicitly and openly. The first candles, those with the names of the most revered men, are sold quickly for high sums, but as the evening progresses the bidding slows and candles are sold for much less. Figures frequently called out are 26, 52, 101, and multiples of other numbers that are equated in mystical thought to the names of God, the prophet Eliyahu, or which have other kabbalistic associations.

The rabbi and lay leaders exhort the congregation to continue to buy, to honor the great rabbis and to support the congregation. Where the rabbi stresses the power of the rabbis—"The day of Shimon bar Yochai's death is a day of happiness and faith," and "He who buys a candle of Rabbi Akiva brings the light of the Torah into his home," the lay leader may stress the reciprocal relationship between the divine realm and the individual: "Whatever you give tonight will be doubled [by God]." "The more you give, the more He will give you," and "If you give charity, you never know how it will be repaid." When in 1980 the president of the congregation cited his own example, that God had repaid his charity the previous year with a beautiful new baby, he was answered with slightly nervous laughter from the more middle-aged group. Three years later, this little boy carried the candle of Rabbi Shimon bar Yochai to the table where his grandparents, parents, and brothers sat clapping and singing.

The purchase of candles at *hillula* is similar to Magen David's sale of synagogue honors on the High Holidays, a practice that is also common in traditional Ashkenazic congregations. This auction of public ritual acts may be seen as an example of a core value of Jewish religion, *tzedakah*, a word whose various English translations suggest the complex interactions characteristic of *hillula*.

Tzedakah is concurrently "righteousness," "good deeds," and "social justice"—"charity" that is a social obligation as well as the verification of the moral individual. *Tzedakah* implies that monies or favors given are rightfully due the recipient as a member of the society. *Tzedakah* also suggests the leveling of differences between individuals, a concept that is especially important in a society that otherwise recognizes and permits distinctions in abilities, class, and learning.

The apparently materialistic act of bidding for candles or honors is, in fact, an act that expresses the highest religious values. The honor of carrying the Torah is one for which a man or woman will pay more dearly than for a coat or a piece of furniture. The child who receives an honor because his father bids for it and is brought to the Ark or to light a candle apprehends this ephemeral action as one of lasting and extreme value. There are, of course, inequities in the system, and many Jews consider it nondemocratic and also disruptive of the flow and mood of the religious service. However, in a world of traders, money is an obvious and suitable medium for relating individual and community. The rabbi explained: "When you sell a mitzvah, people appreciate it more. [The sale is] for the purpose of endearing: it increases the value of the mitzvah." When the wealthier individual purchases a candle or an honor for a large sum of money, inequality is obvious, but when that sum of money is used to ensure the continuation of the synagogue for all, that same sum is *tzedakah*.

The rabbi's words suggest a more profound understanding of *hillula:* it is an experience of collective mitzvah, of collective and potential good deeds waiting to be realized through an endearing act. The unlit candles are mitzvot waiting to be brought to life and their energy released into the community. The purchaser is not a possessor but an enabler, one who acts in accordance with the mystical understanding that man is to rescue the sparks of God's light that have fallen into the darkness of the world. In the context of the religious community, the purchaser's prosaic act of lighting a candle assumes a sacred dimension and he or she becomes, for a moment, a medium or channel between heaven and earth, just like the holy man who is honored. The excited call *"misheberakh!"* recognizes that because of this good deed, God's blessing may now enter the room.

Purchase of the candles may also serve to convey respect, love, and honor among friends and family. One woman clasped her hands to her chest and remembered how "thrilled" she and her husband were when a friend repaid a kindness by purchasing a candle for them, for a great sum. One year the very well-liked Ashkenazic wife of a Sephardi bought three candles, and then was openly delighted when her husband presented her with the candle of Rabbi Akiba. She was also deeply touched when another congregant presented her with the candle of another famous rabbi. She told me she had "caught the spirit" at Meron, the site of the great pilgrimage in Israel. It is also common for children to display their affection for their parents through the purchase of a candle, especially one enhanced by a shining silver candlestick. And, of course, many people hope that the blessing that accompanies a purchase will help heal someone who is ill. Several persons remarked that "it's all a matter of faith," but faith is only one of many possible motivations for buying a candle.

About half-way through the bidding, an informal kosher meal is served by the women: cold chicken, cold cuts, pickles, potato salad, and cole slaw. American food. The first year I was surprised and disappointed at so ordinary a meal; I had expected more "exotic" North African food. But I was also being unrealistic. Now that so many women work outside the home, few women remain home to prepare the complex, time-consuming traditional food, even for their own families. Furthermore, the quantities necessary for the large group at *hillula* would make the meal very costly and reduce the evening's profit. One year a few traditional treats were ordered from a caterer— sambusa (meat-filled pastry triangles), vegetable quiche, meat-filled "cigars." The next year these foods were once again gone from the menu and no one at my table of twelve seemed to notice.

Whatever the food, the meal offers another opportunity for *tzeda-kah:* often the cost of the food is underwritten by a family in memory of a relative. In 1979 a family combined two deeds of *tzedakah* by sponsoring the dinner "to welcome the *sefer* Torah they have donated to the Congregation in memory of their beloved brother." And in 1982 the inextricable dimensions of personal, communal, and sacred *tzedakah* were extended across time and space when the congregation chose not to keep the needed monies at home but to send them to a poor North African neighborhood, Shmuel HaNavi, in Jerusalem.

As the evening progresses, the collective spirit of religious community fills the room. Even where faith in the holy men is lacking, the open bidding carries a public message of community identification. Those from outside the Maghreb who have been to *hillula* before have demonstrated their willingness to be captured by the spirit of the evening by attending in the first place, and they are very aware that their bids are helping Magen David to survive. A middle-aged couple from Argentina came to *hillula* a few years ago. Ever since he left Istanbul as a child, the husband had been part of an Ashkenazic religious group. He came to *hillula* because he felt a great need to be among Sephardim once again. Even the Moroccan tones of the *mi-sheberakh* seemed to satisfy him and he brought two candles to our table.

The table of Iranian Jews who attended the strange ceremony one year remained silent. Iranian Jews are the most recent non-Ashkenazic group to arrive in the Washington area and, like others before them, they are not yet certain whether their Jewish future lies with this Moroccan-focused congregation, with Ashkenazic-oriented synagogues, or as a separate social group. It may be that those who came that evening were not yet prepared to commit themselves to the community; perhaps this explains their silence.

Ruth Fredman Cernea

My own position at *hillula* is, of course, unique. The other American-born Ashkenazi who comes regularly to *hillula* is married to an active member and is herself now an important part of the community. Even though I come alone, as the anthropologist, I feel at home at *hillula* and it seems only natural to buy a candle. I am still a bit shy about calling out my offer, but I enjoy making my affection for the community public through the light of Rabbi Abu Hatzeira or Rabbi Itzhak Alfassi. Community members are delighted to have me participate and always assure me that I have bought the candle of a particularly good man. One year, after my candle was blessed in honor of my children, a woman from Casablanca who had once invited me to her home for *maimouna*, the post-Passover "open house," assured me that now I would have "good fortune, good luck." And then she added, "I think you really are a Sephardi!" The following year she was too ill to attend *hillula*. Instead, *hillula* came to her: her niece brought the candle of the great miracle worker Rabbi Meir Baal HaNess for her aunt to light at home. Together niece and aunt emulated the kabbalists, who, legend tells, "prayed at the grave of Rabbi Shimon bar Yochai . . . and sent up flaming prayers to God" (Ausubel 1948:207).

Emanations

One year, the "auctioneer" was from Lebanon. Before the auction he paused and noted: "Before we start: This is a Moroccan custom but here I see Iranians, Egyptians, Syrians, Turks, Moroccans, Libyans, Americans. *Am Yisrael khay!* [The people of Israel live!]."

The auctioneer's words are more than a passing observation; they indicate the complexity of contemporary American Jewish social experience. With few exceptions, the people he addressed are all now "Americans." Furthermore, despite his linguistic shorthand, only Jews born in Turkey—a secular state—are comfortable referring to themselves as "Turkish"; the others see themselves more exactly as "Jews from Morocco" (or Syria, or Egypt) or "Moroccan Jews," not "Moroccans," "Syrians," or "Egyptians."

America is a unique experience for most: it is the first time, with the possible exception of residence in Israel, that national and Jewish identities do not seem inherently incompatible. Although he spent his youth in Casablanca, one man said, "In Morocco I never considered myself Moroccan." Another "Moroccan" is now in Marrakesh. Twenty years ago she and her husband left North Africa because they saw no future as Jews in an Arab land. Ironically, her husband later became a United States government official in charge of an energy agency in Morocco. For political and for emotional reasons, "home" in Morocco, for this woman as for the man quoted above, was located in the community but not in the state: "We wanted to belong to something . . . such a craving to belong, you have no idea. We had no part, no country. We were subjects of the Sultan; if the Sultan was nice, it was all right."

In the words of the congregation's president, the issue of identity is "very complicated." In Moslem lands, many Jews held European passports: nationality suggested utility, not communal identification. Culturally and socially they were European and Jewish, even as Arabic folkways colored their lives. Now they must integrate "American" into this complex assortment of identities. All this takes time. Although he is deeply grateful for the opportunities America offers, this businessman cannot yet say he is an "American": "I think it's a beautiful country and I appreciate very much this country. But do I consider myself as "American?" No. No means that I consider myself a Moroccan Jew. . . . I have that roots . . . that pride. . . . It's very hard. You see, I left Morocco at an age that I was marked by it. Although I lived in Israel thirteen years, I matured in Israel, somehow I feel more a Moroccan Jew. I have that flavor, that love."

"How do I identify myself?" reflected a neighbor who has been in America since 1956, when the Suez war broke out. "I'm a Jew, that's all, a wandering Jew. . . . I'm an Egyptian Jew. . . . I don't know. . . . I also feel American. It depends on what is required. . . . I'm also Sephardic." And another man, also born in Cairo, described the blending of personalities so common among the first generation in America when he said: "You see my mentality today is not an Egyptian, it is not an American, it is not a European. I took among the three of them and I made what I am today."

One woman called herself "an American and a half! because America gave me shelter, it gave me opportunity to do anything which other countries don't give," but the woman who did not "belong" in Morocco cannot yet say she "belongs" in America: "I have tried to belong, but frankly, this country is in the process of making. America is such a young country . . . so many identity problems. What is going to be my identity with all this turmoil?"

[185]

Hillula refreshes the past for some; for others, it is the means of contact with people who share the more general Sephardic heritage. At a *hillula* table one year a couple from Turkey on my left discussed the number of languages they speak (five: Turkish, Judeo-Spanish, Greek, French, and English) with the people to my right (six: French, English, Armenian, Farsi, Arabic, and Hebrew). And although *hillula* is new to both couples, they are comfortable with the Mediterranean—or at least, non-Ashkenazic--tone of the prayers and with the concept of extreme reverence for an extraordinary man, whether pious or charismatic. Indeed, by the end of *hillula*, the tables with the most candles are occupied by Egyptian, Syrian, Turkish, and American-born Jews. In the spirit of community, the Armenian Christian relatives of one member have also bought candles. Many Washington-area Moroccan Jews do not attend the ritual.

In his discussion of the *hillulot* among Tunisian immigrants to Israel, anthropologist Shlomo Deshen explains why such memorial celebrations retain their popularity among certain groups. The Israeli *hillulot* offer an opportunity for social interaction and "concentrated acts of piety" (1972:112) for persons who are otherwise suffering dislocation from the traditional culture. They provide an opportunity to meet people of common background and to dip into the pool of shared emotion and cultural meaning. This new, occasional social piety is at the same time offensive to others for whom the traditions have deep associations and profound meanings. They, and those who wish to repudiate their Tunisian cultural heritage altogether, do not come to the *hillulot*.

Unlike in Israel, in Washington the number of North African Jews is small and alternate opportunities for communal association are limited. As in Israel, some Moroccan Jews feel that the celebration in Washington is too altered to be meaningful; others do not participate for practical reasons, such as scheduling conflicts. "Scheduling conflicts," if real, testify to the elective nature of ethnic association among the Washington Sephardim. The *hillula* is always held within a few days of Lag B'Omer; if the gathering had priority over other events, many conflicts could be avoided. Although the cost and the public pressure that results from open bidding are also possible deterents, few will discuss such private considerations with me.

Many come to *hillula* with memories of lantern-lit pilgrimages to cemeteries; just as many others have never experienced the North African *hillula*. Yet the American *hillula* is no less authentic than its

North African counterpart: this new ritual is but one example of the way Jews have continually accommodated their religious practices to life's circumstances. In North Africa, the mystical teachings of the Zohar, which extend the concepts of the Torah, were blended with local custom to produce a unique ritual and worldview. Now this complex of meanings is being reshaped once again by life in a new society.

Hillula may be able to be adapted to a new environment and a diverse population because its central symbol, light, seems to suggest powerful, eternal associations cross-culturally. When the Olympic flame is lit, when candles brighten Scandanavian winter celebrations or a birthday cake, or the president of the United States pulls the switch that illuminates the "National Christmas tree," no scientific exegesis is needed for those who are there. Judaism has further invested this dense symbol with particular meanings drawn from the Torah and other traditional writings, and each Jewish society has added even more dimensions of meaning according to local custom. But no matter where the particular Jewish society is located, it may be seen as "enclosed" in light: the Torah, so frequently referred to through the metaphor of light (Proverbs 6:23), is also the constitution that places moral and social boundaries around every Jewish community and therefore defines the terms of the community's relationship with others.

The multiple experiences of light—the soft rays of early morning, the angry lightening, or the candle with its ascending smoke—also imply avenues of communication between man and God. If the Torah represents the rational relationship, the Zohar expresses the mystical, experiential rapprochement.[6] Central to the Zohar is the concept that the emanations of God's pure, white light into the created universe— the ten Sefirot—are paths to the comprehension of God's hidden nature.[7] Each of these emanations, each refraction of the white light, suggests another quality of God: blue indicates wisdom; green, insight; red, justice; and cream-white, mercy. Thus the colors of the prism, like the rainbow and its substitute, Rabbi bar Yochai, appear to mediate the great chasm between heaven and earth.

In daily life, traditional religious concepts and magic become intertwined, as people use the insights of the Torah to give meaning to everyday activities and to protect themselves at times of perceived danger. Festival candles celebrate God's presence even as they ward against the demons of darkness, and God's protective light accompanies life's crises: circumcisions held at dawn, torch-lit weddings under the stars, childbirth in a room illuminated by candles and by the Book of Radiance, the Zohar (Trachtenberg 1974:171–72).[8]

The many dimensions of this rich symbol come together in the conceptualization of children as inherently pure vehicles of God's light, potential scholars who, through knowledge of the Law and through righteousness, will hasten redemption.[9] Too young to be responsible for full knowledge of the Law, children are as yet free from possible transgressions. This unusual state of unsullied purity links the child with those at the opposite end of life, the great rabbis and scholars honored at *hillula*. Through great piety and study, these men have regained an uncommon state of purity and have become lamps of God. It may have been for this reason that it seemed only natural, and beautiful, for three-year-old Daniel to carefully carry the flame of Rabbi Shimon bar Yochai to his parents' table at *hillula* in Washington.

Another key element of the American *hillula* also expresses a fundamental, cross-cultural experience, that of communicating social cohesion by sharing food and drink. In all historical contexts, the Jewish dietary laws have separated the Jew from the outsider by defining the community as those with whom one may share food. Anthropologist Mary Douglas has observed that in ritual, ordinary food is infused with socially derived meanings—salt represents the covenant, bitter herbs the bitterness of slavery in Egypt, matzah is "the bread of affliction"—and individuals demonstrate their unity with the society by eating and thus "ingesting" those meanings (1973:59–76). While it overworks the argument to see the American food served at *hillula* as laden with imposed meanings, still it is significant that the participants are not at all concerned that at this "traditional" ritual they are eating fried chicken, bologna, and cole slaw. In fact, sharing kosher American food in the context of a *hillula* integrates the Turkish or Syrian-born Jew far more easily than a purely North African meal would, even as it reinforces the changed national status of most of the people present.

Around these tables covered with paper plates, American fast food, tall candles in silver holders, and little candles in glass jars sit Jews born in Meknes and Istanbul, Damascus, Beirut, Cairo, Tunis, Tripoli—and even Philadelphia. They will soon kiss each other "au revoir" and take their candles to homes many miles apart. They will also take with them a feeling of warm community, and this too will become part of the meaning of the candle's light.

Each time I come to *hillula*, I recall the impassioned words of a father who helps to organize the ritual each year:

"I am extremely proud of being a Moroccan Jew—the style of the Moroccan Jew in prayer, the way of life, respect of the family, in whatever you want. . . . I came from a house that I was proud [of]. I cannot ask my son. . . . He [won't] know anything about Morocco. My sister sent her three sons to Morocco; they hated it—they were born here.

"I was in Morocco and I was crying in synagogue. For me it is living history, but how can I ask my children . . . ?"

The more I have come to know the gracious people who welcome me into their homes, the more compelling this father's question has seemed to me. Just how does one transmit a beloved heritage?

For some, this spring ritual is a partial resolution to a profound dilemma. For others, this blend of Jewish mystical thought and North African folk custom is a new but essential part of the process of transforming the strange capital city into a "home." It speaks softly to people who cherish the past but who now must make peace with the present.

Notes

1. In his 1973 article, Rabbi Marc Angel of Congregation Shearith Israel in New York "guessed" that there were then one hundred thousand Sephardim in America (88); four years later, the American Sephardi Federation counted 150,000 (*Sephardi World:* 12); by 1987 the estimates had grown to 200,000–250,000 (*Bulletin,* Congregation Shearith Israel, June–September 1987, no. 8:7).
2. There was actually one Sephardi known to have been in Washington during the nineteenth century. However, because he was alone, he joined Ashkenazic groups and had no part in originating a public Sephardic presence in the area.
3. Black migration patterns differ somewhat from white and Asian resettlement patterns. Despite fair housing laws, upwardly mobile blacks tend to reside in predominantly black, affluent areas of the District of Columbia and Prince George's County, Maryland.
4. Discussion, Congregation Shearith Israel, New York City, 24 November 1981.
5. The Zohar-reading societies have a parallel in the continuous Koran-reading societies of the Maghreb.
6. In Jewish mystical thought, the letters of the alphabet have numerical values. In this system, the Hebrew word for light, *or,* is equivalent to "mystery."

Ruth Fredman Cernea

7. The song sung throughout *hillula*, "Bar Yochai," is divided into ten stanzas corresponding to the ten *sefirot*.
8. Sympathetic magic is implicit in these folk practices and also in the Talmud's association of light with (male) children, potential students of the Torah, and therefore potential conduits for God's thoughts: "He who regularly lights the Sabbath candles, his children will become scholars," and "Thanks to paying attention to the candles, a man will merit that his wife will bear male children" (Patai 1983:401).
9. From the *Code of Jewish Law*: "For the Rabbis, of blessed memory, said: Let the pure (the children) come and engage in the study of purity" (Ganzfried 1961: vol. 4, 10).

REFERENCES

Angel, Marc D. 1973, "The Sephardim in the United States: An Exploratory Study." In *American Jewish Yearbook,* ed. Morris Fine and Milton Himmelfarb. New York: American Jewish Committee 73:77–138.
Ausubel, Nathan. 1948. *A Treasury of Jewish Folklore.* New York: Crown.
Chouraqui, André N. 1973. *Between East and West: A History of the Jews of North Africa.* Trans. Michael M. Bernet. New York: Atheneum.
Crapazano, Vincent. 1980. *Tuhami.* Chicago: University of Chicago Press.
Deshen, Shlomo, and Moshe Shokeid. 1972. *The Predicament of Homecoming: Cultural and Social Life of North African Immigrants in Israel.* Ithaca: Cornell University Press.
Diamond, Luna Ereza. 1976. "The Sephardic Jews." *The Record.* Washington, D.C.: The Jewish Historical Society of Greater Washington, 8, 1: 22–7.
Douglas, Mary. 1973. *Natural Symbols.* New York: Vintage Books.
Ganzfried, Solomon. 1961. *Kitzer Shulhan Aruch: Code of Jewish Law.* Trans. Hyman E. Goldin. New York: Hebrew Publishing Company.
Gellner, Ernest. 1969. *Saints of the Atlas.* Chicago: University of Chicago Press.
Geertz, Clifford. 1968. *Islam Observed.* Chicago: University of Chicago Press.
The Holy Scriptures. 1947. Philadelphia: Jewish Publication Society.
McGrath, Peter, and Howard Means. 1980. "Washington Coming of Age: How Washington Became a Real City." *The Washingtonian* 16, 1:129–60.
Montefiore, C. G., and H. Loewe. 1963. *A Rabbinic Anthology.* Philadelphia: Jewish Publication Society.
Patai, Raphael. 1983. *On Jewish Folklore.* Detroit, Mich.: Wayne State University Press.
Schulter, John J. 1977. "Washington's Moroccan Jews—A Community of Artisans." In *Coat of Many Colors: Jewish Sub-communities in the United States,* ed. Abraham D. Lavendar. Westport, Conn.: Greenwood Press, 289–95.
The Sephardi World. 1977. New York: American Sephardi Federation, 3, 1:12.
Sholom, Gershom. 1965. *On the Kabbalah and Its Symbolism.* New York: Schocken Books.
Slouschz, Nahum. 1944 (1927). *The Jews of North Africa.* Philadelphia: Jewish Publication Society.

Tilly, Charles. 1970. "Migration to American Cities." In *Toward a National Urban Policy*, ed. Daniel P. Moynihan. New York: Basic Books, 152–66.

Torah. 1962. Philadelphia: Jewish Publication Society.

Trachtenberg, Joshua. 1974. *Jewish Magic and Superstition*. New York: Atheneum.

Zohar. N.d. Trans. Maurice Simon and Harry Sperling. New York: Rebecca Bennet Publications.

[8]

Laughter That Hurts: Ritual Humor and Ritual Change in an American Jewish Community

Riv-Ellen Prell

In fall 1973 I was immersed in the first months of anthropological fieldwork, examining what to me was and remains a compelling problem of American life. How is a religious tradition adapted to contemporary life by those who choose neither to foreswear it nor to embrace it entirely? What is their religious life like and what kind of community results? A group of young Jews in southern California who had formed a Sabbath prayer community, the Minyan, became the focus of my study.[1] These forty young men and women, ranging in age from twenty to thirty-five, met every Sabbath in the university area of a large West Coast city to pray, discuss, and celebrate. They were members of the generation whose political activism in the sixties appeared to have been transformed into a quiescent spiritualism in the

The system of transliteration used here is according to the pronunciation of modern Hebrew since it is closer to the speech patterns of this community than the Ashkenazic Hebrew used elsewhere in this volume.

An earlier version of this paper was presented at the American Anthropological Association meetings in 1975. I benefited from the collaboration of Steven S. Foldes in writing that paper, and many of his ideas are reflected here. Harvey Goldberg and Elaine May both made insightful comments on earlier drafts. Professor Goldberg directed my attention to a number of relevant works. Just as I was completing this paper in 1983, I received the sad news that Victor W. Turner had died. Much of what interests me about this community, about humor, ritual, symbolism, and social relations I learned from his work, his seminars, and his vision of life. As my life was immensely enriched by knowing and studying with him, so has his death and the end of his work impoverished me.

[192]

seventies. This community was committed to integrating Judaism with the countercultural values it had embraced and still maintained. They participated in a small but growing nationwide Jewish movement that identified with no denomination, joined no synagogue, and felt considerable alienation from the American Jewish community, their parents' generation, and the institutions they had created. Yet, they were not alienated from Judaism.[2] To the contrary! Some found their way back to a Jewish tradition they believed would more fully express their deepest aspirations as well as their history than anything else they had encountered in the American counterculture. Other members maintained a lifetime commitment to Jewish observance but were enacting it in a new setting and with a new vision of Jewish community.

They were a sober and serious group with a strong commitment to understanding what Jewish tradition meant to them and, through discussion, to resolving conflicts they all felt with that tradition. Each week at Sabbath services, prayers and the weekly Torah portion became the basis for discussions about what constituted a Jewish life.[3] Texts that concerned women, community, war, ritual, and status differences led to particularly lively group conversations because the attitudes and values that the texts expressed compelled the members to understand and react to them. Members looked at these ancient sacred writings neither as irrelevant historical writings nor as being beyond scrutiny and criticism. What ultimately concerned them was both the discontinuity and the continuity of sacred texts with the members' lives. In just two months I had already heard discussions about "the meaning and relevance of prayer in our lives," "the role of women in Judaism," "where is the group going and is it adequately providing a real prayer experience," and "violence and nonviolence in Jewish tradition."

The integration of discussions into prayer services was only one of many alterations they had made in the typical American synagogue Sabbath services. In addition, the group recognized no formal leaders. There was neither a permanent service leader nor a person designated to run the affairs of the group. All responsibilities were shared and rotated from week to week. The tasks of leading services, conducting discussions, bringing lunch, and facilitating quarterly evaluations of the group's concerns alternated among members. None of the four rabbis and ten rabbinical students in the group functioned as *the* rabbi. Initially, even the meeting places were changed weekly. After two years they agreed to use the facilities of an interdenominational religious center on the campus and so created a permanent home for the group, though from time to time they still meet in the larger homes of some of the members.

In their creation of an alternative setting for Jewish worship, these men and women expressed their commitment to a general, rather than a particular, Jewish tradition. They regarded themselves as "traditional Jews," observant of the law, yet they altered Jewish law and openly criticized it. They instituted specific innovations they believed were appropriate for them to make. But they never clearly articulated, nor felt the need to do so, the principles, theologies, or rules according to which they decided when change was appropriate and when it was unnecessary. These articulate men and women paradoxically lacked a systematic ideology. When it was necessary to make changes in the tradition, the correct ones seemed apparent.

Their powerful commitment to the religious equality of men and women is a good example.[4] In 1973 Jews across the United States had barely begun to feel the impact of feminism on their religious lives, an impact that over the next ten years would affect every sector of the Jewish community. The Minyan, in contradiction to traditional Jewish law, was already scrupulously commited from their founding in 1971 to women's equality. They made clear that however deeply they cleaved to tradition, they would not accept laws they believed wrong. By the time I arrived, women were indeed fully accepted members, wearing prayer shawls, leading services, reading the Torah, all activities normally limited to men. Perhaps the most significant of all Minyan innovations concerns gender.

In the fall, as the academic year began for Minyan members and they looked forward to the long cycle of Jewish new year holidays, I looked over my first months of fieldwork with real satisfaction. I found myself among serious "informants," capable of thoughtful and intelligent discussions of their purpose, of what the group meant to them, of their conflicts and commitments. I believed that I was observing people transforming tradition without sacrificing it, and that my task as their ethnographer would consist of showing the truly heroic dimensions of that transformation. They struggled to incorporate women in a new way into a tradition that had excluded them. They struggled to keep alive the tension between tradition and inherited symbols, rituals, and beliefs and the contemporary concerns and values associated with their lives as experienced in a pluralistic, secularized society. They sought both change and continuity in Judaism, because their experiences in America had shown them that America was neither a melting pot nor a haven for hearty individualists. They sought to recover the Judaism of an earlier generation without recreating the isolation or the assimilation of their parents.

I also wanted to understand these issues about this community because of what it might teach me about American Judaism. Social scientists, with some important exceptions, have treated American Jewish religion narrowly and quantitatively. Their research has measured what religious rules Jews have observed and have not observed. The widespread and increasing lack of observance of Jewish law by American Jews has been charted by generation, region, gender, and date of immigration (Goldstein and Goldscheider 1968; Cohen 1983). The data and interpretations are useful, but they are very incomplete. They have led to a few important works on the relationship between Jewish religion and ethnicity (Sklare 1972; Liebman 1973). But it is only in the last few years that scholars have sought to understand what Judaism means to Jews, what happens to them when they participate in their rituals. What do the rituals say or fail to say to them? In the interest of developing a normative picture of American Judaism, one must pay as much attention to what is done as to what is not done by Jews. And those studies have only just begun to appear in print (Myerhoff 1979; Heilman 1983).

As I contemplated all the complexities of the Minyan members' religious observances, I yearned to understand why they found Sabbath prayer an appropriate vehicle to express their attachment to a Judaism they wanted to alter. What was getting said in the prayers, in the inclusion of women as partners in Jewish observance, and in their discussions? And how was continuity with Jewish tradition, as well as the reformulation of that stable bedrock, related to their prayer life?

With what I thought was my own sense of purpose clarified, I found myself unprepared for a series of male-dominated, licentious, and what seemed to me even blasphemous performances that occurred during the celebration of the festival of Simhat Torah (Rejoicing in the Torah) in October. I was startled also to discover that the humor, the sexist jokes, the raucous irreverence of that event was repeated on several subsequent occasions. I was not disappointed, not sad to discover that my "heroes" were in fact real men and women. I was perplexed at the introduction of these puns, slurs, mimicry, and gestures, all of which excluded women, were focused on rabbis, and

[195]

lampooned the Torah, which were all normally treated with great reverence. I discovered some new tasks for myself. I had to understand the other faces of these heroes, which I first glimpsed during the festival. There, in what most members agreed was a normal and appropriate celebration, I heard for the first time—in the guise of jokes—real conflicts, anger, uncertainty, and even anxiety about the whole process of innovation and change in Judaism that the Minyan had undertaken. In all the straightforward discussions of conflicts with tradition, the members had never expressed such strong sentiments about their community and about the Judaism they practiced.

I realized that any interpretation I would make of their religious experience would need to account for its contradictory and complex nature. I had not anticipated the fact that for them ritual would unify the oppositions that characterize the dominant symbols of traditional societies and religion.[5] Rather than presenting an elegant and symmetrical cultural picture of their religious lives, an analysis of Minyan members' ritual observances seemed to yield contradictions and conflicts. Indeed at times what seemed to unify them most effectively was their shared ambivalence about traditional Judaism. They were unwilling to abandon liturgy and unable to avoid adapting and altering it. A picture of their religious lives could not emerge until I understood what continuity meant to them and what threatened it. Gender-related humor provided that key insight for me.

Simhat Torah

Simhat Torah marks the annual completion of the year's weekly readings of the Torah. On this ritual occasion, the final verses of the Book of Deuteronomy and the first verses of the Book of Genesis are read to mark the end and beginning of the Torah cycle. The festival is also the climax of weeks of new year and harvest festivals. The entire period is an intensely holy and serious time. The imagery of the New Year's festivals focuses on God's judgement of each person, the responsibility to repent, and the renewal of life.

Simhat Torah stands in contrast to these events because its sacredness is celebrated joyously rather than solemnly. Dancing occurs, as do parades of merry people carrying all the synagogue's Torahs around the sanctuary, while children wave flags and eat candy and fruit during the parade. In some settings, adults drink alcohol, though drunkenness is not encouraged. The synagogue, normally a place of re-straint involving a carefully prescribed distance from the Torah scroll and careful etiquette for all who come near to it, is transformed.[6] In the evening, along with parades, the Torah is read, the only night reading in the yearly cycle. In the morning the gaiety continues and the Torah cycle is begun anew as Genesis is read following another series of circular parades around the synagogue.

Simhat Torah is not a saturnalia (Gaster 1950). The numerous prohi-bitions associated with Jewish holy days are not relaxed. For instance, one still cannot drive, carry money, or do any form of work. Yet in reading and celebrating the Torah, there are unusual elements of lightheartedness, of uncharacteristic intimacy with sacred objects, and considerable sensuality in embracing, touching, and dancing with the holy scroll. In addition to these widespread customs, in some con-gregations, others have arisen. Simhat Torah is also the occasion for parodies of esoteric knowledge, attacks on authority figures, particu-larly the ritual functionaries of the prayer service. The antics range from drenching the service leader with water as he recites the prayer for rain to parodying the priestly blessing offered to the congregation by those descended from the priestly class by reciting it to liquor bottles.

American Jews who attend synagogue are familiar with the pagean-try of the *hakaphot* (circumambulations with the Torah scrolls). But few Americans have seen people guzzle alcohol in a synagogue, par-ody a serious prayer, or jostle a cantor in the process of a Simhat Torah celebration. Such undecorous activities are unknown in a synagogue. These forms of celebration exist in institutions of higher Jewish learn-ing (yeshivas) or among Hasidim or very Orthodox people. Virtually no Minyan members grew up witnessing such antics at close range. Yet it was these behaviors, about which I had read in descriptions of European Jews, that I saw at the Minyan along with even wilder and more idiosyncratic adaptations.

Simhat Torah in the Minyan was celebrated with the larger univer-sity Jewish community in the evening, and with the more intimate, exclusive Minyan group for the morning portion of the festival. Be-cause work is prohibited on the festival, there is no competing activity for Minyan members and the service is a long and leisurely one. The celebrations focused on the Torah are identical in both the evening and morning services. There are *hakaphot*, dancing, expressions of happiness, singing, and drinking. The morning differs only in that the

[197]

beginning section of Genesis is also read and that special honors are extended to the people who recite the blessings for the final portion of Deuteronomy and the first portion of Genesis. The honored ones are called *hatan* or "groom" of the Torah and Genesis.

On this particular fall morning, members gathered at Jacob and Rachel's home. A distinct sense of celebration was in the air, more lighthearted and happy than a regular Sabbath service. The festival morning prayer service proceeded as usual until the Torah was to be read. At that point a drama unfolded in which women, sacred knowledge, and the Torah itself became the targets of jokes and abuse.[7]

What initially struck me about the merriment was that although all members participated in praying and then received *aliyot* (honors) to bless the Torah, only a few actually participated in any of the joking. Rather, there was an event within an event, and while one was inclusive, the other was exclusionary. The chief actors of the inside event were the *gabbai* (the officiant charged with assigning ritual honors) and the Torah reader, the two men designated as *hatan Torah* (groom of the Torah) and the *hatan breshit* (groom of Genesis). The two Torah service leaders who orchestrated the event were not rabbis; the two honorees were.

From the moment that the Torah was unwrapped from the prayer shawls (*taleysim*) that cover it during a service and separate it from even the holy activity of prayer, it was the target of uncharacteristic physical attention. The usual stately march of the Torah around the room led by Harvey, the reader, was replaced by him race-walking the scroll around the room, dodging furniture and people until it was put on the table with some jostling. At that point Michael, the *gabbai*, intoned a complex series of rules. "Each person who takes an *aliyah* will then have a drink [he pointed to the bottles of hard liquor on a table standing nearby]. The *gabbai* will then have a drink and the reader will follow him in a drink. After an *aliyah* a person is free to take as many drinks as he or she likes." Michael emphasized that he and Harvey would have as many drinks as there were people in the room, which would have totaled about fifteen drinks each before 11 A.M. They did not consume half that amount of liquor, but by establishing the rules, they linked their subsequent behavior to the effects of alcohol. Michael also took the center stage by introducing his rules as a contest between him and Harvey to see who could consume the most alcohol. In this way their roles were transformed from ritual functionaries to key actors.

Each Minyan member was serially called to receive an *aliyah*. Because there were more people than verses to read, Harvey simply read the verses again and again, stopping short of the last, chanting until his voice was so hoarse that he could barely be heard. Rather than exclusively chant with a *trop*, a traditional melody with which the Hebrew verses are read, he occasionally used nursery melodies that verged on the taunting songs of preschoolers. Each Minyan member took his or her *aliyah*, had a few small sips of liquor, listened to the lengthy Torah reading, and occasionally chatted with a friend quietly amidst the jovial and relaxed atmosphere.

At times, Sima or Donna, two founding members of the group, played a prank of the sort children might have done in a *shtibl* (a small storefront synagogue). While the reader read the scroll or the *gabbai* called up members, one of them would tie the ritual fringes of his *tallit* to the *bimah* (the reading table). When he tried to move he found himself tied to the table and had to unknot the fringes to get free. Everyone laughed at the awkward predicament in which the men found themselves and the prank was repeated several times until the participants tired of it.

After all the other members were given their *aliyot*, Jay, one of the group's rabbi members, was called up as "bridegroom of the Torah" to bless the final section for the last time. A large man, Jay strode authoritatively to the *bimah* after his Hebrew name was called, his long prayer shawl gently swaying about his body as he walked. When he reached the table he told the *gabbai*, "Call me *rav*; you have not shown sufficient respect." And then, when Michael complied, he laughed and said, "Don't call me rabbi; I still owe the seminary a paper." Harvey responded, "You're not married Jay, how can you be the Torah's bridegroom?"

Jay then approached the scroll, covered with the Torah cover. He slowly and suggestively picked up a tiny corner of the velvet cover and peeked beneath it. His face registered a look of shock and then a leer. He cleverly affected the behavior and expression of a man peeking beneath the dress of a woman. His pantomime was so effective that the woman seated next to me whispered, "Is he going to fuck it next?" Her tone expressed her anger. Her anger and lack of amusement indicated that not all members participated equally nor were they equally intoxicated. The side remark particularly underlined the difference between the central actors and the sideline observers.

"She is a poor bride," Harvey commented, in response to Jay's gesture, acknowledging the worn and faded condition of the cover. Jay chanted his *aliyah* and as Harvey read the final verse, the "bridegroom" crawled around under the table on his hands and knees, slightly shaking the reading table, and distracting attention from the much-repeated readings of the verses.

Jay remained at the *bimah* while Jacob, another rabbi, was called to be the "bridegroom of Genesis." The words of praise and honor the *gabbai* is prescribed to read after bestowing the honor were read with ridicule and mockery, so that Jacob's *aliyah* in fact became a debased honor. As he approached the *bimah*, Michael and Harvey teased, "You are so old to be a bridegroom. Can you make your way up here? Can you manage?" Jacob, in his early thirties and one of the older members, feigned the behavior of an old man. He walked stooped over, pantomimed carrying a cane, and struggled to the Torah. Jacob read the blessing seriously and remained at the *bimah*. While Jacob and Jay stood at the *bimah* as the Torah was read, there was a momentary pause. Jacob wandered off, distracted by someone tying his *tallit* to the reader's table. "Come back, Jacob," said Jay. "This is the closest you will come to *aliyah*." Group members shouted "boo!" It was the first time they had failed to act as an appreciative audience to the small and exclusive drama of the four men who now stood in the center of the room.

Jay had made a pun, and one whose tone appeared sharper and more cutting than all the preceding insults and jokes. *Aliyah* means both a call to go up to the Torah and to migrate to Israel, or to literally "go up to Israel." Those who leave Israel permanently are called *yordim*, "those who go down." Both a call to the Torah and to Israel are movements to higher spiritual planes, and Jay's implication was that Jacob, who was not planning or contemplating a permanent move to Israel, as was Jay, was mistaken and possibly less completely Jewish.

Harvey then read the first verses of Genesis. He announced another set of rules. "Each time we read one day of God's creation we will pause and sing this melody." He then introduced a nursery melody. And the group followed suit. After properly chanting, for example, "And God called the light day, and the darkness he called night. And there was evening and morning, one day," the people paused and sang a tune using "la, la, la," disrupting the continuity of reading. After Harvey read about the creation of man and woman, he said in an aside to Michael, "It is clear that men are superior. It says so right here." Beth retorted, "It's odd we didn't have a female bridegroom in the Minyan." Harvey answered, "A female bridegroom is impossible and women in the Minyan should be pleased they are even allowed near the Torah. You should know your place." Harvey exaggerated his statements with pomposity and everyone laughed, some louder than others, at this continuing parody of sexism. In fact, throughout the day Harvey had feigned the role of the stern Torah reader, who in the face of noise and whispers in a synagogue pounds his fist on the *bimah* shouting, "Quiet, quiet, you must be quiet or I will not read." And on occasion he added, "The women in the gallery must stop the gossiping," referring to the separation of the sexes during traditional worship and his own memories of immigrant-dominated synagogues where women were labeled disruptive talkers and curtained away from the proceedings of prayer.

Following the Torah reading, the section of prophets (*haftorah* readings) was read in English by a Minyan member. He exaggerated certain sentences, raised his voice and lowered it, but he failed to engender much laughter. The service then ended routinely. Everyone stayed for a brief lunch, during which the atmosphere changed. Harvey's hoarse voice prevented him from engaging in much conversation. The Yom Kippur war in Israel was still under way and there was little else anyone discussed at meals, in private conversations before and after services, and even in formal discussions. The group broke up immediately following the service, and over the year, several people reflected back on the service as a somber one because of the war.

I spent the afternoon thinking about what had happened and I was very excited. I called a friend who was an anthropologist in the area and blurted out immediately, "The Minyan had a real rite of reversal." "What are you talking about?" she asked uncomprehendingly. "Today, during Simhat Torah. They broke rules; they were licentious with the sacred. They were like the Swazi and the Iatmul inverting and reversing normative sacred behavior. I've never seen anything like it. I had no idea Jews still did things like this."[8] "You wrote it all down I hope," she said. "Well, of course I couldn't write there; it was like *Shabbat* (the Sabbath). But I did afterward and I've gotten most of it."

Since I was conducting urban American research, I had not expected to encounter behavior that matched that of the groups studied in the classic ethnographies of British or American anthropologists.

[201]

But I had seen precisely what I had read about; special occasions when high-status people are ridiculed by low-status people, when the sacred is almost defiled, when sexual references are rampant, when humor and joking dominate every interaction, the more outrageous the better (Babcock 1978). I went to Sabbath services eagerly a few days later, watching to see if there was any indication, any hint, any sense that all that had transpired on the morning of Simhat Torah would affect the rigor and order of the Sabbath. There was no mention of it, except by one member, who said to me, "What did you think of Simhat Torah? It was a real saturnalia, no?"

Because Minyan members were not Swazi and not even Orthodox Jews, I wondered what their "ritual reversals," humor, and celebration signified to them. They had chosen by their own behavior and beliefs to break with many of the norms of traditional Judaism. Some Jewish laws went unobserved by everyone in the group and the observance of other ritual requirements and prohibitions varied considerably among them. Minyan members did not require "ritual license" to challenge the social norms or sacred demands of normative Judaism. Their own parents, if not their grandparents, had begun the process of change long ago when they immigrated to the United States. Change was not difficult for them to imagine. Yet the most outrageous examples of ritual license are most often associated with societies where stability and timelessness are the perceived norms. These rituals diminish and often disappear in pluralistic societies, where neither norms nor attacks on them are uniform and straightforward (Turner 1977).

In addition, I subsequently discovered that the Minyan's humor was in many ways idiosyncratic.[9] Although this occasion for merrymaking was shared with other Jews, the actual content of Minyan humor and intimacy with the Torah was not. The Torah was handled in an unthinkable manner for either a deeply observant group of Jews or even for more acculturated Jews, who found such antics "undecorous." The explicit attribution of sexuality to the Torah was particularly unprecedented. And the content of the humor, rather than resting on standard esoteric wit, was unique to the people involved.

I watched these events with volatile emotions. The anthropologist in me delighted at finding rites of reversals. The feminist in me was sensitive to women's responses. They laughed less heartily; some looked very uncomfortable. Only a few commented under their breaths. The pain and anger I heard subsequently made it even clearer to me that I could not see the apparent fun of the key participants uncritically. These events were painful for half of the room. Women were not included. Had I been a member, I would also have sat on the sidelines, silenced and awkward. As the anthropologist of the group, I had often identified very closely with the most powerful men of the group, who had dominated the joking. They had much to tell me and I was an eager listener. But I was also a Jewish woman, and I had to realize that I would have had none of the power necessary to dominate the Torah and the humor that morning.

This sobering realization made me search harder to understand the contradictions that seemed to dominate the humor. The events unfolded from two perspectives. Those who joked controlled the tradition. Those who remained silent were excluded from it. As I observed the events I could not observe the rendering of tradition without seeing the exclusion. These cleavages had never appeared on the Sabbath.

Because I had identified with all members in fieldwork I felt both the exclusion and the power of active participation. In experiencing both I felt the threat of each to the other. Those at the center felt they had to push away those at the margin who wanted change. Those at the margin felt they had no place at the center. It was the complexity of these positions that humor revealed better than any other aspect of Minyan life.

The *Minyan* performance was a symbolic attack on both the traditions of Jewish life and on their own community-constructed ones as well. For example, they crossed the boundaries of properly respectful treatment of the most sacred of objects, the Torah. Members literalized its symbolic feminine attributes through touching and ridiculing it in ways other Jews do not. In the process they slurred women as well, by treating the feminine as exclusively sexual and subservient. In the latter case, they attacked one of the key components of their group—a commitment to the equality of men and women. Similarly, considerable ridicule was directed toward the men in the group who are rabbis. While rabbi/layperson statuses are central to the American synagogue, they were not acknowledged in the ideology of the Minyan or in its highly egalitarian formal structure. The rabbi/nonrabbi distinction was also not an operative distinction in the Minyan, because not all of the group's ritual experts were rabbis. Yet *gabbai* and reader introduced the distinction by focusing the humor at the *bimah*, where they emphasized who was a rabbi, who was a very knowledgeable Jew, and who had been in the group the longest. These categories also marginalized women from any participation at all. The women who momentarily participated by tying men's *tzitzit* to the *bimah*, as peripheral as this activity was, were among the founders of the group. Hence the humor not only blurred the distinctions between sacred and profane that is typical of such rituals, but it introduced distinctions into the Minyan that group members did not normally acknowledge; male/female, rabbi/layperson, Minyan founder/Minyan member, knowledgeable/less educated. Such ritual occasions are normally antihierarchic, reversing statuses and roles to equalize, even if briefly, all members of a society. The effect in the Minyan was the opposite. Hierarchy and differentiation were repeatedly introduced, above all by the control of the humor by four men.[10]

What I had first perceived as a rite of reversal because of its form—parody and inversion—I came to understand as well as ritual expressions of complex ambivalence. Tradition was used by some members to attack some of their own deeply held convictions, convictions such as equality, which were integral to the group's creation. But hostility was directed at tradition too through the unprecedented irreverent treatment of the Torah. Their behavior toward the Torah was more aggressive than in any comparable setting. Categories of behavior and persons defined by tradition were made articulate through humor that expressed the complex tensions between the normative Jewish tradition and the Minyan's innovations. Caricatures of synagogue decorum—the shouting reader, gossiping women, the poor bride, rabbis, lay people—populated the Minyan with a cast of characters from synagogues of their childhood. The antics themselves—joking, drinking, mischievous childish behavior—evoked a past that had not been experienced by all but was appropriated as part of the collective memories of European Jewish life that Minyan members claimed as their own.

There was a paradox in their humor. The jokes and gestures that ridiculed the Minyan's commitments to religious innovation dominated. Each witticism introduced hierarchic, patriarchal Judaism as the norm. Normative Judaism then was the medium of all humor. To participate one had to be familiar with the most conservative elements of Judaism. Inevitably then, not all members could participate.

Although Minyan members returned to their orderly lives and to their commitments regarding how Judaism should be lived, the same jokes resurfaced from time to time. The jokes about women's place, about the female attributes of the Torah, and about the synagogue found their way into a variety of Minyan settings. I witnessed another dramatization of their humor eight months later during a twenty-four-hour Sabbath retreat. The full-scale parody was arranged by Mark, the one rabbi in the group who did not participate in the festivities of Simhat Torah. He had left the service prior to the celebrations of the Torah in order to monitor a potential campus crisis. Jewish Defense League members were organizing a rally in support of Israel in the Yom Kippur war and he was concerned that violence might erupt. He later told me that he had been relieved to miss the festival Torah service. He said: "No one in the Minyan grew up with these events on Simhat Torah but me and Michael. I don't know where people picked these up—from college maybe. They did baby shit, pranks and tricks, instead of sophisticated parodies. The Minyan should find a different form to celebrate what gives us joy. Simhat Torah belongs to those who seriously study Torah, not to us." Despite the remark some months later, Mark created just such an event. He called it the rebbe's *tish*.

The Rebbe's Tish

At the end of the school year, Minyan members celebrated an entire Sabbath outside the city at a local camp. Following the Friday night prayer service, dinner, and singing of *zemirot* (Sabbath songs), Mark announced without prior discussion that a special event, a *rebbe's tish* would be held at midnight. A rebbe's *tish* is an event celebrated by hasidic Jews, for whom their rebbe, or spiritual leader, occupies a unique role.[11] He is a charismatic person whose followers believe that his spiritual qualities, advice, and blessings yield great power because of the insight and understanding available to him as a result of his exceptional piety and his particularly intense relationship with God. A *tish*, held on the Sabbath, is an event in which a rebbe shares wine, food, and song with his *Hasidim*, or followers. He comments on the weekly Torah portion, shares his insights, displays his knowledge, and draws out a moral point or lesson to guide their lives.

The *tish* is not an occasion for humor or the inversion of norms. It is, however, joyous. First, it occurs on the Sabbath, when normal work ceases and celebration takes over: good food, lovely clothing, sexuality, and leisure are all customary or prescribed. The singing and drinking during the *tish* are part of Sabbath celebrations. In addition, the rebbe's followers are close to him, bask in his knowledge, insights, and presence. The *tish,* then, shares certain but far more restrained practices with Simhat Torah and even Purim.

Mark is not a Hasid, though he grew up in a part of New York near where many of them lived. He is knowledgeable about Hasidism, and as a rabbi who works on campus, he is personally acquainted with a hasidic community oriented toward attracting alienated and troubled college students to Judaism. Masquerading as a Hasid, he expressed a radically different view of Judaism, its emotional power, its vision of the Torah, of men and women, and community. It was a vision that seemed to resonate with most members and allowed them to enter the parody, to participate in it, and to ridicule it as well.

At midnight everyone gathered around the table in the central room of the lodge where the retreat took place and where the Sabbath events had just occurred. Mark took from his briefcase a bottle of brandy identical to one that would be served at a real *tish.* As he set the bottle on the table, he told his "followers" that he was the Munkatsher rebbe. "My Hasidim," he began. "I was your rebbe in Hungary before the war and now we are together here. I am very pious, more religious than even the Satmar rebbe. And yet here we are in *goles* [exile], where I am responsible for the sins of my followers. Here in America we all know it is impossible to be a good Jew. The more you, my Hasidim, sin the more I am driven to drink because I must take your sins on me. Oy, this is a hard life." Mark communicated a number of cues to the Minyan members in this role. He chose Hungary not simply because part of his own family is from there, but because Hungarian Hasidim are notoriously extremist, pious, and ultraobservant. The Satmar rebbe is the head of one of the largest groups of Hasidim in the world. They do not recognize the state of Israel because they believe Zionism is a secular ideology that distracts people from religious observance.

Mark established himself as pious, and, of course, in the Minyan's view, as "extreme." He enhanced his performance by changing his speech. He used the singsong cadences of Jewish immigrants and changed his Hebrew pronunciation from Sephardic to Ashkenazic.[12] This change meant that words normally pronounced in the Minyan using a *t* sound, based on the Hebrew letter *tav* (*sav*) were now pronounced with an *s* sound. Mark's reference to *goles* (exile) was funny simply because the familiar and more "modern" pronounciation of Minyan members is *galut*.[13] Mark's emotional statement about the difficulty of his life and that of his followers also imitated an intense emotionalism associated with Eastern European Jews, where Stoicism and emotional restraint are not highly valued. Mark's performance, then, resonated with members' memories of their own grandparents, or with films, stories, or other sentimentalized representations of Eastern European Jewish life. Mark was effective. Members laughed loudly, appreciatively, and with recognition of all that he imitated.

Mark continued: "But despite the fact that we are in *goles* there are still *simkhes*. David and Chaim are celebrating the anniversary of their *bar mitsves this very shabes,* and Rachel is celebrating the anniversary of her *bas mitsve.* Though we suffer and cannot be where we want, some of us still succeed. Bluma, David, and Zahavah all have completed their MA degrees. We can still thank God for our successes and celebrate. Because I live in America now I looked over the Torah portion for a few minutes before I sat down and I have also asked David to offer a few comments." Mark did offer real information to the Minyan about the various celebrations and successes of various members. But he referred to all of them by their Yiddish as opposed to their Hebrew or English names. He continued to imitate the emotion and style of a rebbe in his announcements. And his final comment invoked the most laughter, many laughing until tears rolled down their cheeks. A learned scholar, of course, studies the weekly portion of the Torah at length, for many hours each day. The rebbe's statement was funny because few people in the Minyan devote much time to Torah study, and those who do at all literally do so for a few minutes. The joke, playing on American life and its effect on piety, was literally a joke on themselves. It was particularly funny when spoken by a Hungarian Hasid.

Harvey, who Mark called David, had been forewarned and began to discuss the Torah portion. His jokes were all sexual, but since I could not record them because of Sabbath prohibitions, and my Hebrew was not good enough to understand the sexual innuendos, all that transpired had to be explained to me both during and after the event. Naturally, I was not alone in this disability. Many people who had laughed heartily moments before felt lost during this performance. Whispered explanations buzzed up and down the tables: The few who "got" the subtlety of the jokes explained them to the many. Harvey talked about the prophetic reading that paralleled the Torah portion for this Sabbath. It described the prostitute Rahab, who hid Israelite spies, an act for which she was rewarded.[14] In the previous year, some jokes had been casually made about this section during a Torah discussion as well. But at the *tish* the joking was more elaborate and Harvey was joined by others in expanding the puns. The hilarity became focused on Jacob, Mark, Harvey, and Jay, who because of their expertise understood the most and made the most jokes. Jay, for example, referred to Rahab as "the lay of the land," implying both her role as a scout, looking over Israel, and as a prostitute. Her identity as a prostitute evoked snickers and laughter and the references to her status were made repeatedly.

These textual references were interrupted by comments the key participants made about one another. "We need a wedding," said Harvey. "Jacob has been married a year now so, since the Munkatsher Rebbe is the oldest, he should get married."

"No, no," declared Mark. "I want to drink at the *bris* [circumcision] of Jacob's son." Jacob and Rachel had no children yet and no immediate plans for any.

"No," responded Jacob. "First at the rebbe's wedding."

Finally, one woman, Sharon, entered the joking: "Harvey, you have just completed a degree, started a new job, and moved into a new apartment. You seem the likely one to be married." Harvey blushed a deep red, but Sharon did not remain a principal participant in the joking. The patter continued only a short time longer until everyone had had a small sip of brandy and then they retired for the night.

The content of the humor on this occasion resembled that on Simhat Torah. The form the events took differed. The *tish* was a play that transformed the audience into actors. Mark used props and language to make himself a rebbe and members Hasidim. Simhat Torah was a festival where the inversion of norms was sanctioned. Therefore, the *tish* parodied a real event, while on Simhat Torah members enacted a basic script. They embellished it with their own idiosyncratic jokes. Both the *tish* and Simhat Torah events coincided with the end of an intense period of concentration—New Year festivals in the latter and academic exams in the former.

The striking feature of both events is the sharp division of men and women in the performance. Women were virtually excluded from the humor, certainly from the sexual humor. Females were included as the butt of jokes concerning the Torah portion and were portrayed as entrappers in commitments of marriage or having children that men wanted to avoid. In the *tish* there was no simple distinction between rabbis and nonrabbis, as there had been on Simhat Torah. Instead, a distinction was drawn between the learned and nonlearned. Those who understood Hebrew, knew the Torah portion and the Haftorah, and knew various sexual references in the Bible were in a position to participate in the event. Those with less knowledge still formed an essential audience but either laughed unknowingly or required interpreters. The one and only woman who managed a successful joke was "learned," a graduate student in Jewish history. The learned principals of the *tish* were virtually the same participants as on Simhat Torah, with the exception of Michael, who did not attend the Sabbath retreat.

Obligation and Sentiment

In the course of my observations of these events, I saw two minyans; the Minyan as it appeared week in and week out, and the Minyan where joking, masquarade, and ribald performances occurred. The first Minyan never acknowledged the second, never discussed what occurred there, except for the few disgruntled women who made covert references to these events.[15] The two minyans were, however, virtual mirrors of one another. What they reflected were the two faces of the Minyan's contradictory enterprise: to maintain and to change normative Judaism. Almost all Minyan members spoke of themselves as traditionalists. To varying degrees they observed the dietary laws, the Sabbath, and in many comparable ways distinguished themselves from more assimilated Jews. Yet, their membership in the Minyan bespoke not only their criticisms of American mainstream Judaism, but their commitment to change Jewish laws and rituals.

They remained commited to Jewish practice and Jewish community because they believed that innovation could be integrated into a Judaism that maintained a continuity with the past. Their position was a paradoxical one. Without both a sense of continuity and of alteration of tradition, there could be no Judaism for them. They had discussed these conflicts through particular Jewish texts. They had taken decisive action by instituting changes. Yet, the most profound contradictions in what they had attempted only surfaced in the humor enacted in these events. The humor expressed the force of sentiments associated with memory and continuity as well as anger at laws that required change. Humor was the vehicle for the expression of such paradoxes, because, like play, it establishes a boundary of "let's pretend." It acknowledges that what is said is not to be taken at face value, that any other circumstances than these would make the statements or actions entirely unacceptable (Basso 1979:37). On these occasions, humor provided the principal participants with license to articulate for themselves and the whole group the tensions between their lives as a community of innovators and as maintainers of the tradition.

Minyan members constantly used humor derived from the tradition as they focused attacks on the tradition. They exaggerated, caricatured, distorted, and even ridiculed symbols of both the tradition and of themselves as innovators in order to lampoon all the forms of religious action in which they were engaged. In the expression of those tensions, they formulated and reformulated what they did in the Minyan, ultimately creating a comment upon their basic enterprise. They expressed, consciously or unconsciously, what they do. Every Sabbath they enact Jewish ritual and Minyan ideology. On occasions when they joke, they enact their ambivalence about their efforts to be a minyan. Clifford Geertz's (1973) analysis of a Balinese cockfight and Victor Turner's (1977) discussions of traditional ritual suggest that societies create occasions for reflexivity. The secular world is punctuated by events that both reflect and express the key concerns of a culture. Similarly, the fundamental "business" of the Minyan is the exercise and transformation of traditional Judaism. Therefore, it is likely that just that "business" will come under scrutiny during occasions dominated by humor.

These events expressed, even if they did not articulate, these tensions within the Minyan. Humor became for them an agent capable of allowing Judaism to be questioned while strengthening its fundamental premises. Normative Judaism may have been the source of considerable ridicule, but it was also the source of considerable power, emotion, sentiment, and shared experience. In displaying the arbitrary nature of all forms of their Jewish life, they also emphasized the unique power that tradition rather than innovation held.

Indeed, their performances were complex for this reason. The content of the humor and forms of joking they used on these two occasions are not easy to analyze. They were neither simple inversions of communal norms nor attacks on the sacred premises of the tradition. Such forms of humor would be characteristic of the rituals of traditional peoples, at least as represented in anthropological ethnographies.16 Nor were members adapting to a contemporary situation and elaborating on basic patterns of ridicule of higher status groups and people, as reported by anthropologists in urban contexts (Basso 1979; Miller 1967; Handelman and Kapferer 1972). Rather, by combining distinct types of humor in a single performance, their humor seemed to turn back on itself. Participants joked in so many ways that the humor seemed to turn back on itself. Participants joked in so many ways that the humor never focused on a single topic and never delivered a devastating sting.17 The many forms of jokes represented the numerous visions of what their religious community was to be. As one man joked, another would follow, only to joke at the expense of a markedly different issue. A parody of sexism was followed by a near assault on the Torah. They acted like sexist-traditionalists, only to act afterward like blasphemers. The joking amounted to the expressions of contradictory experiences in many forms of humor. What I was left with was a sense of the utter arbitrariness they must have felt about any of their religious expressions. In their humor, the jokers moved from Torah readers, to Hasidim, to ultra-Orthodox believers, to rabbis, to sexists with fluidity and equal comfort and discomfort. Their humor attacked all types of Judaism and all forms of Jewish authority. This variety implied their uncertainty about what form Judaism could or should take.

The jokes and humor fall into three categories: impersonal slurs, distortions of the sacred, and the adoption of traditional forms of humor. They encompass humor directed at people and sacred objects in forms provided by the tradition and from American society. The simplest is the impersonal slur, the jokes directed by Minyan members at one another. The slurs are mild and tend to focus on status and social roles.18 The second type is far more complex. It grows out of mimicry or the attribution of qualities to sacred symbols or subjects that become symbols. The treatment of the Torah, the rebbe's performance, and the attributions made to the Torah are all examples. These exaggerations and distortions produce humor that lies in the elaboration of associations to the key symbols. The idiosyncratic nature of the Minyan's elaborations are clearest here. The third form of humor rests in the adaptation of traditional occasions for and forms of humor. Here, esoteric humor follows a traditional script, which on particular ritual occasions licenses ridicule of the cantor, nonsensical disquisitions on sacred texts, and enactments of stories. This script is loosely followed on Simhat Torah and appears in the various jokes on textual passages.

In these three forms, juxtaposed against one another in the Minyan's joking performances, the traditional norms and values of Judaism were both attacked and upheld. Innovation was attacked and upheld as well. For example, the use of traditional scripts for humor, elaborating on an Orthodox Simhat Torah, not only introduced traditional values, but allowed those with the most knowledge of normative Judaism to dominate. They introduced and imitated the characters of the traditional synagogue. They excluded women who were never center stage on such occasions in a synagogue. Yet, simultaneous with the expressions of the value of tradition was the attack upon it. [The qualities they associated with the Torah and rabbis evoked barely disguised hostility.] Torah and rabbis are the foundations of traditional authority. The Minyan humor exhibits and debases that authority. The Munkatsher Rebbe is a fraud. He doesn't study and he drinks too much. He is laughable. The sacred Torah is a poor bride capable of evoking salacious intentions. The traditional synagogue is not only the domain of childhood memories but a bastion of contemptible sexism and ludicrous figures. The humor constantly turns back on itself, first inverting one order and then another, using such Minyan ideals as sexual equality to attack the synagogue, and such traditional values as sexual segregation to attack the Minyan and its "marginal members."

The humor flaunts and reenforces traditional authority. Authority, and who has access to it, is made overt in the joking performances when participants who are closely identified with normative Judaism carefully control events. Those in the center of the performance are associated with those at the center of a Judaism that excludes women, the uneducated, and those less certain of their religious commitments. Yet the assertion of their authority is also undermined. They control the humor and direct it at one another, making themselves most visible. But the form and content of the humor largely depends on denying the essence of the authority they represent. They accuse and protest through their status relations. The statuses valued and recognized by traditional authority are the ones they deny. They assert their independence from what they consider to be constraints rather than statuses. Fatherhood and marriage, even age, are consistently treated as undesirable. The access to knowledge that gives them priority in the joking performance is eschewed through the status relations they invert and slur. They flaunt their power not only to attack traditional authority, but those in power control the attacks. This is not the usual inversion of power in which the powerless briefly attack the powerful through humor. It is the powerful attacking the ideas that support their status.

What is particularly dizzying about the combinations and recombinations of such wit is the continual opposition between traditional authority and the continuity of Jewish tradition. Tradition is symbolized by Torah, text, and law; in short, the obligatory. Continuity, while obviously also associated with Torah, is expressed by reenacting childhood experiences that evoke sentiment, memories, and emotions that remain powerful. For the men who control the performances, for example, sexism expressed in the parodies of rebbe and synagogue simultaneously pushes away the past while drawing it closer. In any joking performance focused on women, the principals are in fact sexists, because they exclude women and undermine their claims to equality. But simultaneously the actors demonstrate the need for innovation. The attitudes and behavior of the traditionalists the Minyan abhors is displayed. But the abhorrent behavior carries the weight of not only obligation but affect as well. It is apparent in the humor that despite Minyan commitments, normative Judaism is not only embraced "in general," but very much in the particulars that are so objectionable. Childhood experience is not easily severed from the range of religious expressions, even when it contradicts the ideals of innovators. The humor attacks and evokes meanings that carry powerful feelings for these men and women. The world of childhood and its potent memories are evoked through references to the childhood synagogue, by the use of Yiddish personal names, by the rebbe who represents prewar Europe, even by the humor of Simhat Torah itself. The use of this "childhood language," even if the memories are acquired abstractly—through Yiddish, altered Hebrew pronounciations, and changed synagogue decorum—evokes an unchanging Judaism that lays claim to an authentic, unbroken Jewish tradition. Members' free use of that language of images, normally excluded from Minyan interaction, constitutes what linguists label "code switching," intimating a particular set of meanings aimed at particular social relationships. The response evoked by the code switch is the laughter of shared recognition of images from a past whose shared content is in part constructed. The characters, language, and affect are nevertheless real. They embody the authority and power of a Judaism that

transcends the individual experience of Minyan members and demonstrates their part in and access to a timeless people and religion.

Yet Minyan members have chosen to break that link, to undermine
the code, to transform the sexism of that tradition, and to modify the
constraints and obligations of the law they do not entirely accept.
Hence they attack that powerfully evocative "code" as well, ridiculing
and taunting it through jokes and gestures toward the Torah, the
potent representative of the unbroken tradition of Jewish law from
Moses the lawgiver to the present.

The humor that makes attributions of gender to symbols in texts
(which is virtually all of it) is, not surprisingly, the most powerful.
Here the ambiguity of the task of the religious innovator is nowhere
more apparent. The most significant innovation made by Minyan
members concerns gender. They have changed these laws because
they believe they are wrong. Making men and women equal represents their most direct attack on authority. Yet, paradoxically, their
humor directs hostility at the feminine and ignores the real women in
the room. Women are doubly attacked. They are marginalized and
slurred. The feminine is associated with unwanted obligations, with
entrapment, and with the trivial. Sexism is parodied throughout the
performance, but the hierarchic principles of the tradition that differentiate male and female are reenforced as well. Women, unable to
participate in the humor, become the butts of it, tolerating the event
in exchange for the equality available the rest of the year.

Humor was not, however, only the occasion for expressions of conflict. Another holiday joking performance I observed united affect and
obligation. The obligatory, in lighthearted form, became the occasion
for unifying members and expressing the success of their efforts at
maintaining continuity and introducing innovation. Purim, the Jewish
masquerade holiday, was the occasion for a *shpil* or play that embodied humor that was shared rather than divisive, sexual without making
gender or sexuality its butt. The play's affect and humor were derived
primarily from the applicability of a story derived from normative
Judaism to contemporary events. The humor was unambiguous and
reenforced Jewish tradition without sacrificing Minyan ideology. In
fact, it expressed and proved their compatibility.

While reading the *Megillah*, the biblical story of Esther that recounts
the putatively historic events in which mighty Persia fights against the
Jewish people, several Minyan members enacted the roles of culture
heroes and enemies. Minyan members were both scroll readers, chant-

ing the story from the Hebrew text, and actors, silently performing and dramatizing it. Minyan members, as well as university students, faculty, and people from the community at large attended the event at the university religious center. A Purim audience is never made up of polite bystanders. They boo and make noise with noisemakers each time the enemy, Haman, is mentioned, hence drowning out and effacing his name. Mark, the rebbe of the *tish*, is a rabbi at the campus Jewish organization where this took place; he played Haman.[19] He took the role explicitly because he is the assistant director and rabbi of the organization; he chose a "reversed role." There was no need to deny his expertise and prominent role in his work life as there is in the egalitarian Minyan. In the role he parodied current American events to create a powerful relation between text and American life. He masqueraded not as the biblical Haman, but as Watergate "villain" H. R. "Bob" Haldeman. He walked onstage dressed in a three-piece business suit, wearing a hat, and carrying a briefcase on which was written H. R. "Bob" Haman. Audiotape trailed out of his briefcase, and he spent a good deal of the performance snipping it.[20] Haldeman/Haman is hanged in the end when his plot to kill all Jews is discovered and he himself is destroyed. Mark had no spoken lines: His entire performance was visual and succeeded because of his ability to effectively associate Haldeman with Haman and Haman with Haldeman. The enemy of the Jews was cast as the enemy of America, the American Left in particular. The Persian conspiree who holds high office in the court of the king was doomed when his evil intentions were uncovered. So Haldeman, whose access to presidential power was considerable, was also stripped of power through the public Watergate investigations. Mark's performance was successful precisely because everyone present recognized the connections he created, and they appreciated and shared his juxtapositions of a contemporary and an ancient story.

The *shpil* expressed the connection between two phemomena that Minyan members are committed to integrating: a shared interpretation of American life and a shared interpretation of Jewish history and ritual. Haman and Haldeman could be simultaneously portrayed because Minyan members could readily identify heroes and villains. They also shared the belief that a sacred text may help one see the key issues in contemporary politics. Texts may also be understood more vividly when looked at in light of those politics. In this performance, affect is shared and undergirds both poles of experience, the contemporary-political and the textual-traditional.

[215]

The obligatory, in the guise of recognized authority, is also sup-ported. The Purim event, shared by a wider university Jewish com-munity, does not challenge the authority of tradition. Mark, and in other years, Jacob, the director of the organization, gave a "Purim Torah," explicitly using wit to parody sacred texts.21 Their "license" was sanctioned by the tradition and the shared community. Authority is basically supported and the humor rests in a shared interpretation of text in light of modern life. Gender relations are reinterpreted with-out challenging their entire structure because Purim is not an occasion for stringent separation of the sexes. Indeed, Purim is a holiday that to some extent invites the relaxation of rigid rules and separations.

By contrast, all other Minyan performances challenged all forms of authority, debasing and ridiculing them. Authority was set off against other forms of attachment to Judaism. Though much of the humor was "scripted" by traditional license, its enactment was coarser and more idiosyncratic, bearing the unique stamp of conflicts in the Minyan. Because the Minyan participated in rather than provided the ex-clusive setting for the Purim celebration, its particular conflicts were restrained, while its "approach" to Judaism was maintained.22

All forms of Minyan humor seem to be categorical.23 Though they concern social relations, the butts are rarely real people in the Min-yan. Rather, the crucial themes of Minyan members' religious lives are formulated in the humor embodying expressed and unexpressed feelings about members' histories, identities, aspirations for and anx-iety about the future of a changed Judaism. The feelings are frankly and unmistakably ambivalent, even as the altered context of the Pu-rim celebration shed some of that ambivalence. They are shared by people whose community rests on the assumption that Judaism can be changed and will remain recognizable and potent. The humor rests on the potential contradictions in just that formulation. As such, the joking performances constitute a constructed metacommentary on the process in which they are engaged.24 What occurs in the humor is a construction, formulation, undermining, and reconstruction of tradi-tional Jewish authority, affect, and a transformation of authority that undergirds every Sabbath service.

The metacommentary or enactment of their most important com-munal drama is derived from setting, social relations, and metaphors. Humor that is occasioned by traditional events (Simhat Torah and the Sabbath) sets a safe context for such commentary. There will be no confrontations. The most engaged participants are also those who are associated with normative Judaism. But the wit is anything but safe. It is not a simple inversion of the daily events of life. It does not even represent an agreed upon construction of some portion of members' experiences.[25] It is a statement of the ambiguity and difficulty of the Minyan enterprise, formulable only because humor allows each participant to disavow his or her role as butt, principal, or aggressor. In the metaphoric attribution of gender to symbols, of religious obligation to status, and religious feelings to childhood experience, the jokes intimate that religious change is impossible and essential. In their performances, Minyan members witness and participate in the very contradictions that create their community. They have distorted their story in order to enact it.

Notes

1. Minyan is the Hebrew word for prayer quorum. While Jews may pray privately, many central prayers of the liturgy and obligations can be performed only among ten men. Jews of the Conservative denomination have counted women as part of a prayer quorum since 1972. Orthodox Jews recognize only males. Reform Jews do not require a minyan for prayer.

2. *Havurot* (fellowships) are a North American Jewish phenomenon that gained prominence in the early 1970s. Sleeper and Mintz (1971) and Neusner (1972) describe the initial movement. Bubis and Wasserman (1983) and Reisman (1979) describe the later development of *havurot* within synagogues. Prell-Foldes and Weissler (1983) have both conducted ethnographic studies of such groups. Like the Minyan, most *havurot* were made up of graduate students and faculty members. The Minyan had a number of members who were nonacademic professionals, many of whom were alumni of the university near which they met.

3. The Torah is divided into weekly readings, publicly read twice on Saturday (during morning and afternoon prayer services), on Mondays, and on Thursdays. Each weekly portion is divided into seven sections so that each Saturday morning seven adult males (in traditional communities) may be called to recite blessings (*aliyot*) appropriate to the occasion of the public reading. In other services, only the first section of the weekly portion is read, and this is subdivided into three blessings. There are special Torah portions read for festivals that do not follow the chronological cycle of the Torah reading. The entire Torah is read each year.

4. Traditional (*halakhic*) legal Judaism differentiates male and female obligations. Women are freed from the positive mitzvot (laws) that obligate adults to time-bound duties, such as reciting prayers for the prayer services that occur three times a day, and wearing a prayer shawl. Women must observe all negative mitzvot with minor exceptions. Non time-constrained positive mitzvot are also required, again with the exception of biologically specific ones. Because women cannot be obligated to participate in public activity, they are not counted in the minyan. See Saul Berman (1976).

5. Classic examples of this approach to symbolism are Turner (1967), Myerhoff (1975), and Kapferer (1983).

6. A description of such etiquette may be found in Kirshenblatt-Gimblett (1982).

7. The ethnographic events recorded on pp. 198-201 also appear in Prell (1987:177-8).

8. Ethnographies describing these rituals are Kuper (1963) and Bateson (1958).

9. I have not found any written references to this form of joking on Simhat Torah, and I am indebted to Rabbi Moshe Adler for his description of it in a variety of settings.

10. Handelman and Kapferer (1972) are particularly useful in analyzing how spontaneous humor emerges out of "category routinized," that is, prescribed occasions for, joking. They also discuss why some actors are able to control such events.

11. Hasidism was an Eastern European Jewish movement originating in the eighteenth century whose followers rebelled against rabbinic and legalistic interpretations of Judaism. It developed a written and oral tradition, heavily influenced by mysticism, which reinterprets traditional texts. Today Hasidism is associated with extreme Orthodoxy. See Scholem (1941) for a historical discussion.

12. The Ashkenazic pronunciation is characteristic of Eastern European Hasidim. The Hebrew spoken in contemporary Israel has adopted some salient features of Sephardic communities and has thus come to be known as "Sephardic." Since the establishment of the state of Israel, there has been a trend among Jewish communities in the United States to switch from an Ashkenazic pronunciation to modern Israeli Sephardic. In the synagogues of the parents of the Minyan members, however, the prevalent pronunciation was most likely still Ashkenazic.

13. Ashkenazic pronounciation was used extensively in the joking on Simhat Torah the following year in the Minyan.

14. The Torah section referred to is from the Book of Numbers, beginning with chapter 12. A parallel story is told in the Book of Joshua, chapter 2. It is in this chapter, constituting the *haftorah* of the Sabbath in question, rather than the one in Numbers, that the reference to prostitution is made.

15. A group of women, partially motivated by the humor used in these events, organized an entire service focused on women and Jewish ritual. See Prell-Foldes (1978a).

16. An extensive discussion of the key interpretations may be found in the "Introduction" in Babcock (1978).

17. Mary Douglas (1975) understands ritual humor as the articulation of the joke form and the social system. In that analogue she finds the potency of humor. The message of the joke, she argues, is often the "escapability" of patterns of social life. [The variety of forms Minyan humor took, and the contradictions between them are key to this analysis. Members lampooned every aspect of Jewish religious observance; their grandparents', their parents', and their own.] Hence the ambiguity of authority in the group and the constant ambivalence about structure makes the humor constantly ambiguous, one form often undermining the other.

18. Radcliffe-Brown (1975a and b) concentrates on the social relationships in his analysis of joking. He emphasizes that the slur acts to join people in apparent acts of antagonism. Humor does partially function this way in the Minyan by allowing the key actors to differentiate themselves from others.

19. Mark's performance was the central one, but it was surrounded by other significant ones. Two characters are women—Esther, the wife of the king and savior of the Jewish people—and Vashti, a rebellious woman whom the king divorces before he marries Esther. The woman who played Vashti dressed herself in a costume that included a women's liberation symbol drawn on cardboard and draped over her back. She was played as a feminist hero rather than the failed wife

portrayed in the text. Gender did enter the Purim *shpil*, but it made women visible and able to articulate their perspective on the tradition. The *shpil*, like textual discussions, allowed women to reinterpret traditional characters. There were other male characters as well.

20. Haldeman's tape-snipping was a reference to the extensive tapes made of all presidential meetings by Richard Nixon, which included discussions of the Watergate break-in. Twenty-one minutes of particularly important conversations were inexplicably erased. That fact was revealed the year of the Purim performance.

21. Purim Torah is the name given to the witty, esoteric parody of text that scholarly men usually perform on Purim.

22. Weissler (1982) describes a Purim performance at a time of conflict in a *havurah*. The parodies were all directed at social relations in the group.

23. They are, however, relevant to social relations in the group. The humor on Simhat Torah directly followed a discussion in the Minyan that revealed the extensive discomfort members felt about prayer, its truth, and its relevance for them. By the festival, the group had decided to hold classes instead of preprayer discussions to formally learn about the prayerbook. They assigned teachers, three of the four principals on Simhat Torah, thus instituting their first formal leaders. The humor obviously embodies many of these themes and issues. See Prell (1988).

24. In his article on the cockfight, Geertz introduces the notion of a metasocial commentary (1973: 448) arguing that the cockfight "interprets" the process of humans assorting themselves into hierarchical ranks and organizing collective experiences around it. He emphasizes the deep sentiment evoked by the cockfight, and how that sentiment allows the experience of the key themes without the consequences of normal daily social encounters. As play, the cockfight allows people to experience the public social order and the imagined possibilities of various ways of participating in that order. I use the term *metacommentary* to emphasize that the joking is not "functional," but instead expresses the critical themes in Minyan members' construction of religious life. Basso (1979) also focuses on how humor enables the "construction" of critical experiences in his analysis of Western Apache imitations of white people.

25. Minyan members cannot agree on shared constructions of themselves, as Basso argues that the Western Apache do.

REFERENCES

Babcock, Barbara, ed. 1978. *The Reversible World: Symbolic Inversion of Art and Society*. Ithaca: Cornell University Press.

Basso, Keith. 1979. *Portraits of "The Whiteman": Linguistic Play and Cultural Symbols among the Western Apache*. Cambridge: Cambridge University Press.

Bateson, Gregory. 1958. *Naven*. Palo Alto, Calif.: Stanford University Press.

Berman, Saul. 1976. "The Status of Women in Halakhic Judaism." In *The Jewish Woman: New Perspectives*, ed. Elizabeth Koltun. New York: Schocken Books, 114–28.

Bubis, Gerald, and Harry Wasserman. 1983. *Synagogue Havurot: A Comparative Study*. Washington, D.C.: The University Press of America.

Cohen, Steven M. 1983. *American Modernity and Jewish Identity*. New York: Tavistock.

Douglas, Mary. 1975. "Jokes." In *Implicit Meanings: Essays in Anthropology.* New York: Routledge & Kegan Paul, 90–114.

Encyclopedia Judaica. 1971. "Purim." Vol. 13. New York: Macmillan.

Gaster, Theodore. 1950. *Purim and Hanukkah.* New York: Henry Schuman.

Geertz, Clifford. 1973. "Deep Play: Notes on the Balinese Cockfight." In *The Interpretation of Cultures.* New York: Basic Books, 412–53.

Goldstein, Sidney, and Calvin Goldscheider. 1968. *Jewish Americans: Three Generations in a Jewish Community.* Englewood Cliffs, N.J.: Prentice-Hall.

Handelman, Don, and Bruce Kapferer. 1972. "Forms of Joking Activity: A Comparative Approach." *American Anthropologist* 74:484–517.

Heilman, Samuel. 1982. "The Sociology of American Jewry: The Last Ten Years." *Annual Review of Sociology* 8:35–60.

———. 1983. *People of the Book: Drama, Fellowship, and Religion.* Chicago: University of Chicago Press.

Kapferer, Bruce. 1983. *A Celebration of Demons: Exorcism and the Aesthetics of Healing in Sri Lanka.* Bloomington: Indiana University Press.

Kirshenblatt-Gimblett, Barbara. 1982. "The Cut That Binds: The Western Ashkenazic Torah Binder as Nexus between Circumcision and Torah." In *Celebrations: Studies in Festivity and Ritual,* ed. Victor Turner. Washington D.C.: Smithsonian Institution Press, 136–46.

Kuper, Hilda. 1963. *The Swazi: A South African Kingdom.* New York: Holt, Rinehart and Winston.

Liebman, Charles. 1973. *The Ambivalent American Jew.* Philadelphia: Jewish Publication Society.

———. 1982. "The Religious Life of American Jewry." In *Understanding American Jewry,* ed. Marshall Sklare. New Brunswick, N.J.: Transaction Books, 96–124.

Miller, Frank C. 1967. "Humor in a Chippewa Tribal Council." *Ethnology* 6:263–71.

Myerhoff, Barbara G. 1974. *Peyote Hunt: The Sacred Journey of the Huichol Indians.* Ithaca: Cornell University Press.

———. 1979. *Number Our Days.* New York: Dutton.

Neusner, Jacob. 1972. *Contemporary Jewish Fellowship in Theory and Practice.* New York: Ktav.

Prell, Riv-Ellen. 1988. *Prayer and Community: The Havurah Movement and the Recreation of American Judaism.* Detroit: Wayne State University Press.

———. 1987. "Sacred Categories and Social Relations: The Visibility and Invisibility of Gender in an American Jewish Community." In *Judaism Viewed from Within and from Without,* ed. Harvey Goldberg. Albany: State University of New York, 171–94.

Prell-Foldes, Riv-Ellen. 1978a. "Coming of Age in Kelton: The Constraints of Gender Symbolism in Jewish Ritual." In *Women in Ritual and Symbolic Roles,* ed. Judith Hoch-Smith and Anita Spring. New York: Plenum Press. 75–100.

———. 1978b. "Strategies in Conflict Situations: Ritual and Redress in an Urban Jewish Community." Ph.D. diss., University of Chicago, Department of Anthropology.

Radcliffe-Brown, A. R. 1952a. "A Further Note on Joking Relationships." In *Structure and Function in Primitive Society.* New York: Free Press, 105–16.

------. 1952b. "On Joking Relationships." In *Structure and Function in Primitive Society*. New York: Free Press, 90–114.

Reisman, Bernard. 1977. *The Chavurah: A Contemporary Jewish Experience*. New York: Union of American Hebrew Congregations.

Scholem, G. G. 1941. *Major Trends in Jewish Mysticism*. Jerusalem: Schocken Books.

Sklare, Marshall. 1972. *Conservative Judaism: An American Religious Movement*. New York: Shocken Books.

Sleeper, James, and Alan L. Mintz, eds. 1971. *The New Jews*. New York: Vintage Press.

Turner, Victor W. 1967. *The Forest of Symbols: Aspects of Ndembu Ritual*. Ithaca: Cornell University Press.

Turner, Victor W. 1977. "Variations on a Theme of Liminality." In *Secular Ritual: Form and Meanings*, ed. Sally Falk Moore and Barbara G. Myerhoff. Assen: Van Gorcum, 36–52.

Weissler, Lenore. 1982. "Making Judaism Meaningful: Ambivalence and Tradition in a Havurah Community." Ph.D. diss., University of Pennsylvania, Department of Folklore and Folklife.

SECTION THREE

Us and Them

[9]

A Goy in the Ghetto: Gentile-Jewish Communication in Fieldwork Research

William E. Mitchell

Early in my career as an anthropologist, I joined a small team of social scientists planning a study of New York City Jewish families. An important part of my work for the study was to interview family members in their homes. As a Gentile from Kansas, I knew that my cultural background was very different from theirs, so I asked two Jewish male social scientist friends born and raised in New York City for advice. With devastating frankness I was told that my "cool WASP manner" would "scare the wits" out of my interviewees. As Kansas men are generally open and friendly—we smile a lot—I was discomforted by their view of me. But that was only the beginning.

My body language, they said, was too detached, too placid. They were concerned that I rarely gestured and, when I did, the gesture was so small and anemic that it was barely discernible. Besides, my gestures were all wrong; they were woodenly symmetrical rather than creatively baroque. They insisted that if I were to work successfully with New York City Jewish families of Eastern European background, I must look more "bright-eyed" and act "more lively." And, while they assured me that my speech patterns were not as retarded and heavily accented as those of some midwesterners, it was obvious that I must "speed it up."

For comments on a draft of this essay, I am grateful to Jack Kugelmass, Annette B. Weiner, and Jonathan B. Weiner.

If I could not make these important behavioral accommodations, the research, according to my friends, would be a disaster. The families would find me "strange" and feel "uncomfortable" and "anxious" as long as I was around. In other words, if I wanted good rapport I would have to change. "Sure you're a Gentile," they seemed to be saying. "But you don't have to act like one!"

The personal experiences on which this chapter is based come from two separate but related studies of New York City Jewish families of Eastern European background (Leichter and Mitchell 1978; Mitchell 1980). The parent research project, "Studies in Social Interaction," was carried out with a large group of families who were clients of the Jewish Family Service of New York. Our primary research interest was in the extent and nature of the relationships these households of parents and children had with their other relatives and in the ways social workers assigned to the families intervened to support or change these relationships.

During this research we "discovered" an unusual kind of urban descent group, organized as clubs called "family circles" or "cousins' clubs," and I made a separate study (Mitchell 1980) on the history, organization, and functioning of these groups, which included individuals and families completely unrelated to the parent project. In both studies, I made interview visits to my informants' homes or places of business and also attended some of the family clubs' meetings and parties.[1]

How one "acts" in the research role, as my two friends knew, is a significant factor affecting rapport in behavioral research, which may directly affect the outcome of the research itself. Behavioral scientists often consider "good rapport" as the *sine qua non* for "good research." It is an especially crucial dimension for an anthropologist who is studying cultural groups that in some ways are very unlike one's own. In these instances, the anthropologist must be overtly sensitive to the customs and behavioral nuances of his own culture as well as that of one's hosts.

I was aware, as were my two friends, that they were informing me about my own subculture as well as telling me about theirs, because anthropological rapport is a culturally symbiotic relationship. There must be a behavioral "fit" between the anthropologist and his informants for trust and understanding—essential ingredients in all anthropological research—to grow. If the anthropologist's behavior signifies a culturally antithetical persona, the informant will warily withdraw and the research most certainly will flounder. So it is the anthropologist as "cultural guest" who must make the accommodating moves in order to win the approval and cooperation of informants.

Depending on the society studied, these behavioral accommodations may take a variety of forms. For example, on my first research project, I worked with college-educated Chinese from mainland China living in New York City (Hinkle et al. 1957). To gain their respect and establish rapport, I learned to sit much more quietly than is my usual wont and to ask personally sensitive questions indirectly. Fortunately, I already knew how to maintain a smile, because that too was important.

An even greater challenge for establishing behavioral rapport came on a field trip to Papua New Guinea (Mitchell 1987). Although American men generally avoid touching one another except for a ritual handshake or an occasional brusque slap on the back, men of the Wape tribe with whom I lived have close physical relationships. Gathered together in the men's house, they visit amiably with legs intertwined and arms draped across one anothers' bodies as if they were their own. And among the Iatmul, another New Guinea group I lived with, young men who are good friends sometimes stroll through the village holding hands by clasping their little fingers. To the men of these societies such actions are commonplace, but for me they were emotionally charged experiences. I was not aware of the affective strength behind the touching taboo of American males until I was in New Guinea and felt my personal space and body being "violated" by my new friends. My response was an almost overwhelming desire to pull away and draw myself in. Although I did not withdraw from their friendly touching and holding, it was only gradually that I learned to relax and enjoy their intimate camaraderie.

These fieldwork experiences may strike some as essentially trivial or inconsequential and not, as I perceive them, critical examples of building rapport. Or some may view the anthropologist's behavioral adaptations to the host culture as contrived and manipulative. That would be unfortunate, because the motivation for "fitting in" goes far beyond the constraints of research methodology, important as that is. It also is intrinsically related to the strong humanist concern of anthropologists who spend years in the field augmenting their understanding of human nature, culture, and themselves. These behav-

[227]

iorally transforming fieldwork experiences serve the anthropologist as powerful entrées into the host culture. By adapting one's behavior to that of one's informants, a sense of empathy may be generated and the work of learning the culture gets under way. This does not mean, however, that the anthropologist goes "native," nor am I espousing the "sentimental view of rapport as depending on the enfolding of anthropologist and informant into a single moral, emotional, and intellectual universe" that Clifford Geertz justly criticizes (1967:12).

These personal fieldwork experiences are important because they help give the anthropologist a sense of the host culture and its behavioral parameters. The fieldworker begins to get the "feel" of the culture almost unwittingly as he succeeds in occasionally "fitting in" or else receives a polite rebuke. Once, as a large group of New Guinea village children rushed onto our temporary and dangerously rickety porch, I called out loudly for them to get off. The children fled in terror. A nearby villager turned toward me, his hushed voice filled with embarrassed anguish, and said, "Speak gently!" My face burned with shame. But it was a lesson in Wape manners I never forgot.

This problem of how to communicate with one's informants and establish rapport in the field is an important methodological issue in modern anthropology.[2] "Communication," or more properly in this context, "interpersonal communication," specifically refers to face-to-face or two-way communication. It is concerned with the transmission of behavioral messages and how these messages are interpreted by others. In other words, the interpretation or "meaning" is separate from the act or "messages." In this sense, communication is the process of creating a meaning from a message (Tubbs and Moss 1974:6). As my two Jewish friends had wisely advised me, the meaning my Jewish informants undoubtedly would give to my behavioral messages was "this man is a *goy*, beware!"

When I joined the Jewish family research project I had little personal experience regarding Jewish-Gentile relations in American society. I did know that anti-Semitism was a chilling reality in American life, and, as an anthropologist, I was certainly aware of the importance of cultural differences. But in my personal life I tended to play down ethnic differences among my friends and was impressed by the common humanity of New Yorkers amid such polyglot cultural diversity. So it came to me as a surprise when my two Jewish friends found my behavior and style of interaction so disturbingly different.

[228]

The social division between Gentiles and Jews is an ancient one, although what is meant by "Gentile" depends upon the context. The term comes from the Latin and means "of the same clan or race." Formerly it was used by Christians to refer to "heathens," is presently used by Mormons to refer to non-Mormons, and of course by Jews to refer to non-Jews, especially Christians. But for this paper I will use the Yiddish term *goy* (*goyim*, pl.) to refer to the non-Jew because it is a more culturally salient concept for the problem at hand. While "Gentile" is a somewhat neutral term, *goy* is loaded with cultural meaning based on the Jewish experience as a persecuted minority in the Diaspora. As used by Jews, it is a pejorative term, referring to someone who is "dull, insensitive, heartless." As Leo Rosten points out in his discussion of the term, centuries of Jewish persecution have left a legacy of bitter sayings about the *goyim;* for example, *"Dos ken nor a goy,"* translated from the Yiddish means "That, only a *goy* would do!" Or the exclamation of exasperation *"A goy!"* is used "when endurance is exhausted, kindliness depleted, the effort to understand useless" (Rosten 1970:142).

It was during my research that I first became aware of the Jewish view of a distinct Jewish-Gentile cultural dichotomy characterized by the *goy* as a symbol of callousness and danger; the kind of person one tries to avoid if possible. As my informants led me into their perceptual world, I too, albeit reluctantly, began to see individuals in terms of this dichotomy. I was so deeply imprinted with this ethnic duality during the research experience that it has been one of the most enduring personal effects of the study. Learning firsthand about the inexorableness of ethnic divisions was an emotionally powerful experience because it challenged and in some ways shattered my youthful "one world" idealism. An early response is recorded in my notebook:

This family circle meeting was the first time I was accosted with a Jewish-Gentile dichotomy. It was presented to me in several quite personal ways. Some pleasant and some joking; others that were to me of a negative tinge. Aunt Edith, who is fifty, kept coming up to me and telling me how fine the Jews were, that the Jews and Gentiles should learn to get together, that the Jews want to get along with the Gentiles, that most Jews are fine people like here at the family circle; all they want to do is to be friends with the Gentiles, isn't it a shame the way the Jews are sometimes treated, etc. I was quite amazed by all of this talk and even more at a loss at how to handle the indomitable interaction

[229]

entrances. It all seemed quite irrevelant and annoyed me that I was being accepted—provisionally—as a "good" Gentile rather than as a fellow human being.

In my research with other cultural groups, for example, with the Chinese and the Papua New Guineans, it was obvious to them that I was an outsider because of my light skin color, but with my Jewish informants, the situation was not so clear. Racially we were Caucasians, but culturally speaking, there were significant differences.[3] While I doubt if any of my informants seriously believed I was Jewish, it still was very important to them that they be absolutely sure. They knew that the research was sponsored in part by a Jewish social-work agency and that we were studying Jewish family-kin relationships. The question seemed to be "What's he here for if he's not Jewish?"

During the interviews at the beginning of the research, an informant would usually pause at some point and, eyebrows raised, diffidently ask, "You Jewish?" During one interview, an informant's elderly mother came into the room, and after listening to our conversation for awhile asked the inevitable question. When I said, "No," she shook her head sagely and replied in a strong Yiddish accent, "You don't look Jewish!" The point is that an unambiguous ethnic placement of me was very important to my informants. They needed to know if I was an "insider" or an "outsider." Did I "belong" or didn't I? So I learned to volunteer during our first meeting that I was not Jewish and to offer other personal information about myself. While the New Guinea Wape were singularly uninterested in my cultural background, my Jewish informants seemed pleased when I gave them information that placed me in a fuller and deeper social perspective. So instead of waiting to be pumped for personal data, I could always count on an amused expression, for example, when I volunteered that I was born and raised in Wichita, Kansas.

In some of the Jewish homes that I visited, I was something of an "event" because I was the first *goy* guest. Many of my informants lived in an almost entirely Jewish world—socially ghettoized, if not physically so—in all their significant relationships with their neighbors, fellow-workers, friends and, of course, relatives. This is possible in a city of several million Jews, where large sections of the city and even certain industries have become predominately Jewish in composition. For persons who have spent most of their lives in an almost totally Jewish milieu, social relations with *goyim* are unusual, and when they do occur, they are touched with apprehension. After a pleasant visit with a Jewish family accompanied by an informant, I learned that I was the first "WASP" to have entered the home. My informant's comment about our hostess was, "I bet she sighed a sigh of relief when you went out the door!"

This sort of apprehensiveness was reflected in most of my initial interviews with informant families. There was always an initial hesitation on my first visit, a kind of cautious stiffness that I interpreted as manifesting misgivings, perhaps even overt suspiciousness. But that mood was never sustained. I found that the best way to break it was to begin collecting a genealogy as soon as possible. As we set to work on the family's genealogy, with brown wrapping paper spread out on the kitchen table and usually a soft drink and cookies on the side, the tension would subside. Most of my informants became intensely engrossed in watching the social and cultural dimensions of their family network unfold before their eyes. "My," one woman exclaimed with enthusiasm, "isn't this interesting!"

However, there was always a certain amount of bemusement that I, a *goy*, was studying Jews. There was something wrong—intrusive maybe—that this *goy*, this outsider, was trying to get "inside" Jewish family life. This "wonderment" regarding my involvement in the research project was primarily expressed to me via joking comments. Not only did my informants seem a bit muddled and amused about my research role, but so did my New York Jewish friends and colleagues. At the time I did not know how to interpret this levity; I know I failed to see the humor of my role to the extent that they did. For me it was a serious and fascinating research project and my involvement did not strike me as odd or "funny." I could not help but feel that the smiles and laughter were tinged with disapproval; that the joking response was covering up at least some resentment toward this presumptuous *goy* trying to penetrate Jewish family life.

But once I was accepted, family members went out of their way to make me feel as though I were not the relative stranger that I obviously was. Still, there were often problems if my informant had to go beyond her or his immediate family to get information or to grant me permission to attend a specific family function. That entailed the inevitable explanation of who I was and why I wanted what I wanted. Sometimes the explanations didn't make much sense to older family members whose suspicions about the *goyim* had been documented not just by social discrimination and negative insinuations but by

[231]

horrifying personal experiences in Eastern Europe and the genocidal murder of close relatives.

Because of my own idealism regarding intergroup interactions and because I was an "integrated" member of a Jewish social agency, I initially was unaware of any emotional connection between the Holocaust and my research role. I could remember as an impressionable teen-ager the photos and newsreels of the German concentration camps and the terrifying impact they had upon me, so it never occurred to me that such heinous events could be associated, even remotely, with my research. I can recall the sickening feeling I had when a male informant during the last week of interviewing wise-cracked that I was collecting Jewish genealogies for "a giant Manhattan concentration camp." I laughed, but I was so struck by the monstrousness of the comment that I wrote it down. I was puzzled how a man of my own age and American-born could bring such a macabre association to my research. Then three days later, while interviewing another informant, the "concentration camp" image appeared again. I wrote in my notebook: "[My informant] said that he had asked his uncle, who is president of their Family Circle, for the documents and explained what I was doing. The uncle was skeptical and joked about my collecting all of the family names for a concentration camp. [My informant] said it was doubtful if he could get the documents for me."

The *goyim* issue was a pervasive problem that influenced all of my informant relationships. Establishing rapport undoubtedly would have been easier had I been a Jew, but as an outsider, I was able to see some things more clearly and with less distorting personal involvement than would a member of the group.[4] However, there were other problems less specifically ethnic in origin that in some instances also affected my relationships with informants.

Informant disapproval is not a unique response to anthropological research, especially in literate societies. To be "studied" is seen by some people as demeaning; that one is being treated as an object rather than as a human being. I occasionally ran into this type of resistance, especially when I tried to gain access to family social events and was turned away because some family members didn't want to be "studied." Family affairs, including meetings of family clubs, were generally considered private activities where relatives could relax and have fun. The presence of a researcher, I was once told, would be "a damper" on the festivities.[5] There was also the problem of the popular view that anthropologists are primarily interested in "primitive peoples," hardly a flattering observation to a "civilized" person and his group. "A sociologist," said one informant, "I can understand, but why an anthropologist?"[6] Morton Fried had a similar problem when, on beginning his anthropological fieldwork in east-central China, he was summoned to appear at the office of the county magistrate. "The magistrate was polite but cold: an anthropological study of his country was an affront; anthropologists, said the magistrate, studied only savages and barbarians" (1959:351).

There are, however, communication problems other than those directly related to informant rapport that have an impact upon the research process and on the anthropologist's understanding of what is happening. Among these is the way the anthropologist interprets an informant's "interaction style," that is, the culturally patterned actions that characterize how a person initiates or responds to others. The anthropologist, like all other human beings, is culturally trained from infancy to interpret and to respond to behavioral patterns of her own culture in a specific and often unconscious way. So when working in another culture, the anthropologist is always at risk of projecting a behavioral interpretation from her own culture onto the one being studied.

Anthropologists call this phenomenon "ethnocentrism," and they recognize it as a common cause of distortion and misunderstanding between individuals of different ethnic backgrounds. Although a behavioral act in two different cultures may appear to be the same, the social meaning of the act can vary; what looks like one thing in the terms of one's own culture may have a very different meaning in the terms of the host culture. During the first months of the research, as I was learning about the culture and its characteristic interaction style, I frequently misinterpreted an informant's behavior.

Initially, I was somewhat abashed by my informants' familiarity and verbal frankness. As a group they were quick to express their personal views, even very negative ones, about their relatives and family affairs. Their extreme candor about "family skeletons" as well as their boasting about family accomplishments occasionally embarrassed me. I was unaccustomed to such bold forthrightness—it was almost the reverse of my own subculture and of the Chinese I had previously studied. And while I might marvel at their unreserved and seemingly uncensored presentation of themselves and their families, I wondered how family members could endure such brashness without alienating one another.

Although they treated me kindly as a guest in their homes, they felt no constraint or need to defer politely to me, as my Chinese informants had done. If I made some passing and to me innocuous comment, I might be directly challenged with an opposing view. If they thought I had misunderstood or not comprehended a point in the interview, they would abruptly correct me or ruefully continue their explanation. They were excellent informants, willing to instruct me in details but ever-ready to chide me if they thought I didn't understand completely. Most of them quickly grasped the nature of my study, even anticipating my next question and volunteering data before I had the presence of mind to ask for it. It was exciting research, fast-paced and fully developed, but it wasn't what I would call "easy." It demanded a great deal of mental discipline because the data and their nuances appeared so rapidly. It was very different from my later work with the New Guinea Lujere (Mitchell 1977), in which some of my informant interviews moved so slowly that I could occasionally daydream about home and still keep track of what was being said in a foreign language.

But there was no time to daydream with my Jewish informants. I was too busy keeping abreast of the interview's action. At first, I tended to misinterpret their avid outspokenness and abrupt corrections and comments as "put-downs" of myself. It seemed as if I could do nothing right and that nothing was sacred; if they had a view, it existed to be expressed. Even my own cultural background did not escape critical commentary. Once, in an interview on Jewish weddings I commented that the gift-giving of money was different from my family's custom:

MRS. X: Well, you are not Jewish, or no?
WM: No.
MRS. X: No, then that's the difference. The style is entirely different! I know in your case they usually bring gifts in their display.
WM: That's right.
MRS. X: And everyone brings a piece of junk, and by the time you get through, half that stuff is thrown out. You don't even use it. Am I right?

This kind of critical forthrightness, to my chagrin, would sometimes throw me off balance. However, as I learned not to withdraw—for that only made the interviewee more impatient and anxious—my interviews became both more interesting and more valuable. My informant seemed more comfortable because she had someone to "push" against or disagree with. I also learned that it wasn't really important for us to agree; no one had to "win." It was the disputation or "status jockeying" that was important; it made the interaction sequence exciting, and, I can't help thinking now, not blandly *goyish*.

Learning this disputatious interaction style was a challenge because it was different from my own more circumspect cultural style, in which one should protect the feelings of the other person and open disagreements, especially with relative strangers, are avoided. There is, however, a special exhilaration in the disputatious style. It is bold and assertive and intellectually stimulating. One must think quickly to marshall evidence for a convincing riposte. What once would have seemed like an inappropriate argument came to feel like a stimulating discussion about a disagreement. Later, when I asked an informant about conflicts or arguments in relation to her family circle organization, I knew exactly what she meant when she smilingly replied, "Oh, we don't have arguments! We have disagreements!" Nevertheless, because a disputatious interaction style involves interpersonal conflict, it flirts with danger. A lively discussion may easily move into genuine quarreling if a participant "pushes" too hard, is too intractable, or is insulting. [7]

Related to this assertive interaction style is the phenomenon of "overtalking," that is, two or more individuals speaking simultaneously. Again, this was different from my own subculture where it is considered either "rude" or "aggressive" to speak when another person is talking. To keep from losing control of an interview when my informant interrupted me, I learned how to "overtalk" by raising my voice as I persisted in asking a question or making a comment. However, I never succeeded in feeling at ease with this tactic. The problem was even more difficult when I did a family interview with parents and children. Verbatim transcriptions of these interviews presented a complex methodological problem when, for example, the wife, husband, teen-age daughter, and I were each verbally competing for attention.

In an important way, then, this essay is about language—language used in its widest application to include the symbolic displays of both the voice and the body. I have emphasized the differences in these communicative displays between Gentiles and Jews as exemplified by my personal experiences as an anthropologist studying New York City Jewish families of Eastern European ethnic background. It is an anthropological truism that our culture helps to shape the way we perceive ourselves and others. It is also true that intimate experience with another culture can affect one's perceptions and understanding. In the Jewish research, I learned that I was a *goy*, a pejorative term signifying that I was a callous outsider and potential enemy. My physical appearance and style of interaction further corroborated the cultural differences between myself and my informants. These were cultural facts embedded in deep and compelling cultural histories. Nothing I might do could completely change or transcend them.

There is an old Yiddish saying *"A goy blaybt a goy!"* that translates loosely as "Once a *goy*, always a *goy!*" I was a *goy*, but in my role as an anthropologist, I made a concerted attempt to modify my *goyisher kop*, my "Gentile ways." By consciously working to accommodate my behavior and interaction style to that of my Jewish informants, I was able to feel my way into the host culture and gradually to develop a sense of empathy and "connectedness" that facilitated the communication process. Although I never completely attained the easy verbal and gestural expressiveness of my Jewish informants (or, for that matter, the easy physical intimacy of my Wape male informants), I did attain an approximation that made me feel and look less behaviorally foreign. And once I understood that my informants' disputatious interaction style was not a personal attack but an elaborated form of provocative play, I could enter into the exchange without fear of hurting someone's feelings or suffering a damaged ego myself.

At the end of this project, I moved to northern Vermont to work with rural and village families and there I encountered yet another problem in cultural adaption. Compared to the placid mien of many rural Vermont Yankee males, my indigenous Kansas style of interaction was rather lively, and when it was augmented by the expressive behaviors learned during the Jewish project, it became explosively dynamic. My wife, a native Vermonter, admonished me to modify my interaction style. There, it was the "village idiot," not the successful man, who cultivated verbal and behavioral expressiveness.

Communication problems are a "given" of anthropological fieldwork. The nature of the problems and how they are revealed depends upon the culture of the anthropologist and the culture of the informant. The extent to which the anthropologist is successful in adapting his behavior patterns to those of the host culture will vary greatly. It is a problem area that has had little, if any, formal discussion among anthropologists, although it is a crucial dimension of fieldwork that may have enduring effects on the anthropologist's life. Each group with whom an anthropologist works, if he is sensitive to the kinds of communication problems explored in this essay, helps to change and/or augment his behavioral repertoire. In this sense, fieldwork research is a transforming experience.

My research with New York City Jewish families was no exception. Like most anthropological fieldwork, it has had a lasting influence upon me. Learning about the profound rigidity of ethnic divisions was, in spite of my Kansas optimism, a disillusioning experience. But my personal life also has been enriched by learning a lively cultural style of interaction quite different from my own. Perhaps of even more significance, I learned something my Jewish informants and their families have known for centuries: how it feels to be a dangerous outsider.

Notes

1. The parent project was cosponsored by the Jewish Family Service of New York and the Russell Sage Foundation. The project was directed by Hope Jensen Leichter and the regular research staff included Fred Davis, Judith Lieb, Alice Liu Szema, Dianne Tendler, Candace Rogers, and myself. A detailed account of the samples, methodology, and findings of this study are reported in Leichter and Mitchell (1978). For similar information on the study of Jewish family clubs, see Mitchell (1980). The majority of the data for both studies was collected between 1958 and 1962.
2. See, e.g., Freilich (1970); Hammersley and Atkinson (1983); Lawless et al. (1983); Mead (1970); and Pelto and Pelto (1973). More recently, some anthropologists, e.g., Marcus and Fischer (1986), Ruby (1982), and Stocking (1983), have developed a critical interest in the anthropologist's fieldwork experience in a particular society and how this is reflected in resulting publications.
3. Although Jews are sometimes collectively called "the Jewish race," this term is scientifically incorrect. Race is a biological concept. The great variation among Jews in terms of physical characteristics disqualifies them from being counted as a race per se. See, e.g., Newman (1965:21–30) and Shapiro (1960).
4. For example, even Jewish social scientists who were members of a "family circle" or "cousins' club" did not recognize the uniqueness of these urban descent groups in the ethnographic record or their importance for kinship theory, but tended to react to them as annoyances that demanded an occasional appearance at a meeting or special event.
5. This negative response to anthropological research has become a frequent response in the Third World, where anthropologists are sometimes viewed as having been handmaidens to an exploitative colonialism and are now barred from doing fieldwork. See, e.g., Strathern (1983).
6. It is true that it is very unusual for a Gentile to study and publish on Jewish life. As Mayer has noted, "the sociology of Jews has been written almost exclusively by Jews" (1973:152).

7. For substantive data on conflict among Jews of Eastern European descent and on their cultural background, see Leichter and Mitchell (1978:166–84), Mitchell (1978:155–68), and Zborowski and Herzog (1952).

REFERENCES

Fried, Morton H. 1959. *Readings in Anthropology.* vol. 2. New York: Thomas Y. Crowell.

Freilich, Morris, ed. 1970. *Marginal Natives: Anthropologists at Work.* New York: Harper & Row.

Geertz, Clifford. 1967. "Under the Mosquito Net." *New York Review of Books* 9:12–13.

Hammersley, Martyn, and Paul Atkinson. 1983. *Ethnography: Principles in Practice.* London: Tavistock.

Hinkel, Lawrence, et al. 1957. "Factors Relevant to the Occurrence of Bodily Illness and Disturbances in Mood, Thought, and Behavior in Three Homogeneous Population Groups." *American Journal of Psychiatry* 114:212–20.

Lawless, Robert, et al., eds. 1983. *Fieldwork: The Human Experience.* New York: Gordon and Breach.

Leichter, Hope Jensen, and William E. Mitchell. 1978. *Kinship and Casework: Family Networks and Social Intervention.* New York: Teachers College Press.

Marcus, George E., and Michael M. J. Fischer. 1986. *Anthropology as Cultural Critique: An Experimental Moment in the Human Sciences.* Chicago: University of Chicago Press.

Mayer, Egon. 1973. "Jewish Orthodoxy in America: Towards the Sociology of a Residual Category." *Jewish Journal of Sociology* 15:151–65.

Mead, Margaret. 1970. "The Art and Technique of Fieldwork." In *Handbook of Method in Cultural Anthropology,* ed. Raoul Naroll and Ronald Cohen. New York: Columbia University Press.

Mitchell, William E. 1977. "Sorcellerie chamanique: Sanguma chez les Lujere du cours supérieur de Sépik." *Journal de la Société des Océanistes* 33:178–89.

——. 1980. *Mishpokhe: A Study of New York City Jewish Family Clubs.* 2d ed. Hawthorne: Aldine.

——. 1987. *The Bamboo Fire: Field Work with the New Guinea Wape.* 2d ed. Prospects Heights: Waveland Press.

Newman, Louis I. 1965. *The Jewish People, Faith and Life.* New York: Bloch.

Pelto, Pertti J., and Gretel H. Pelto. 1973. "Ethnography: The Fieldwork Enterprise." In *Handbook of Social and Cultural Anthropology,* ed. John J. Honigmann. Chicago: Rand McNally.

Rosten, Leo. 1970. *The Joys of Yiddish.* New York: Simon and Schuster.

Ruby, Jay, ed. 1982. *A Crack in the Mirror: Reflexive Perspectives in Anthropology.* Philadelphia: University of Pennsylvania Press.

Shapiro, Harry I. 1960. *The Jewish People: A Biological History.* Paris: Unesco.

Stocking, George W., Jr., ed. 1983. *Observers Observed: Essays on Ethnographic Fieldwork.* Madison: University of Wisconsin Press.

Strathern, Andrew. 1983. "Research in Papua New Guinea: Cross-Currents of Conflict." *Royal Anthropological Institute News*, no. 58:4–10.

Tubbs, Stewart L., and Sylvia Moss. 1974. *Human Communication: An Interpersonal Perspective.* New York: Random House.

Zborowski, Mark, and Elizabeth Herzog. 1952. *Life Is with People.* New York: International Universities Press.

[10]

"Salim's Going to Be Muslim Someday": The Negotiated Identities of an American Jewish Ethnographer

Shalom Staub

On Rosh Hashanah, September 1975, I attended services in a Yemeni Jewish village in Israel. A young American Jewish graduate student, I had taken up residence in a village household to conduct field research on Yemeni Jewish music and dance. Despite our common bonds as Jews, the village elders were suspicious of me. As an American, they associated me with everything that pulled the young people away from their traditions. By attending services at the village synagogue regularly, I sought to dispel this suspicion and to demonstrate the sincerity of my purpose. Observing the auctioning of *aliyot*, the honor of being called to the Torah, I hit upon a strategy to demonstrate the level of my interest in Yemeni cultural traditions. I would read from the Torah on the following day. Since I had studied the passages on the binding of Isaac some years before, I had virtually memorized the Torah portion for the second day of Rosh Hashanah. I also knew the proper Yemeni pronunciation of the Hebrew, and I had a basic mastery of the traditional Yemeni Torah cantillation.

I practiced with Haim, my host, and we agreed that he would bid on my behalf for the honor of reading the Torah on the second day of Rosh Hashanah. It was a presumptive plan. As an Ashkenazi Jew, the

Editor's note: The system of Hebrew transliteration used here reflects the pronunciation of Modern Hebrew rather than the Ashkenazic pronunciation used elsewhere in this volume.

villagers would not expect me to be able to read according to Yemeni custom. In the Yemeni tradition, all Jewish men are expected to be able to recite from the Torah on any occasion. Biblical verses are chanted according to a cantillation specific to the Yemeni community and pronounced according to the Yemeni Hebrew dialect. When Ashkenazi guests visit the village synagogue, the Yemeni Jews honor their guests by allowing the Ashkenazim to recite the Torah blessings in Ashkenazi Hebrew; however, the villagers will not permit the Torah to be recited in anything but the Yemeni style.

The second day of Rosh Hashanah arrived, and I started to get nervous. If I didn't meet the community's standards on this occasion, I risked losing the villagers' respect. I listened carefully as the first reader recited the blessings and biblical verses, rehearsing the proper pronunciation and melody in my mind. I waited impatiently as Haim outbid all others for the *aliyah*. As I stood up to approach the Torah, the men around me assumed that I had gotten up to leave. They cautioned me not to leave during the Torah reading. It didn't occur to them that Haim had purchased the *aliyah* for me. I put my *tallit* [prayer shawl] over my head, as I had seen all the Yemeni men do as they approached the Torah scroll, which stood in its hard case on the reader's table in the center of the room. One man pointed to the place, about five lines that were left uncovered by the brightly colored scarves draped over the parchment. Just as I was about to start, there was a commotion over allowing me to recite the verses. Haim lobbied to let me read and he prevailed in the argument. I touched the scroll with my *tallit*, recited the blessings, and read the biblical verses.

As I returned to my seat, Saadya, a village leader, took my hand on the right and Mori Yaish, the village rabbinical authority, took my hand on the left. "*Ḥazak barukh* [May you be strengthened and blessed]," said Saadya, using the traditional congratulatory greeting for the synagogue setting. Mori Yaish added, "*Kol hakavod* [All the honor]," the equivalent modern Hebrew phrase. Many more men greeted me after the service. I became the day's topic of conversation, particularly because I had read in "the true Yemeni accent." Saadya later added, "You don't know how much you raised yourself in the eyes of the community for doing this." The following week in synagogue, one of the men asked me if I wanted the honor of reciting the Torah in his place. I declined, not having practiced beforehand. Saadya declared to the other villagers, "He's already a *ḥaver moshav*," a full member of the village.

Of course I was never really a *haver moshav* in a strict sense, although I did enjoy a close relationship with the villagers over the fifteen months of my residence and contact with them. I lived with several different families, was taken into their homes, and felt like a family member. Some villagers affectionately called me "Salim," the Yemeni form of my name. As I participated in village activities and gained extensive knowledge of particular folkloric expressions, villagers called me *yamani abyadh,* "a white Yemeni." I had a genuine interest in participating fully in village life. As a Jew and as an anthropologist, I wanted to experience the richness of daily, weekly, and yearly rites in this Yemeni Jewish agricultural village. In the course of my stay, I decided to pursue a career in Jewish ethnography.

After returning to Wesleyan University to complete my thesis, I considered various options for doctoral training in anthropology and folklore. I finally decided to pursue my interest in Middle Eastern Jewish folklore by enrolling at the University of Pennsylvania's Department of Folklore and Folklife. I began to study Arabic, since older Yemeni Jewish men and women continue to speak Arabic. Many of the traditional songs are in Arabic, and many Yemeni Jews tell stories whose punchlines are delivered in Arabic.

As I began to think about my dissertation plans, one of my professors, Ray Birdwhistell, urged me to consider doing field research with a non-Jewish community. He argued that my interests in Jewish folklore would remain strong and that I needed the experience of working in a non-Jewish community. I countered that although I shared a common religious background with Yemeni Jews, there was a world of difference between my experience as an American Jew and theirs as Middle Eastern Jews. Birdwhistell responded with several good arguments. A new setting would expand my understanding of cultural dynamics. I would become more versatile in my research and teaching interests, and therefore I would increase my employment opportunities.

I strongly resisted Birdwhistell's arguments, yet I wondered whether or not my setting up a professional boundary encompassing only Jewish communities was intellectually justified. Was I simply unable to reconcile my own observance of Jewish tradition with the role of a participant observer in a Gentile environment? By studying only traditional Jewish communities, no one would challenge my observance of the Sabbath and Jewish dietary laws. Despite my initial resistance, I did feel a growing curiousity to follow Birdwhistell's suggestion. My definition of a "Jewish folklorist" began to change from one who works exclusively within Jewish environments to one who also works within a Gentile environment. Indeed, working in both affords a useful comparative framework that enhances an understanding of Jewish culture.

Once I allowed for the possibility of not working with Yemeni Jews, I began to consider an appropriate new topic of study. I was reluctant to waste my three years of studying Arabic, so I had a strong interest in working with another Middle Eastern community. But my wife's career and our desire to start a family ruled out overseas field research. I remembered hearing of a community of Yemeni Muslims in New York City. Since I had already done fieldwork among Yemeni Jews in Israel and in New York City, working with Yemeni Muslims had a certain allure. I was interested in studying immigrant culture and I would utilize the Arabic I had learned. At the time, I had no immediate intention of linking my earlier work on Yemeni Jews with the work I was planning on Yemeni Muslims, but I knew that ethnographic research with one group would add greatly to my understanding of the other. Despite the fact that working among Muslims might pose a real challenge to my personal Jewish observance, I now felt that this new project would round out my training as a Jewish folklorist.

The decision to attempt an ethnographic study of a Middle Eastern Muslim community through participant observation would challenge my Jewish identity and ritual practice in ways I could not anticipate at the outset. I recognized that this fieldwork would inevitably force me to confront choices, for I knew that in some cases, the appropriate behavior for an ethnographer was bound to conflict with my practice as a Jew. There would be some limits to this conflict (Islam forbids pork consumption as does Judaism, for example), but the daily schedule of fieldwork and vital personal interactions revolving around food consumption would force me to negotiate my identity and make compromises in these situations. In a sense, this fieldwork situation would represent an extreme version of the everyday accommodations and choices that characterize living as an observant Jew in an open pluralistic society like America.

In my research in Israel, my identification with Yemeni Jews, my adoption of some of their customs, and my resulting integration into that community facilitated my study. In preparing for fieldwork with Yemeni Muslims, one of my chief concerns was whether I, as a Jew, would be able to establish the level of intimacy necessary for ethnographic research with Muslim informants. I assumed that Yemeni Muslims' reactions to me would be partly based on their traditional image of Jews in Yemen and partly on their attitudes toward current Middle Eastern politics. I knew that before the Jewish mass emigration to Israel between 1948 and 1950, Muslim-Jewish relationships in Yemen had varied greatly over time and in different locations. Discriminatory decrees had been issued periodically by the *Imams,* Islamic religious-political rulers. Jews' relationships with their Muslim neighbors in the capital and other large towns were restricted, and yet in small villages in the mountains and valleys of Yemen's countryside, Jews and Muslims often had amicable associations. Muslim immigrants from different areas of Yemen were likely to have different images of Jews, and I did not know how Yemeni Muslims would view Jews in general after a thirty-year absence of contact. Although I pretty much knew the official stance of the Yemen Arab Republic in the United Nations regarding Middle Eastern politics, I had little idea of the individual views held by emigrant Yemeni villagers and townsmen.

Like any anthropologist, I would have to contend with an assigned status of "outsider," viewed with a moderate degree of suspicion or as an outright threat; however, there were some factors that I thought might be in my favor. I was familiar with many aspects of traditional Yemeni culture (albeit from a distance and in part through the eyes of Yemeni Jews), and I spoke Arabic. I considered Middle Eastern politics outside the domain of my work and therefore intended to avoid potentially divisive discussions.

Since the late 1960s, many Yemeni villagers from the rural southern highlands have come to the United States seeking jobs in the industrial centers of Detroit and Buffalo, the farmlands of California, and in service occupations in New York City. Single and married men, ranging in age from their late teens to their fifties, spend several years at a time away from their families. Men follow their relatives and covillagers in search of employment, intending to earn as much money as possible and spend as little as possible in order to send their earnings home. Most immigrants return to Yemen periodically and a small number bring their families to the United States.

Although Yemenis work and live throughout the greater metropolitan New York area, the Yemeni community in New York City is most visible in downtown Brooklyn. The area is closely associated with many Middle Eastern communities; one recent book on ethnic New York (Stern 1980) identifies this area as "Arab New York." Known for its Syrian and Lebanese bakeries, groceries, gift stores, and restaurants, this area also houses two mosques, two Yemeni clubs, and seven Yemeni-owned restaurants.

The restaurants provided a reasonable point of entry into the community. They are a public presentation of Middle Eastern culture where Yemenis routinely interact with outsiders. Walking south on Atlantic Avenue past Court Street one spring day, the Near East Restaurant caught my eye. I read a restaurant review displayed in the window and learned that this former Syrian restaurant had been bought by two Yemenis. I noticed the other messages on the painted sign that bore the name of the restaurant: a misspelled reference to a well-known Middle Eastern dish, *shisk kabob*, and a saying, "It Pays to Eat Well." The restaurant review noted that the restaurant's name, the *shish kabob* reference, and the maxim were all carryovers from the former owners. I was amused by the maxim and curious to learn how the Yemeni owners had put their distinguishing mark on the restaurant. Looking at other items in the window, I saw evidence of the Yemeni identity of the restaurant owners. Plants and Middle Eastern cut-brass lamps provided a backdrop for a picture calendar, issued by Yemen Airways, showing a view of stone houses and terraced fields on steep Yemeni mountainsides.

I entered the restaurant and waited for a waiter to show me to a table. I noted that the interior decor was simple, with Islamic calligraphic designs and Middle Eastern scenes covering the wood-paneled and brick walls. Lebanese music was playing through speakers at the back of the restaurant. I was seated at a small square table covered with a white tablecloth and paper placemats. The waiter, a teenager dressed in a red waiter jacket, black pants, white shirt, and a dark tie brought a menu, together with a basket of hot pita bread and butter. The menu included such foods as *shish kabob* and *kibbe*, which are popular Middle Eastern dishes but are certainly not native to Yemen.

Since I was interested in the restaurant as an entry into the Yemeni community, I wanted to explore any specifically Yemeni elements in the restaurant. When the waiter returned to take my order, I addressed him in Arabic: "Do you have any *ḥilba?*" referring to a traditional Yemeni condiment made from fenugreek, garlic, and coriander.

"How do you know about *ḥilba?*" he answered, surprised by my request. "Are you Israeli?"

[245]

"No," I answered, again in Arabic. "I'm from Brooklyn, but I'm familiar with Yemeni customs." His reference to Israelis told me that others, perhaps Yemeni Jews, had asked for *hilba* before, but I didn't know what his associations with Israelis might be.

"Well, we eat *hilba* at home; we don't serve it in the restaurant," the waiter said, concluding our opening conversation.

I engaged the waiter in conversation every time he stopped by the table. He eventually introduced himself as Abdal Aziz. He had come to the United States with his immediate family three years ago, though most of his family still lives in Yemen. He goes to a Brooklyn high school and works in the restaurant evenings and on weekends. I indicated that I would enjoy speaking with him again to improve my Arabic. He wanted to improve his English. We agreed to meet again. Before I left, he commented that I was not the first American to ask for the Yemeni spices, but I was the first he had met who could speak Arabic.

Encouraged by this first meeting, I went back the following week. In the middle of a weekday afternoon, the restaurant was quiet. I greeted Abdal Aziz as I walked in, and I sat down with him at a back table at his invitation. We began to speak, mixing Arabic and English. Some of the waiters and kitchen workers sat down with us; others stood by briefly until they resumed their chores. Curious about my presence, the restaurant workers questioned me when they sat down at the back table.

"*Aysh ismak?* [What's your name?]," they asked.

"*Ismi Salim Staub*," I answered, giving an Arabic equivalent of my name. I continued in Arabic, "I'm a University student and I'm interested in Yemeni culture."

"Where did you learn to speak Arabic?"

"I studied Arabic at the University of Pennsylvania."

"Have you gone to Yemen?"

"No, I've never been to Yemen, though I'd like to go someday."

"Besides Arabic, what do you study?"

"I study 'folklore'—the songs, stories, customs, and traditions of different cultures." I used the English word "folklore," since there is no single word in Arabic that has come to encompass the broad range of activities that contemporary folklorists study. Anticipating that "*al-folklor*" might be an unfamiliar term, I also mentioned Arabic terms for specific folkloric genres. The Yemenis nodded in recognition as I referred to their traditional songs, dances, and stories.

"What are you doing in Brooklyn?"

"I'd like to speak to Yemenis about their experiences here in the United States."

"Where do you live?"

"I live in Philadelphia, which is about two hours away by car. When I come to New York I stay with my parents."

"Are you married?"

"Yes, I've been married almost two years."

"Do you have children?"

"No," I answered.

"In the future, *insha allah* [God willing]," they commented.

This round of general questioning naturally seemed to lead into another series of more personal questions.

"Are you a Muslim?"

"No," I answered, wondering how my response would shape the course of this conversation.

"Where were you born?"

"I was born right here in Brooklyn."

"Where were your parents born?"

"Both my mother and father were born in New York."

"Where were their parents born?"

"My father's parents were born in Hungary; my mother's parents were born in Poland. They came to the United States when they were young."

The questioning restaurant workers paused. One worker, a middle-aged man named Ahmad, began to speak about Yemeni Jews, praising them and mentioning the good feelings that Muslims and Jews had in Rada, his home town. I was surprised by his description of Jews in Yemen. I didn't have any idea what had prompted this new subject. I had not mentioned that I am Jewish.

Ahmad's sentiments seemed positive, so I decided to mention that I had lived for some time in a Yemeni village in Israel. I added that Salim is the name the Yemeni Jews gave me from my Hebrew name Shalom.

"Yes," Ahmad said. "Salim is a common Jewish name."

"Do you have an American name?" asked Saad, a waiter in his early twenties.

"Steven," I answered.

"This would be Sayf, meaning 'sword,'" Saad responded. Despite this suggestion of the name "Sayf," I continued to introduce myself and be addressed as Salim.

As I met and spoke to Yemeni Muslims in Brooklyn, I realized that my initial presence was more of a puzzle than an intrusion. By means of their questions, the Yemeni workers were trying to make sense of my identity. I didn't fit into the categories of ordinary Yemeni social interaction. I spoke Arabic, but was not an Arab. I was familiar with Islamic beliefs and practices and did not disdain them, yet I was not a Muslim. I could describe many details of life in Yemen, but I had never been to Yemen. As a graduate student, I appeared to be unemployed, and yet I presented myself as a professional.

The one social category into which I fit neatly was the category of Jew. The Yemeni workers probably guessed my Jewish identity as soon as I had introduced myself as Salim. Though Salim is not an exclusively Jewish name throughout the Middle East, in Yemen it has a strong association to the seventeenth-century Jewish poet, Salim Shabazi, who was revered by Jews and Muslims alike as a saint. By referring to the good relations between Muslims and Jews in Yemen, Ahmad indirectly confirmed his awareness of my Jewish identity. Following his cue, I linked myself to Yemeni Jews by recalling my experiences in the Yemeni village in Israel. As a Jew and in my association with Yemeni Jews, I had placed myself in a social category familiar to Yemeni Muslims. Despite Saad's suggestion of Sayf as an alternative name to Salim, those who already knew me began to introduce me to others by saying, "This is Salim; he is Jewish, he speaks Arabic, and he is a frequent visitor at our restaurant."

My identity was not always so evident to the people I met along Atlantic Avenue. By speaking Arabic and by acting as a participant observer, my "presentation of self" (Goffman 1959), was sufficiently ambiguous for some people to project various identities onto me. One Lebanese Christian merchant was convinced I was Christian. He refused to call me either Salim or Shalom, but consistently called me Steve. During Ramadan, when Muslims fast from sunrise to sunset, the young son of one of the Yemeni restaurant owners asked me if I had fasted that day. I replied that I had not fasted because I am not Muslim. The youngster said that he thought I was Muslim since I was eating their foods, particularly the foods they eat in the evening to break the fast. An adult present at the table looked at me in surprise. Because I had been participating so often in a variety of events, he had also assumed I must be Muslim.

As a Jew, I was generally seen as a potential convert. When one restaurant worker who had thought I was Muslim learned otherwise, he asked me, "Then why don't you become Muslim? Do you want to go to hell or paradise? When a Jew converts to Islam he automatically enters Paradise when he dies!" Islam is a religion that seeks converts and Yemenis in Brooklyn could point to one young American who had converted to Islam. Although he was a disaffected Irish Catholic and I a proud and somewhat observant Jew, the Yemenis saw his conversion as evidence that young, white, middle-class American males were candidates for conversion.

As I made acquaintances in other restaurants, one of the first conversations I had with them invariably turned to religion and the superiority of Islam above all others. To avoid a personal confrontation during such discussions, I often switched from the first person, "in my opinion," to the third person, "Jews believe." Sometimes an informant would interrupt a conversation and direct me to "pray to the Prophet" or tell me, "Salim, you and I are going to make *ṣalat* [Islamic prayer ritual] today." Throughout the eighteen months of fieldwork, there was a general expectation that, in the words of one Yemeni, "Salim's going to be Muslim someday."

Some of my interactions with informants were governed by proscriptive rules. "A Jew cannot touch a Qur'an," I was told, and "Only a Muslim or a person planning to convert may enter a mosque." Respecting these boundaries, I never attempted to accompany any Yemeni worker to the Brooklyn mosques. My presence was acceptable, however, when an individual performed *ṣalat* privately. The proscriptive rules weren't always clear. Once when I sneezed I was instructed to say *Ilḥamdu lillah* [Praise to God], to which the appropriate response would be *Yiraḥamuk allah* [May God be merciful to you]. Another Yemeni present vigorously objected to this exchange, saying that it is inappropriate if I am not Muslim. The Yemeni who introduced these phrases defended his position. "God is God," he said "and Muslims and Jews both believe in one God."

On some occasions my Jewishness was treated as an identity with its own independent validity. I was questioned about my own practices. "Do you eat pork?" "Do you drink wine?" Both are forbidden to Muslims. "What do Jews believe?" "Why don't Jews believe in Jesus?" "When you say that you pray to God, what do you do?" During the month of Ramadan, I was asked if Jews fast, and if they do, for how many hours. My description of my observance of the twenty-six-hour fast of Yom Kippur accorded me a certain respect among those who questioned me. Even when it was not the explicit topic of conversation, my identity as a Jew often provided a framework for

[249]

interaction. In a discussion about traditional music and dance, one worker asked me in Arabic, "How do you say 'dance' in your language?"

"Dance," I responded.

"No, no, not in English, in *your* language," he said.

"*Rikud*," I answered, this time in Hebrew.

The Muslim-Jewish boundary was ever-present, though not always divisive. There were times when the boundaries shifted, encompassing both Islam and Judaism, Arab and Jew. Commenting on the endlessness and futility of Arab-Israeli conflicts, Yemenis asked why this had to be. "After all, the Jews are our cousins; we are *bani Ismail* [children of Ishmael] and they are *bani Ishaq* children of Isaac]." Faced with the difficulty of mastering the English language, Yemenis commented to me that "our" languages, Arabic and Hebrew, are so much clearer, easier to speak, read, and write. I encountered comments about how similar Islam and Judaism are to one another and how different Christianity is from both. In New York City, it is difficult to obtain *halal* meat, slaughtered and prepared according to Muslim practices. Some Yemenis seek kosher meat, knowing that it was slaughtered by a man who believes in one God. It was not unusual to pass by the local kosher delicatessen and greet Yemenis leaving or entering the premises.

The Yemenis viewed me with considerable ambivalence. Though I was generally received cordially and was treated with traditional Arab hospitality, socially I was held at a distance. In the restaurants, this social distance was often expressed in physical terms. I was routinely granted access to the semiprivate back table where the Yemeni workers relaxed. In fact, the bulk of my research was spent sitting for hours at the back tables of several restaurants, talking informally with the workers and observing their interaction among themselves and with customers. The kitchen, basement, and back courtyard were more private areas, where social interaction was dominated by family and village associations from the old country. At times I was invited back to these areas to talk or to share food, and yet on other occasions the workers made it clear to me that my presence was not welcome there. While they were working, there was no room, and when the workers wanted privacy during their leisure time, I had little choice but to remain at the back table, sometimes sitting alone.

Language was another instrument of social distance. I understood their Arabic when they addressed me, but if they chose, they could

speak quickly or in local Yemeni dialect that precluded my understanding entirely. One night after the last customers had gone, I sat at
the back table of the Near East listening to a lively session of joke
telling. One man began: "Three men are in terrible danger and fear
for their lives. Suddenly, a helicopter arrives to save them. The first
man catches a rescue rope, the second catches on to the first man's
legs, and the third man catches on to the second man's legs. When the
helicopter began to lift off, taking them away from the danger, all
three men were relieved. The first man exclaimed *Ya layl* [Oh, night],
the second uttered *Ya ayn* [Oh, eye], and the third clapped his hands
in joy!" I caught the gist of this joke at the time with the help of the
narrator's hand motions, but as the joking continued and intensified, I
understood less and less. I did hear the phrase, "Yemeni jokes,"
repeatedly, but no one answered my inquiries about the jokes being
told.

The next day I looked for Ali, a young man in his early twenties who
had been present at the joke session the night before. I visited him
regularly, and I hoped that this time he could tell me more about the
joking that I didn't understand. I found him seated at the back table of
the Mareb restaurant, where he worked with his brother as a waiter. I
asked about the "Yemeni jokes" told the night before, but Ali responded evasively. "We used those words," he said, "but no jokes
were told." I asked specifically about the one joke that I had partially
understood. Ali retold the helicopter rescue joke, but he claimed that
that was the only joke he remembered. Six weeks later, I got my first
clue to the "Yemeni jokes" I had heard but had not understood.

Walking along Atlantic Avenue, I happened to meet Hassan, another of the men who was present that evening. At the end of our
casual meeting when we were leaving each other's company, Hassan
said, "You remember the last time I saw you, when we were telling
jokes? Those men were asking about you and saying that you are a spy.
They were laughing and talking about you while you were sitting
there."

If they really thought I was a spy, their laughter and mockery
suggested that they didn't take me as too serious a threat. Still, if there
were illegal immigrants within the community, there was bound to be
some suspicion of outsiders. How could they know for sure that this
stranger who speaks Arabic and asks about Yemeni folklore is indeed
what he says he is? Ali's evasive responses to my inquiry about the
"Yemeni jokes" perhaps revealed his own suspicion of me. Or perhaps

he felt that propriety didn't allow the revelation of the precise contents of an insult.

There were other occasions when my presence was incongruous and potentially suspect. In the course of my fieldwork, I attended two annual events to celebrate the Yemeni revolution. One summer evening, approximately 150–200 Yemenis and Palestinians gathered in a small auditorium decorated with Yemeni flags and banners bearing nationalistic slogans to hear speeches about the unification of North and South Yemen as a single socialist state, and about the solidarity between Yemenis and Palestinians. I went with Abdal Aziz, the teenage waiter who was my first contact in the community. We sat down together toward the back of the room, but I sensed a certain discomfort on his part. In the course of the evening, Abdal Aziz switched his seat several times as a way of distancing himself from me. I sat alone through most of the politically charged speeches. After two hours of speeches interspersed with nationalistic songs, the Yemeni musicians began to play traditional dance music. Most Palestinians left at that time, and the Yemenis who remained enjoyed the festive mood. Some danced; many listened to the music, continued their conversations, perhaps commenting on the dancers.

I approached the front of the room to get a better view of the dancing. When the dancers and observers noticed my interest, they began to encourage me to join in. Eventually one of the dancers came over, took hold of my arm, and pulled me into the dance. I was confident that my active participation in the dancing would go smoothly, since the dances were quite similar to those I had studied among Yemeni Jews in Israel. Many Yemenis were impressed by my participation and it became a topic of conversation in the restaurants for several days afterward. My presence at this event troubled only the one Yemeni who had accompanied me.

About a year later, approximately three hundred Yemenis and Palestinians attended another event held in a Brooklyn public school auditorium. I went unaccompanied on this occasion, though I came at the invitation of Muhammad, the featured Yemeni musician whom I had met the year before. Having spoken to Muhammad beforehand, I brought equipment to record the music and film the dancing. I sat alone near the front of the room in the corner, waiting as people slowly drifted in. The first row center was filled by the speakers: representatives of three Palestinian liberation groups and one Lebanese group. Before the speeches started, the men in the front row sent someone over to ask me who I was and what I was doing there. I explained that I came at the invitation of Muhammad to record the singing and dancing. Later, when the first Palestinian speaker began, someone came over to tell me not to record the speeches. I shut off my tape recorder. The speeches celebrated the Yemeni revolution and criticized American imperialism and reactionary governments in the Middle East. Through two hours of speeches, I was questioned repeatedly by various members of the audience about my presence and purpose. I was relieved when the program switched from politics to traditional dance music. Muhammad later confirmed that my presence had generated tremendous suspicion. Someone had gone backstage to ask him if he knew the Jew in the audience with the tape recorder and camera. Muhammad vouched for me, but some of the men in the auditorium clearly harbored their suspicions throughout the evening.

In the course of my day-to-day fieldwork in the restaurants, I knew that discussions of Middle Eastern politics could be divisive and raise suspicions. Although I refrained from raising the subject of politics, I responded when asked about my opinions of Middle Eastern politics. I had developed a standard response to these questions. Yes, I had visited Israel several times; no, I am not an Israeli citizen; I am an American. The day I spoke to Ali about the late-night joke session, he questioned me about my opinions on current Middle Eastern politics. If he had shared in the joking about my being a spy, his decision to initiate this dialogue may have been his way of testing my integrity.

"So, Salim," Ali began, "how do you think this conflict between the Israelis and Palestinians can be resolved?"

"You know of those two moderate West Bank mayors who have spoken about an Israeli state and Palestinian state?" I asked Ali, seeking the most conciliatory position available without compromising my support for Israel's right to a secure existence. "Maybe there is some hope that a two-state solution can guarantee peace and homelands for both Israelis and Palestinians."

"Two states would be fine," responded Ali, "but what about Jerusalem? What will be its future?"

"Even now, while Jerusalem is united in name, it remains divided socially. There are strong feelings that Jerusalem must remain united; maybe its future lies in an approach that provides unity without imposing uniformity among its diverse population."

"That's fine," said Ali, "but who will hold the keys? Who will be in charge? It must be the Muslims," he continued. "After all, it is a Muslim city."

"You may think of Jerusalem as a Muslim city," I responded, "but Jews think of it as a Jewish city, and Christians as a Christian city."

"Forget about the Christians," Ali exclaimed. "They have no power in this conflict. Jerusalem has been a Muslim city from the earliest of times."

"But Jerusalem was founded as a Jewish city in the Torah by Abraham, by David, and by Solomon."

"What! Do you think Abraham and Solomon were Jews?" asked Ali, apparently shocked by my ignorance. "They were Muslims. It is written in the Qur'an."

"But the Jews will say that their Torah was written before your Qur'an," I answered switching from first to third person as the conversation spiraled toward the unresolvable.

"But we know that the Jews changed the Torah from what was revealed to Musa [Moses]," Ali countered, citing Islamic teaching.

"What do you do when two peoples believe that their way is right, but the belief of the one contradicts or denies the other?" I asked.

"This is the reason that Jews and Muslims cannot be friends," concluded Ali.

"Can you and I be friends?" I asked testing a personal relationship against categorical reasoning.

Perplexed at the first instant, Ali answered, "Yes, we are friends, but that is different. We can talk to each other and understand one another." I wondered whether our "friendship" and understanding of each other wasn't more a function of my responsibility as a fieldworker to accommodate and explore the views of informants and less a reflection of a more encompassing relationship between us.

Five days later, Israeli warplanes destroyed the Iraqi nuclear reactor. When I went to see Ali soon after that incident, I found him sulking at the back table. He said he was angry. I asked Ali what was troubling him, but he didn't respond. After a long pause he answered me.

"Someone told me that you are planning to write bad things about the Yemenis."

"Do you think what you heard is true?" I wondered who was trying to discredit me.

"No," Ali said, "but the possibility troubled me."

"I have always been honest with you, and you know that my intentions are to learn about Yemeni traditions and the life of Yemenis in the United States. I would never write anything to harm the Yemeni community."

"I too have always been straight with you, and when I heard this thing about you, I knew I had to talk to you," Ali responded.

"Do you remember our conversation last week, when you said that we are friends because we understand and respect one another? Don't you think that's true?" I asked.

"Yes, it's true. If we were government leaders we might be fighting one another, but as two ordinary people we can be friends and be straight with each other," Ali concluded.

Such moments as these with Ali were gratifying, but they were rare. Much more typical were the long periods of frustration and feeling shut out. One year into my fieldwork, I reviewed my notes and decided to narrow my focus of inquiry. I wanted to collect life histories of individual informants in order to identify patterns in the Yemenis' emigrant experiences. For my first attempt to elicit formally a full life history, I approached a man who had been helpful to me on an earlier occasion, when I was collecting oral poetry.

I entered the Adnan restaurant one mid-afternoon in July 1981 as the lunch crowd was thinning out, taking a place at the back table beside Salah and Abdu. They continued a lengthy conversation, which I neither participated in nor fully understood. As Abdu was getting ready to leave, I turned to him.

"Abdu, I'd like to ask you something. Can we sit down together at your convenience so that I can hear about your experiences: how you came from Yemen, and how you established yourself here?"

"This time you've gone too far," he answered. Addressing the other men seated or standing around the back table, Abdu added, "He wants to talk to me and ask about my life from the beginning to now."

At that point, Abdu angrily walked away. Somewhat stunned, I was left at the back table with Salah and Muhsin, who added their comments immediately.

"Salim, why do you go so far?" asked Salah.

"Salim, you have no right to ask this. You go too far," said Muhsin. "Salah is my cousin, and I would not ask him questions like these."

"I answered you at first when you asked if I go to the Yemeni club," Salah continued, "and I also told you that I go to Coney Island with my friends. But I thought to myself later, what right does he have to ask me these questions? What business of his is it to know where I go?

People may be involved in illegal activities, or a man may go to a prostitute. We are all free of illegal involvements, but what right do you have to ask where people go with whom and when?"

"As you know, I am a student at a university writing about Yemeni life in New York. I try to speak to Yemenis and ask about their life here."

"Did you ever ask anyone here if they wanted you to write this book?" Salah asked. "Until just now, I never knew that you were working on research and writing a book. I never knew why you asked so many questions."

"I'm sorry I asked an offensive question before. I did not intend to insult Abdu," I said, wondering exactly what were the implications of my question that had provoked such a strong reaction. "I have had other conversations with Abdu and I have asked him other questions. I thought this question would be acceptable. Now I am not sure what questions are allowable. What can I ask you that is not offensive? I have been honest with you about my intentions here, and I would not write anything to damage anyone. I am not connected to the government or the police, and I'm not interested in finding out about legal and illegal activities. I want to learn about traditional Yemeni culture and about Yemeni life in the United States."

"Ask about stories and jokes," Salah suggested. "We have many good stories and jokes, also poetry and songs. This would be much more interesting than the words of people about their own lives. Everyone has the same experience anyway: coming to America, finding a woman, getting a green card, becoming a citizen, and working."

Muhsin began a story about a donkey that escaped from its pen and the ensuing search that the villagers conducted. Taking great pleasure in his own story, Muhsin concluded with the donkey's owner proclaiming, "Praise Allah that I am not riding the donkey, otherwise I would also be lost." The tension of the moment passed as we all laughed at the silly villager.

"We've got a story," Salah said after the conversation resumed. "There was a poor man walking in the street, and a rich man stood on the roof of his house. The poor man called out to the rich man, and the latter descended all the steps of his house to the street. The rich man met the poor man at the door. The poor man said, 'Give me, in the name of Allah.' The rich man answered, 'You called me for this? Wait here.' The rich man returned to the roof of his five story house and called to the poor man, 'Come up to the roof.' The poor man climbed all the stairs to the roof, and when he arrived, the rich man said to him, 'Allah is generous.' The poor man said, 'Why didn't you say this at the beginning when I was at your door?' The rich man answered, 'You brought me down the stairs to ask alms for Allah; I brought you up to tell you that Allah is beneficent.'

Not knowing why my question about life history had evoked such a negative response, at the time I felt that this confrontation would determine the possibility of continuing my research. By the time Salah had finished his story, the tension of the interaction had dissipated. The Yemenis present laughed at the outcome, though I wondered if Salah, well known for his stories and jokes, had used the safety of storytelling to voice his perception of me.

I was intrigued by Salah's use of storytelling, but I also needed to understand why my attempt to collect a life history had failed. A colleague who had conducted anthropological field research in Yemen suggested that my questions about the circumstances of leaving Yemen and getting established in the United States may have touched on possible illegal activities. Months later I realized that my "failure" related only in part to the substance of my questions. How and when I had asked my question also contributed to the Yemenis' blunt refusal to respond. I found that in informal private conversations, Yemenis revealed personal details about their lives for which I never would have considered asking. The formality of my questions, the desire to arrange an interview, and the request for public disclosure of private matters were all factors that ensured the dismissal and censure I experienced.

Following my aborted interaction with Abdu, Salah and Muhsin offered a definition of a proper area of inquiry for me. "Ask about stories and jokes," Salah had suggested. Following their own advice, they offered two stories. Muhsin's story about the silly villager and his lost donkey momentarily eased the tension and allowed us to mock a situation outside of our immediate concern. Salah's story provoked laughter too, but I suspected that his story was a metaphoric representation of his view of my research and possibly of his attitude toward me as a Jew. Salah most likely identified himself with the rich man and viewed me, the researcher, as the beggar. Drawing on my familiarity with the ethnographic literature, I recalled Yemeni cultural associations to Jews and beggars as involving inferior social statuses within the traditional social hierarchy.

The rich man and the beggar in Salah's story evoke cultural values associated with generosity and neediness, two qualities that feature prominently in Middle Eastern culture in general and Yemeni culture in particular. The demonstration of generosity and need introduce superior and inferior social statuses based on the accrual of social debts. Yemenis often pride themselves on their generosity and view it as a claim to superior social status. Salah frequently demonstrated his generosity among his family and strangers alike. He extended his hospitality to me when I visited the Adnan restaurant.

If Salah identified himself as the rich man in the story, he clearly identified me as the poor man. After all, I was coming to his restaurant often, accepting his food, asking questions, and seeking information. In Salah's eyes, I was the one in the relationship who asked for things and had little to offer in return. As a general rule, I accepted the hospitality of the restaurant workers. I was usually offered a hot or cold beverage when I took a seat at the restaurant back table. I paid (or tried to pay) when I ordered a meal for myself, though there were many occasions when workers insisted that I join them in their meals. On several occasions I offered tangible gifts, though most often I offered services: running errands or transporting people in my car, offering informal English tutorials, filling out official forms, and other activities generally related to translations from English to Arabic or the reverse. For several weeks I helped to edit the English version of the weekly sermon delivered in the local mosque.

Wanting to maintain his own social superiority, Salah played down any favor I offered and refused to accept any material item from me as a return on the social debt. Shortly after he finished telling the story of the rich man and the beggar, Salah asked me to help him with an application for a pistol permit. After some revisions, we left the restaurant to find a notary public. Caught in a sudden downpour with only the small umbrella I had in my bag, we found a hardware store where I bought a second umbrella. When we returned to the restaurant, I asked him to accept the umbrella as a gift. He refused. Earlier that afternoon, he had also refused to let me pay for my lunch. Apparently, I was not allowed to reciprocate his generosity.

The rich man in Salah's story is not generous in the end. He deceives the beggar, denies his request, and mocks him. Like the poor man in Salah's story, I too found that Yemeni generosity occasionally crossed into ridicule. Indeed, I sometimes became the butt of the very jokes my informants directed me to collect. On one occasion, Salah and I were sitting at the back table with several other restaurant workers. Salah pointed to my neck and asked me to name it. I responded in Arabic. Salah wanted me to name it in English, so I said "neck." Salah then pointed to my knee, and asked me to name it. I said "knee." Salah then told me to say it several times quickly. I did: "neck-knee; neck-knee; neck-knee." By this time all the Yemenis were laughing. When I inquired what was so funny, they told me that I was saying, "fuck me!"

Several minutes later, Salah started writing a series of letters on a spare piece of paper: E, D, B, T, Z. He asked me to read the series. I read them slowly. Salah told me to read them faster, and I did, "E-D-B-T-Z." Again, all the Yemenis were laughing. Again, I inquired what was so funny, they explained to me that I was saying, *yadi btizi,* "my hand is up my asshole."

For several days after the confrontation at the back table of the Adnan restaurant, I returned to begin to repair the damaged relationships by reestablishing a more low-keyed presence. Four days after the original incident in the early afternoon, several Adnan workers were sharing a wealth of stories and jokes. Salah was there too, telling a humorous story about an immigrant who has not yet mastered the English language, a long moral tale about how a sheikh discerned a deceitful woman, and later, another long tale about two disciples of Muhammad. Salah had allowed me to tape record the first two stories, but when I asked him to repeat the last story for a recording, he declined, seeming to have had enough of my questions. I pressed him, citing his own instructions to me to inquire about stories and jokes. Instead of repeating the story about Muhammad's disciples, Salah told me another story about two travelers who met each other on the road. One of them had many provisions, the other had nothing. When it was time to set up camp and prepare a meal, the second traveler became very generous, saying to the first traveler, "You provide the flour for the bread and I'll provide the fire to cook on."

Like the earlier tension about eliciting oral history, this minor confrontation over the persistence of my questioning provided Salah with another opportunity to draw upon his story repertoire. Similar to his earlier tale about the rich man and beggar, this story of two travelers echoes the theme of generousity and need, commenting clearly on our respective roles in this fieldwork interaction.

Salah left the restaurant to go up to his apartment to take an afternoon nap. I stayed in the restaurant at the back table, talking to one of the waiters about Yemeni jokes and proverbs, life in the old country, and life in the United States. A couple of hours later, Salah returned. He saw me sitting at the back table with my tape recorder talking to his coworker. As Salah approached the back table, he commented aloud, "Ahah! Salim is asking for more donations."

Salah's exclamation confirmed his identification of our real life interaction with the story characters. But here, his comment was like a private joke among friends. Much of the tension was gone and Salah good-naturedly confirmed the positive side of his ambivalence about my presence.

I continued to follow Salah's advice to ask about songs, stories, jokes, and proverbs. Though I never once attempted to elicit stories about Jews or with incidental Jewish characters, I was told many such stories. There was a curious mixture of references to Jews. One man matter of factly quoted a stanza of oral poetry in which an adversary is insulted with the line, "A Jew fucked your mother." I was stunned at first, but soon I felt a perverse satisfaction that I had been given access to this aspect of the Yemeni Muslim-Jewish relationship. Another man with a reputation as a master storyteller told his version of a well-known story that comments disparagingly on the intelligence of Bed-uoin tribesmen. I had heard the story before, with its memorable alliterative ending, *"Ma aqalla aql al-bidwi ma aqalla"* [There is nothing less than a Bedouin's intelligence, nothing less], but in this telling, the master storyteller cast a Jewish character for the role of disparaging the Bedouin's mental faculties!

Apart from traditional stories and jokes, I was told many personal narratives of meetings with American and Yemeni Jews. New York is a site of renewed personal contacts between Yemeni Muslims and Yemeni Jews, since the Jewish mass emigration to Israel in 1948. Some Yemenis assumed that I knew the Jews they had met. While some of these meetings are planned, most are fortuitous. When recounting the experiences, the Yemeni Muslims expressed their amazement at hearing strangers speak their local Arabic dialect.

The interaction between Yemeni Muslims and Jews is often focused on a shared town of origin. Rada in the Yemeni southern highlands is a town that before 1948 had a significant Jewish population. For the older Rada Muslims in New York, meetings with Rada Jews are reunions; for the younger generation, the meetings provide a glimpse at a part of Yemen they have never witnessed before. I was told of these meetings, which sometimes included singing, dancing, and the traditional Yemeni habit of chewing the narcotic *qat* leaf. I was shown

[260]

pictures and letters from Yemeni Jews, momentos carried by the
Yemeni Muslims with pride. The name Yihye was repeatedly men-
tioned, a Rada Jew who has on occasion provided *qat* cultivated in
Israel to New York Yemeni Muslims.

I wanted an opportunity to observe a meeting of Yemeni Jews and
Muslims. I asked to be told in advance about such plans, but the
Yemenis treated this inquiry like my requests for advance notice of
many other events. I was usually the last to know when anything
happened, so it was just by chance that I entered the Near East
restaurant one evening and found three Yemeni Jews seated at the
back table: Yihye's wife, his brother Shlomo. and his son Yossi. The
woman, in her late fifties, wore a dress and head covering, indicating
her traditionalist orientation. Shlomo, in his fifties, and Yossi, in his
late twenties, wore no head coverings. Qa'id, the owner of the Near
East, introduced me to Shlomo and brought four Yemeni coffees from
the kitchen. Shlomo placed a telephone call to his brother Yihye in
Israel. As the Jewish family spoke to Yihye, Qa'id and several other
restaurant workers gathered eagerly around the phone, waiting their
turns to greet their former townsman.

While the restaurant workers spoke to Yihye, the three Yemeni
Jews questioned me in Hebrew about my presence in the restaurant. I
explained how I had lived in the Yemeni Jewish village in Israel and
that now I was doing research among the Yemeni Muslims. The woman said repeatedly that the "Yemeni Arabs" are good people and that
they had always had good relations with them in Yemen, unlike the
Arabs in Israel.

When the workers gathered once more around the back table,
Shlomo performed, regaling his listeners with stories and jokes told in
their shared local Yemeni Arabic dialect. The workers encouraged
him, laughing and enjoying the reminiscences of Yemen's earlier
days. Yossi leaned over to me, commenting in Hebrew that although
he could understand much of what was being said, he didn't really
have the command of the Arabic dialect. I myself could not follow the
rapid talk in dialect, and I found it difficult to switch between the
Arabic of the general conversation and the Hebrew of the private
interactions between me and the Yemeni Jews.

Shlomo showed pictures of his family and house in Israel, including
some of a recent Yemeni Jewish wedding. One of the young Yemeni
Muslims was startled when he saw a photograph of what he took to be
a Yemeni Muslim bride: a woman dressed in gold robes and jewelry,

wearing a tall headpiece, with her hands decorated with patterns made by applying henna. The older workers pointed out that the bridal gowns worn by Muslim and Jewish women were different; nevertheless, the younger workers were curious to learn that Yemeni Jews have continued the Yemeni custom of the prenuptial party to dye the bride's hands with henna. Shlomo went on to describe the henna evening celebration in Ra'as al-Ayn [Rosh Haayin, outside Tel Aviv] in great detail. The conversation turned to Rada, their mutual town of origin. The Yemeni workers remembered the house in which the family had lived. Shlomo impressed everyone with his recollection of scenes throughout Yemen, even describing the tribal areas close to the Saudi Arabian border, an area of the country to which the workers had never traveled.

Qa'id and the other workers did not join us in drinking the coffee that he had served. It was the middle of Ramadan, and the Muslims were awaiting the end of the day's fast. The Jewish woman encouraged them to eat. "Go ahead already, you look hungry!" Turning to me she added in Hebrew, "These Arabs, what kind of crazy religion they have, fasting like this for a whole month!" Shlomo spoke to the men about obtaining *qat*, and the woman spoke about Yemen, referring to it in Arabic as "our country, our home, the place where I grew up." When I asked her in Hebrew if she misses Yemen, she responded, "Not really, I say that to the Arabs. Israel is our home now."

Soon food was brought out for all the workers to break their fast. Qa'id offered his guests a bowl of meat broth. The three Yemeni Jews politely refused. After some futile coaxing, Qa'id eventually acquiesed. He took their bowls away, but left a bowl for me. Qa'id proudly said, "Salim is like one of us." The Jewish woman criticized me: "How can you eat this unkosher food? This is what happens in America, you forget your religion!" I didn't respond to either comment, and I thought to myself that Shlomo and Yossi would probably have also eaten the broth if the woman had not been present. When the soup bowls were cleared, Qa'id brought out trays of fresh fruit for his Jewish guests, from which they ate freely.

I observed with fascination how the Muslims and Jews balanced their mutual identifications with Yemen and Rada with their mutually exclusive religious and national affiliations. Speaking a local Arabic dialect facilitated their common identification. Shlomo's stories of the old country allowed him momentarily to present himself as more

Yemeni than the Yemeni Muslims. Food was an expression not only of traditional Arab hospitality but also a negotiation of the Jewish-Muslim boundary. The Jewish woman gently mocked the Muslim observance of the daily fast during Ramadan. At the break fast, Qa'id urged his Yemeni Jewish guests to eat the meat broth out of his sense of responsibility as a host. When the Jews refused the meat dish due to their own religious observance, Qa'id knew that by offering fresh fruit he could preserve his honor as host and theirs as guests.

In the presence of Yemeni Muslims and Jews together, my own status shifted in ways it never had with either Muslims or Jews alone. Although the Yemeni Jews were puzzled by my presence at first, I quickly became their confidant. Our speaking Hebrew was a private communication, and they revealed attitudes that at times openly contradicted the appearances they fostered in their conversations in Arabic. It was a confidence that left me uncomfortable, as if I were betraying the Yemeni Muslims who had taken me within their community. When Qa'id served the broth, I knew I had to make a public choice between honoring my host or demonstrating my observance of Jewish dietary laws. Qa'id fully expected me to eat, since I had shared other meat dishes with him in the past. How could I suddenly change the rules and refuse the food on this occasion? And yet, I felt disloyal to the Yemeni Jewish woman who represented the strength of traditional Jewish values and observance.

While conducting fieldwork, I occupied an ambiguous position, suspending my own cultural practices and values yet never fully integrating those of another culture. In Israel, I was never a *ḥaver moshav*, though I thoroughly identified with the common Jewish heritage I shared with the Israeli Yemenis. I did not become a Yemeni Jew, but I spoke, ate, lived, and worshiped like no other American Ashkenazi Jew. I relished the villagers' inventiveness of a new social category: *yamani abyadh*—"a white Yemeni."

Only on rare occasions in my research in the Yemeni Muslim community did I experience a degree of integration and identification. Even the name Salim, which indicated integration on one level, was a constant reminder of outsider status. I did not share a Muslim identity nor did I ever express a willingness to convert. And yet, despite my marginal status, I began to experience New York through the eyes of an immigrant Yemeni. I reached a certain fluency in Yemeni language and behavior. I was told, "You are Yemeni" or "You must be Yemeni"

[263]

by Muslims who watched me dance traditional Yemeni dances. Despite the incongruities, I identified with the Yemenis among whom I was spending so much time.

Long before I ate the unkosher meat broth, I had reconciled within myself the disparity between my own observance of Jewish laws and customs with the demands of my fieldwork. I had separated my identity as a folklorist from my identity as a Jew, the latter existing in a kind of suspended animation, to return to life upon the completion of my fieldwork. For the time being, I had a responsibility to act appropriately toward the Yemeni hosts. Qa'id's comment, "Salim is like one of us," was a powerful statement of integration for both of us. The Yemeni Jewish woman could not understand that for a certain period of time I had chosen to be more the ethnographer than the Jew.

REFERENCES

Goffman, Erving. 1959. *The Presentation of Self in Everyday Life*. Garden City, N.Y.: Doubleday.

Staub, Shalom. 1978. "The Yemenite Jewish Dance: An Anthropological Perspective." M.A. thesis, Wesleyan University.

Staub, Shalom. 1985. *A Folkloristic Study of Ethnic Boundaries: The Case of Yemeni Muslims in New York City*. Ann Arbor, Mich.: University Microfilms.

Stern, Zelda. 1980. *The Complete Guide to Ethnic New York*. New York: St. Martin's Press.

[11]

Surviving Stories:
Reflections on *Number Our Days*

Barbara Myerhoff

Ernest Hemingway is reputed to have remarked that all stories that go on long enough have the same ending. The question, then, is not how things finally end, but how they unfold, and how much time there is for the unfolding. This essay is the story of how things have unfolded in the allegedly doomed, small community of elderly Eastern European Jewish immigrants who live at the edge of the Pacific Ocean in Venice, California.

They have lived there for nearly three decades, scratching out a precarious existence that is as vibrant and intense as it is fragile, built out of the historical and symbolic riches of the people's common Yiddish background in the *shtetls* of the old world, which they left as young people. Coming to America at the turn of the century—before the Holocaust destroyed their culture and their kin—they escaped the intractable poverty and anti-Semitism that had restricted them, to make a new life for their children, to provide them with the freedom

This essay, which Barbara Myerhoff left unfinished at the time of her death, was edited by Marc Kaminsky.

The "Life Not Death in Venice" exhibition was produced and coordinated by Vikram Jayanti in conjunction with the Center for Visual Anthropology, Department of Anthropology, University of Southern California; Alexander Moore and Timothy Asch, Department chair and center director.

I am particularly grateful to Marc Kaminsky for his leadership in exploring the area of survivor stories. The conference he convened in 1983 on survivors' narratives was the occasion for my examining this genre more closely.

and educational opportunities that contributed toward making those children one of the most successful immigrant generations in American history. On retirement, the elders moved west, to enjoy the *yidishkeyt* at the beach community and to develop a new, syncretic culture that freely mixed Jewish, European, and American elements, combined to help them meet the difficulties of old age: poor housing, inadequate transportation, frail health, dangerous neighbors, insufficient income, remote medical attention and the like. Cut off from their highly assimilated children and wealthier Jewish neighbors, they turned to each other and revitalized their common values—Judaism, socialism, Zionism, social justice, learning, philanthropy, community, solidarity, autonomy, and American patriotism—and used these as the basis for a way of life well-suited to meet the severe hazards of old age. Their social life has long been focused on the Israel Levin Senior Adult Center, a Jewish community day center, sponsored by Jewish Federation of Los Angeles, directed by Morrie Rosen, whose dedication to this group qualifies him for designation as one of the *lamed vov*, the thirty-six just men who exist in each generation and who by their compassion and generosity help hold up the world.

The community has been amply documented, and in many media. In 1972 I began an ethnographic study there, funded in part by the National Science Foundation. This study was the basis over the next ten years for a film, book, play, and cultural festival. The film, called *Number Our Days*, appeared in 1977; it was directed and produced by Lynne Littman for KCET, the public television station in Los Angeles, and to everyone's astonishment it won an Academy Award for Best Short Documentary Film, assuring it wide visibility. My book by the same name was published in 1979. In 1980 the University of Southern California Center for Visual Anthropology mounted an exhibit of the elders' art works and folklore as part of a cultural festival of *yidishkeyt*. And in 1981 the Mark Taper Forum of Los Angeles dramatized and performed the play *Number Our Days*, directed by John Hirsch. I have lectured widely about the Israel Levin Center people, conducted scores of discussions, received hundreds of letters.

Everyone eagerly asks: "How does the story end? What has become of them?" If the discussion goes on long enough, they also ask: "How did they respond to seeing themselves portrayed? How has the publicity affected them?" Then: "How has the work changed you?" These are among the questions that I explore here, in 1984, twelve years after the work began. At first I was reluctant to look back and plow

[266]

well-furrowed fields, but the longer I considered it, the more I realized that the unfolding of their story concerns more than the mere
passage of time. It concerns the way they have lived and changed and
stayed the same. It is full of teachings: about the importance of stories
and visibility as essential to meaningful survival; about the values and
problems of participatory anthropology; about the nature and process
of cultural invention and transmission; about the necessity and power
of performance and witnessing. None of these ideas is new; all are
implicit in the book, but they have become clearer and stronger for
me and easier to document over time. That is the unusual benefit of
having such a long timeframe within which to observe a group: change
can be seen in the making, rather than inferred from the before and
after.

What has become of them? They have not died out. This, then, is a
collection of surviving stories, which tell how the elders have survived; a collection of persisting, not-yet-told stories, offered in response to the questions these studies and portrayals have raised. All
stories of surviving are miracle tales, and these are no different. The
seniors of the Israel Levin Center were expected to have died out
years ago. How could they continue? From the beginning their circumstances were perilous. Twelve years later, they are more burdened and imperiled than ever. Housing is more expensive. They are
older—now in their nineties and up—more cross, more frightened
and fragile with each passing year, but sharpened, honed by the
burden and blessing of knowing how remarkable they are in their
heroic and improbable persistence. They have outlived statistics and
enemies.

Morrie Rosen has allegedly retired and that worries everyone, but
the center has more members than ever. No one knows exactly who
they are or where they come from, because no new members can
move into the area, given the unavailability of housing. Perhaps the
isolates among the original people have been flushed out of their
rooms by needs made more extreme by age. Perhaps those who previously were marginal have decided to join and participate, since the
center is livelier than ever before and locally famous to boot. Perhaps
those who remain are so strong, biologically and psychologically selected for survival so many times, that they constitute a genuine elite,
a blessed group that like their biblical predecessors are meant to live
to be a hundred and twenty. One becomes very humble in making any

predictions in such circumstances. All that can be said definitively is that the center membership has slowly but steadily continued to rise and that the new members are like the old members, culturally and socially. There is a contingent of younger members, in their seventies for the most part, but there are not enough of them to have substantially altered the face of the center population.

Somehow, the Israel Levin Center still brings in close to five hundred people for major events. The boardwalk and benches along the beach still accommodate the arguing Zionists, socialists, agnostics, Orthodox men and women who have not ceased to participate in local and national political and cultural events, as if their debates and critical evaluations are all that keep public life on course. And still in the center there are singers, poets, musicians, declaimers, dancers, teachers, artists, those who circulate *pushkes* and hold rummage sales for charity, always on the lookout for ways to raise money for Israel, for the poor and the needy. That they themselves are alone, poor, in delicate health, ill-housed, threatened with expulsion by developers, rapacious landlords, and entrepreneurs, physically endangered by winos, muggers, self-absorbed youths on bicycles and skateboards— this in no way alters their sense of commitment to their community, defined as anyone in need, preferably but not necessarily Jewish.

Of course, many individuals have died; many have left for board and care, old age homes, or convalescent hospitals. But the number of familiar faces—people that I have recognized or known well since 1972—is endlessly reassuring, whenever I return.

Since these people do not die when predicted, the problem of severing relations with them becomes very complex and painful. Lynne Littman and I struggled with it continually. After our documentary film, Lynne went on to work on feature films (considered a defection by the elders), and I to study the larger, more complex regenerating Jewish neighborhood of Fairfax (considered as choosing youth over age by the members). Both of us return periodically and experience culture shock each time we come back. Reentering this arena resonant of our own grandmothers, filled with people who continue to inform our choices and imaginations, is a wrench: always the fear that a cherished face will be missing, a lively friend confined to a walker. And there is always their anger if we have stayed away too long; there are accusations of infidelity. (Who has replaced them in our affections? Now that we are "rich and famous," do we no longer need them?) The rush of grateful familiarity and the sense of belonging are always accompanied by floods of guilt. We are children again, eager for their approval, achingly imperfect and vulnerable. And for me, the anthropologist, there is always the problem of having missed information as well as people whenever I am away. It is only our monographs that end. The lives of our subjects persist after we have stopped looking and listening.

The elders somehow have become our touchstones, the fixed and reliable planets by which we navigate our lives and morality. After a particularly materialistic and vulgar bar mitzvah or a skeptical, shallowly felt religious service, I find myself rushing back to the center to reground myself in their changeless, fully lived, deeply embedded forms of Jewish practice. Lynne returned there for a blessing before her marriage, and although it was not spoken, she wanted their acceptance of her non-Jewish husband. Their children would be raised as Jews. The elders liked her husband's socially committed politics, which he practiced at that time as an investigative reporter. Lynne was called to light the Sabbath candles that day. Their union was approved. To whom else would Lynne go for a blessing? Her mother lives in New York. Her grandparents are dead. We need the grandparental generation for such occasions, and if we do not have our own, we borrow them. It reminds us of Foucault's remark that when we trace our forebears back far enough, they diffuse and dissolve. Genealogy branches out and results in a wider commonality. *Mishpokhe,* the family, expands as the directness and limitation of lineality fades.

I returned on one memorable day to touch base before undergoing surgery. It was to be a hysterectomy, a personal operation. I whispered news of this to Morrie, who, to my astonishment and acute embarrassment, announced it over the loudspeaker and asked people to pray for me. It took all my self-control to sit through the little ceremony, reminding myself that all prayers are statements of good will and, as such, useful, even powerful. Anyway, I was an anthropologist, trained to locate objectivity when I needed it. As I left, several women shouted to me that all would go well, they or their daughters had had such an operation, it was nothing. "Besides," yelled Manya, "how could you fail to recover when you got two hundred atheists praying over you?" Thus they gave me their blessings, laughed at themselves, and demanded a little gratitude, all at the same time. Theirs is not a world in which something is given for nothing. Everything is built around exchange. There are no beggars, no charity, only webs of donors. And so their irony made me laugh, restoring my perspective, mending my embarrassment. We were in this together, and I left them knowing why I had come. This attitude of theirs was what I had so often seen carrying them through the worst of times; it was the subtle, sturdy stuff of surviving.

In April 1984, Lynne and I attended Morrie Rosen's retirement party at the center. This was the really serious separation. It was inconceivable that he could continue without them or they without him. Over five hundred people attended. The senior chorus sang. People recited their poems and tributes. There were plaques and mountains of gifts. Morrie was given a piece of luggage by the members. "You should really try to get away, Morrie. Get some rest. It will be hard for you to leave us, but you should try." They were still his teachers, his elders. They would make out on their own.

A month later, news came to me from a legal aid society. Morrie had led a delegation to a meeting at City Hall, protesting an attempt to evict center members from the Cadillac Hotel in violation of zoning restrictions. Was I willing to be called in as an expert witness and testify to the damage done to the community and to the well-being of the elderly, displaced from their homes? Was the man I called "Abe" in my book Morrie Rosen? Was the hotel in which Basha lived the Cadillac? Would I waive the anonymity I had tried to preserve in order to testify? Of course I said yes. It was reassuring to know that Morrie still hadn't retired and would probably be on duty as long as he was needed. And, as usual, the request raised some important anthropological issues. Here was a major one—the importance of attaching names to stories, of allowing witnesses to proclaim what they had seen and lived through, not anonymously, but personally.

Their names and images needed to be recorded to attest to their continuity. This is a particularly sensitive issue to elders whose children have not carried on their heritage, whose peers and natal culture have been extinguished by the Holocaust. And just as important is their perpetual struggle to be noticed in the simple, basic sense of being still among the living, members of a society that tries so often to push them off their little edge of land, from neglect into oblivion. In our society, perhaps all societies, unwanted members are rendered less disturbing by being overlooked, made into nonpersons, erased; and here were people who were pariahs three times over—old, poor, and Jews. Their ceaseless determination to perform their own lives, garner audiences, and be noticed was not mere petulance or immaturity. It was the very expression of their life force, which dictates that one must be seen by others to experience oneself; existence, to be experienced, depends upon membership in the human community. In *Number Our Days*, I talked about the search for "arenas of visibility" in which elders could present themselves to each other and outsiders; this necessity became clearer, fiercer, and more difficult to obtain with the passage of time.

This bore directly on the problem of anonymity and the protection of people's privacy. As an anthropology student, I had always been taught that subjects' names should be changed in one's publications and insofar as possible, their circumstances carefully disguised in order to avoid identification, for legal and ethical reasons. This is not too difficult when one is studying distant peoples, isolates, or nonliterate groups. Disguising people in one's own backyard is another thing. And it was for my sake as well as theirs that I attempted, in the book, to detach their stories from their personal lives and names. My subjects wanted the last word on how they should be understood, and I had decided to reserve that interpretation for myself. Anything else would have resulted in each one writing his or her own book. Some people's stories or personalities could not be disguised, but all of these were dead at the time of writing. Still, I changed their names. Then there was the problem of the existence of the movie. There, real names and faces appeared. The center, Morrie, the center president, Harry Asimov (called Heschel in the book), the student rabbi, Andrew Ehrlich, were all identified.

What I had not been taught was that there are circumstances when ethics call for identification rather than disguise. The anthropologist is a witness, must bear witness, when no one else is available. The question "How did the publicity, the many portrayals of these people, affect them?" is complex. If there is a single truth to be offered, it is that they would always rather be seen than be invisible, even if they disagree with the portrait. This was borne out repeatedly. During the Festival of Yiddishkeit presented at the University of Southern California in 1980, one of our presenters, Tillie Olsen, was determined to read her entire novella, "Tell Me a Riddle," to the elders, who had been bused in for a series of performances. I pleaded with her not to. "They are too old to sit still so long. And how will they bear hearing a story about an old woman dying of cancer?" "You'll see," Tillie answered. "They will be rapt. I know what I'm talking about." I was

dreading the evening, but Tillie was right. The several hundred center members in attendance sat more quietly, for longer, than they had
done in all the time I had known them. They were enthralled. Afterward, I asked one of the elders if it was not hard to bear. "Of course it
was painful. Who likes to look at his own death? But after all, it was
well written. And it was about *us*."

This teaching recurred, most dramatically and poignantly, when I
discovered that in order for the Mark Taper Forum to present the play
Number Our Days, Rebekkah Goldman, Shmuel's widow, the only
living, identifiable person in the piece, had to sign a new release form
giving permission for her portrayal. The release form would allow the
theater to present her "fictionally, anonymously, without any claims."
I was uneasy from the start. For so many of the elderly, their very
lives depended on making claims, on not releasing their identity. I
sensed trouble. I searched everywhere for Rebekkah. She had not
been seen at the center for months. I left the permission form with
Morrie while I was out of town for a couple of weeks. When I returned, Morrie greeted me with the devastating news. She wouldn't
sign. She wanted money, a thousand dollars or maybe fifty thousand
dollars. "After all, my husband's writings and my life are priceless.
And these are the real heroes of *Number Our Days*."

The day before Thanksgiving I reached her by phone. "May I come
and talk to you, Rebekkah? Is Friday okay?"

"You can come any time," she said. "What about 11:00 A.M.
Friday?"

"Okay, Rebekkah, I'll be there."

"But that will only give us two hours."

"Tell me what time, Rebekkah. I'll be there."

I remembered Rebekkah scolding me for spending so much time
with Shmuel, her husband.

"Don't you think my life is interesting too? Have you ever heard me
read Peretz? I can bring poetry to life like no one else. . . . You gave
me Shmuel's tapes to keep, but I can't work the tape recorder. Also, I
can't listen to them alone. Come sit with me to hear them."

"But Rebekkah, there are thirty hours of tapes there." Her demands always escalated. Later: Rebekkah told me she could no longer
go to the center parties because the clothes Shmuel made her were
wearing out. My long skirts were so lovely. Did I have any others? I
brought three, one an orange velvet, one from Lynne.

"The ones you gave me were so drab, not like the one you are wearing." Did she want me to take it off there in the center and give it to her? Another time: We are videotaping an interview with a center member. There is much excitement. Rebekkah looks on, scowls, then plucks at my sleeve. "You should come over today. I found more poetry of Shmuel's. Come *now*. I will show it to you."

I had long known that the worst thing we had done to the center people was to exclude them from the film, to change their names in the book. Manya was incensed. "You interviewed me for hours, I told you everything. Then you left me out of the movie." Contrite, I gave Manya an immense photograph of herself, publicly, with honor, in front of her friends, and I asked her pardon. "It's no good," she said. "I don't forgive. It's wrong of you to ask me to forgive now, between Rosh Hashanah and Yom Kippur, the Days of Awe, when not to forgive is a sin." Then the film was shown on national TV. She was more annoyed and hurt than before. "I still don't forgive. It wasn't enough you left me out of the film when it showed in Los Angeles. Now it showed in Detroit where my children live. You left me out also in Detroit."

Nervously, I arrived at Rebekkah's apartment. Two television sets sat one on top of the other, neither working. But she didn't like TV. She preferred reading. "These things I read: *Jewish Currents, Spanish for Beginners*"—she still worked on behalf of Mexican migrant fruit-pickers—"petitions, political journals, books by Balzac, Chekhov."

"I don't take *The People's World* anymore. Too politically narrow. Will you eat breakfast? I made fresh squeezed orange juice. Myself, I can't eat. I've been so aggravated about all this, I didn't sleep all night."

It dawns on me. Of course. It isn't money she wants, it's my time. "You never come and see me. Let me tell you the trouble I have been having with my lower dentures." We talk for forty-five minutes about her teeth. I drink my orange juice, resigned, summoning patience. Then there is a sudden turn from teeth to politics. "You know, I still work with the Emma Lazarus Club. We were never, what do you call it, subversive. Only for freedom. All my lower teeth were broken out when those boys tripped me last month."

"Rebekkah, wasn't that last year?"

"Whenever it was, I haven't been able to eat meat since then, because of the lower dentures. . . . You always spent so much time talking to Shmuel. He knew a lot, but I too know a lot. Do you

[273]

remember the first time you met me? I was reading Mendele for the Emma Lazarus. How I can read Yiddish, it is as if you never heard the words before. I don't get myself between the poet and the words. I bring a life into it. I could have been professional." Her hands tremble as she makes me coffee. Her blouse is soiled. Her reading is powerful and her Yiddish is indeed a poem. My heart breaks again along different fissures.

After two hours, we begin to discuss the issue of the release. "You don't know what Morrie did to me, in front of everybody. He made it sound as though I wanted money. Money, for Shmuel's work. I was so embarrassed. No one else in the book is like Shmuel. Everyone says so. Do you know, some of my relatives won't read it. Too narrow. No vision. I didn't spend Thanksgiving with them. I sat here in my apartment and brooded about these things. The center was closed."

I go over the release word by word. There will be a character based on her, fictionalized, an actress portraying her who may or may not look like her. No claims. Everything is all right until we get to the part about changing her name. "You mean you wouldn't use my real name? How would anybody know it was me? My children, my grandchildren. It will all be lost. You and I know Shmuel's greatness. Without your book, it would have remained hidden. By your work, you put it out to the world. Now, you take that away if you change the name. Why couldn't you use our real names?" Because the Taper requires a release that calls for anonymity. Because there would be Byzantine legalities, issues of invasion of privacy. I explain that this is to be a work of fiction, based on the center people, but not exact copies. Liberties would be taken. It was moving from anthropology to art. "Rebekkah"—I am pleading now—"you will come to the play. We will invite your son and the center members, and they will see and know your part in this. Opening night you will come with Morrie, in a long, beautiful skirt. You won't be anonymous. I can promise you that. You will be honored. But I can't promise you will be named in the play." "But if you don't put in my name it passes away. Anyway, Morrie is now mad at me. Will you fix it up with him? Otherwise I can't go back to the center. It's too hard. I can't eat there if Morrie is mad at me. What will I do?"

"Rebekkah, please just sign this, and I'll go right now and explain to Morrie. He won't be mad at you, I promise."

Her hand hovers endlessly over the page. "Won't I get any money for this at all, even if it goes famous? If it's commercial? What do you mean people don't make money, it's nonprofit? Don't they pay an actress for being me?"

"Rebekkah, if you don't sign this, there will not even be a play. Or there will be a play with you left out altogether. The play will bring attention to the center, and that brings in the meals on Sunday mornings, the donations for food from the temples. The Weiss family, Mickey Katz, and the Eddie Cantor B'nai B'rith Lodge—all those people have told me they knew about the center because of the movie. The publicity brings in money, meals, programs. We *need* the play, not just for you and Shmuel but for the center, for the other older people, and not just for Jewish people—for Mexicans, for all the poor old people, for the grape workers. So sign, or there will be nothing."

"Will this be a good play? Will it be correct? How can you be sure it will be true, if they make it a fiction?"

"I'm working very closely with the writer and director, Rebekkah. They love the material. They love you and Shmuel and are making it very carefully, full of respect and understanding. Art has its own truth. Trust me, Rebekkah. Sign. It's getting late. Morrie will be gone."

"But the name you will use in the play—it must be my real name. It should say 'Rebekkah and Shmuel Goldman.'"

"But those are the names in the book that I substituted for yours."

"That's right. That's where the story is. My own name, no one knows. What difference would it make. In the book I am known. I can show that's me. Let them use those in the play."

"I don't know if they will. Let's try. I'll put down that this is your request, that we use Rebekkah and Shmuel Goldman, not your actual names or any others. I can't promise, but we'll try."

"How should I sign this paper? I'm also known as Regina, it was my name when I lived in Paris."

At noon she signs. I dash to the center. There is chaos in the kitchen. Morrie had to argue with the mayor to get meals served on an official holiday, the day after Thanksgiving. Everyone is shouting, three hundred old people waiting for lunch, having lived through Thanksgiving alone. Morrie is furious. "Do you know what Rebekkah did to me? Do you know what you have asked me? This is the most difficult thing I have done for you. Three hours I spent with her. I pleaded, threatened. The others were there. They advised her not to sign. 'You're giving away everything. You'll lose a fortune. Everyone else will get rich on your life.'"

"Morrie, never mind. She's on her way over. She signed and I promised you wouldn't be mad, I promised I'd make it up between you two."

"You want me to make it up. *I'm* not even in the play. I'll tell you what *I* want. After the performance when they applaud and call up the author, I want to be up there with you, alone, on the stage."

Rebekkah appears at the kitchen door. The soup has been lost. Was it thrown away as dishwater? Morrie approaches Rebekkah. She has put on lipstick. She wears a gray knitted pilot's cap. She is four feet ten or less. She stands, silently, apprehensively looking at us. Morrie kisses her. "Rebekkah, it will be wonderful. I will take you out to dinner beforehand. I'll drive you opening night. You and Barbara and I will sit together in the front row." I love Morrie all over again. I blush for my own complaining and anguish. Four people accost him, asking for their soup. Bessie wants to know if he knows who took her umbrella. "You see, Rebekkah, Morrie isn't mad at you."

"That's fine. Now would you go out and tell the others, the people out there, that I wasn't just out for money. I have principles, I have ideals. They should know."

"No, Rebekkah, actually I won't. I'll write to invite your son to the play. Now I'm going home."

Morrie walks me to the car. "I'm retiring in a year and a half."

"You can't, Morrie. They can't live without you. I can't live without you. Morrie, how can I thank you?" We embrace. We laugh and cry.

"Isn't she wonderful?" Morrie says. "Look at her, at this age, in these circumstances. How she still has all this power. She's not a victim. You have to admire her."

The play was a qualified success. The audiences loved it; the critics had reservations. The center members, bused in for a benefit performance, took over as usual. Jennie informed one of the wealthy patrons in the front row that he should change seats with her. It was wrong that the center members were given seats farther back, with their problems in hearing and seeing. He agreed with some embarrassment and soon the first few rows of patrons had been replaced by the elders. As soon as the play began, Bessie shouted to the actors that she couldn't hear them. "Speak up. We don't hear so good." "Good," echoed John Hirsch, the director. "It's what I've been telling them all along." After intermission, the sound of crackling cellophane was heard from all over the theater. The elders had come from a breakfast in their honor just before the play and had brought along extra lox and bagels for a snack later in the day. They unpacked their leftovers, and the theater was pervaded with the unmistakable smell of fish. The play continued with a heightened atmosphere of realism. At the end Morrie and I did indeed stand up on the stage together and were given flowers. And at a formal and glorious reception afterward, Rebekkah entered on Morrie's arm, flashbulbs going off, in a room full of elegant and admiring people. The actress who played Rebekkah rushed up to her to tell her how inspiring she found her character. Some of the audience members complained about the "unnecessarily exaggerated immigrant characteristics" of the people in the play. In one of the scenes, a newcomer complained about the elders to the anthropologist. "But why must they always shout and gesture?"

"Because they can't hear," she replies in exasperation. Nevertheless, at the reception, a well-dressed, late-middle-aged Jewish gentleman could be overheard complaining to his wife, "But I still don't see why they had those terrible accents. And why do they have to shout all the time?" And the center elders argued all the way home on the bus as to whether the representation had been faithful to them. "We don't really argue that much, do we?" "Some would say yes, some would say no. . . ."

The selective identification and recognition of themselves by the elders, by other Jews portrayed in the play, and by the audience was a fascinating phenomenon. The elders wanted more control over their portrayals, though they more or less agreed that the depiction of them was faithful. Still, they wanted the play as a platform upon which to mount their ideals. Younger Jews in the audience reacted to the elders in ways that suggested a reflection of their accommodations to the immigrant generations of Jews in general and to their own immigrant past. Those who had eschewed it were embarrassed and annoyed. Those for whom it struck a nostalgic and sentimental response were warmed, even thrilled, rather than dismayed by the overt display of Jewish "ethnic" markers of identity. More than was the case with the film or book, it was possible to read Jewish responses to the play as a kind of barometer of people's adaptation to their social history, their degree of assimilation and, at a deeper level, their attitudes about very complex and personal issues such as their relationships with parents, grandparents, the elderly in general, and the prospect of their own aging.

Later, what stood out in my mind as I assessed the play's impact on the center people was the subject of Rebekkah's release. In the beginning, her resistance had seemed some combination of narcissism and stubbornness, a desire for power by a person who had, as Morrie pointed out, few occasions for being able to give or withhold something of value. Slowly, it dawned on me that there was something loftier than that involved. She wanted the stories remembered more than her name. She was willing to keep the name I had given her in my book because that was the name attached to her and Shmuel's tales. The tales were her chance for an enduring identity, more than her personal, actual unknown name. She could make it clear to her immediate friends and family that they were hers, using her real name. The protracted and careful rendering of hers and Shmuel's stories presented in the book must remain attached to the names used there. That was where her identity and her chance for some immortality were located. To substitute another name, or to use her "real" name in the play, where the stories would inevitably be changed and abbreviated, would be a loss for her. The character in book and play must be the same, that woman and the stories inseparable. She had become Rebekkah, not in any blind or confused fashion, but because she agreed to let herself be rendered as Rebekkah. She had authenticated that rendering and identified with it. She had few choices. She could remain anonymous or call herself Rebekkah Goldman, since she could not write, publish, and distribute her own interpretation of herself. Thus whenever I brought a stranger or guest to the center, she introduced herself not by her real name, but as Shmuel Goldman's widow, Rebekkah, so that she would be "recognized."

Members' reactions to their portrayals often demonstrated an almost bewilderingly close identification with them. This was particularly evident in center people's responses to the film—by its nature the most concrete, repetitive, public, and affective of all the portraits we made of them.

Film and photographic images are overwhelmingly persuasive mirrors, relatively recent inventions in the array of reflecting surfaces people have used to know and identify themselves. There have always been many kinds of reflecting devices used for this purpose. The importance of mirrors for human self-recognition has been widely explored in studies of performance, reflexivity, and ritual, all topics bearing on the nature of observation and the emergence of self. When it was discovered that higher primates could recognize and respond to themselves in mirrors and could distinguish themselves from fellow apes, it was argued that they were closer to human consciousness than scientists had previously expected. Self-recognition is requisite to self-awareness, an attribute humans usually think is reserved for their own species. Pictures, mirrors, and movies are known to allow primates to identify or, perhaps, create "a self," that unique, steady bundle of distinctive attributes, appearances, and behaviors that allows one to say "I am I." This is, of course, true of humans, who recognize and reflect on themselves through performances in all the rituals, ceremonies, and religious and aesthetic forms they invent to tell themselves who they are (and by extension what they are doing there, and what the point is, in the end, of their existence).

Perhaps the most powerful reflecting surfaces that provide self-recognition are other people, as social interactionist theory has long indicated. We see ourselves in others' eyes. We can erase, even slay, a fellow by looking away often enough or looking with eyes that mirror hate; thus curses and the "evil eye" can be efficacious even without words.

In simpler, stabler times, occasions for reflection were assured, the birthright of all who lived within the web of meanings and tales that constitute a coherent culture. Then all the heroes and demons, animals, deities, plants, and stones are variations of oneself, like a dream in which a single dreamer retells versions of himself/herself in all the characters and situations imagined and envisioned. Then every story told is "my" story, about my family and predicaments, past and future. But now surfaces and stories are provided not from within the indigenous reservoir of agreed-on understandings in the group; they are given, and withheld, by outsiders. Accidents, displacing people from their native countries and cultures, may loosen the web of meanings that held people together and thus may destroy the occasions in which they find themselves "properly" (familiarly and appropriately) understood and reflected. And politics plays an immense role in this destruction: disenfranchised, disdained, marginal people are at a loss for mirroring media, and thus often cannot recognize themselves anywhere. If they are seen at all, it is likely to be in caricature, in simple and negative stereotypes that are disorienting and damaging.

In our time, the stories we hear and the pictures we see that give us

[279]

images of ourselves are most often out of our hands; they have been centralized, packaged, mixed, and sold. It is not unusual to meet, as I did lately, an educated, very intelligent young woman who confessed that she was addicted to television soap operas because "they are realer than my own life." The characters move faster; they are more sharply etched, simplified, exaggerated; they come right to the point; the plot unfolds more powerfully, dramatically, coherently; motives are clear, emotions unmistakable. Whether she likes it or not, those tales have more punch than her own meandering, erratically unfolding story in which the plotline and the outcome are obscure and slow in their revelation. The television image holds the experienced reality of a life, and we, the "originals," are the faded, bored copies.

Peoples' responses to themselves on film have long fascinated ethnographic cinematographers for ethical as well as theoretical reasons. When people who are unsophisticated about technology die after their "images have been taken," their survivors sometimes ask: has the photographer stolen their souls? If a whole village disappears in a slow pan shot across a horizon, how is it to be brought back? When people are shown photographs, or more powerfully, movies, they can often be observed to shape themselves kinesthetically into the person they see on film, verifying the "authentic" filmic version. The French cinematographer Jean Rouche has written on this subject extensively, noting that among Africans he was filming in a documentary on trance behavior, individuals that saw themselves in a possessed state on film were likely to fall into trance again. The replay of the original trance triggered a secondary one. What is the relation between them? Is the original behavior authentic and the second trance a replication, somehow false because it is not spontaneous? Is one real because it is unself-conscious, and the other more real because it is more conscious? Societies tattoo certain markings on their citizens to show them to themselves in a new light: "Now you are an adult, you are marriageable, a full member." These are lessons made palpable, literally embodied. We become emblems; we are what we display. Likewise, the secondary trance, induced by the camera's presence, inscribes societies' teachings and, at the deepest physiological level, recreates its images. Perhaps it is a "cine-trance," manufactured by the camera's eye, or an "ethno-trance," an expression of a culture's interpretation of itself, made more sharp, triggered by the heightening of reflexive consciousness that is one of the hallmarks of human experience and one of the points of all cultural performance.

The same process can be observed in interviewing. When one takes a very long, careful life history of another person, complex exchanges occur between subject and object. Inventions and distortions emerge; neither party remains the same. A new creation is constituted when two points of view are engaged in examining one life. The new creation has its own integrity but should not be mistaken for the spontaneous, unframed life-as-lived person who existed before the interview began. This could be called an "ethno-person," the third person who is born by virtue of the collusion between interlocutor and subject.

Subjects know this intuitively, and for some, the emphasis comes to be on how they are changed by being interviewed, while for others the interest is on how the interview changes the interlocutor. One of the center members whom I had chased for nearly a year, trying to pin him down to do a life history session, faced me at last and explained his refusal. What I wanted was a serious thing, almost like making a *golem*, an idol, he said. It would forever alter both of us.

"If I would tell you my life and you would really listen, it would change you, and what right have I to do that? On the other hand, if I would tell you my life and you would really listen and not be changed, why should I waste my time?" For him, it was not worth the risk, but that was unusual. Most center members wanted desperately to be included. They had very few remaining opportunities for being seen, remembered, attended to. And being left out, particularly being left on the cutting-room floor, was a real trauma.

"It's bad enough that you left me out in Los Angeles. Now the movie shows in Detroit where my daughter lives, and you left me out all over again." Manya never forgave us. Each replaying was a fresh erasure of her existence.

Mr. Stoller, on the other hand, was thrilled. "You gave me back my wife by this film." He was referring to the close-up of a photograph of his wife of nearly fifty years, focused on during an interview with him in his room. "After all this time, she comes back to me." The photograph sat on his dresser in his room facing him every day. How, then, had we given it back? It could only be that seeing it blown up so very large had an impact on him, making it more alive than the version in his room. But more than that, it seemed to me that viewing his wife's picture in a public setting, seeing her being seen by all his friends and fellows there in the center gave her image a heightened reality. Additional life was breathed into her photograph when it was held up to the watching world. There were witnesses who could attest to her existence, to their marriage, who could see his continuing love for her. The audience cospectatorship brought her back into living society, and briefly, magically, returned her to him with a power the picture lacked when, standing mutely on the dresser, it was viewed by him alone.

Whenever we showed the film in the center, we were struck with people's consistency. Those who watched themselves clapping in the film were clapping in the room. Over and over the same people got up and actually left the center at the point they were shown departing in the film. And after the first time we showed it, three of the women, having just heard me reflect on how often I was asked, "Who's with your children, madam Professor?" called me aside, said they liked the film on the whole, then asked me who was with my children.

Everyone was happy about the Academy Award and the public validation of them it offered. But Lynne and I were urged not to become too inflated about it. They had, after all, told us on the first day we began filming that if we did our work well, we would get an Oscar. It was clear that we were only the recorders, and it was *their* lives, *their* survival, that was the material to be acclaimed. (And of course if we had failed, it would have been just as clear whose fault that was!)

The film brought the center immediate attention—visitors, donations, the establishment of programs, some of which went on for years. The capacity of film to change consciousness has always been clear; what had not been so clear to me previously was the extent to which film can be a service as well as a record. And it was and continues to be a source of research information. Now, years and hundreds of viewings later, I still find things in it I hadn't noticed before. And watching people's responses to particular moments is also a source of research data. In one scene, an older woman without a partner dances tentatively at first, then picks up momentum and ends up dancing with great verve, alone and grave, slapping her thighs to the music. It is an emblematic moment in which one can see the crystallization of years of experience: the steps, leading up to the courage to be so alive though alone, are laid out like pebbles marking a path. Audiences of all ages and both sexes often gasp at that image. And Gita, the proud ballerina who is accompanied in her dance by her blind husband, becomes another such emblem. He holds her wrist with reverence, and it is evident that he still sees her beauty. They demonstrate the way two people can use all their artistry and love and years of experience in living together to display *her,* a tiny bent woman, still a coquette, eternally feminine; they execute their routine with the dedication and care one sees in the partnering of Margot Fonteyne by Rudolph Nureyev. At this instant, the center is no longer a miniature arena; it swells to become as immense as the grandest stage in one of life's most exalted enterprises. The common human impulse for beauty and an exhibition of grace are identified; the couple is not any longer cute or endearing but magnificent. Such a transformation can only be *felt* through film, and audiences consistently find that a mysteriously moving moment.

Some acute observers notice the saxophone player's hands in the dance sequence: he is crippled with arthritis. He has no lower teeth. Yet the music we hear is wild and sweet. Viewers respond to this subliminally, moved by more than the music but unable to say why. Jewish audiences laugh or weep at certain words, certain events that do not similarly move non-Jews. But to our amazement the film managed to cross the ethnic barrier. "That's my Armenian grandmother!" "It's just like my Greek grandfather!" We hear this over and over. It has seemed that the commonalities of the immigrant experience override the ethnic specifics.

One of the lessons of the film, which I incorporated into the book, emerged from my decision to include myself overtly as part of the story I was telling. The decision to include me had been made on strictly utilitarian grounds: it sped things up and allowed us to discuss some of the invisible issues. Serendipitously, exposing the way I learned about the elders' lives and how theirs affected mine turned out to be of great interest not only to anthropologists but to lay people as well. That the observer is a part of all she witnesses has long been a truism. That the process of the witnessing is very interesting and instructive was not as clear when we began. Unexpectedly, the film's presentation of my discovering and responding to the members' lives proved to be a model and a teaching. Somehow, audiences were less removed from the elders because I was a more familiar figure—American-born, middle-aged, a bridge. Since so much of the receiving of cultural traditions requires a witness, since so much of what the older people lacked and needed were witnesses, it was absolutely right that I filled that role in the film. None of this was evident to us at the time. In retrospect, the showing of the listening and receiving was as important as showing the offering and telling of stories and traditions. The transmission of culture requires two parties in a complex process, and the role of both parties should be made explicit.

This lesson from the film was incorporated into the book. The decision to include myself was immensely liberating. I was able to expose and explore my conflicts and choices instead of presenting them as hardened, closed states or facts; I could unfold them as processes, resonant with elements originating from the research situation and my own personal reactions. It felt more honest, deeper, and finally simpler than any anthropological work I had ever done. I felt more of my reactions being used, wholistically, the way we are taught to study societies. I was thinking with my viscera, feeling with my brain, learning from all my history and hunches and senses. This notion of wholistic knowledge was part of the lecture I was used to giving my students when introducing them to the idea of participant-observation, but it felt as though I was practicing it for the first time, and I could never imagine trusting my own or anyone else's work as fully again without some signposts as to how the interpretations were arrived at and how the anthropologist felt while doing so.

The book was much less important to the center people—another sort of disappointment entirely. People were either in or out of the film. In the book, such absolutes did not obtain: people were disappointed not to be able to find themselves easily. The careful observers among them noted that the film was the simpler portrait. It was, in fact, a more idealized portrait—the elders seen more as they wanted to see themselves—edited so that there would be no fools or even people who were simply mean. But, of course, such people existed. And the film downplayed the extent of quarreling and dissension within the community. This was a conscious choice. In thirty minutes, it is not possible to present a sufficiently complex picture of an entire group of people; simplistic images, spontaneously presented by "real life" appearances and performances, are inevitably transmitted. The very concreteness of film presents a clearer, misleadingly precise version of reality. It is much more difficult to control, to shade, to turn over for another perspective. That multicolored interpretation was reserved for the book. Both had different messages. The subjects enjoyed the film much more; it was really theirs. Outsiders, social scientists, younger people were more affected by the multiplex and more protean situations found in the book. And they attached themselves to Shmuel—who was in the book but not the film—with intense devotion and even inspiration.

Disguising people in the book was always difficult, a conventional and practical choice originally, but finally futile. Shmuel's son telephoned me sometime after the book came out. "Is the man you call Shmuel in fact my father?" "Yes it is," I confessed, my heart pounding. Would he recognize and approve of this portrayal? Had I really understood the man? The son was as nervous as I was, and about the same issue. Had *he* really known his father? Had his father been closer to me, confessed more to me than what had appeared in the book? Had his father known he was going to die, and had he, the son, somehow been unaware of that? I was immensely relieved to be able to tell him the only one who really knew his father, to whom Shmuel really opened himself, was his wife, not me, an outsider. And no, his father had not known he was going to die. The son had not missed the reality of the man, Shmuel, that showed in my sustained portrait; it matched, but it was not identical with the man the son experienced in the course of ordinary living. "Your picture of him is not false, but it is too sharp. Distilled. My father was an outstanding man, but there was so much else, so much of no clear consequence. You left out the mundane." "Yes," I agreed; as Shmuel said, "I exaggerated." That is the purpose of framing an individual or an event; there are only choices, no faithful copies.

The final arena of visibility in which the elders "appeared"—an exhibition and celebration titled "Life Not Death in Venice: From Victims to Victors"—grew out of an incident described at the end of the book. One of the center members was killed by a bicyclist who ran her down. "I didn't see her," he said, though she was directly in front of him. It was emblematic of all that had grown increasingly apparent to them over the years—the elderly were invisible. After the extensive coverage and attention provided by the film, many members had become very sophisticated about manipulating their images and had grown sensitive to the power they could mobilize by reaching a broader, sympathetic outside public. An article in the newspaper titled "Death in Venice" decried the death. The elders took up the headline as a battle cry, made placards reading "Life Not Death in Venice," and led by Morrie Rosen's always deft political sense, they arranged a procession down the boardwalk, accompanying a mock coffin (a refrigerator carton painted black, carried on a child's wagon), calling attention to their need for some safety zones where they could walk without being imperiled by bicycles and skateboards. Much media coverage assured them the attention they desired, and indeed, they were successful. A city ordinance prohibiting wheeled traffic in the area was enforced. The photograph of the parade became the logo for an exhibition of folk art and a celebration of *yidishkeyt* that we mounted at the University of Southern California in 1980. The title was our own mnemonic device for remembering how important it was that these people were learning to empower themselves by appearing in public and commanding attention.

Increasingly fascinated by their self-depictions, I began to pay more attention to a mural painted by the elders along one entire wall of the center, portraying their peregrinations, from the *shtetls* of Europe, through the sweatshops of New York, ending up at the beach in Venice. It is a complex piece of self-portraiture, worthy of an extended analysis. For our purposes here, two features are striking. At the heart of the mural they had painted a picture of themselves as young people, parading, marching in union demonstrations, picketing, carrying placards, much as they had done in response to the Venice death. Here, then, was an old model, one that existed on their very walls, alive in their history and imaginations as painting and performance. Second, two of the figures in the last panel were mere outlines, empty of color. I had assumed that the mural was simply unfinished at that point. Then I overheard two women discussing it. "It shows us before we came together, so we really didn't exist completely." "No," the other woman rebutted. "It's because we are unfinished. No matter how old, we are still growing and new things can come in."

We underestimate folk art. I had looked at this piece for years without fully understanding it. How much else would they have to say about their paintings and drawings, which hung about on the center walls? What were the visual images that accompanied or elaborated the stories that I knew in much greater detail? Periodically, some of them would bring in a few paintings. I had known them as consummate storytellers. Now I became aware that their visual pictures were rich and vivid too. Completely self-taught, overcoming a religious tradition that forbad portraiture and the depiction of images, nevertheless, they made art objects.

I became even more intrigued on the day I accompanied the members to an exhibition of the works of Marc Chagall at the Los Angeles

County Art Museum. The docent led us through the corridors, politely reciting the text that had been provided for her. When she got to one of the last paintings, she announced that what we saw was an example of "true art," a work, in short, which was incomprehensible. "You see, there is a tablecloth, floating upside down in the air. Only the free and inexplicable imagination of an artist would have thought of such a thing."

"Excuse me, Miss," Beryl interrupted politely, "but on this I would explain a few other things. What you see here is on the day we call *Simkhes Toyre* [Simhat Torah]. We celebrate the joy that comes when we begin to read the Torah all over again. It means the Torah has no beginning and no end, neither is there an up or a down. So everything is backwards and upside down, or the opposite, to show how special it is, to show the wonder and the happiness and that it is a day unlike any other. This thing that you call a tablecloth, we call a *talis*, a prayer shawl. The painting is not so mysterious as you think. Maybe it is even a little bit familiar."

"But none of this is in my guidebook. How do you know it?" she asked him.

"Myself, I am from Vitebsk, which is Chagall's town, and we knew him. So if you have the time I will take the liberty and show you a few other things you have overlooked." And he did, with the members following along approvingly, full of additional interpretations.

If there was this kind of knowledge inside these people about the visual arts, what else was there to be fathomed? I began to sense the importance of looking more closely at their drawings and hearing their interpretations of them. They were portraying a vanished world, personally felt visions with profound cultural correlates. Their techniques and symbols were not at all self-evident, despite the seeming simplicity and rough technique.

And just at this time, as I was becoming more aware of the meaning of their visual images, the opportunity arose that would provide an arena in which to exhibit their art works and give them a chance of offering a public exegesis, for they would have to be their own docents. The Skirball Museum of Hebrew Union College (HUC) at the University of Southern California (USC) announced an exhibition about the elderly of Venice ("The Golden Age of Venice"), by a photographer, Bill Aron and a fine artist, Carol Tolin. I felt it was essential that we also provide a space where the elderly could present their own depictions of themselves, to complement and complete the HUC show. The USC Davidson Conference Center, which specializes in programs for adult students, offered the space, its lobby upstairs and auditorium below. Locating and collecting the art work began in earnest in March 1980.

At that time we began to develop a cadre of young people, students in my anthropology life-history class, whose semester's work would be to locate elderly artists and storytellers and document their lives. The young people gathered the elders' life histories, preserved in written form, and at the same time trained them to interpret their art and experiences to the unfamiliar audience of outsiders that we hoped would attend the exhibit. The search was not too difficult; using local teachers in senior citizens' centers and classes we soon found seventeen people between the ages of sixty and ninety-two, all of Eastern European background, all self-taught and nonprofessional, with one exception. Over a hundred pieces were gathered and displayed, representing a great range of styles and media, but all depicting some aspect of the culture of Eastern European Jewish life in the old world and in America.

During the spring, we ran a series of all-day workshops in traditional storytelling, intergenerational journal work, and intergenerational dramatic improvisation. In these we included the elderly artists whose works we had selected for the exhibition as well as those whose works were not used but who expressed a desire for contributing to making a record of their lives.

Young people enrolled, some volunteers, some relatives and friends of the elders, along with other university students interested in art, anthropology, history, Jewish studies, and social work.

The second phase of the project took place over a six-week period in May and June during which we developed a folklife celebration: a series of weekly performances to accompany and interpret the art work. These consisted of a set of rather glamorous events, held in the downstairs auditorium, designed to attract the widest possible audience, which would have to pass through the elders' art exhibit upstairs to attend the evening events. It was a way of gaining a captive audience of people who, we felt, would not ordinarily pay attention to the artists or folk art of the kind we had assembled.

The events consisted of the works of scholars, fine artists, and performing artists that drew upon, interpreted, and universalized the original Yiddish sources portrayed by the elderly folk artists. The refined, inflected expression of the Yiddish themes—in the form of films, stories, readings, concerts, lectures, and plays—were readily available to those who were estranged from or strangers to the "Little Tradition," the basic, mundane cultural life of the *shtetl* that was the living experience of the elders. The folk art exhibit and the cultural events juxtaposed origins and interpretations, actual historical experiences of the elderly and the assimilated, imaginative versions of those experiences by people who had lived it for a short time as children or at one remove through their parents' or grandparents' memories and stories. The performances were selected to show the immense richness and variety distilled from the culture of *yidishkeyt*. Abba Eban opened the art exhibit. Isaac Bashevis Singer told stories of his family life in pre-Holocaust Poland; Lee Strasberg reminisced about the *klezmer* music of his childhood; Barbara Kirshenblatt-Gimblett showed home movies of Poland between the wars; Jerome Rothenberg read poetry from his anthology, *A Big Jewish Book*; Mickey Katz and His Octogenarians offered Catskill and vaudeville music and humor of America in the 1920s and 1930s; The Traveling Jewish Theater performed stories of the hasidic master, Reb Nachman of Bratzlav; Tillie Olsen read "Tell Me a Riddle"; Georgie Jessel and Baruch Lumet gave stand up one-man shows, comic and dramatic readings in English and Yiddish, respectively. The Israel Levin Senior Adult Chorus opened and closed the series.

Audiences were large, enthusiastic, and heterogeneous. Many were young people who were astonished at finding themselves for the first time among so many old people. "I never dreamt they had so much energy!" was a commonly heard remark. "Where did this stuff come from?" was also a staple comment. "Grandma, you never told me you could draw!" "You never asked," was the reply. The exhibit was full of discovery and surprise, particularly when the young found themselves pressed into providing transportation for old people who found it easier to ask for concrete services than for a more direct and open form of attention. We capitalized on this development by providing free admission to all intergenerational couples who came to the events together. Some lasting unions were established, and our audiences soon included many more elderly people than we were able to bring to the exhibit on our own.

The audience was broadened further when PBS produced a special segment on the exhibit as part of its *Over Easy* television series aimed at the elderly. The visibility we had hoped for allowed us to present the exhibition and celebration as a model, adaptable to people of any cultural group. There is no doubt that there are ethnic elderly people all over America, waiting to be asked, to be discovered, whose art works sit on boxes in the cellar, in trunks, in the attic, whose poems are jammed in drawers, whose reminiscences need to find a witness, a receiver, so that they may complete the interchange that is requisite to all cultural transmission.

In our time we have come to realize that the concept of "image" is not a shallow or trivial affair. Images are the coins in terms of which we are known and valued by the world, and ultimately they are internalized; as such they become the basis for self-evaluation. Appearance becomes "reality," and nonappearance may mean oblivion. When disdained or ignored, people are taught how to control their images, to shape them in accord with their view of themselves and life, despite often contradictory views presented from outside, they acquire a set of skills that are nothing less than the means for gaining enhanced power and self-determination.

Work that is built around portraying a people's interpretation enriches the society to which it is addressed. We have come to accept our multicultural, multiethnic world as a richer one than the imaginary homogeneous "melting pot" once desired. We enrich the total culture and the members of ignored groups when we aid them to "be themselves," publicly and powerfully. It is significant that the elderly provide a model here, since they represent a human universal, crosscutting specific ethnic and regional membership. Assisting them in their movement from victims to victors is a fitting way to bring about internally generated social change.

We were able to demonstrate the use of folk art as a means by which the elderly communicate to successor generations and establish autonomy over their own images, creating their own artistic works and interpretations of their culture in a context in which they see themselves as major figures. They became, for themselves and the outside world, people who must be seen, with important images to show and stories to tell, and so they escaped, however briefly, from their position as invisible victims. The exhibition also called attention to the riches they provide in their role as repositories of history and vanished cultures. The entire body of work provided occasions when young and old came together, to face each other in the giving and receiving of the lore, the lives, which ultimately link the generations; and it is only through exchanges of this kind that we become part of the ongoing stream of history, which makes our lives comprehensible, coherent, and finally gives us the consolation to continue.

We did not, unfortunately, have the means or facilities to publish a catalogue of the artists' works and excerpts of their comments on the meaning of their art and their artistic process. The closest approximation to conveying the discoveries of the project can be seen in some of the captions selected to accompany particular art works. Here are some examples:

"This is a self-portrait, how I look to myself. My friends say, 'Sadie, look in the mirror.' I see my face and it's wrinkled. But the heart, the heart is not wrinkled. Could you see that in the painting?"

"What I find worthwhile in this effort is a sense of identity and self-worth, and to be able to say I have made a contribution, however modest, to the enrichment of the human spirit."

"In drawing, like music, you're trying to express. When you're drawing a face you try to bring out something in the face, like you want to say something in music. After all, there you have black notes on white paper and have to make those notes come alive. Now it's the same thing in drawing. You have black lines on white paper and you have to make those lines say something. A curve, even a twinkle in the eye can say something. I like faces because every face is like an unopened box. But each one has to be opened. Each has something to say. Of course, some you open and they are blank."

"When you look at this picture of Anatoly Shcharansky's mother, you see a mother in grief. As a mother, anyone can understand, all the mothers whose children have suffered. You understand? It is perhaps a Jewish theme but it is about yourself. You have that experience. So you don't have to be Jewish to be Jewish."

"My chief aim in sculpture is to express my fellow man with dignity, understanding, and with as much perfection as I can command. I hope that I am able to give others some measure of joy and pleasure through my work."

"When you design, you are an artist. So many things in your head, and you could yourself create the style. An architect, a tailor, and it's the same thing. There are patterns in things, like blueprints. When you put it together, you have made it for the first time. Do you understand what I am saying? Everything has a pattern. You didn't make it, but you brought it out, so you make something new in the world."

[291]

"I've been drawing as long as I could remember. We used to live upstairs from my papa's bakery, that was in New York. I remember— he would close the store about 11:00 P.M. at night and come upstairs and shake his head. However tired, there I would be—sitting, drawing still."

"Art to me is life itself, like the children is to the parent. It is my history. It tells a story and I love it."

"A person who works only with her hands is a laborer. A person who works with hands and head is an artisan. But a person who works with hands and head and heart is an artist."

"Painting for me is turning inward. It is how I find who I am. I may start a painting with an idea but in the process that gets lost and I just permit myself to be led by what's happening on the canvas. Most start one way and become something else."

"This what you see is a dead tree, found in Hollywood, come back to life. This particular tree represents the beginning of life. What I have carved from it is the statue of Adam and Eve, inside the trunk of the dead tree. It is placed to overlook the playland of Hollywood, right in our garden—the garden which my wife made our Garden of Eden with all kinds of fruit trees, vegetables and beautiful flowers. So I put this in. It is a real Garden of Eden."

"What does it mean to draw my *shtetl?* It means you can't forget. They always said to me, 'You should not forget our history, ever, you must remember.' There's sadness in this scene, sure, but also happiness too, because you see I did my job. I survived."

"Let the person who looks at my paintings interpret for their own. I have nothing more to say."

The center members, I am convinced, will remain indomitably themselves, impervious to outsiders and to intrusions on their customs and morality as long as they live. One of my most vivid memories of a recent visit with them reinforced my realization of the extent of their self-determination. I was going to Jerusalem, where I had agreed to take their messages to put in the *kotel*, the Western Wall of the Temple, along with their notes to relatives, used clothing, old jewelry, a used set of dentist's tools, a pair of drapes, and other miscellaneous items to be given to friends and family. As I was trying to juggle the implements, feeling very much like a refugee myself, Beryl called me aside. "I will give you here one dollar. When I left Russia seventy years ago, my father did this for me. 'Beryl,' he said, 'take these ten rubles and find a poor man in America who needs them. That way your trip will be safe. You will be a *shaliekh mitsve,* a blessed messenger on a sacred journey.'" Others overheard him, and before I knew it, I had nearly two hundred dollars in crumpled bills to deliver to the needy in Israel. An intense argument immediately began as to who should receive the donation. "Not the anarchists!" "Whatever you do, not the ultra-Orthodox. They're against Israel!" "You should find the Arabs who need it the most—that's true charity!" The blind, war orphans, for education—all were passionately urged on me as the proper cause. With no consensus, I felt free to decide for myself, realizing that no one would be happy with my choice.

After much searching, I settled on an organization that provided care and work for elderly Jews and non-Jews who were unable to live on their own, "Lifeline for the Elderly." Founded by Miriam Mendilow, the original group had been comprised of homeless and helpless elderly people, caught in the crossfires of various wars. They knitted, crocheted, embroidered, bound old books, made cards, and raised funds to support themselves in a sheltered workshop. They were very appreciative of my offering and insisted on giving me dozens of items they had made to return to the Jews in Venice who had kindly sent them the donation.

I came back to Venice, bearing the return gifts and filled with apprehension. "What do you mean you gave it to the elderly? What good does that do anyone? You must support youth, they carry on the future. Besides why have you brought these things back? Don't those people know we don't take charity? We were giving to them!" In the ensuing commotion, I slipped away, but not before I heard a discussion developing as to how they could auction off the gifts I had brought back and use the funds to send money to Israel, to the really needy people, and the ones who wouldn't try to send back anything in return.

This, then, has been a reprise of some of the stories of survivors, the surviving stories not elsewhere recorded. There are scores more; it is endless. There is no telling how much more unfolding will occur or how long it will take. It cannot be called a tragic tale or a predictable one. On the contrary, the people seem to have a boundless capacity for passionate, meaningful, self-determined lives, full of irony, dignity, humor, and conscience. No one who has spent sufficient time

[293]

among them or looked very closely at their lives can feel anything save delight, wonder, and finally awareness that it is a privilege to have shared this time and this place with them.

REFERENCES

Crapanzano, Vincent. 1980. *Tuhami: Portrait of a Moroccan.* Chicago: University of Chicago Press.

Myerhoff, Barbara. 1986. "Life Not Death in Venice: Its Second Life." In *The Anthropology of Experience,* ed. Victor Turner and Edward Bruner. Urbana and Chicago: University of Illinois Press, 261–86.

——. 1984. "Rites and Signs of Ripening: The Intertwining of Ritual, Time, and Growing Older." In *Age and Anthropological Theory,* ed. David Kerzer and Jennie Keith-Ross. Ithaca: Cornell University Press, 305–30.

——. February 1980. "Re-Membered Lives." *Parabola.*

——. March 1980. "Telling One's Story." *The Center Magazine.* Santa Barbara, Calif.: Center for the Study of Democratic Institutions.

——. 1979. *Number Our Days.* New York: E. P. Dutton.

——. 1978. "The Older Woman as Androgyne." In *Parabola: Myth and the Quest for Meaning.*

——. Winter 1979. "The Renewal of the Word." *Kenyon Review* 1, 1:50–79.

—— and Hirsch, John (director). 1981. *Number Our Days.* Dramatized and presented at the Los Angeles Mark Taper Forum.

—— and Lynne Littman (producer, director). 1976. *Number Our Days.* 16mm thirty-minute documentary produced for the Public Broadcasting Corporation.

—— with Virginia Tufte. 1975. "Life History as Integration: An Essay on an Experimental Model." *Gerontologist* 15, 6:541–43.

Rouche, Jean. 1975. "The Camera and Man." In *Principles of Visual Anthropology,* ed. Paul Hockings. The Hague.

Ruby, Jay, ed. 1982. *A Crack in the Mirror: Reflexive Perspectives in Anthropology.* Philadelphia: University of Pennsylvania Press.

[12]

The Making of a Miracle

Jack Kugelmass

In 1983 a one-hour documentary based on my fieldwork at the Intervale Jewish Center of the Bronx was made for British television. The film, *The Miracle of Intervale Avenue*, came about as most things do, by chance. Irving Rappaport, a British film producer, and I had both been invited to a luncheon at a mutual friend's apartment on Manhattan's Upper West Side. It was the first day of Rosh Hashanah, the Jewish New Year.

I arrived late, having gone with Sacks to *tashlikh* (the ceremony of casting off sins). Moishe Sacks is the leader of the Intervale congregation. Although he is already in his eighties, he is extremely energetic and generally gives the impression of being a good twenty years younger. I had long learned to admire the easy way he approaches ritual: he is determined to bend it to suit the needs of an aging congregation. The handful of Jews who come to the Intervale Jewish Center are most of what remains from a once-thriving Jewish neighborhood, the Hunts Point section of the South Bronx. Though once notorious as the home of the beleaguered "Fort Apache" precinct, in recent years, the area has lost much of its former "glamor": vandalism and arson are no longer rampant and the drug situation is no worse than in many other areas of the city. Still, the changed atmosphere has not brought about an influx of younger Jews to replace the tens of

Chapter 12, "The Making of a Miracle," originally appeared in *The Miracle of Intervale Avenue*, copyright © 1986 by Jack Kugelmass, Schocken Books, published by Pantheon Books, a division of Random House, Inc.

thousands who left in the decades following World War II. As the last synagogue still in use in the area, the Intervale Jewish Center provides a weekend sanctuary for the elderly Jews who refused to leave. Despite frequent deaths and departures, the synagogue has been able to maintain a minyan (ritual quorum of ten men). Sacks has long maintained that there is the hand of God in that, and he refers to the continued existence of the synagogue and the minyan as, "the miracle of Intervale Avenue."

Normally *tashlikh* is held late in the afternoon, and I lament not being able to witness the ceremony because of the luncheon engagement. As usual Sacks is willing to accommodate religious custom to personal schedules. After services he rounds up a couple of congregants and we walk to an ugly bridge on a busy expressway that overlooks industrial wastelands on both sides of the Bronx River. Desolate, almost forbidding, the site looks custom-made for casting off sins. Sacks recites the prayer. Tossing the bread crumbs (our symbolic sins) into the water, Lena Zalben shouts down, "Here fishies, eat. We'll be back next year." But I doubt there are any fish alive in those waters. I feel somewhat relieved as we head back to a mercifully sinful little park. Sacks will find a seat among the neighborhood types, the young black craps shooters long familiar with this old Jewish baker, and he will wait for other congregants to lead to *tashlikh*.

Back in Manhattan I apologize to the other guests for being late and take a chair next to Irving, who is explaining the differences he observed between services in New York synagogues and those in London, where he lives. More as a joke than as a serious offer, I suggest that if he were interested in seeing something truly different, he might want to visit the shul I have been studying for the past two years in the South Bronx. The following day he accompanies me to Intervale for the second day of Rosh Hashanah.

We arrive while services are underway. A Jewish policeman from the Forty-first Precinct is present in uniform. He stands several rows behind the other men, looking as if he does not belong, yet holding a prayer book and wearing a *talis* (prayer shawl). I introduce myself, and he rather sheepishly apologizes for being on duty on the holy day, promising not to work on Yom Kippur. I assure him it's of no concern to me and invite him to join us at the table where I usually sit. I then go over to Sacks to introduce Irving.

"*Gut yontev*," I say. "I see we have a cop here. Is everything okay?"

Sacks seems a little surprised by my question. "Oh yeah," he answers, "everything is fine. I always ask for police protection for the holidays."

"You mean," Irving asks more out of curiousity than alarm, "you think there might be some kind of trouble?"

"No. No trouble. Sometimes Dave works at the center, or Mr. Abraham can't make it and I'm missing a man for the minyan. So I call the Forty-first Precinct and I ask them to send me a man. If I'm lucky they send a Jewish cop so we have him for the minyan."

Irving and I wander over to the bench where I usually sit, and I decide to make use of the officer's presence to learn more about the area. The policeman confirms what I already know. The name "Fort Apache" is a vestige from the past:

"I started working in the precinct in 1968 when the gangs were at their height. Today, of course, the gangs are gone. It's the kind of thing that comes back every twenty years, kind of like a cycle. In those days the Savage Skulls were located just around the corner from the shul. They had maybe fifteen hundred members, broken down into divisions, battalions, and a gestapo squad to enforce discipline. A guy named 'Blood' was their leader. There was another gang here that was pretty big too, the Dirty Dozens. They weren't right here, they were over in Longwood about twenty blocks from here. I arrested their leader, Fat Louis, for drugs and homicide. This guy was so well-connected that when I busted him he didn't even call a lawyer. He called the D.A. The D.A. must have owed him favors for helping with evidence on other cases. This time, though, his connections didn't do him any good. He was sent upstate to Ossining for five years." Our conversation is interrupted when the policeman is called to remove the Torah from the Ark. He stands next to Malachi and Mordechai on the platform. I am amused by the palpable sense of astonishment on Irving's face as he takes in what to him must seem utterly outlandish: two black cantors, the light-skinned cantor, a paragon of grace and dignity in an otherwise bizarre shul, and his yeshiva-educated son, conversant in Yiddish, with the mannerisms and worldview of a hasidic Jew. Equally exotic is the presence of a policeman in full uniform with a loaded gun hanging from his hip and a *talis* draped over his shoulders embracing a worn Torah *mantl* (cover). And then there is the shul itself, everywhere displaying evidence of assault— windows covered by wooden planks, huge pieces of plaster fallen from the ceiling forming a vast diaspora of tiny fragments on the rotting wooden floors. Equally outlandish are the signs painted on the doors and hallway walls that read "THANK YOU, COME AGAIN," "GLATT KOSHER," and "KOSHER LADIES ROOM," the latter drawn inside an enormous red heart with Cupid's arrow pointing toward the lavatory. All the handiwork of Dave Lentin, Intervale's eccentric kaddish-sayer who approaches Irving now and then to run through his repertoire of bawdy comments and lewd gestures. And finally there is Mrs. Miroff, hard at work apportioning food onto paper plates for the meal that will follow the service, interrupting her work when we first approach her in order to switch from eighty-four-year-old grandmother to gun moll, describing the latest murder on her block and her affectionate relationship with the street people. Irving doesn't have that much time to gawk. With a shortage of men, and extra *kibbudim* (honors) to give out because of the holiday, Sacks has him scurrying about to perform various parts of the service. "In London," Irving remarks, "I could wait in line for fifty years to be called to the Torah on Rosh Hashanah. I've only been here for a couple of hours and I've already been called up three times."

Irving returned to London soon after his visit to Intervale. A month later he called to let me know that he wanted to produce a film on the community. If I agreed, the filming would take place in the late summer or early fall. In the course of time, the project moved off the drawing boards. Irving approached Ken Howard, a British director who was immediately interested in the project and offered to assemble a film crew. The two men next approached the BBC with the project, and they agreed to coproduce the film. The shooting would take place in the fall around the time of the Jewish High Holy Days. The following June, Irving and Ken arrived in New York. The three of us began to outline the film's structure and I introduced Ken to the people I thought would be most suited to appear on camera.

When Ken and Irving returned home, I asked Sacks whether he was looking forward to the film's production. I found him rather noncommittal: "It's a long way off; who knows whether or not I'll live that long." In any case, neither he nor the other congregants anticipated even the slightest change occurring in their lives on account of the film. Unlike younger people, the elderly do not tack fantasies of Hollywood careers onto the word "film." Their main concern is to keep on living the life they know. Asked about the future, Sacks usually responds, "If I live that long," or, "Young people think about the future. Old people think about the past."

At that time, I had known Sacks for just over two years. I had always considered him an optimist, undaunted by life's various pitfalls. But when the film production began I was suddenly introduced to another side of Sacks, a dark side that I had not noticed before. At a loss how to deal with it, I responded by minimizing its importance and ignoring every warning sign that things might not work out as smoothly as I expected. Little did I know at the time that I was completely misreading a situation so volatile that it threatened not only the film but even the very close working relationship I had established with Sacks over the previous two years. Yet had I known better, I might not have acted much differently, because it was Sacks rather than I who controlled the situation.

Despite his comments, Sacks's disinterest in the film went beyond the usual refusal to look ahead. At the time he had suddenly developed a particularly dim view of life, largely because of an intense pain in his left leg. He reacted with an almost fatalistic resolve:

"Either the pain will get better or it will get worse. Either the pain will go away or the leg will go away. Life is an equation. It's all part of God's plan. It reminds me of what happened to my cat Pinkie. [Evelyn] the boss's wife put down some mouse poison and Pinkie probably ate it and is dead because I haven't seen him all week. So that's a new equation. You know, I had five sons. Two are now alive. I had a three-year-old boy who died of appendicitis. He used to visit me in the bakery and say, 'Hello, Daddy.' Now people don't die of appendicitis. So they die of a double heart attack. No. Not even from that, but from a cancer eating various parts of the body. Whatever it is, you're still going to die."

Sacks's moodiness comes and goes. I ignore it. Amid ever-present morbid thoughts, a glimmer of optimism unexpectedly emerges. Each time I assume the side of Sacks I am more familiar with will prevail. Even his none-too-well-masked ego surfaces now and then. Responding to a question I pose about any specific requirements on his part regarding the film's production, Sacks refers back to his hero and namesake, Moses. "Just remember to put the period in for the things that I do." "What period?" I ask. Sacks has in mind a bit of biblical exegesis:

"The period in the Hebrew word for modesty. Although the Bible is perfect, it left out the dot from the word modesty when it described Moses. The rabbis interpreted that to mean that Moses was so modest that he even hesitated to have himself described as modest. But that doesn't mean you should go so overboard either. Otherwise they'll say that I'm a liar and no one will believe you. You know when I was a young man, besides the different things I would do, I also worked in the bakery. Sometimes when I would see my father I would tell him how much I had made, how many of this or of that I had baked in a day. And he would say, '*Sha*, Moishe! I believe you. But everyone else will think that you're lying.'"

For a while Sacks's mood switches back and forth between feelings of despair and moments of optimism and good humor. But two weeks before the crew is scheduled to arrive from London, his mood plunges into dark pessimism. Besides the continuing pain in his leg, two new developments have contributed to his increased feelings of desolation. Mr. Abraham, his closest friend, learns that he will need surgery to treat a malignant tumor. Mr. Abraham's condition seems to spark off morbid sentiments in Sacks, feelings that lurked just below the surface. Outwardly, Sacks voices his usual optimism, particularly when speaking to his friend. When Mr. Abraham informs him that the surgery will consist of a radioactive implant rather than a removal of the tumor, Sacks is quick to confirm the wisdom of the procedure:

"I had an aunt who was over eighty and was diagnosed as having cancer. The family asked the doctor what her chances were and he told us, 'If we operate she may live another five years. If we don't, who knows? The decision is up to you.' The family decided not to risk the operation and the woman lived another fifteen years. The doctors couldn't explain it. They figured it must have something to do with metabolism. So you see, it's good that they're not operating. They'll put the thing in you and you'll be okay." The optimism is only show. Sacks continues to talk about death a good deal. He seems to fantasize that the circulatory problem in his leg is caused by a blood clot that sooner or later will be dislodged and cause either a fatal heart attack or a stroke. This mood is reinforced by a threatened disruption of his normal routine. Tony, his assistant for the past twenty-seven years, is facing the likelihood of forced retirement because of his increasing blindness. The condition isn't new. Tony's failings have long been a part of Sacks's personal folklore. He is a reliable assistant, but only up to a point:

"Tony came in here unknowledgeable of any baking. He learned to a certain extent and refused to learn anymore for the twenty-seven years that I've been working with him. He learned how to make a roll. He learned how to make *challie* dough but he doesn't know how to braid a *challie*. He learned how to grease for me the pans and even make the mixes for the large cakes and make the butter cream and make everything necessary for the colors. But he will not go to take the cake and decorate it. He put a limit on what he wants to do and that he doesn't want to do anymore. For me he was sufficient. The twenty-seven years he was working here I made him a union man. I made him get all the benefits of the union and everything. And he worked with me straight down. He drives a car and picks me up every night that we worked. . . picks me up at my home. And as he picks me up, the cops in their radio cars follow us. Now Tony is every bit a good man. But there is one thing wrong with him. He has only one eye. And that one eye (the other eye is glass which is nothing) the one eye has been deteriorating till he's now officially blind. He was still taking me back and forth even with the official blindness. Even the vehicle bureau has taken away his licence and everything else. But he is officially blind. He can't see anything. And when we made the turn from Hunts Point down to the block he never hit the cars because the cars had to miss him. Till finally it came to an impass that he doesn't even see the shadow now. He absolutely cannot drive. And if his wife lets him drive from Jersey, she's actually telling him to commit suicide. So we had a discussion in here, in the bakery. We told him about it and everything else. By the way. He still owes me $25. And we told him that he can't come back to work. He's retired."

When Sacks first tells me the story he is quite upset. In his view, Tony's retirement might well mean the closing of the bakery. I try to reassure him that it seems easy enough just to train a new man. Apparently, I hit a raw nerve:

"That's just what's bothering me. If Jerry my boss had mentioned anything about a new assistant I wouldn't be so worried. But Jerry is in semi-retirement. He would like to get rid of the place altogether. What does he need it for? His wife Evelyn, she wants to keep it for the kids, she says. But Evelyn is a very sick woman. Besides, the lease will be up in two years. They had a fifty-year lease so you can imagine what their rent must be like. When they try to get a new lease who knows what will happen?"

"So they'll sell the place," I say. "What makes you think that the new owner won't want you?"

"I don't care even if he does want me," Sacks barks back. "I'm not interested in working for a new owner. If they sell the bakery I leave!"

"How are you going to leave? Where will you go?" Sacks, apparently, had already given a good deal of thought to that very question, suggesting, as I realized only later, the extent of his despair:

Actually, I'm getting used to the idea of retirement. The bakery has been closed for vacation for the last two weeks and it hasn't been so bad. I feel pretty good. My feet aren't bothering me anymore. So I spend the day in the little park over here reading Bashevis Singer. Besides, I'm well taken care of financially. I get social security and a pension. Plus I have income yet from some property I own in Brooklyn, including a bowling alley. I also got stocks and bonds. If I can't make do on that then something is wrong. Besides I got where to go. My son Arthur is thinking of leaving the city. He would like to move near his brother upstate. He's looking for a house. And he's looking for something where I could move next to. I tell him all I need is that I should be in walking distance to a shul where I could *daven* [pray] and a bakery where I could work."

"But if you leave Intervale, won't you miss playing the kind of role that you play here?"

"I don't have to miss it. Look, there's a certain percentage of people who stand out as leaders in any crowd. These people are leaders no matter where they are. Do you think if I were in another shul that I wouldn't be active the way I am here?"

"Maybe you will. But what about the ones who remain here? Who is going to lead them?"

"Don't look to me like that. That's not fair to put so much responsibility on me." Sacks is agitated by my arguments. It exposes something still unsettled in his thinking. But he has thought this through. "Besides," he continues, "Malachi can lead them."

"No he can't." I counter. "People look to you as a leader. Like Moses."

"No they don't. Bloch doesn't consider me Moses."

"Bloch does." I am desperately trying to win the point, even if I have to stretch the truth. But I'm not far off the mark. Although he works on Saturday, Bloch is in all other respects Orthodox, and Sacks frequently defers to him before making decisions on ritual procedure.

"Bloch, for instance, won't go along with me in considering the minyan complete with only nine men." Sacks pauses for a moment, then adds in a self-congratulatory way, "But he respects me enough to accept my dispensation or maybe I should say my not criticizing him for working on *shabes*."

[302]

"It seems to me, that you've just contradicted yourself. Before you were telling me that Bloch doesn't consider you a leader. Now you tell me that he does."

"Maybe. But I'm not as important to Intervale as you make out. Anyway, I don't like people placing so much burden on me. It's not fair. It interferes with my ability to function." Sacks's desire to leave the area surprises me. It seems so much out of character with the man as I know him. He has been resolute almost to the point of arrogance in his determination to keep the shul alive. Several years earlier, when the shul was being repeatedly vandalized, a local minister offered the use of his church for Intervale's Saturday services, even promising "to cover the cross so you can have the service in the way you want to have it." Sacks adamantly refused: "We're not moving from this place. If we're not safe here then no one will be safe anywhere! Besides, you walk down the street, you see a building and you say, 'This used to be a shul.' Then you come to another one and you say the same thing. You come to the Intervale Jewish Center and you don't say, 'This used to be a shul.' Do you know why? Because this still is a shul!"

Since the possibility of his leaving never occurred to me, I feel inclined to dismiss what he is telling me and attribute it to a passing mood. I reassure myself with the thought that the optimistic side of the man that I'm familiar with will soon reemerge. Why not give it a little prompting? I try to cheer him up by talking about the plans for the film. It is a mistake. I do not comprehend the depth of his despair, so I have no way of anticipating Sacks's response. It is like a red flag to a bull.

"I don't know if there's going to be any film," Sacks thunders.

"What do you mean?" I respond, my voice betraying an element of terror.

"Now isn't the right time to make it."

"Why not?"

"Because first let's see what happens in the bakery." Why should the future of the bakery effect the making of a film? I let the matter drop. The statement is ridiculous. The best approach is to continue with the plans. Time will bring Sacks around.

The following week I arrive for Saturday morning services and go over to shake hands with Sacks. He looks even more agitated than when I last saw him.

"Look, Jack. You have to call the whole thing off. Tony is now completely blind, he can't work. Jerry says he's going to close the bakery."

"I don't understand." Stunned by this sudden shift to a more aggressive offense, I feign incomprehension. "What should I call off?"

"The film! Call Irving and tell him he has to change his plans. He can't make the film now." Sacks's adamant opposition is something I hadn't anticipated. I begin desperately looking for some sign of flexibility.

"Well, I don't think it's possible. The crew has already been booked. Everything is ready. I don't think we can cancel now."

"It's up to you. But you'll just have to make the film without me. I can't promise you anything."

"We can't do that. You're central to the film."

"I'm not. You said you're calling it 'The Miracle of Intervale Avenue' not 'The Miracle of Moishe Sacks'!'"

"Well, let's see what happens." I try to get the last word in and leave the issue open. A quasi maybe is preferrable to an absolute no. But even that token victory fades as Sacks warns, "I'm telling you, Jack. You're wasting your time. You better cancel!"

The following day, Irving calls from London. I fill him in on the details of the shooting schedule. Toward the end of the conversation he asks whether I've allotted time for a lengthy interview with Sacks. I explain the problem I'm having, but I predict that Sacks will cooperate once production gets under way.

I sincerely meant what I said. But my reassurance stemmed in part from a somewhat arrogant assumption that what I thought would be good for my informants, they would think was good too. That, however, was the relatively minor misconception. Far more serious was my complete misreading of Sacks's stubbornness and the underlying cause of his behavior. I assumed that Sacks's mood was irrational. True, the "blood clot" was a fantasy, and Mr. Abraham was not nearly as ill as Sacks feared he might be. However, Sacks's concern that the bakery might close was no mere fantasy. Jerry was anxious to retire. Neither of his two sons had much interest in running the place; both had business interests on the side. Evelyn's deteriorating health made her less and less able to keep a tight grip on things. Consequently, supplies dwindled and bills went unpaid. Sacks was waging a constant battle with family members who were waiting impatiently to rid themselves of a business they had no interest in maintaining. So Tony's forced retirement set off omens of immanent doom in Sacks's mind.

[304]

For a man accustomed to seeing the world around him bend to his imaginings, fearsome fantasies are far more worrisome than the most troublesome reality.

The following week I arrived in shul to find Deborah, a black Jewish woman who has recently moved away from the area, visiting with her grandson Haim. I am about to witness firsthand "the miracle of Intervale Avenue." At the kiddush, Bloch announces that he is being transferred to his company's main office in Manhattan and that next week will probably be his last visit to the Intervale Jewish Center. I expect the announcement will be a further blow to Sacks's spirits. I examine Sacks's face, carefully looking for any signs of distress. There are none. I probe. "How do you feel about losing another member of the minyan?" Sacks responds without missing a beat.

"Bloch is leaving, so now we have Haim here. That's Bloch's replacement. It was the same when Horowitz went into a home. We got someone else to take his place," he says, referring to Rashim. "Now we'll just need someone to make the kiddush over wine. That was Bloch's job so someone else will have to do it now."

"How about Malachi?" I ask.

"Malachi? No. He only does *rosh khoydesh* [the new month]." I offer several other names, but Sacks dismisses every one I come up with. It dawns on me that he would like me to volunteer for the assignment. Less the participant than the observer, I do no such thing. Sacks lets the matter go. He is obviously in a better mood than he was last week. When we finish the wine and cake, he asks me whether I plan to accompany him to the bakery. The question is hardly necessary since Saturday afternoons in the bakery have long been a part of my routine. I look forward to the food and the banter, deriving particular pleasure from a sense they give me of belonging to a private men's club. I want to reestablish that intimacy, and I am also hoping for a truce in a battle of opposing wills. Sacks picks up his white plastic shopping bag with its "I love New York" logo, the repository of his valuables—baker's tools, synagogue receipt book, bank books. I pick up mine containing a New York *Times* and tape cassettes. I am vaguely aware that the shopping bag is an affectation on my part, an attempt to be like him. We walk side by side, gradually making our way past the rubble-strewn lots now lush with vegetation and dotted here and there with a plywood *cassita*, the shelters Puerto Ricans use as club houses. I keep an eye out for an occasional rat scurrying across our path. Sacks is mindful of the broken sidewalk, concerned that a fall might permanently rob him of his cherished independence. "Are you still worried about the bakery's future?" I ask. "Not at all. Jerry has already ordered cake from Zaro [a major New York bakery] and Zaro is only too glad to give him what he needs. I just tell Jerry, 'Look. You're the boss. Whatever you decide, you decide.' The three weeks I've spent on vacation haven't exactly done me any harm. I'm feeling good. My leg doesn't hurt. How do I look?"

"You look fine." I am not lying either. He does look good. His face has shed its previous pallor, his cheeks have regained some fleshiness, and the shadows under his eyes are gone. Even his pace is brisk. His leg no longer hurts. I, however, am the one in pain. Thinking about Sacks's refusal to appear in the film is literally causing my head to throb. "I'll need some aspirins when we reach the bakery."

"You don't have to wait until we reach the bakery. I have some with me."

"You're a walking pharmacy."

"I don't know if I'm a pharmacy. Aspirin I carry because I read somewhere that they prevent blood clots." Like many old people, Sacks has a vast repertoire of tricks to cheat death. After an elderly man was struck and killed by a car whose driver claimed not to have seen him crossing the street, Sacks was quick to put into practice the lesson learned from the incident: he began to wear a bright red sweater and scarf. I take the aspirin, feeling protected for the moment from a fifth-column assault from my circulatory system. Sacks resumes the conversation, referring to Bloch's departure and the unexpected appearance of a likely replacement.

"So your miracle is intact," I comment.

"Of course it's intact!" Sacks shoots back. The conversation stops while we concentrate on dodging traffic as we cross Westchester Avenue at Simpson Street. Behind us, just down the street is the Forty-first Precinct, "Fort Apache." It leers at us like a green-eyed monster. The building has become somewhat of a shrine, drawing media pilgrims the world over: German, French, and Japanese film crews, and now the BBC. Above us, casting a serrated pattern of light and shadow on Westchester Boulevard, stands the archaic steel framework of the El. We wind our way through a maze of steel pillars and aggressive automobiles, piloted by strutting Latin males, greeted as we reach the opposite side of the street by a tinny, Salsa-blaring loudspeaker mounted over the door of a butcher shop. The shop window has a prominent display of skinned pigs. Like the music, they are unkind reminders of change. I sense that Sacks, too, has the urge to seek refuge from the blaring noise and the dead animals so we move rapidly like ships at sea, our progress hampered now only by the need to chart a zigzag course through street vendors with mounds of plantains or avocadoes stacked in grocery baskets. We turn the corner and we are on Southern Boulevard. Home turf. Its many Jewish storeowners are a great reservoir of potential congregants for the shul. The street is dense with shoppers, but the sidewalk is very broad. We can walk side by side. I resume the conversation.

"You know something? Today even with my headache I was sitting in shul and thinking that the place in its own peculiar way is kind of beautiful."

"That too is a miracle!" Sacks responds.

"What do you mean?"

"I mean it's a miracle that you, even with your headache, can open your eyes and look at the building inside and see that it's beautiful. Isn't that a miracle?"

"I don't know. Maybe it is." I begin hoping that if Sacks is so freely dispensing miracles perhaps he'll throw one my way and agree to participate in the film.

"Anyway," Sacks continues, "I was telling you about Jerry and the bakery. So I stopped worrying about it. Whatever happens, happens. In the meantime, I'm getting the dough ready for when we start baking. Tuesday we open for business. And let me tell you, Intervale isn't the only miracle. Tony showed up at the store yesterday. His eyesight improved."

"So he'll be back at work?"

"Maybe. And there's another miracle too. Remember José?"

"You mean the guy you lent a thousand dollars to, so he could go to Mexico to see his wife and children?"

"Yeah. Well, he came back and gave me the thousand dollars. Imagine that. Would anybody believe that someone would go away for a year and return to give me back the money? Tony did the same thing. On the last day he worked he gave me back three hundred dollars, the last installment on the money I loaned him for the mortgage on the home he bought in New Jersey." Sacks's stories about money always have a hidden meaning in them. They are boastful reminders of his net worth, a sign of worldly success. But they are also reminders of another sort. Here he is needed. Tony's reappearance has apparently sparked some optimism in Sacks; the blindness may not be permanent after all. We jaywalk our way through the heavy traffic of Southern Boulevard, sneaking across to wind the corner onto Hunts Point Boulevard. Another block and I can spot the bakery, looking like a way station before a wide vista of abandoned buildings. Once inside, we set to work preparing lunch. Mr. Abraham joins us. I do not mention the film.

The following day I again visit Sacks at the bakery. I pound away at the gray metal door with its thick glass window. An impenetrable barrier to the world outside, the door cannot distinguish friends from enemies. The noise of my pounding goes unheard. I continue to bang on the door, many times, harder now. Sacks is in the rear in a separate room. Now and then I can see him scurrying about moving huge encrusted wooden trays. Perhaps out of the corner of an eye he sees me or perhaps the pounding has had its intended effect. Sacks heads to the door to let me in. I follow him past the cafeteria section with its torn red Naugahyde chairs and equally worn linoleum floor tiles. The floor changes from linoleum to ceramic tile as we approach his work-bench in the rear, as if it were stripping down for serious work. I remove my camera and tape recorder from my bag while he resumes his activity. The room is dark. The lone fluorescent bulb works hard, its light absorbed rather than reflected by the gray-painted walls and tin ceiling. A huge skylight occupying a sizable chunk of the ceiling and a small window attached to the back wall are now covered over to prevent unwanted entry. Light does not penetrate, as if it too were suspect. The only relief from the dungeonlike atmosphere is a lighted clock that hangs crooked, high on a wall. On its face in red and blue lettering is the name of a prominent kosher meat firm. Sacks looks perfectly at peace with himself, as if he were relaxing in his living room. A scratchy sounding radio near the workbench is tuned to classical music. The rhythm and tempo of sonatas create an illusion of art rather than craft, as Sacks takes a gooey mound of dough from the refrigerator and rolls it out with an enormous rolling pin. He seems to dance as he cuts the flat slab into small squares less than a quarter-inch thick. When the slab is completely rolled out and cut up, he lifts a large plastic container of cheese, holds it close to his nose, then takes a deep breath: "I think it's still good."

"Well," I comment, "You'll find out for sure when your customers taste it."

"I haven't had any complaints yet."

"Maybe they never live to talk about it."

Sacks laughs, and as usual manages to get in the last word: "You know I've never heard of anyone dying from baking, only from not baking."

"You're talking about your father who, you once told me, lost his interest in working when his third wife died?"

"That's right. She was his downfall. He loved her so much that after she died he didn't want to live anymore."

"Is that why you've never considered remarrying?"

"I've never considered remarrying because I'm married to the bakery, to my job. This is all I need. And besides, the right person hasn't come along. When I quit here and I'm ready to retire and if the right person comes along, I'll get married again." At his age, it seems to me he's pushing his luck. I keep the comment to myself. As we talk, Sacks is busy cupping his hands to squeeze small gobs of cheese filling from between his palms, then tosses them like projectiles onto the squares of dough. When all the squares are filled, he takes the opposite ends of each and pulls them to stretch the dough, then folds each corner past the middle before proceeding to the next diagonal to form a neat miniature box. Baking is Sacks's link to the universe, his way too of praising his Creator through imitation. I watch, both fascinated and envious. Years earlier I had worked as a potter. Reminded now of the tactile pleasure, I ask Sacks if I can try to make a few. Sacks humors me but corrects my first try. I make another one. He casts a disapproving glance: "They'll see that, they'll think, 'The old man is slipping in his old age!'"

To distract Sacks's attention from my "handiwork" I try to resume our conversation about his father: "Did you learn to bake these from your father?"

"Yes. But I also learned several other varieties." Again Sacks casts menacing glances at my work. I remain undaunted. Sensing that Sacks is in a better frame of mind and determined to divert his attention elsewhere, I decide to head the conversation gradually in the direction of the film and the benefits he might derive from it. I mention the question of legacy.

"Do you see your children as an extension of yourself?"

"What do you mean, an extension of myself?"

"I mean a legacy."

"Nothing I do will last permanently. The only thing that will last are my children and the contribution they make to the world. That's my legacy."

"What about the shul?" I ask, curious about the omission.

"The shul doesn't need me. The 'miracle of Intervale Avenue' as you call it is a miracle without me. I'm not even sad or worried that Bloch is leaving. In a way I'm glad, because he'll be able to be *shomer shabes* [observe the Sabbath] as he believes and that's good. So we're not losing Bloch. God is gaining him. Anyway we have Haim, the young colored boy to take his place. So God makes the miracle, not me!"

"You keep denying the fact that you have an impact on other people."

"I have an impact on other people? Well maybe on those women who come there to shul. They come in and know nothing about the Torah and on Sundays I go over the *parshe* [weekly Torah reading] and that way they learn something. I don't know if you want to call that a legacy. Da Vinci's "Mona Lisa," or Rodin's "The Thinker," or Michaelangelo's "Moses"—those are legacies. They are great works of art that people remember, that the world is better for." Sacks's humility seems a little out of character, so I try to press the point.

"Don't you think that the film also might be a legacy?"

"No. The film is a financial venture and not a work of art."

"Well, then, how about my writing about you?"

"That may be a legacy of sorts, but not necessarily my legacy. You're writing about the story of the Intervale Jewish Center, not Moishe Sacks."

"So you don't see yourself as central to the story?"

"No!" Sacks barks back. I still do not believe that Sacks is determined to write himself out of his own story, to disavow the central role he plays in the miracle. Exasperated by a logic I cannot understand, I decide to stop beating around the bush and to get a commitment of cooperation from him. "Now that the issue is settled with the bakery, will you appear in the film?"

"We'll see," Sacks replies. "Remember, I'm not promising you anything." The answer is less reassuring than I had hoped for. But I accept it gratefully as a grudging nod to move ahead.

The following week Irving arrives. After attending services, he asks to make a short speech to the congregation. Sacks is in excellent spirits; he even advises Irving how to tailor his speech. "As you all know by now," Irving begins, "tomorrow we start filming. I just want you all to realize that we are doing this from our hearts. . . . "

"Stop right there," Sacks interrupts. "That's a perfect closing line for a speech."

Irving ignores the advice, and continues: "I just want people to know that they should act as if we aren't there and to understand that if anything goes wrong, it's our fault and not theirs."

"Well," Sacks comments, "that was an okay ending too. But the other one would have been better."

Although in most synagogues the penitential Slichot service is held at midnight on the Saturday before Rosh Hashanah, few of Intervale's congregants will venture out at night, so their Slichot service is held on Sunday morning. A series of prayers rather than a holy day, the service offers none of the proscriptions on filming or similar activities that accompany most Jewish holy days. We decide to make good use of the occasion. To give us ample time to film, Sacks announced that members of the congregation should show up promptly at 9:30 A.M., much earlier than their usual arrival time for services. I was very pleased by Sacks's announcement. I was particularly pleased by the levity of his mood. It seemed to bode well for the two weeks of shooting that lay ahead. Then, as if from out of nowhere, Sacks turns to me and Irving and in an uncompromisingly firm way adds: "You can film me in the shul tomorrow but that's it. No way will I let you film me at home. I'll only let you in as far as the entrance to the front door downstairs. You can film Tony or the cops giving me a ride, but you can't come upstairs to the apartment. And no filming in the bakery."

Sacks's sudden shift away from the good-spirited mood catches me by surprise. The proviso he adds about filming him at home and in the bakery seems artificial. I suspect that it will be rather easy to ignore. I was already familiar with similar provisos regarding my photographing him at work in the bakery. In fact, the proviso was repeated years later, even after numerous occasions on which I had photographed him inside the bakery. Once, after entering the work area with my camera, Sacks told me straight away, "You can stand here and talk as much as you want, but the moment you start taking pictures, I'm walking out of here." I explain why I need the photographs. Sacks is adamant: "You take pictures in here and you're liable to get a rat in one of them!" "I should be so lucky. I've been trying for years to get a picture of a rat at the Intervale Jewish Center without any luck. They refuse to pose."

"Well, the rats in here pose!" I have a good laugh at the absurdity of the image and Sacks joins in. The humor reinforces a common bond. Sacks begins to change into cleaner work clothes. Donning a fresh apron and hat, he asks, "Why aren't you taking any pictures?"

"You told me not to."

"So who's telling you not to now?" In the course of time I learned to ignore the provisos and Sacks learned to ignore the camera. I assumed that his refusal to be filmed in the bakery was simply for the record. He could deny his culpability in case of a reprimand from his boss. So, for the moment, I choose to let the matter drop.

When the kiddush is over, Sacks and I begin our walk to the bakery, while Irving as "producer" must double as driver of the van. On the way, Sacks reviews the merits of Irving's speech, repeating once again his suggestion that "from the heart" would have been a better closing line. "You seem to be getting excited about the film," I comment.

"Excited? No. What will be will be. I have a very fatalistic attitude in general. When a young child dies in your arms after the nurse tells you the child is going to die unless you can get him to defecate and he can't, and your wife also dies in your arms after a heart attack, at first you say, 'Why me?' Then after a few minutes you accept it." A typical Sacksism; fierce resilience in the face of adversity. Little wonder I respect him. But that continuing morbidity, what should I make of it? Will his fatalism work in our favor or against us? I don't know. At the bakery, Sacks delights us with stories of his past. The New Year is approaching and his reminiscences are closely honed to memories of New Years' past. The food and banter puts us all in a relaxed mood. Sacks seems pliable enough, although he does not give a firm commitment to participate in the film beyond tomorrow's shooting. Soon it is time for us to leave. The film crew is about to arrive and Irving and I are off to meet them. Heading toward the airport, we recount some of Sacks's anecdotes, wondering as we do which of them will find their way into the film.

The following day, Sunday, we begin to film. Sacks repeats his previous condition: he is making himself available to us for that day only; a fair compromise by his reckoning. For the rest, we are on our own. We shoot a sequence of Dave opening the shul. As we film, other congregants begin to arrive, and Irving, the producer, has the unenviable task of trying to keep a cantankerous group of elderly Jews outside, so that they will enter only one by one; the sequence could serve as a way to introduce the various members of the congregation. Suddenly, the calm entry scene is transformed into bedlam as people burst through the door and fall on top of one another in a mad panic to get downstairs. Lena is yelling, "They're shooting! They're shooting!" I assume she is referring to the camera crew, but the rush of frightened, screaming people and the panic in their voices tells me something else. A moment later, a pudgy man in his late twenties wearing cut-off blue jeans and a white T-shirt, his leg oozing blood, lunges through the entrance, stops for a moment to peek through the crack of the door that he is clutching like a shield to see if he is still being pursued, then hobbles madly through the sanctuary and flees out the rear into the yard, where he falls to the ground, unable to move. The man has been shot several times through his left thigh, apparently, we learned later, as a warning about his passing information to the police regarding drug deals. I am completely bewildered by the incident. Well trained in the dos and don'ts of documentary filming, the crew keeps the film rolling throughout. I join them outside the rear exit of the shul to interview the wounded man: "Who shot you?"

"Four guys in a gang."

"Why'd they shoot you?"

"It's a long story." I am sure it is, but I let the matter drop. In considerable pain, the man is in no mood to talk. When the ambulance arrives, I head to the front of the shul, where a crowd of neighborhood people has gathered. Awed spectators to a drama of life and death, they linger to consider events so engrossing that they need to be reviewed again and again. A pool of blood dominates the entrance fo the shul. Its message is as transparent as a flashing neon light on a cheap motel. The smell of blood is overwhelming. I have all I can do to stop from vomiting. I accompany the ambulance driver to help him carry the stretcher. His assistant is busy elsewhere. Sacks has steered him inside the shul to examine Rose Cutler, who has a rag pressed to her neck. She has been nicked by a ricocheted bullet, but she prefers to be left alone: "I'm not going to no hospital. I don't need no hospital. Look even the blood it doesn't come. I'll be all right." Sacks convinces her to let the medic examine her, then apply a bandage to the wound. It is typical of the tenacity of these people. Hospitals are stages en route to nursing homes. They avoid them until severe illness or infirmity leave them no choice.

Later, when the police, paramedics, and various sleezy neighborhood types who had wandered inside the shul leave, Sacks goes to the *bima*. He is Moses now, the leader who guides his people through the Sinai wilderness. Sacks explains to the congregation that the synagogue is not only a holy place but it's also like the towns that Moses designated as places of refuge: "Even a non-Jew knows it's a place of refuge. The man was shot and he came into the synagogue for safety. I can assure you that if a non-Jew knows this is a place of refuge, that is exactly what we have known all these years. Anyway the excitement is good for you. It's good for your blood pressure. Nobody jumped up. We're used to it."

Sacks is in good humor. He seems to enjoy performing before the camera. He continues, still exuberant, while we film a sequence during which his son and daughter-in-law arrive to give him his birthday present, a hat. Sacks tries the hat on. It's too big and it sinks until it drowns his ears. "That's all right," Sacks announces. "By the end of the day my head will have swelled enough so the hat will fit." Later the bus arrives to take the congregation for an outing to the Plainview Jewish Center. On the bus he continues playing to the camera: he is funny and charming. At the outing he is even more flamboyant. Asked by the hosts to give his usual review of the weekly Torah reading, Sacks begins to orate much like a fire-and-brimstone preacher. His mood, though, is already changing. The humor is gone. As we prepare to leave, the film crew asks the bus driver to delay until they can finish filming some "cutaways" for the leaving scene. Concerned with his own work schedule, Sacks becomes increasingly agitated by the delay. When we arrive in the Bronx and he steps off the bus, he advises us that he has done for the film all he intends doing: "That's it. I've given you everything I'm going to give you. You can forget about filming in the bakery or in my home. I got work to do now. I've got a lot to do to get ready for Rosh Hashanah. The rest you'll have to get from someone else, not from me. Okay?"

"There is no one else to get it from." I reply. "Anyway, right now we're all tired. We'll fight this out tomorrow."

"There's nothing to talk about tomorrow. This is it." I try to argue, but it's no use. "The bakery is off-limits. Jerry and Evelyn are against any filming in the bakery," he insists. "They're looking to sell the place and they don't want any publicity, particularly not something that might be seen by the health department."

He refuses to budge from his position. I try joking with him, hoping I can charm him out of his obstinacy. That doesn't work. I try reason: "Well, if the bakery is a problem then we'll film after work on a Sunday or someplace else."

"There's no place else. You're not filming inside my apartment because I've had more leaks than Noah and I don't want anyone to see how I live." When his son offers the use of his own apartment in Queens, Sacks still refuses. Uncertain of how to get around the obstacles Sacks is throwing at us, we decide that familiarity might breed some form of acquiescence, however grudging. It's a technique I've used before, so I have some reason to believe it will work now.

The front of the bakery is a self-service Jewish-style delicatessen. The only restaurant of its kind in the area, when it opens for business at 3:30 A.M. the place is like neutral territory in a war zone. Cops, muggers, sanitation workers, truckers, pimps, prostitutes all line up for fresh danish and hot coffee. We figure we will have no problem blending in. The following day we arrive at the bakery for lunch. Bad luck. Sacks is in the front area talking to a customer. As soon as he sees us, he begins to scream loud enough for Jerry and Evelyn, who are sitting close by, to hear: "You're not filming inside the bakery!" I explain that we have come only to eat lunch, but Sacks keeps shouting and leaves the eating area to shut himself off in his private domain— the back room.

The episode leaves a pall on the film crew. I am utterly bewildered, unable to explain Sacks's behavior, and even worse, I feel completely unable to change it. Mercifully, my sense of frustration is spared by a shooting schedule that channels our efforts for the next few days into other scenes in the film. But in the back of my mind the nagging thought remains that Sacks's obstinacy might hold throughout the film crew's entire two-week stay. I begin a furious campaign to line people up on our side, to bring pressure to bear on Sacks. Everyone is reassuring: the cops from the Forty-first Precinct, "We'll talk to him." Other members of the congregation, including Mr. Abraham, "Give him time. He'll come around. He's just got his hands full now with what's going on in the bakery." Mrs. Miroff, "He left me the keys to his apartment so the painter can get in to fix it up. Then he'll let you take pictures." Jerry, his boss, "It's my wife who doesn't want you to film. She leaves at 3:00 P.M. After that, do what you want." Sacks's son and daughter-in-law, "We'll talk to him." Then later in the week, "We'll keep trying but there's a limit to what we can do." The strategy is a dismal failure: it only challenges him to match his obstinacy against our pressure. Mountains are easier to move. For Sacks to concede would be an acknowledgment of weakness.

Strangely enough, Sacks's ambivalence is evident throughout. About a week into the filming we become desperate for a solution; we

[315]

walk into the bakery and set the camera up on the table pointing at the counter area where Sacks often meanders. We order lunch. The cameraman can film while we eat, his head far enough from the viewfinder not to generate suspicion. Sacks comes out from the work area and sits down in the center of the room, right in the camera's line of vision. He acts as if he normally sits there to rest (although he does not), and as friends enter the bakery, he motions them to join him at the table. Never once does he look directly at the camera, nor does he acknowledge our presence. The following day, still discussing his refusal to be filmed, he comments that he knew perfectly well that we were filming. A few days later, on Saturday, he unexpectedly allows us to film him inside the bakery (the bakery is closed on weekends). We are having lunch with him, ostensibly to discuss the problem his refusal to be filmed poses for us. Suddenly he comments: "So who's stopping you from filming now?"

"You don't mind if we film now?" I ask stunned.

"No." We whip out the camera, tape recorder, and lights. I ask questions. Sacks responds. The crew films. But it's all mechanical. It doesn't feel right. Sacks's affable mood slips away, a hopeful spark that lights no fire. The interview is over as unexpectedly as it began.

Toward the end of the two weeks, just after another futile round of bargaining in the bakery, Sacks calls me aside and asks me to deliver a message to a social worker assigned by the Jewish Allied Services for the Aged. Sacks has received a phone call that Lena Michaels, a black member of the congregation, is dying, and friends of hers are concerned that she receive a proper Jewish burial. Extremely busy, Sacks asks whether I would pass the message on? I promise to do so. The conversation feels like a truce to care for the wounded and bury the dead. But it serves, I think, as a reminder to both of us that our battle is quite trivial in the face of life's larger dramas. A day or so later, Sacks mysteriously relents and agrees that we can film him just before closing time in the bakery. "But for one hour only. After that I'm throwing you out whether you got what you need or not!" At any rate, the one hour inside the bakery stretches into two. This time there is real magic. Sacks busies himself at the workbench, rolling out dough and simultaneously fielding questions. This is his show now. The storyteller has reemerged and he is playing to an audience, wooing, teaching, scolding.

Although the crisis passed once Sacks allowed us to film him at work, the incident had created a serious enough breach in our relationship to cause him to ask me ten days later, when the film crew had already returned to England, whether I was still mad at him and whether I would keep coming on Saturday. I assured him that I had every intention of continuing to come. The truth of the matter is that I was never angry at Sacks. I felt bewildered and somewhat humiliated by the futility of my efforts to change his mind. Unlike the film crew, however, I saw Sacks less as a culprit than as a mysterious and enigmatic figure who in the end would, as in fact he did, give in.

Sacks's concern that I remain in the minyan may have had a good deal to do with his eventual participation in the film. It also had a lot to do with my willingness to push him into participating. After three years of my attending services on a regular basis, neither Sacks nor I believe that I keep coming back for purely professional reasons. In fact it was Sacks who suggested without my prompting that I come for my own personal reasons: "As an intelligent person, you recognize your own mortality, just like the old people. So you feel compelled to participate in the shul sort of as a way of making your peace with God." There is more than a grain of truth in Sacks's statement. I had long ago gathered enough information about the service. Most of the information I still needed could be learned during occasional visits to Sacks's bakery or through telephone interviews. I continued attending services because I still enjoyed the company of various congregants long after I stopped needing them for information. So, while as an anthropologist I might have had reservations about interfering in the life of an informant, pressuring him to do what he was so adamantly refusing to do, it wasn't the anthropologist who pressured: it was the part of me that felt like "family." I felt justified in crossing certain boundaries of professional propriety because I felt that I was apprenticing in the "family business" (i.e., Sacks's specialty) of finagling God, Jewish relief organizations, and city agencies. There are, of course, good reasons for me to have felt like family here, beyond the bounds of the normal informant/anthropologist relationship. Elderly people, particularly when they share the same ethnic background, with the anthropologist, readily project a family relationship onto a young person and the anthropologist may very well project the same family relationship too. Consequently both expect certain favors and make certain demands that they would be less inclined to make with someone from another ethnic background. But I think my relationship with Sacks went beyond that, and its particular quality stems from the fact that in the course of this project I began to see the anthropological enterprise as an apprenticeship in another culture. More than just accumulating knowledge, it involves the internalization of that information so that the anthropologist learns to think like his informants and thereby becomes an interpreter—a conduit for knowledge to pass between cultures. Particularly when certain cultural groups are disappearing, the anthropologist who studies them must assume the role not only of a conduit but also of a repository. His knowledge may be the only surviving traces of a culture. And this, I believed, was precisely the case in my relationship with the Intervale community. Consequently there developed a certain blurring of identities, particularly on my part, so much so that I sometimes saw myself as Sacks. What I did not understand at the time, however, was that the relationship was only partly reciprocated: when Sacks assumed my role, he generally had a hidden agenda. While filming, for example, Sacks refused to explain the "miracle" of Intervale Avenue in his usual fashion, that God guaranteed the minyan despite the deaths or departures from the neighborhood of individual congregants. He insisted now that "there is no such thing as miracles. The synagogue serves the needs of each person who comes there." Sacks was playing anthropologist. Indeed, he had begun to attribute the idea of the "miracle" to me, since I had used the word in the title of an article about the shul. This seemed like a peculiar disavowal on his part, but upon reflection I believe that he had considerable motivation here, although he had hidden it perhaps like a puppeteer pulling strings. By attributing his thoughts to me and by assuming the role of the outside observer, Sacks and I had in effect switched roles. Right at the outset, when he made it clear that he would not participate in the film, Sacks suggested that it should be me whom the director should interview, since "Jack has all the information anyway." But this was not the only case of Sacks's asserting the ambiguity of our respective roles. Eight months later, a few days before a sneak preview of the film in New York, I asked Sacks what he planned to say to the audience when he gets up to speak:

"That's easy. I'll just tell them the story of the Khofets Hayim who was traveling from town to town with a *balegule* [coachman]. After hearing the Khofets Hayim give the same speech in town after town, the *balegule* says to him: 'You know what you do isn't so hard. At the next town let me do what you do and you be the *balegule*.' So they switch places. When they come to the town, someone comes to the 'Khofets Hayim' and asks him a very difficult question on the Talmud. The 'Khofets Hayim' has no idea how to answer the question. So he thinks for a moment, then he answers the man, 'You know that question is so easy that I won't even bother with it. I'll just let this simple coachman over here answer it.' So you see, if anyone asks me something I can't answer I'll just tell them that it's too simple for me to bother with and I'll tell them they should ask you."

That night, when I was asked to say a few words following the screening, I stole Sacks's lines from him. I told the audience the same story Sacks had told me, and then I introduced him as the simple coachman. Never one to be upstaged, Sacks later told me that he knew I would steal his lines and that's why he told me the story. So here was the puppeteer again. And I was just another of his marionettes.

The story of the coachman continues to have a certain appeal to me, perhaps because I feel myself acting out the coachman character through my relationship with Sacks. After all, I am the one who drives Sacks out of his own environment onto film or the printed page. And I suppose I envy him, too: his knowledge of rabbinic lore, his sense of completeness, and his satisfaction in the self-contained world of Moshman's bakery. So I have a "secret" longing to become Sacks, that is, to be a wise old Jew and a master craftsman.

For his part, Sacks probably has a longing to be young. He certainly has a desire to be a teacher (he was unable to pass the entrance exam on account of his "Lithuanian" accent). And I suppose, just like the Khofets Hayim who agreed to make the switch, he probably has a secret yearning to determine his own fate, entirely unaided by the coachman/anthropologist. But more than vanity is at work in Sacks's assuming the role of director/writer/anthropologist. Because he is my chief informant, it is through his eyes that all of my research on the Intervale Jewish Center is filtered. Moreover, the bulk of my information comes directly from him during our Saturday afternoon feasts.

The closer my relationship with Sacks became, the more my observations took on the quality of what Clifford Geertz calls "looking over the shoulder" (1968) to jot down what he had to say. This was not something I had to do on the sly. Sacks was not only aware of what I was doing, he began to save tidbits of information for me. But in the course of time, a more subtle and unspoken agreement arose between us, particularly after Sacks first saw me lecture and read my articles about the shul. He began to take a more direct role in gathering information and making sense out of it. So the line between us became over time increasingly thin.

But the blurring of identities is only a phase of ethnographic research. Empathy can get you only so far, distance and the reemergence of the self is vital, too (Shaffir et al. 1980). The struggle with Sacks speaks to a more general point in the relationship between a chief informant and an anthropologist: through the conscious articulation of two distinct and often mutually contradictory worldviews, ethnography gains the quality of a dialogue between two discrete cultural universes. Indeed, the breakdown within our relationship was a necessary reminder that the common identity I imagined existed between us was an ethnographer's fantasy: the agenda of informant and anthropologist can never be entirely the same.

Still, there is more here than just the personal dynamics of an ethnographer/informant relationship. There were after all numerous instances when our respective agendas were very much in sync. Sacks needed me for the minyan and I needed him to answer questions. Moreover, my presence within the community contributed something to Sacks's (and the others') self-esteem. It gave them a sense, to use Richard Schechner's words, that "someone else is interested, is listening (1982:80)." Since old people need the life review as a way of establishing and reaffirming the meaning of their lives (Myerhoff (1988), the questions that encouraged Sacks and the others to be reflexive served the community well. Why were our respective agendas out of sync now? Did Sacks have a hidden agenda during the making of the film or was his behavior mere fist-flailing?

What becomes increasingly clear to me in reviewing these events is that the stories men fabricate to impute meaning and order to their lives sometimes falter. If Sacks's grueling work pace, despite his advanced age, represents a heroic defiance of death, being deprived of the opportunity to work because of the possible closing of the bakery is a rather clear symbol of the futility of that struggle. So Sacks's difficult behavior at the time of the filming represented a momentary disavowal of a narcissistic belief that he had control over his own life, that he could conquer death. And it hinted perhaps at the possibility that even his miracle minyan might be on the verge of tottering. Sacks responded by seeking some way of restoring his sense of control. Consequently, the more we pressured, the more stubborn he became. At the same time, the problems he caused for us were a way of lashing out, of generalizing what was to him a specific problem that he alone faced. Sacks's principal problem derived from the limitations old age imposed upon him. If the bakery closed, he would have a hard time finding comparable employment. Even if he could find work, he would lose the status he enjoys as a man who almost singlehandedly produces Moshman's baked goods. Opening up his own shop was out of the question. Although he had the funds to do it, he could feel his strength ebbing. "Besides," as Sacks once explained, "it's one thing to work in a place and take on some of the responsibility of running it. It's another thing to own the place and have all the responsibility. I'm too old for that." The situation with the bakery brought Sacks face to face with the chilling realization that his options were limited. His ability to effect the world around him was decreasing. The film crew, by comparison, was full of vigor and in good health. Its members, for the most part, were coming into their own as successful directors, cameramen, soundmen, and producers. The world to them was limitless. So they would take what they needed from Sacks and then move on in life. By behaving the way he did and setting irrational limits, Sacks forced the film crew to experience life the way he was experiencing it—as limited. For a brief two weeks, we were all old people. We were all groping for a way to deal with the unfairness of life's circumstances. And since the crew would return to London at the end of their two-week stay, time became like a grim reaper, threatening to cheat us of what we had set out to make. The whole situation had the quality of a metaphor for the eternal struggle within each of us between the will to live and the need to accommodate ourselves to the inevitability of death.

But there is another level here, one in which the narcissistic belief in omnipotence is not at all denied, but rather is confirmed. By denying that the "miracle of Intervale Avenue" is the "miracle of Moishe Sacks," Sacks was actually affirming and proving that very fact. He not only identified himself as the central character without whom there could be no "miracle," but also by extention, he staked his claim to being the creator of the film. By refusing to participate, he was implicitly directing the film. And when he finally agreed to take part, it was entirely on his terms, leaving us to wonder whether he might suddenly change his mind and throw us out. Sacks had effectively wrested control of a very complex situation, and it probably helped to restore his overall sense of power.

Nor is Sacks's assertion of control limited to the making of the film. Sometimes, in our relationship I have felt a certain disloyalty on his part, his using the advent of a journalist or photographer to drive home the fact to me that whereas he is crucial to the story, I am

expendable. The truth is that when Sacks comments that a poorly
written article about the shul has some good lines in it—the ones in
quotes (meaning his own) he is both vain and correct. His is the only
indispensible role. As storyteller or mythmaker for the community, he
literally fashions through his imaginings a world of refuge for those
around him. As storyteller, Sacks gives these people a place to come
to and be needed, their individual eccentricities as integral parts of
the miracle. Without them there would be no miracle, just as without
Sacks there could be no myth of a miracle. In Sacks's mind, I too am
part of the miracle. Sacks repeatedly denies that he invented the
phrase "the miracle of Intervale Avenue." By attributing the term
"miracle" to me, Sacks is legitimizing it's existence: "It's not a miracle. It's scientifically verifiable. In all the time you've been here,
hasn't there always been someone new to take the place of a man who
leaves the minyan?" But by denying authorship of his own creation,
Sacks is actually "mystifying" it—giving it greater credence as a miracle. Therefore, I play a critical role in the legitimization and mystifica-
tion of Sacks's myth. In that sense, my relationship with him is totally
reciprocal. I have remained at Intervale these many years to verify
Sacks's miracle. I also wanted to see what would happen to the "miracle," as congregants die or leave the community. How would Sacks
respond to a situation that mocks his peculiar view of reality? I discovered that the mockery is reversed: Sacks's fertile imagination generally got the better of reality. So I have come actually to believe in his
miracle—not so much as a "miracle" but as a part and parcel of Sacks's
overall worldview, or what the psychoanalyst Erik Erikson (1978) calls
wisdom—the balance in old age between despair and hope. The real
miracle is one of old people believing that they can take control of
their own lives and make things happen, that "*amuno*" (faith) as Sacks
maintains can indeed "make the miracle." Sacks's genius does not
simply lie in his ability to overcome despair. It emanates rather from
his ability to convince others to think like him, to believe in the same
miracles he does, and in that way he extends one man's view of the
world outward to encompass an ever-widening circle of people. In the
final analysis, this may well have been at the root of Sacks's capitula-
tion. Despite his protests, he was and still remains captive to his own
miracle. Myths once created do not easily shatter. Instead, they take
on lives of their own, their credibility confirmed and enhanced by the
number of their adherents. Perhaps it was his continuing faith in the
miracle that whittled away despair and forced him to return to the

fold. Or perhaps it was simply his desire to reassert a sense of control. For storytelling is the only enduring source of his or of any man's power. And for a man who is neither politically powerful, wealthy, nor in his prime physically, to be able to exert so much control over his surroundings, particularly over such bleak surroundings, could indeed be "the miracle of Intervale Avenue."

Nine months after the film was finished, I decided to go to London for the premiere. My flight was on a Saturday night, so I was able to spend the early part of the day at Intervale. During the kiddush, Sacks and I discuss my itinerary. While we talk I manage to eat most of the pieces of chocolate babka, and I suspect that Sacks sees that as a sign that when I return from London I will continue to attend the minyan. When the plate is empty I get up to leave. As I do so, Sacks asks me about the plans for the premiere.

"I'm not sure what Irving's planning, although he did ask me to say a few words to the audience."

"Have you decided yet what you're going to say or will you do like I do, be extemporaneous?"

"Actually I meant to talk to you about it. What do you think I should say?"

"Say what you think at the time. I told you I do things extemporaneously."

"Yes, but even when you speak extemporaneously you have some idea of what you plan to say."

"That's true."

"Well, if *you* went to London what do you think you would say?"

"I'll tell you what you can say. Tell them that we should all thank God that we have lived to see this day."

"You mean I should say the prayer *shekhiyanu?*"

"Yes. Say *shekhiyanu.*"

"I will." I shake hands with everyone and wish them a *gut shabes.*

When I shake Sacks's hand he says, "Jack, I want you to have a good time in London. But don't have such a good time that you forget about us. So drop us a line from time to time. Not too often, though. Otherwise we'll think that you're having a terrible time and you spend all day in your room writing letters."

"I'll write. And I promise not to write too often." I head to the stairs.

Before I reach them Sacks calls out: "And one more thing. When you talk to the audience, remember to tell them that in case any of them is ever in New York, we're saving a place for them here at the Intervale Jewish Center."

REFERENCES

Erikson, Eric. 1978. *Adulthood*. New York: W. W. Norton.
Geertz, Clifford. 1968. "Thinking as a Moral Act: Ethical Dimensions of Anthropological Field Work in the New States." *Antioch Review* 28, 2:139–58.
Myerhoff, Barbara. 1988. "Surviving Stories." In *Between Two Worlds: Ethnographic Essays on American Jewry*, ed. Jack Kugelmass. Ithaca: Cornell University Press.
Schechner, Richard. 1982. "Collective Reflexivity: Restoration of Behavior." In *A Crack in the Mirror*, ed. Jay Ruby. Philadelphia: University of Pennsylvania Press.
Shaffir, William, et al. 1980. "Introduction." In *Fieldwork Experience: Qualitative Approaches to Social Research*. New York: St. Martin's Press.

Index

Library of Congress Cataloging-in-Publication Data
Between two worlds.

   (Anthropology of contemporary issues)
   Includes index.
   1. Jews—United States—Identity.   2. Judaism—
United States.   3. United States—Ethnic relations.
I. Kugelmass, Jack.   II. Series.
E184.J5B525   1988   305.8'924'073   88-47735
ISBN 0-8014-2084-9 (alk. paper)
ISBN 0-8014-9408-7 (pbk. : alk. paper)